Mechanics of pre-industrial technology

*An introduction to
the mechanics of
ancient and
traditional material
culture*

Mechanics of pre-industrial technology

BRIAN COTTERELL
*Department of Mechanical and Production Engineering
National University of Singapore*

JOHAN KAMMINGA
*Department of Prehistory and Anthropology
Australian National University*

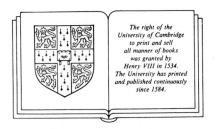

The right of the
University of Cambridge
to print and sell
all manner of books
was granted by
Henry VIII in 1534.
The University has printed
and published continuously
since 1584.

CAMBRIDGE UNIVERSITY PRESS

Cambridge

New York   Port Chester

Melbourne   Sydney

Published by the Press Syndicate of the University of Cambridge
The Pitt Building, Trumpington Street, Cambridge CB2 1RP
40 West 20th Street, New York, NY 10011-4211, USA
10 Stamford Road, Oakleigh, Victoria 3166, Australia

© Brian Cotterell and Johan Kamminga 1990

First published 1990
First paperback edition 1992

Printed in Great Britain by the University Press, Cambridge

British Library cataloguing in publication data

Cotterell, Brian
Mechanics of pre-industrial technology.
1. Industrial antiquities to 1750
I. Title   II. Kamminga, Johan
609

National Library of Australia cataloguing in publication data

Cotterell, Brian, 1934–
Mechanics of pre-industrial technology.
Bibliography.
Includes index.
ISBN 0 521 34194 9.
1. Mechanics. 2. Material culture. 3. Industries,
Primitive. I. Kamminga, Johan. II. Title.

620.1′009

Library of Congress cataloguing in publication data

Cotterell, Brian, 1934–
Mechanics of pre-industrial technology: an introduction to the
mechanics of ancient and traditional material culture/Brian
Cotterell, Johan Kamminga.
    p.   cm.
Bibliography.
Includes index.
ISBN 0 521 34194 9
1. Mechanics. 2. Material culture. 3. Industries, Primitive.
I. Kamminga, Johan.   II. Title.
OC125.2.C68 1989
620.1′009 – dc19   88-29238   CIP

ISBN 0 521 34194 9 hardback
ISBN 0 521 42871 8 paperback

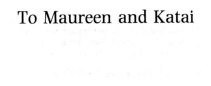
To Maureen and Katai

CONTENTS

Contents

FIGURES

TABLES

PREFACE

This book is about the material culture of ancient and non-industrial societies. The topics covered range from the fragments of siliceous stone that are the earliest known hominid artifacts to the development of watermills and other artifacts up to the Industrial Age. Our case studies are selected from as wide a range of societies as possible to try to avoid the Eurocentric bias that can be seen in some histories of technology. We consider not only archaeological artifacts but also ethnographic and historical evidence from traditional hunter-gatherers and other non-Industrial peoples such as, for example, the Australian Aborigines, the Polynesians and the Ottoman Turks. Some enthnographic artifacts can be of great value in reconstructing or inferring the properties and performances of archaeological ones. We encompass all modern artifacts used in non-Industrial societies under the label 'traditional'. Many of our examples of hunter-gatherer artifacts are from the material culture of the Australian Aborigines. Our bias is partly because we are most familiar with the traditional material culture of our own country, but it is also because the Aborigines comprised the world's largest population of hunter-gatherers in modern times and therefore much research has been done on their material culture.

The idea of a book about mechanics of early and traditional technology occurred to us during an archaeological conference on stone tools that was held in Vancouver some years ago. We gave a joint paper about the mechanics of stone flaking, a topic that drew on our two areas of special interest: engineering fracture mechanics and prehistoric stone technology. While the audience of archaeologists appreciated what we were saying most of the delegates did not know sufficient mechanics theory to understand how we had arrived at our conclusions; nor was there much comprehension of mechanics terminology. This general lack of familiarity with mechanics theory is not surprising. The structure of college and university education does not particularly encourage students in archaeology or anthropology, or in the humanities in general, to study the sciences. While the study of artifacts is a fundamental part of archaeology and cultural anthropology, the study of how they perform mechanically has a patchy history. Franz Boas was the first anthropologist to write a general account of the mechanics and performance of traditional artifacts, in the introduction to a general book on anthropology (Boas 1938:238–81). However in recent decades there have been few general accounts of mechanics in material culture studies, though there have been many that deal with specific applications, a large number of which we refer to in this book. Mechanics serves anthropology not only in providing an understanding of artifacts and technological processes but in its applications to problems in biological evolution as well – as shown in recent biomechanical studies of the hominid face and cranial architecture (e.g. Demes 1982; Russell 1985).

This book is not a history of technology, nor one of mechanical science, though in our presentation of mechanical principles we have taken a partly historical approach. Mechanics forms the basis of many branches of science, including engineering, and is necessary in the development of much new material culture – be it a component for an artificial hip or a new transport system. In this book we present the interdisciplinary study of the mechanics of material culture. Interdisciplinary studies involving mechanics are not new. For example biomechanics is now a firmly established interdisciplinary field and mechatronics, the study of both the mechanical and electronic aspects of robots, is a fast expanding field.

This book, which illustrates the applications of mechanics in archaeology, should also serve a wider readership in disciplines such as cultural anthropology, engineering, history, and physics. Because our book embodies the first contemporary review of the field we introduce basic mechanical concepts in the earlier chapters and bring in other mechanics in later chapters as they become relevant to the various analyses. Because a number of our readers do not have a grounding in advanced mathematics we have kept our calculations reasonably elementary so that they should be understandable to anyone who has completed secondary school mathematics. Those of our readers who are uncomfortable with equations can still grasp the essentials of the mechanical concepts we present. The mathematical details of the mechanics of any artifact or technological process can be passed over lightly without losing continuity in reading the text.

In developing our style we were influenced by Lloyd Taylor's book, *Physics, the pioneer science*. We also much admired the lucid style of J. E. Gordon's two books, *The new science of strong materials* and *Structures*, which we found valuable sources of information. We would have found it difficult to begin the mechanical studies of the wide range of artifacts without the two monumental works: *A history of technology* edited by Charles Singer and colleagues, and *Science and civilisation in China* written by Joseph Needham and his co-authors.

For permission to publish photographs and drawings we
thank the following individuals and institutions: Fig. 1.2,
Carnegie Museum of Natural History (photo by Rudyerd Boulton);
Fig. 2.7 and 2.8, Vatican Museums and Art Galleries; Fig. 2.10,
Wilkinson Sword Group Australia Ltd., Melbourne; Fig. 5.2, Paul
Popper Ltd., Photographic Agency, London (photo by Paul
Popper); Fig. 5.14, The British School at Rome, Exhibition Road,
London; Fig. 6.2, F. P. Dickson; Fig. 7.6, Bibliographisches Institut
and F. A. Brockhaus (copyright Associated Press); Fig. 7.12, Dr
Felix Hess, Rijksuniversiteit te Groningen; Fig. 8.3, National
Museum, Copenhagen; Fig. 9.7, John Coates and CUP; Fig. 9.17,
University Museum of National Antiquities, Oslo; Fig. 10.10,
Jennifer Steel Photography, North Sydney.

The progress of our work has depended very much on the
interest and generosity of our colleagues. To those who have
helped and encouraged us we extend our thanks. Various drafts of
this work were commented on by Kim Akerman, John Coates,
Barry Cundy, Frank Dickson, Brian Hayden, Yiu-Wing Mai,
Vincent Megaw, Andrée Rosenfeld, Leonn Satterthwait and Roger
Tanner. We are especially indebted to Leonn Satterthwait for his
patience and good humour during our revisions. We also thank
Naguib Kanawati for procuring handmade Egyptian rope; Jenny
Astridge, for her invaluable help in hunting down obscure texts;
Trevor Shearing, whose photographic skills are evident in a
number of the plate pages; and Stephanie Frost, Lyn Kennedy and
Marichu Agudo, who with patience prepared the typescript. We
acknowledge the support of the Australian Research Grants
Scheme, which has funded a number of the experimental studies
described in this book, and thank the Department of Mechanical
Engineering, Sydney University, for supporting this rather esoteric
project for an engineering department.

1

Introduction

The material culture of our earliest hominid ancestor who inhabited northeast Africa some four million years ago was probably on about the same level as that of the modern apes. The first identifiable hominid, *Australopithecus afarensis*, was a small primate, less than a metre and a half tall, with a brain about the same size as a chimpanzee's. This hominid probably made use of only slightly modified natural objects, much as apes do today. Unmodified objects such as rocks used to crack a nut are sometimes called *naturefacts* (Oswalt 1973:14), and their use is by no means limited to the primates. On the Galapagos Islands Charles Darwin observed a species of ground-dwelling finch (now named after him) that used a cactus spine or twig held in its beak to pick insects out of crevices in tree trunks. Many animals also purposely modify natural objects for immediate use in a task – for example the Darwin Finch modifies a twig by shortening or trimming it (Beck 1980:24–5). However impressive animal tool-use may be, it is the range, complexity and sophistication of modified objects, or *artifacts*, that is the hallmark of humanity.

The first evidence of a material culture appeared some two million years ago with the stone artifacts of *Homo habilis* (literally, 'handy man'). As hominids evolved so did their material culture. Early technology was simple, but with the evolution of *Homo erectus* and the emergence of modern man, *Homo sapiens*, these species spread to populate even the most challenging environments. The human species is the most adaptable and successful of all the higher animals and its ability to develop sophisticated and complex material culture seems almost boundless.

Invention and diffusion

Culture is a shared body of learned knowledge transmitted from one generation to the next. It is through culture – material and otherwise – that humans adapt to different environments, though not all such learned behaviour is adaptive (Huffman 1984). Innovations in the form of local inventions or ideas derived from outside the social unit can be added to the pool of learned knowledge. While land animals other than humans learn little from individuals outside their social units, they can also make innovations. For example one group of macaques on the Japanese island of Koshima learned that unhusked rice scattered on the beach for them by scientists could be separated from sand if thrown into a rock pool and collected from the surface of the water. This and other innovations were made by a three-year-old female, who was perhaps the macaque equivalent of a Marie Curie, and quickly learnt by other members of her group (Kawai 1965).

Today almost all the world's societies are linked by a sophisticated communication network so that most changes in a region's material culture occur by diffusion. It is only a rare society, like the Jarawa of North Sentinal Island in the Andaman group, that is almost entirely cut off culturally from the rest of the world, and even in this case the Jarawa accept gifts of mirrors and metal basins left by the Indian government patrols. Although there has always been some communication between social units in the form of trade, the speed by which innovations could be diffused must have been comparatively slow in prehistoric times. Hence innovations in the form of simple artifacts such as most stone tools, or artifacts suggested by nature itself, like cords and ropes, would be more likely to occur by invention than by diffusion. There is less possibility of inventing a relatively sophisticated and complex artifact, such as the rotary quern, and these kinds of artifacts are more likely to have appeared in a particular area because of diffusion rather than independent invention. Today when independent inventions are made in more than one place they are more likely to have come about because of the topicality of the subject; for example many researchers around the world are currently attempting to invent a material that will be superconducting at higher temperatures. In today's industrial societies a high value is placed on useful innovation which, to varying degrees, is in contrast to the cultural values held by prehistoric and non-industrial societies. Nevertheless even in the most conservative societies innovations were possible when material and social prerequisites were in place.

Very little is known about invention and diffusion in prehistoric and non-literate societies because evidence such as reliable oral traditions is sparse. The archaeological record can reveal the presence of a new artifact in a particular time or place, but the process of how it occurred and the reasons why it was adopted and developed in a particular direction is usually open to different interpretations. Much of what is written about culture history is concerned with just this problem. One topical example is the origin and development of the Lapita cultural complex in the western Pacific that is associated with the ancestors of the Polynesians. The Lapita complex belongs to recent prehistoric times; when one proceeds further back in time the evidence for resolving problems of this kind becomes even more scarce and tests the strengths of archaeological theory.

The innovation by macaques discussed earlier had immediate application and reward in the food quest and one can see why it became established as a group norm, but certain other apparently beneficial innovations that were also seen to occur were not acquired by the rest of the macaque group (Kawai 1965). Many factors operate to condition the response of individuals or groups to changes in material culture. Whether a change is seen to be beneficial to an individual or group is in part a subjective opinion of the observer. Thus not all innovations are adopted, be it in macaque or human society. For an innovation to be accepted there must be an appropriate social, political, technological and economic environment. It is a common observation that people tend to resist cultural change because it often requires shifts in established cultural values. Resistance to change is not limited to non-industrial societies, and indeed a warning about this aspect of human nature is often sounded to aspiring engineers early in their university training (e.g. Beakley and Chilton 1973).

It is worthwhile to review a number of historical case studies to grasp the context of change in material culture. The importance of religious factors in the response to some innovations cannot be overemphasised. One outstanding example of religious proscription is that of the Old Order Amish community in the United States which bans its members from using automobiles and electricity. There are also economic, technological and other cultural factors to consider. For instance the wooden screw press, which we discuss in Chapter 4, was not used by the peasant farmers of Corfu because they were unable to make the capital investment (Sordinas 1974). While this machine had been invented by the Alexandrian Greeks in the first or second century BC, and was therefore well known to the inhabitants of Corfu, the crushing of olives continued to be done by the technically less-efficient and truly antiquated direct beam press. While most people think that the jet engine is a modern invention, the original concept can be traced to Heron of Alexandria, an avid inventor of the first century AD, who made a toy steam jet engine. In 1791 a British patent for a gas turbine was granted to John Barbar, but it was not to be until the late 1930s that the first practical jet engine was produced. The earlier attempts to develop this artifact failed because a strong heat-resistant material needed for the turbine blades still had to be developed. When suitable materials became available, the first practical jet engines were produced independently within a year of one another by Sir Frank Whittle in Britain and Hans von Ohain in Germany. This example highlights the need for an appropriate technological environment for change to occur. A more personal and contemporary example of an unsuitable environment for the acquisition of new material culture is provided by a group of Agta Negritos which one of us recently studied in an isolated part of the Philippines. While gin and cigarettes were seen as appropriate and affordable purchases from trade stores, items of Western medicine that were highly desired were uncommon purchases because they were perceived as being too expensive (though comparable in price to the gin and cigarettes) and could not be administered because no one was able to read the instructions about dosage.

In the cases cited the reasons for an innovation not being exploited are known because there are sufficient historical records available, but there are also many instances where the evidence allows only speculation. One of the most notable of these cases is the absence of wheeled vehicles in the New World. While the Incas had more than 3000 km of made roads with suspension bridges for pedestrian traffic, and llamas for carrying loads, they failed to develop wheeled vehicles. Similarly the absence of the bow and arrow among the Australian Aborigines is difficult to explain when the materials for making them were certainly available, and when these artifacts were in common use among their neighbours in New Guinea and the Torres Strait islands. In contrast to this evident disinterest in certain new subsistence technology, the Australian Aborigines copied the outrigger canoe from New Guinea and were unhesitating in their acceptance of the steel hatchet and other artifacts brought by white settlers, such as blankets and glass bottles.

The appearance in the archaeological record of a new type of artifact or a design change does not necessarily imply a novel invention, but may simply reflect a technological or social change that promotes or allows the general adoption of an obvious idea. An invention can be conceived countless times before it becomes established as a cultural norm. Making stone tools by grinding rather than flaking is a low order innovation about on par with making simple flaked stone tools; it has direct correspondence to observable processes in nature and the phenomenon of abrasion and grinding must have even been within the experience of hominids – our old friends the macaques rub pebbles together as a form of play (Huffman 1984:726). Yet ground stone technology did not appear in the archaeological record until as recently as 20000 to 30000 years ago. Among the Australian Aborigines the primary use of ground stone tools was to extract small game hidden in tree trunks and to process the new and important food resource of grass seeds, while the first appearance of ground stone tools in the Middle East and Europe was as an element of farming technology.

Some changes in material culture that occurred in prehistoric time were due entirely to fashion, just as today many changes in the shape of automobiles have little to do with improving their aerodynamics. In the Kimberley region of northwest Australia the Aborigines made delicately shaped stone spear heads called Kimberley points (Fig. 1.1) that were the finest

Fig. 1.1. A Kimberley point.

examples of flaked stone implements made on the continent. Much time was spent in their execution, and they were highly regarded in adjacent regions where the process of their manufacture was not understood and where they acquired a new status as ritual objects (Davidson and McCarthy 1957:435; Tindale 1965:155). Yet the most aesthetic specimens appear not to have been particularly efficient because they frequently broke on impact, and their popularity may well have been due to social factors of status and fashion.

Theories of cultural evolution

In the eighteenth and nineteenth centuries navigators, adventurers and colonial officials were returning to Europe with artifacts from many different traditional societies. In the light of Darwin's theory of biological evolution parallels between these artifacts and ancient ones were quickly drawn and grand schemes of cultural evolution began to be defined. One of the most popular early theories of material culture development was conceived by Augustus Henry Lane Fox (1906), who later changed his name to Pitt-Rivers and became Britain's first Inspector of Ancient Monuments. Lane Fox was a military man and his conception of cultural evolution emerged from his observation of the changes in bullet design and their effect on the rifle's accuracy and range (Lane Fox 1858). His proposition was that the most 'primitive' or basic types of artifacts had prototypes evident in natural objects and that material progress followed a path of increasing specialisation and complexity.

The models of cultural evolution proposed by Lane Fox and other scholars such as Otis T. Mason (1895), a curator of the US National Museum, and Henry Balfour, curator of the Pitt Rivers Museum in Oxford (see Rogers 1962), relied to a large extent on the mechanism of diffusion – an innovation would appear in one place and, if it was useful, be conveyed into distant regions where it was subject to modification to make it more suitable for local conditions. In describing how these evolutionary schemes worked one of the best examples one can cite is that of stringed musical instruments. It was reasoned that the simplest stringed instrument, the one-string musical bow, must have evolved from the hunter's bow. The next postulated evolutionary step or advance on the basic design was the addition of a resonator, as it appears on traditional African musical bows (Fig. 1.2). Further postulated design modifications were thought to have led to the development of the whole family of modern stringed instruments.

While the diffusion of ideas from single sources was emphasised, it was recognised that similar forms could and sometimes are known to have evolved independently of one another in quite different regions. For instance there is no evidence to indicate that the material cultures of the complex societies of Central and South America derived in any way from

Introduction

those on other continents. However the degree to which cultural evolutionists accepted independent development as a major factor in culture change varied considerably.

The emergence of the 'historical method' in ethnology at the turn of the century marked a reaction to the extremes of grand theories of cultural development and promoted an appreciation of material culture in its local context. The most prominent proponent of the new approach was Franz Boas (1858–1942). Today there is no robust theory of evolution of material culture. Certainly the grand theories of the nineteenth century were too simplistic. What appears to have happened is that material culture began in a simple form over 2000000 years ago with the hominid ancestors of modern humans. In time, possibly relatively recently, the general material culture inventory of the species grew larger and the artifacts became progressively more complex in form and more efficient overall. World prehistory is framed in terms of evolutionary phases that are based on a combination and predominance of subsistence modes (hunter-gatherer, agricultural and pastoral, industrial) and the type of material for hardware artifacts (stone, bronze, iron and steel). The general changes in subsistence mode and metal technology are

Fig. 1.2. Gubu player.

evolutionary, but they did not occur uniformly throughout the world; nor did all material cultures develop in the same direction. In Australia the hunter-gatherer way of life and stone technology lasted for over 40 000 years into the nineteenth century, and in more isolated parts of the continent until the late twentieth century, when the traditional Aboriginal material culture was superceded by an industrial material culture with a technology based on steel and other metals and a range of diverse synthetic materials. In the New World flaked and ground stone technology continued as a major part of indigenous technology until the colonial era, though in some regions the soft metals – copper, silver and gold – were exploited, while in remote Greenland the Eskimos made iron implements from a huge 30-tonne meteorite they called Abnightito (Weaver 1986:410).

Cultural, environmental and geographic factors have combined to cause the development of material culture to be diverse within the context of broad global changes, so that the material culture increased in complexity even in hunter-gatherer groups like the Australian Aborigines (Lourandos 1983; Kamminga 1985:20–1). The various material cultures were often specific to the physical environments in which they operated. For instance the artifacts possessed by the inhabitants of cold temperate and Arctic lands made possible the human settlement of those inhospitable parts of the world. Likewise the artifacts of the Aboriginal tribes who inhabited the deserts of the interior of Australia fulfilled the essential needs of people who were required to travel as unencumbered as possible over long distances; for this reason their artifacts were often multipurpose – their spearthrower was not only used to cast spears but also used in firemaking, and a small stone flake fixed on one end served as a chisel. Thus it is virtually meaningless to compare artifact inventories from different parts of the world as if they represent development stages in one progression towards the material culture of the Industrial Age as was the common belief of the grand theorists. In Australia hunter-gatherer technology developed over tens of thousands of years in relative isolation. A developmental sequence is evident from the archaeological record, certainly in the stone technology (Kamminga 1985:21). Other developments in material cultures in different parts of the worlds are also clearly indicated by the archaeological record. However material cultures are not always accumulative. Innovations are sometimes discarded by societies when, for one reason or another, they no longer suit the physical and cultural environment. Cultural loss can come about by proscription due to social or political change, but in most documented cases the causes are cultural isolation or environmental change.

It has been suggested that the Tasmanian Aborigines, who had one of the least complex material cultures in the world (Jones 1977; Oswalt 1976:189), became culturally pauperised because of geographic isolation. Only 8000 years ago the island was part of the Australian continent and its inhabitants at that time are presumed to have shared some of the material culture of their more northern neighbours. However at the time of first contact with Europeans they had no idea of how to make fire (like the Andaman Islanders), and they had no stone tools hafted with wooden handles, such as hatchets and adzes, and no boomerangs or spearthrowers. One pundit has proposed that the Tasmanians suffered a 'slow strangulation of the mind' (Jones 1977), but the mechanisms responsible for this simplification of material culture are yet to be fully understood.

A second example of material culture loss is provided by the Polynesians, the descendants of coastal Asian people who had pottery and possibly knew about metal when they began their odyssey eastwards into the Pacific. These Asian seafarers brought fine pottery with distinctive decoration, and pottery technology remained in the material culture of Polynesian descendants in the western Pacific. But further east, on islands like Hawaii and Easter Island, pottery is completely absent. Again, while geographic and cultural isolation must have played a part in material culture change, the precise causes of this artifact loss are as yet unknown.

An example of material culture loss due to a change in the environment is provided by the Polar Eskimos of the Thule District of northern Greenland. In that high Arctic latitude the subsistence technology is largely concerned with ice-hunting since the ice remains practically throughout the year. When this Eskimo group was discovered in 1818 the normal summer-hunting technology had disappeared and the kayak and umiak were unknown to them. It was not until the beginning of the 1860s that the forgotten elements of Eskimo material culture were restored in the Thule District through the immigration of some families from northern Baffin Island (Gilberg 1974).

Artifact sophistication and complexity

Attempts have been made to gauge the technological complexity of artifact inventories (e.g. Oswalt 1976; Satterthwait 1980) to enable general statements to be made about change in different material cultures. One such gauge is based on the structural complexity of artifacts, that is, their interrelated parts, patterns or elements (Oswalt 1976:42). In this system each individual part of an artifact is called a technounit, and the number of technounits that comprise a complete artifact is a measure of the artifact's complexity. Defining artifact complexity in terms of the diversity of its parts or structural units is a very simple gauge of an artifact's status. Although the measure of technological complexity depends on how one defines complexity, whatever definition is used it is obvious that on a worldwide scale artifacts have increased in complexity with time, especially since

the end of the Pleistocene period about 12 000 years ago
(Fig. 1.3). However increased complexity can be considered an
evolutionary progression only if it reflects greater efficiency. While
artifacts are becoming more complex in the contemporary world,
improved efficiency can also be gained by structural simplification.

Fig. 1.3. The development of material
culture.

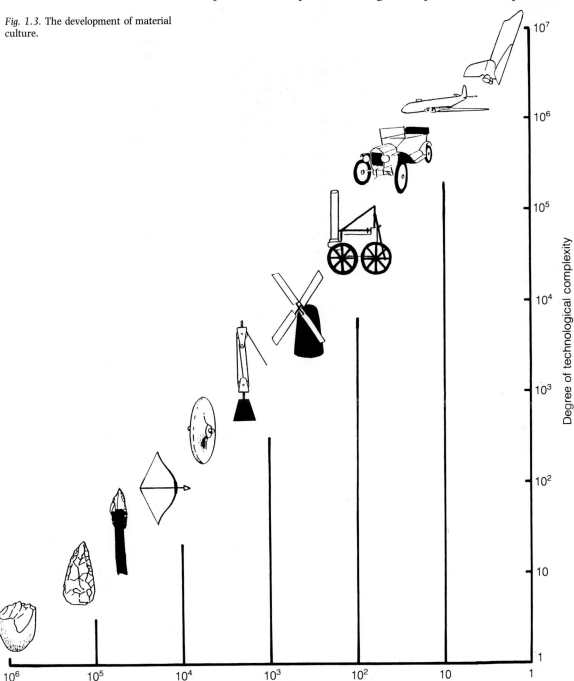

There are three main regions of the world where complex societies and material cultures developed as an outcome of the adoption of farming, animal domestication and the process of urbanisation – in East Asia, the Middle East, and Central America. With the advent of the Industrial Age many elements of the material culture of complex societies in Eurasia and North America were exported, through political and technological dominance, to most other regions of the world. In the last two centuries much of the traditional material culture of non-industrial societies has been swept away and replaced by both simple and complex artifacts of American, European or Japanese design – for instance the Coca-Cola can must now be one of the world's most widely recognised artifacts.

The exponential increase in material culture occurred because of the development of highly organised economic structures that enabled tasks to become highly specialised, ideas to be communicated easily and the cooperation of large workforces. Today new artifacts or modifications to pre-existing designs that come into common usage are the product of the cooperative efforts of sometimes countless thousands of humans drawing on, and contributing to, a common pool of knowledge (Altshuller 1984:3). The pace of research is increasing at such a phenomenal rate that in some areas, like computing technology, obsolescence of artifact types occurs within only a few years.

In the contemporary world, many artifacts are both complex and sophisticated in design. Artifacts of earlier times were on the whole much less structurally complex, though not necessarily unsophisticated. Let us examine the wheel as a way of demonstrating these qualities. The basic conceptual sophistication of the wheel is the idea of rotary motion about a fixed axle. Obviously a wheel is more distant from a natural object than a roller is, and it is therefore more sophisticated. The earliest wheels were solid timber discs, less complex than a wheel constructed from a number of separate pieces of wood. As well as being structurally more complicated, a spoked wheel has the added design sophistications of lightness and resilience. The fitting of an iron tyre introduces further mechanical sophistication by strengthening the wheel, and structural complexity by adding an artificial material, iron. The early Chinese wheelwrights learned to dish their wheels so that the spokes formed a shallow cone; this increased the strength of the wheel and is therefore an additional design sophistication. The wheel is just one example and obviously it does not show all the possible kinds of complexity and sophistication an artifact can possess.

The sophistication and complexity of an artifact must be judged against its efficiency. Mechanical efficiency will be discussed in Chapter 4, but we must first consider the broader aspects of efficiency which relate to an artifact's fitness for purpose and cost effectiveness in all the activities for which it is used, as well as its efficiency solely in a mechanical sense. The use of a pulley to lift water from a well is actually less efficient mechanically than hauling the bucket up directly, but in lifting a bucket out of a well it is physiologically easier to pull down on a rope. Likewise large wheels on a chariot are more efficient mechanically, but if because of their size they interfere with combat, large wheels would be impractical. Careful consideration must be given in determining whether design change really reflects greater efficiency. In engineering, artifact designs and technological processes are evaluated and compared by methods of analysis called 'attribute listing' or 'value analysis' (Beakley and Chilton 1973). The basic method of evaluation is to assess the artifact's relative efficiency and its suitability for a particular market. Perhaps a similar approach based on conceptual input evident in artifact design can be devised for evaluating non-industrial artifacts and processes. Reasonably objective measures of conceptual input in inventions can be devised (see Altshuller 1984:42–3).

The development of mechanical science

Mechanics is the basis of much of both early and modern technology. During most of human existence mechanical phenomena were recognised and utilised without much in the way of theoretical understanding. The dominant role of science in the creation and production of technology is a recent phenomenon. With virtually no mechanical theory the ancient Egyptians built the pyramids and transported monoliths weighing several hundreds of tonnes. The advances in technology were based on empirical observations and not on theory. The size of wagon wheels increased in diameter not because it was deduced that a large diameter caused less friction, but through the knowledge that wagons with large wheels were easier to pull. Despite their obvious importance to society the constructions of artisans were regarded by Confucian scholars and classical philosophers as unworthy of attention. Plato (*Gorgias* 512b–e) wrote of the engineer: 'at times he has no less power to save lives than the general...do you place him in the same class as the advocate...You disdain him and his craft and you would call him engineer as a term of reproach and would refuse...to give your daughter to his son'. Plutarch (*Marcellus* XVII, 3–4) claimed that Archimedes held the practical arts in disdain, 'regarding the work of an engineer and every art that ministers to the needs of life as ignoble and vulgar'. While it is unlikely that Archimedes, who contributed so much to both the theory and practice of mechanics, held these views himself, it does represent educated opinion in Plutarch's time. In fact many Roman engineers were slaves, graduates of a technical school established for them by the wealthy Crassus, a member of the First Triumvirate (Straub 1952:29–30). Even Vitruvius, a renowned engineer and architect of early Imperial Rome, reveals his plebeian origins in the poor Latin of his *Ten books on architecture*.

Mechanical science as it is known today began with the ancient Greeks. The first great contribution was made by Archimedes (287–212 BC) who firmly established the principle of the lever and the theory of buoyancy. The Greeks were less competent with problems concerning the motion of bodies. The attempts by Aristotle (384–322 BC) to explain motion were more of a hindrance than a help because, in common with most Greek philosophers, he was only concerned with the question of *why* a physical phenomenon occurred; it was not until the Rennaissance period that philosophers began to ask the more testable question of *how* it occurred. During the Roman era mechanical science continued to develop in the Graeco–Egyptian city of Alexandria. In the Dark Ages that followed the fall of Rome knowledge of mechanics was maintained and developed by the Arabs through whom the Greek treatises were eventually transmitted back to Medieval Europe.

The emergence of contemporary mechanics theory was heralded by the studies of Galileo Galilei (1564–1642). Prevented from continuing his work on astronomy by the Inquisition, Galileo turned his attention to the less-controversial study of mechanics, and in doing so he paved the way for Newton's discoveries. The foundations of classical mechanics were laid by Isaac Newton (1642–1727) in his famous *Philosophiae naturalis principia mathematica*, which is the most significant single publication in the history of science. Newtonian mechanics allows one to predict the actual motion of all bodies both heavenly and earth-bound with, as Einstein put it, 'a delicacy of detail little short of wonderful'. The *Principia* fired the imaginations of many educated Europeans and created the readership needed for the publication of popular books on mechanics. The most interesting of these earlier works was *A course of experimental philosophy* written by John Theophilus Desaguliers (1683–1744), a Huguenot refugee who was a friend of Newton and, in later life, chaplain to the Prince of Wales. Desaguliers' book is a lively introduction to the science of mechanics and some of the data in it has been invaluable for our work. An influential but poorly attended course of popular lectures on mechanics was given by Thomas Young (1773–1829) at the Royal Institution during 1802. Young's lack of success was not entirely due to his subject matter. His turgid style disappointed the audience, and Young also had competition from the handsome Humphrey Davy whose lively lectures on chemistry, complete with spectacular experiments, were far more appealing, especially to the young ladies.

The nineteenth century saw the spread of mechanical science to the working class through the Mechanics Institutes. This very British self-help movement owed much to George Birkbeck (1766–1841), the Professor of Natural Philosophy at the

Andersonian Institute in Glasgow. Birkbeck was aware of the keen interest of the tradesmen who made his apparatus and arranged to give a course of lectures for them on mechanics and science. Birkbeck's first lecture was given to an audience of 75 mechanics in the autumn of 1800 – by his fourth lecture the audience had grown to 500. Independent Mechanics Institutes spread quickly through Britain and the idea was exported – mainly to the east coast of the United States and to Australia. The original purpose of Mechanics Institutes was to instruct factory workers in subjects that directly related to their jobs. However these aims were modified as clerks and shop assistants started to attend and eventually dominate the audiences. Gradually the liberal arts began to oust the sciences, and in time the vitality of the Institutes declined. Now all that remains are the sad buildings with their ornate inscriptions proclaiming their original status, and which now only offer bingo on a Wednesday night.

There have been few attempts to popularise mechanics in the twentieth century. Most modern basic texts on mechanics for engineers and scientists are regrettably boring and unlikely to be read by people outside the field. It is therefore not surprising that few scholars outside the physical sciences understand even basic mechanical terms like mass or acceleration; yet, as C. P. Snow (1962:15) said some years ago, this lack of scientific knowledge is the equivalent of being illiterate.

Some knowledge of mechanics is essential for a proper understanding and appreciation of material culture. Mechanics is not a sword that unaided can cut through archaeological knots. However it can be used to assess the role or efficiency of artifacts and technological processes and to understand their design.

Mechanics of material culture

Mechanics plays a fundamental role in the study of material culture, but because it is not normally part of teaching in the humanities many scholars and students of material culture are unaware of how it can be applied. In simple terms, mechanics can explain how artifacts operate technologically and how efficient or effective they are. From this information artifacts and their functional and stylistic attributes can be better identified, making it possible to devise more meaningful artifact classifications. These kinds of data can then be used to reconstruct culture history, to measure material development and to develop theories of cultural change.

One of the basic analytical tools of archaeology and cultural anthropology is artifact classification, and it is this area of study on which these two disciplines were originally built. In the nineteenth century many of the collections held by antiquarians were opened to public view for the first time and the question of how to display them meaningfully became an immediate one. Christian Thomsen, Denmark's first museum curator, separated his collections into three groups representing successive cultural phases which he called the Stone, Bronze and Iron Ages. Thomsen's presentation soon became standard in museums throughout Europe, and with some elaboration it is still current.

The number of attributes of an artifact that can be chosen as criteria for constructing a classification can be enormous and the selection will depend on the kinds of information that the classification is expected to provide. Some attributes tell us about style changes and fashion, while others can tell us about function and performance. For many artifacts – such as weapons, lifting devices, boats and musical instruments – some of the most significant functional attributes reflect mechanical behaviour. The basic attributes of artifacts are those of material, shape and function. Sometimes the attributes chosen to reveal an informative patterning in an archaeological collection are not at all well considered. One of the major problems encountered in selecting the more informative attributes is that often artifact function and performance are poorly understood. Because of this difficulty many typologies of prehistoric flaked stone tools are flawed. In archaeology there has been a consistent tendency to construct over-elaborate stone tool typologies based primarily on attributes of artifact form. Stone tool typologies of artifacts from western Europe, North America and Australia usually rely on formal attributes like size, plan-shape and location of retouch on the stone tool. By providing the information that archaeologists have often never had – how artifacts functioned – classification will be made a far easier exercise, as well as being far more informative.

Methods of mechanical analysis

A mechanical problem in material culture studies can be analysed either theoretically or experimentally. In this book theoretical methods are emphasised because we are aware that there is a need to introduce basic mechanical concepts to our readers. The first and most important step in an analysis is mathematical modelling. It is the normal procedure in mechanical studies to simplify an actual physical situation to enable easy analysis, and many times in this book we have done just this. For example, when dealing with problems of levers, one can usually assume that they are rigid and can ignore their deformation. On the other hand, if one is considering a beam supporting a roof, attention is focussed primarily on the beam's deformation and strength. Mathematical modelling is not always an easy art and in an introductory book such as this we do not pretend to teach all the tricks.

Once the physical problem has been modelled one then needs mechanical data for its analysis. Much basic physical data can be taken from the engineering sciences. It is, for instance, easy to find the density of air or viscosity of water, but some data is not directly available and there is room for much more experimental work. In some cases, the data is unavailable because the mechanical application or process is now antiquated. For example since human power is no longer important in technologically developed societies, there is little modern data on the performances of people engaged in a wide range of traditional tasks. Even the discipline of ergonomics, which is the study of a person's efficiency in a work environment, concerns itself with the force a person can exert on a fixed object, or in the total energy expended, but not with the *useful mechanical work*. There is some data on human power available from sport's medicine, but mostly we have had to rely on our own experiments or on nineteenth-century data. Another example of reliance on 'old' data concerns the friction of ropes over pulleys, which was a topic of vital interest in the nineteenth century but not studied at all now. Some data relating to the behaviour or performance of artifacts is not available, and it is therefore necessary to carry out replicative or model experiments. For instance, in Egypt, ropes are still made by hand from palm fibres in the same way that they were during Dynastic times, so by testing the strength of these ropes one has a fair idea of the strength of comparable ancient ones. Whenever possible we provide tables of available data which will enable reasonable calculations to be made.

Mechanical experimentation
Mechanical experiments on the performance of artifacts are of two kinds: field and model experiments. To resolve the mechanical aspect of a particular problem it is often necessary to study a much simpler situation than the real one. In the analysis of microscopic wear on the cutting edges of stone tools one needs to identify the significant characteristics of small fractures called flake scars (Cotterell and Kamminga 1979, 1987). Understanding these scars and deriving useful information from them to identify the uses of stone tools cannot come about by studying only the scars on archaeological specimens. First one has to perform model experiments in which the variables that effect the shapes of the fractures are isolated and controlled, so that meaningful patterns can be derived from the infinite variety of edge fractures. Sometimes model experiments are forced on us by economic restraints. No one is ever again going to attempt to move a monolith like the 800-tonne Colossi of Memnon by manpower alone. Often in experimental modelling, where the model is smaller than full-scale, mere geometric scaling down is not enough. It is also necessary to ensure that the physical processes involved are properly scaled. For example, if we want to test a model spear in a small wind tunnel, the air speed must be scaled so that the pattern of air flow is similar to that around a full-size spear.

Introduction

Definitions and units

All disciplines of necessity acquire technical words to make description easier and more precise. Unfortunately this means that there are different terminologies for each discipline. While the difficulty can be alleviated a little, it is inherent in modern science and cannot be avoided. A person who wants to understand mechanics simply must learn the appropriate vocabulary. To add to the problem many everyday words have acquired a precise technical meaning. For example we shall see that, in mechanics, the word *work* has a limited meaning that excludes many common events like office work. In the various chapters that follow we have tried to introduce technical definitions in as painless a way as possible.

Since mechanics is above all else concerned with measurement, standards for comparison are necessary. Even in the earliest civilisations there was a need for standardised measurements, though their recognition was only local and often the measure changed with the commodity being measured. It is only within the last few years that a sensible and systematic set of universal units, the *Système International*, has been adopted. This – we hope – final standardisation has taken a long time to establish.

Table 1.1 *SI units*

SI basic units

Quantity	Name	Symbol
length	metre	m
mass	kilogram	kg
time	second	s
temperature	degree celsius	°C

SI derived units with special names

Quantity	Name	Symbol	Expression in terms of other units	Expression in terms of SI base units
frequency	hertz	Hz		/s
force	newton	N		kg m/s^2
pressure, stress	pascal	Pa	N/m^2	kg/m s^2
work, energy	joule	J	Nm	kg m^2/s^2
power	watt	W	J/s	kg m^2/s^3

Preferred SI multipliers and submultipliers

Multiplying factor	Prefix	Symbol
10^9	giga	G
10^6	mega	M
10^3	kilo	k
10^{-3}	mili	m
10^{-6}	micro	μ
10^{-9}	nano	n

The first General Conference of Weights and Measures met as far back as 1889 in Paris and it was at this time that the international prototypes of the metre and kilogram were defined. There were moves in 1935 to establish the metre, kilogram and second as the basic set of units, but World War II intervened and it was not until 1954 that they were formally accepted as the basic international units. The name, Système International, with the abbreviation SI, was adopted by the Eleventh General Conference of Weights and Measures in 1960. Since the 1970s most countries have adopted the Système International and it is now used in all scientific publications. The basic SI units and those derived from them are introduced in the text where they are first met, and a list of those with special names is given in Table 1.1.

A glossary of important mechanical terms (Appendix I) together with a list of the major symbols used (Appendix II) is included to provide assistance to the reader in understanding the technical content of the book. A list of simple trigonometrical and geometrical relations is given in Appendix III.

2

Basic mechanics

The principles of mechanics are so basic that people rarely think about them. By simply picking up this book the reader is involved in a mechanical action. As Leonardo da Vinci wrote, 'mechanical science is the noblest and above all the others the most useful, seeing that by means of it all animated bodies which have movement perform their actions' (Hart 1925:101). In this chapter we outline the basic mechanics of bodies. Although many advances were made in mechanics before the seventeenth century, it was Newton who first gave a structure to the science.

Space and time

In Newtonian mechanics space and time are absolute. For the purpose of understanding the mechanics of terrestrial bodies we can disregard the fact that, as Einstein has shown, they are never strictly absolute. Even the orbits of the space satellites can be calculated with extreme accuracy solely by classical mechanics. Only incredibly minute deviations from classical mechanics can be found within the solar system, such as an advance in the perihelion[1] of Mercury by 43 seconds of an arc per century (Dampier 1968:409).

To describe space one first needs a unit of length, which in the Système International is the metre (m). Until 1960 the metre standard was a bar of platinum-iridium kept in Paris and was conceived as being one ten-millionth of the distance between the equator and the North Pole; but the surveyors got their sums slightly wrong (Dampier 1968:207). Today the metre is defined as the distance travelled by light in a vacuum during the fraction 1/299,792,458 of a second.

The early standards of length were based on parts of the human body (Table 2.1). For example the cubit was the length of the forearm and extended hand, and was represented as such in Egyptian hieroglyphics. As in the Imperial System the measures of lengths used in the early standards were a variety of multiples of each other. China was like any other country in this respect prior to the unification of the states under the Emperor Qin Shihuang in 221 BC. The first emperor's advisors acquired decimal notation from the Mohist school of philosophy and arranged their units of length in powers of ten, pre-empting the French decimalisation by 2000 years (Needham and Wang 1962:17,18).

[1] The perihelion is the point in a planet's orbit nearest to the sun.

To study the motion of a body it is necessary to specify its position relative to a fixed reference point. We all understand how the location of a geographical feature can be described by stating that it is so many kilometres north and so many west of a certain

Table 2.1. *Ancient units of length*

Region	Sub-units	Unit	Length (mm)
Mesopotamia	30 shusi	kus or cubit	530
Egypt, from about 3000 BC	7 palms	Royal cubit	524
	6 palms	short cubit	450
	4 digits	palm	75
Greece, Classical	24 dactyls	Olympic cubit	462
	16 dactyls	foot	308
	12 dactyls	span	231
	4 dactyls	palm	77
Rome	12 unciae	foot (pes)	295
	16 digits		
	3 unciae	palm	74
	4 digits		
China, after unification	10 chi	zhang	3333
	10 cun	chi	333
	10 fen	cun	33

Fig. 2.1. Cartesian system of coordinates.

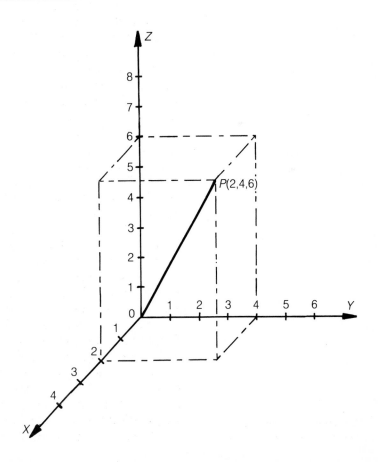

position. This method of location is a particular case of a general system first developed by René Descartes (1596–1650). In this system three mutually perpendicular axes *X,Y,Z* passing through a particular point *O* are taken as reference axes (Fig. 2.1). The position of any point *P* can be given in terms of the distances from the three references axes. These three distances are called the *coordinates* of the point *P*. Thus in Fig. 2.1 the point *P* is shown as having coordinates 2,4,6. There are other methods of defining position, all of which need three measurements, but the cartesian system is the most versatile.

Precise measurement of time was not possible before the invention of the pendulum clock. It is said that Galileo realised that a pendulum could be adapted for time-keeping by observing the swinging of suspended lamps in the cathedral at Pisa. By timing the oscillations with his pulse Galileo found that they were constant. Experiments later showed him that the period of a pendulum's oscillation is independent of the amplitude of the swing. Just before his death Galileo realised that a pendulum could be combined with a pin-wheel escapement to make an accurate clock. By this time he was blind, and so gave the instructions to build the clock to his son Vincenzio. However Vincenzio was not particularly diligent and he died before he completed the clock. The Dutch astronomer, Christian Huygens (1629–1695), was aware of Galileo's discoveries and had the honour of building the first pendulum clock, although he used the inferior verge escapement (Lloyd 1957:662). The pendulum clock had a time-keeping accuracy an order of magnitude better than any other clock of the period. These days atomic clocks which measure the oscillations in individual atoms of caesium achieve accuracies so great that the cumulative error is only one second in a thousand years. The second (s) is the SI unit of time.

Mass

Mass and *weight* are terms that are frequently confused. The distinction eluded all philosophers until as late as the seventeenth century. Newton described mass as the *quantity of matter* in a body. An object has the same mass wherever its location – be it on earth, the moon or in outer space. Weight, which varies from place to place, is the gravitational force acting on the mass. The common method of measuring mass with a beam balance actually compares weights but, since both the standard mass and the object being weighed are subject to the same gravitational field, the masses are exactly proportional to their weights. The modern spring balance measures mass by the deflection of the spring caused by the weight, and gives slightly different values in different parts of the world. Hence a person who weighs 70 kg on bathroom scales in Paris would weigh about 60 g less on the same scales in Washington.

Having, we hope, thrown some light on the difference

between mass and weight, we use the terms mainly in their normal English sense in the rest of this book. The problem is that no verb derives from the noun, mass, and to be strict about its usage leads to very clumsy English. So we shall say that particular objects weigh such and such when strictly we should be referring to their mass. The confusion between mass and weight was compounded by the old Imperial System in which the pound was used as a unit for both. In the Systéme International the kilogram (kg) is the unit of mass. Unlike the units of length and time, the unit of mass cannot be defined in terms of standards that are forever renewable, but is the mass of a standard cylinder, of platinum-iridium, kept at the Bureau International des Poids et Mésures in Paris.

Standard masses, which date back to the beginning of the third millennium BC, were first used to weigh gold. Prior to about 1450 BC standard masses were made of stone which means that most of those found have not deteriorated through the centuries. Even in early times efforts were made to maintain the uniformity of the standard. There is, for example, a weight in the British Museum that has a cuneiform inscription certifying it to be a standard that King Nebuchadnezzar II (605–526 BC) had copied from a weight of King Shulgi dating to about 2100 BC. The Chinese during the time of first unification made an effort to decimalise the Chinese system of weights. The new system, however, was not accepted nationally, and the decimal system for weights was officially fixed much later in AD 992 though the older measures survived until the Ming Dynasty. The modern approximate equivalents of ancient standard masses are shown in Table 2.2.

Table 2.2 *Ancient units of mass*

Region	Sub-units	Unit	Mass
Mesopotamia, 2400–600 BC	50 shekels	mina	489–680 g
Egypt, 2900–300 BC	10 debens	sep	933 g
	10 kedet	deben	93 g
Biblical Palestine	60 minas	kikar	49 kg
	50 shekels	mina	818 g
	2 bekas	shekel	16 g
	10 geras	beka	8 g
Classical Greece	60 minas	talent	26 kg
	100 drachmas	mina	437 g
	6 obols	drachma	4 g
Roman Empire	80 librae	talent	26 kg
	12 unciae	librae	327 g
	8 drachmas	unciae	27 g
China, after AD 992	100 jin	dan	50 kg
	10 liang	jin	500 g
	10 qian	liang	50 g

Force

People have a commonsense understanding of force. When
we pick up a book our muscles tense to resist its weight. We
perceive the degree of force by the tension our muscles are put
under and how it registers in the nerves of our fingers. The
experience of force is so fundamental that during recorded history
there have been innumerable attempts to define it. Aristotle
ascribed violent motion to a force. By violent motion he meant
motion away from the object's natural place, such as when a
stone is thrown in the air. Aristotle failed to realise that the
'natural motion' of a stone falling back to earth was also due to a
force. The contemporary Chinese Mohists had a more general
conception of force as an agency for causing things to move
(Needham and Wang 1962:19). Leonardo da Vinci went further,
observing that 'nothing whatever can be moved by itself, but its
motion is effected through another. This other is the force' (Hart
1925:79). Elsewhere in his notes da Vinci seems to grasp that
force does not in itself have reality but is a manifestation of
motion. In an endeavour to explain this metaphysical aspect of
force da Vinci wrote: 'Force I define as a spiritual power,
incorporeal and invisible...spiritual because in this force there is
an active incorporeal life, and I call it invisible because the
body...does not increase in weight or size'. Galileo in his *Dialogues
concerning the two new sciences* came close to the classical
conception by proposing that a force accelerates a body. It was of
course Newton who first gave the complete relationship between
force, mass and motion.

The laws of motion

All of classical mechanics derives ultimately from Newton's
famous three laws of motion. A free translation of these laws from
the Latin of the *Principia* goes as follows:

  I Every body continues in its state of rest or uniform motion
    in a straight line unless it is compelled to change that state
    by forces applied to it.
  II The rate of change of momentum is proportional to the
    applied force and is in the direction of that force.
  III To every action there is opposed a reaction; in other words,
    the mutual actions of two bodies upon each other are
    always equal and opposite.

Newton's major innovation was his second law. The first
law, which is really only a special case of the second, was already
anticipated by Galileo in his treatment of projectiles (Galileo
1638:268), while the third law was already understood to apply
to bodies at rest or in uniform motion; for instance, the Mohists
in China realised that a suspending force acts in the opposite
direction to the force that pulls downwards (Needham and Wang
1962:19); similarly, Leonardo da Vinci in his notes on the
parachute wrote that 'an object offers as much resistance to the

air as the air does to the object' (Hart 1925:150). Newton's contribution was his appreciation that the third law applied equally well to bodies in unsteady accelerating motion.

Newton defined momentum as the product of the mass of a body and its velocity. Therefore the rate of change of momentum is the product of the mass (m) and the rate of change of velocity, which is called acceleration (**a**). The second law can be expressed in mathematical terms by:

$$\mathbf{F} = m\mathbf{a}. \tag{2.1}$$

This equation enables us to define and quantify force (**F**) as that which, when imposed on a unit mass, produces a unit acceleration. In the Système International the unit of force is the newton (N), which is the force required to accelerate one kilogram by one metre per second. It is rather appropriate that a force of one newton is approximately equal to the weight of an apple.[2] Newton's first law follows from the second. If no force is applied to a body then there is no change in its momentum and the body remains either at rest or travelling with a constant velocity.

Newton's third law is evident in simple physical acts. In picking up a book we have to exert an upward force. At the same time the book exerts an equal and opposite force on our hand. If we hold the book still, the force applied by our hand must equal the weight of the book. To accelerate the book upwards we must apply a force greater than its weight, and Newton's second law tells us the acceleration. The third law applies throughout, and the force we exert on the book is equal and opposite to the force exerted by it on our hand whether it is being accelerated or not.

The main sources of force in pre-industrial technology

There are two types of force: one performs a task, the other resists its performance. In pre-industrial cultures muscles and gravity provided the most readily available forces. We shall also briefly discuss the harnessing of water and wind power to generate forces.

Two forces have to be overcome in performing a task: friction and gravity. Friction arises because of the resistance to relative motion between two solid objects, as we discuss in this section, or from the motion of a body through air or water (see Chapters 3, 7 and 9). Gravity, which can assist in the performance of a task, can also be a force that has to be overcome. An obvious example of the latter type is in any task that involves lifting an object.

Muscular force

The force most readily available to us is that provided by our own muscles. Until mechanisation people relied almost entirely on their own strength to overcome gravity and friction and, because of the physical versatility of human beings, this source of power has

---

[2] Although there is no direct evidence for the tradition that Newton suddenly realised the universality of gravity by observing an apple fall, the adoption of the newton as the unit of force in the Système International makes it particularly apt. The story apparently stemmed from Hannah Barton, Newton's favourite niece, and housekeeper during his later years (Voltaire 1785, III:175).

remained important right into the present century, even in developed countries.

When a muscle receives the appropriate nerve signal, it shortens in length and can produce a tensile force of up to 0.3 N per square millimetre of muscle cross-sectional area (Hertzberg 1972:548). The major muscles of the human body are attached either directly or by tendons to a lever system formed by the bones, and the force that we can apply depends on the mechanics of that system as well as on the sizes of the muscles involved. We can exert our greatest effort while pushing or pulling against an immovable object such as a wall (see Table 2.3). In the case of pressing on a wall our muscles tighten but do not change their length. Although we perform no external work – that is, we do not move the wall – we do expend energy in maintaining our muscles in a state of tension; we tire quickly and our maximum effort can only be maintained for a few seconds. Over a period of hours only 15–20% of the maximum force can be sustained (Hertzberg 1972:550).

If we perform external work, such as pulling a sledge, then the force that we can exert will be greatly reduced. Because contemporary writers on manpower in prehistory have little direct experience of manual labour they often grossly overestimate average human strength. Earlier writers and engineers had a much more realistic idea of human capabilities. In the late seventeenth century the French academician Philippe de la Hire (1640–1718) wrote that a man could exert a force of 27 livres (132 N), or one-seventh that which could be performed by a horse (de la Hire 1699:98). Jean Baptiste Le Bas (1797–1873), commissioned in 1833 to erect the Egyptian obelisk in Paris (a topic we shall return to in Chapter 8), decided on a figure of 98 N as the force that his soldiers could exert on a capstan (Gorringe 1885:89). Other nineteenth-century writers give values of up to 130 N for pushing or pulling tasks (Rankine 1889:251). The largest force quoted by the Scottish engineer William Macquorn

Table 2.3 *Maximum effort pushing or pulling against a fixed object*

Mode of exerting force	Force (N)
pushing horizontally with one hand	130
pulling horizontally with one hand	100
pushing vertically upwards with one hand	150
pulling vertically downwards with one hand	250
pushing with both hands horizontally against a wall using a foothold	700
pushing with shoulder against a wall using a foothold	860
pushing with both hands while braced between two walls	860

Source: Hertzberg 1972

Rankine (1820–1872) in his *Useful rules and tables* is 178 N for hauling up weights with a rope (Rankine 1889:25).

All the estimates we cite are for the force that a man can exert over an extended period, but even over short periods of less than a minute the maximum force is not especially great. One afternoon a number of engineering students performed an experiment to determine the maximum force they could exert in an experimental situation. The task was to raise a weight 3·4 m from the ground by pulling on a horizontal rope that ran over pulleys. The students quickly found that the stance of anchorman in a tug-of-war allowed them to lift the heaviest weight. In this position the heaviest man could pull the hardest, and the slightly overweight middle-aged lecturer could impress his students by being able to lift more than they could. The maximum force exerted by the students varied from 325 to 590 N, which was 0·56 to 0·72 (average 0·65) of their body weight. We stress that these forces represent the maximum that the students could exert while drawing the rope a short distance, since after their performance it was necessary to revive them with a liberal supply of Australian beer. When many hundreds of men were assembled to perform such tasks as moving heavy statues they would have been expected to work for a number of hours and could not have continually exerted forces as large as the students did in our experiment.

Gravitational force

It was Aristotle's belief that heavy bodies fell to earth because that was their natural place (Aristotle, *De Caelo* III, 2). The property that these bodies possessed to make them fall Aristotle called gravity. It was thought that the heavier the body the more gravity it had, and consequently the faster it would fall. Before the Renaissance period philosophers denied the relevance of experimental observation to the understanding of natural phenomena, and it was not until 1590 that heavy and light weights were shown to fall together. These experiments, carried out by Simon Stevin (1548–1620), were repeated by Galileo (1638) who dropped balls made of different materials (Dampier 1968:130). Galileo found that balls of denser materials did fall slightly faster, but rightly concluded that the differences were due to the resistance of the air and that in a vacuum all bodies would fall with the same speed. Importantly, Galileo demonstrated that in free fall the velocity of a body increases with constant acceleration.[3] It is of course the force of gravity that causes a falling body to accelerate.

Newton's great achievement was his realisation that the earth's gravity extended to the moon and beyond. Making use of the observations of the German astronomer Johann Kepler (1571–1630), that the square of a planet's year is proportional to the cube of its mean distance from the sun, Newton deduced that

---

[3] Galileo (1638) overcame the problem of accurately observing free fall by rolling the balls down an incline and weighing the water issuing from a water-clock to time the event.

the forces which keep the planets in their orbit are inversely
proportional to the square of their distances from the sun. Gravity
is a ghostly tug-of-war between distant masses. Newton's universal
law for the gravitational force F separated by a distance r can be
written algebraically as

$$F = G\frac{m_1 m_2}{r^2} \qquad\qquad (2.2)$$

where G is the constant of universal gravitation, which
experiments show to be 6.67×10^{-11} m³ kg s². The universal law
of gravitation was fully understood by Newton as early as 1666,
but he delayed publication for 20 years until he could prove that
the mass of a spherical body like the earth acted as if it were all
concentrated at its centre.

  According to the universal law of gravitation the force acting
on objects on the earth's surface is in proportion to their mass.
Hence from Newton's second law all objects in free fall accelerate
at the same rate (which as is usual will be denoted by g). We can
use the universal law of gravitation to calculate g as 9.82 m/s²
from the earth's mass (5.976×10^{24} kg) and mean radius
(6.371×10^6 m). Calculating in this manner the acceleration due
to gravity neglects the effect of the rotation of the earth and the
more usual value quoted is 9.81 m/s². Because the effect of the
earth's rotation varies from zero at the poles to a maximum at the
the equator, and because the earth is not a true sphere but is
slightly flattened at the poles, the acceleration due to gravity is
about half a percent greater at the poles than at the equator. The
proximity of large land masses and variations in the density of the
earth's crust also slightly affect the local value of the constant of
acceleration. Variation in the acceleration due to gravity was first
observed in 1672 when Jean Richer was sent by Colbert, a
minister of Louis XIV, to Cayenne, the capital of French Guiana,
to carry out astronomical observations for the purpose of
improving navigation (Dampier 1968:150). While the pendulum
clock Richer took with him had kept correct time in Paris, it lost
2.5 minutes a day in Cayenne.

  Gravity acts on a body whether it is in free fall or at rest,
and the gravitational force of a body is called its weight. The
weight of a one kilogram mass which under free fall would
accelerate at 9.81 m/s² is therefore 9.81 N. The weight of a body,
unlike its mass, varies slightly from place to place on the
earth's surface because of the variation in gravity and speed of the
earth's rotation; hence the possibility of losing weight merely by
travelling from one place to another. In this book we shall take
the weight of a body in newtons as 9.81 times its mass in
kilograms.

  The gravitational force acts through a particular point
which is called the centre of gravity. The concept of a body's
centre of gravity is very old. Archimedes wrote a book specifically

on the centre of gravity which unfortunately has been lost, but his treatise *On the equilibrium of planes* identifies the centre of gravity of many two-dimensional shapes (Heath 1897). The first surviving theoretical study of the centre of gravity in a solid body is contained in the manuscripts of Leonardo da Vinci (Hart 1925:103).

Frictional force

Frictional forces are unlike muscular or gravitational forces in that they cannot initiate motion but can only resist it. In many circumstances friction is undesirable, but if it were suddenly to disappear entirely from the world we would be unable to do normal things like walk or light matches. Of course the energy absorbed by friction can be costly in economic terms and ways have been sought of reducing it; for example an Egyptian chariot dating to about 1400 BC, found in the tomb of Yuaa and Thuiu, had animal fat on its axles that was presumably for the purpose of lubrication (Dowson 1979:30).

Although the two most fundamental statements on friction are attributed to Guillaume Amontons (1663–1705) they had already been made some 200 years earlier by Leonardo da Vinci (Dowson 1979:99). Amontons reported to the French Royal Academy that the frictional force between two sliding surfaces was proportional to the force pressing them together and independent of their contact area. The Academy accepted Amontons' first observation, but the second caused some astonishment and the senior academician de la Hire was motivated to check his experiments (Dowson 1979:156, 157). De la Hire's experiments confirmed Amontons' findings. The modern explanation for the apparent paradox is that surfaces – even precision-ground steel ones – only make contact over a finite number of asperities. The force pressing the two surfaces together deforms the asperities so that their actual area of contact is proportional to the force. Therefore the total area of the surfaces is unimportant.

When a sledge is on the level the perpendicular contact force F_c between its runners and the ground is equal and opposite to the sledge's weight mg (Fig. 2.2). If we pull horizontally on the sledge with a force F an opposing frictional force F_f is developed. The sledge starts to slide if the applied force is greater than the critical value of the frictional force F_f^*. It takes a larger force to start the sledge sliding than that necessary to keep it moving. The first observation that static friction is greater than sliding or dynamic friction was made by the Greek philosopher Themistius (390–320 BC), but the difference must have been known to the ancient Egyptians, who moved quite enormous masses on sledges. According to Amontons the ratio of the critical frictional force to the contact force (F_f^*/F_c) is a constant which is now called the coefficient of friction μ. Often it is more convenient to use the

28   Basic mechanics

Table 2.4 *Typical values of the coefficient of sliding friction*

Surfaces in contact	Condition of surfaces	Static or dynamic friction	Coefficient of friction
ice on ice	at 0 °C	static	0·05–0·15
		dynamic	0·02
ski on snow	at 0 °C	dynamic	0·1–0·3
wood on wood	dry	static	0·25–0·5
		dynamic	0·2–0·5
	slightly unctuous	dynamic	0·15
	lubricated with lard or tallow	dynamic	0·1
wood on grass	green	static	0·5
		dynamic	0·35
	dry	dynamic	0·25
wrought iron on wood	dry	dynamic	0·25–0·6
	wet	dynamic	0·25
	lubricated with lard or tallow	dynamic	0·10
leather on wood	dry	dynamic	0·3–0·35
	wet	dynamic	0·3
leather on bronze	dry	dynamic	0·55
	wet	dynamic	0·35
	oiled	dynamic	0·15
bronze on bronze	dry	dynamic	0·2
	lubricated with lard or tallow	dynamic	0·07–0·08
bronze on wrought iron	slightly unctuous	dynamic	0·15

Source: Bowden and Tabor 1950, Clark 1878:722, 723, and the authors' experiments

Fig. 2.2. Forces acting on a Sumerian sledge.

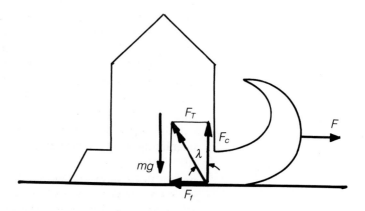

friction angle λ, which is defined as the angle between the perpendicular to the surface and the total force F_T, instead of the coefficient of friction μ (Fig. 2.2), where λ is given by

$$\mu = \tan \lambda. \tag{2.3}$$

The static and dynamic coefficients of friction are given in Table 2.4 for a number of materials likely to have been used prior to the Industrial Age.

Scalars and vectors

The mechanical quantities we introduce in this chapter are of two types: scalars and vectors. Scalar quantities only have magnitude and they can be added using the ordinary rules of arithmetic. Mass and time are both examples of scalar quantities. Vectors, on the other hand, need a direction as well as magnitude to describe them completely. Force and acceleration are vectors. In this book we indicate vectors by bold face type and scalars, or the magnitude of a vector, by italics.

In common speech velocity is synonymous to speed, but in mechanics velocity is a vector quantity. Speed is only the magnitude of the velocity. For example, to determine the velocity of a ship, one needs to know both its speed and course. A special arithmetic is needed for vector addition. Let us examine the addition of two velocities. Consider the actual velocity of a galley being rowed at a speed of 10 km/h in a north-easterly direction while the tide is running in a southerly direction at a speed of 5 km/h. Although the steersman keeps the vessel on a northeasterly course, because the tide sweeps it south its actual course is more to the east. The actual velocity of the galley can be found geometrically. If the galley is kept to a steady speed, then after an hour's row the distance covered by the galley relative to the water can be represented by making the line *OG* in Fig 2.3 proportional to 10 km. However because of the tide the water will have travelled south by 5 km during the same time. Hence the actual position of the galley is at *R*, where *GR* is in proportion to 5 km. The actual velocity of the galley to an observer on land is therefore proportionate to the length *OR* (7.4 km/h) and has the direction of *O* to *R*. A way of expressing what we have done is to say that *OR* is the resultant of the addition of the two vectors: *OG* representing the velocity of the galley relative to the water and *GR* representing the velocity of the tide. So vector addition can be accomplished graphically by using the two vectors as adjacent sides of a parallelogram and taking the resultant vector (which we signify by a double-headed arrow) as the diagonal.

An alternative method of vector addition obtains the components of the vectors in any one direction so that they can be added by simple arithmetic. Any vector can be split into two components acting in the same plane. While the components of a vector can be taken in any two directions, it is usually most

convenient to take them at right-angles. In Fig. 2.4 we illustrate
the forces acting on a sledge carrying a large vessel that is being
pulled by a rope at an angle of about 40° to the horizontal,
depicted in an Egyptian bas-relief in the tomb of Sheshonq at
Abusir.[4] If we resolve the tension T in the rope into horizontal
and vertical components we can more easily apply Newton's first
law to determine its value. The horizontal and vertical

Fig. 2.3. Vectorial addition of velocities.

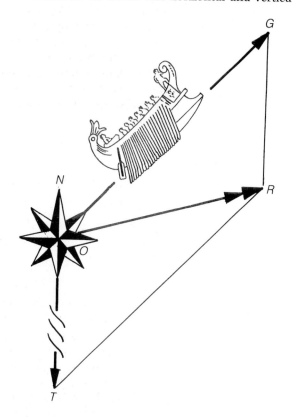

Fig. 2.4. A large vessel being pulled on
a sledge (based on a relief in the tomb
of Sheshonq at Abusir).

[4] We realise that the inclination of the
rope in this bas-relief is exaggerated;
Egyptian illustrations of some similar
scenes actually show the rope vertical.
This example was not chosen for its
exactness of representation, but because
it has all three kinds of forces we have
discussed – muscle, gravity and friction.

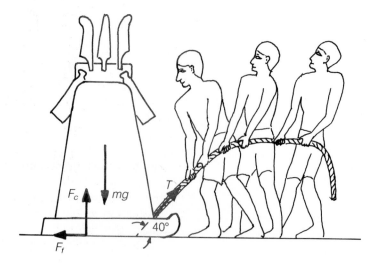

components of the tension T are $T \cos 40$ and $T \sin 40$
respectively. For uniform equilibrium motion Newton's first law
states that the total force must be zero. If the total force is zero,
then its component parts in the horizontal and vertical directions
must also be zero. Let us assume that together the vessel and
sledge weighed about 250 kg. If the wooden sledge was being
pulled over an unlubricated wooden track, then a reasonable
value to take for the dynamic coefficient of friction is 0·35
(Table 2.4). For steady sliding the frictional force F_f will be
0·35 F_c where F_c is the perpendicular contact force between the
sledge and the track. We can now express the conditions for
equilibrium by equating the sums of the horizontal and vertical
components of the forces acting on the sledge to zero. Hence,
taking account of their direction, we have for the horizontal
components

$$T \cos 40 - F_f = 0$$

or $\quad F_c = 2 \cdot 19\,T$

and for the vertical components

$$F_c + T \sin 40 = mg.$$

Hence on substitution for F_c we find that to keep the sledge
moving the three men must together produce a tension of 870 N
in the rope.

Acceleration
Velocity, because it is a vector, changes with both speed and
direction of motion. In mechanics we define acceleration as the
rate of change in velocity and it too is a vector. Let us consider
first acceleration due to change in speed.

A free falling body accelerates at a constant rate g and after
t seconds will have reached a speed $v = gt$. The distance s fallen in
time t is the average speed $v/2$ multiplied by the time t. That is,

$$s = \tfrac{1}{2} vt \qquad\qquad (2.4)$$

and if we substitute for the speed in terms of the acceleration we
obtain

$$s = \tfrac{1}{2} gt^2. \qquad\qquad (2.5)$$

This equation was first derived by Galileo (1638) to show that
bodies fall with a constant acceleration. Galileo went on to prove
a corollary that must have pleased his friend Kepler who believed
that God created the world in accordance with the principle of
perfect numbers (Dampier 1968:127). From equation (2.5) it can
be seen that the total distance fallen *in* equal time intervals is in
proportion to the squares of the real numbers, that is,
$(1:4:9:16:36\dots$ The distance fallen *during* each interval obtained
by differencing these squares is therefore in proportion to the
series of odd numbers $1:3:5:7\dots$

A body traversing a circular orbit of radius r with a

constant speed v provides an important example of acceleration that is caused by a change in the direction of motion. In this case the acceleration is not immediately obvious, but if we swing a weight around on a string we can feel the tension that accelerates the weight. While the body moves a distance vdt from A to B during a small time interval, dt, a line joining the body to the centre sweeps through the small angle $d\theta$ (Fig. 2.5). It is possible to measure this angle in degrees, though it is often more convenient in mechanics to use another unit called the radian (rad). In this system instead of dividing a full circle into 360 degrees it is divided into 2π radians, and one radian is approximately $57 \cdot 3°$. Because the circumference of a circle of radius r is $2\pi r$, the magnitude of an angle in radians is obtained by dividing the arc of the circle it subtends by the radius r. Hence the small angle $d\theta$ in radians is vdt/r. We define the angular velocity ω of the body as the rate of angular movement $d\theta/dt$; therefore

$$\omega = \frac{v}{r}.$$

(2.6)

During the time interval dt, the velocity vector rotates through the angle $d\theta = \omega dt$. To accomplish this rotation the velocity of the body must suffer a change of dv in a radial direction. Hence

$$dv = vd\theta = v\omega dt.$$

The acceleration a which is the rate of change of velocity is given by:

$$a = v\omega = \omega^2 r = \frac{v^2}{r}$$

(2.7)

and is directed towards the centre of rotation.

Fig. 2.5. Centripetal acceleration

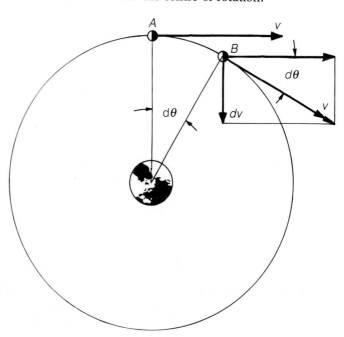

Newton probably derived this expression for centripetal acceleration in 1666 to test his universal law of gravitation.[5] The moon is held in stable orbit around the earth by the force of gravity which provides the necessary centripetal acceleration. The lunar month lasts just under 28 days ($2 \cdot 36 \times 10^6$ s), hence its angular velocity is $2\pi/(2 \cdot 36 \times 10^6) = 2 \cdot 66 \times 10^{-6}$ rad/s. Since the moon's mean distance from the earth is 384 400 km, its centripetal acceleration can be calculated from equation (2.7) to be $0 \cdot 00272$ m/s². Thus from Newton's second law of motion (equation 2.1) we know that the earth's gravitational force on the moon must be $0 \cdot 00272 \, m_m$, where m_m is the mass of the moon. On earth, bodies fall with an acceleration of $9 \cdot 81$ m/s², and hence the gravitational force on a mass of one kilogram on the earth's surface is $9 \cdot 81$ N. So the ratio of the gravitation force of the earth on the moon to that on a mass of one kilogram is $0 \cdot 000277 \, m_m$. The universal law of gravitation (equation 2.2) predicts that the ratio of the forces should be proportional to the ratio of the masses and inversely proportional to the square of the ratio of their distances from the centre of the earth. Since the mean radius of the earth is 6371 km, the ratios of the gravitational forces should be $0 \cdot 000275 \, m_m$. The small discrepancy between the two calculations is mainly due to the fact that the moon's orbit is slightly elliptical.

Work and energy

Work has many common meanings. No doubt all of us would agree that lifting a bag of cement is work. However office staff would be rather unhappy with us if we suggested to them that they did little work. Certainly in the everyday sense of the word they may perform a good deal of useful work and become quite fatigued, but the mechanical work they do is extremely small. Supporting a bag of cement on the shoulder, even for a few minutes, is quite hard work for the average person, but in fact no *mechanical* work is performed whatsoever in this task. Mechanical work is defined as the product of the force exerted on a body and the distance it moves in the direction of that force. The distinction between work in its technical sense and its common meaning must be clearly understood. It does not matter how fatiguing or useful the task is, in mechanics work has only one technical meaning: the product of the force and the distance through which it moves. One must also be careful to measure the distance in the direction of the force. So, if we carry a bag of cement up a slope to a set height, the work performed against gravity is equal to the weight of the bag multiplied by the height it is raised, irrespective of whether the slope is gentle or steep.

Work is a scalar quantity and its unit, the newton-metre (Nm), has the special name of joule (J) after James Joule (1818–1889). If we carry a 40 kg bag of cement to a height of 10 m, the work done on the bag is $40 \times 9 \cdot 81 \times 10 = 392$ J. Work

[5] Newton finally published his result in the *Principia* in 1687. Christian Huygens in the meantime had published the same result in 1673 (Dampier 1968:152).

can be performed either *against* a force or *by* a force. For example if we haul up a weight on a rope we do work against gravity, and if we lower it back down again an equal amount of work is done on us. By raising the weight from the ground it has been given the capacity to do work. The capacity of a body to do work is its energy. In the example we have just described the weight possesses *potential energy* equal to the work done in raising it. If we let it fall the weight will accelerate, losing potential energy but gaining *kinetic energy* by virtue of its motion. The pendulum is another instance where potential energy is converted into kinetic energy. Apart from a small loss due to friction and air resistance the potential energy of the pendulum bob swinging about a fixed point (*A* in Fig. 2.6) when it is at its highest point (*C*) is converted into kinetic energy as it swings down (to *B*), and then back into potential energy as it rises once more to its original height (*D*). Galileo (1638:206) realised that the essential point was that the pendulum bob reached its original height at the end of the swing. He illustrated this point quite dramatically by hammering nails in the path of the thread of the pendulum; whether the nail was positioned at *E* or *F* the pendulum bob still returned to the same height at which it was released (*G* and *I* respectively). If the nail was placed so close to *B* that it was impossible for the bob to rise to its original height, the thread would leap over and twist itself around the nail. What Galileo was demonstrating in this experiment was one of the most important principles in mechanics – the *principle of the conservation of mechanical energy*. If no work is done on a mechanical system nor any extracted in useful work or dissipated in friction, then the total energy of the system remains constant. A corollary of this principle is that if work is done on a mechanical system it will reappear as an increase in energy.

Let us consider the exchange in energies that occurs when a mass *m* falls freely to the ground through a height *h*. The potential energy *V* of the mass before it falls is equal to the work required to raise it to the height *h*.[6] That is,

$$V = mgh. \tag{2.8}$$

Fig. 2.6. Galileo's demonstration of conservation of mechanical energy in a pendulum (after Galileo 1638).

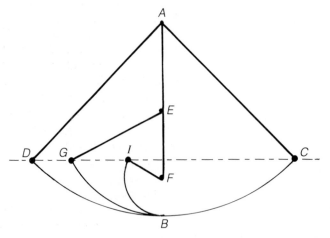

---

[6] Actually it does not matter what is taken as the datum level since different levels only introduce a constant.

At the moment of release the mass has no velocity, hence its kinetic energy is zero and the potential energy is the total energy. When the mass hits the ground the potential energy is exhausted and the kinetic energy constitutes its total energy. Therefore the potential energy is exchanged for kinetic energy and

$$T = V = mgh.$$

Kinetic energy arises from the motion of a body and must be a function of the mass m and its velocity v. From equation (2.5) the height through which the mass falls in time t is given by

$$h = \tfrac{1}{2}gt^2.$$

Since $v = gt$, this equation can be rewritten as:

$$h = \frac{v^2}{2g}.$$

Hence the kinetic energy of a body is given by

$$T = \frac{mv^2}{2}. \tag{2.9}$$

The principle of the conservation of mechanical energy is actually a special case of a far wider law. Julius von Mayer (1814–1878) was the first to realise that mechanical work could be converted into an equivalent amount of heat. Lacking the facilities for his own experiments Mayer used data already available to calculate a value for the mechanical equivalent of heat and his figure is not far different from today's value. However this achievement was the lesser part of Mayer's contribution. In the same paper in which he published the mechanical equivalent of heat Mayer also wrote, 'energy once in existence cannot be annihilated; it can only change its form' (Taylor 1959:291–303). At the time this statement of what is now called the *first law of thermodynamics* was ignored. It was the work of James Joule that finally made physicists realise that heat and mechanical energy were convertible. Joule was so obsessed by his idea of the mechanical equivalence of heat that on his honeymoon he visited the waterfall at Sollanches, in Switzerland, not for the romantic setting, but to measure the temperature at the top and bottom of the falls. The first law of thermodynamics indicated that the potential energy of the water would be converted into heat at the base of the falls, causing a temperature rise of about 1 °C. To his dismay, Joule found the water broke into spray before reaching the bottom of the falls and any increase in temperature was lost to the air (Wood 1925:54). We now know that all forms of energy, not only heat, are equivalent. Even mass is a form of energy; one so enormous that it threatens the very existence of humanity.

Power

Power (P) is the rate at which work is performed. Its unit, the joule per second (J/s), is called a watt (W) after James Watt

(1736–1819) who developed the first efficient steam engine and defined *horsepower*, the first unit of power. In 1782 Watt made a calculation in his notebook of the power of a horse based on the observations of Mr Wriggley, a millwright, that a millhorse walked a 24 ft (7·6 m) diameter circle making $2\frac{1}{2}$ turns a minute, or roughly at a speed of 180 ft/min (0·9 m/s). Estimating that the force exerted by the horse was 180 lb (800 N), Watt obtained its power as 180×180, or 32 400 ft lb/min (732 W). Watt later rounded off his figure for horsepower to 33 000 ft lb/min (746 W), a value it has kept to the present day (Dickinson and Jenkins 1927:354–5). Watt overestimated the force that an average horse could exert, and hence its power during a full day's work – perhaps deliberately since he was anxious that his steam engines performed better than the horses they replaced. Nineteenth-century measurements show that a horse can only develop about 570 W over an eight-hour day. An average horse can only sustain an output of one horsepower (746 W) for about three hours (Clark 1878:720).

The power figures that we quote are for a modern horse in a collar harness. In earlier times the horse was no bigger than a large pony, and certainly in the Western world was not fitted with such an efficient harness (see the discussion on harnesses in Chapter 8). The useful power of the horse in the past would therefore have been less than that of a modern horse. However, because it was expensive, the horse was not used for regular draught work until comparatively late in history. One exception was in mills where broken-down horses, 'with but three feet' as the fourth-century writer Ausonius bluntly puts it, were used (Moritz 1958:100). The commonest mill animal was the ass, which was cheap to maintain. Although horses were much more expensive to feed, presumably the low purchase cost of broken-down ones and their higher output more than compensated for this. Rankine (1889:251) quotes 410 W as the average power that a horse can develop in a mill. Desaguliers (1734:252) a century earlier drew attention to the fact that horses cannot give their best performance in a mill, especially if the turning circle is less than 12 m in diameter. Space has always been at a premium in urban areas and the turning circles of mills were very small. In Pompeii, where the bakeries can still be inspected, the animals had to walk as close to the millstone as possible, as the distance between the millstones was only about a metre (Moritz 1958:82). These mills would mostly have been powered by asses, but a stone relief uncovered in Rome (Fig. 2.7) reveals that horses had no better conditions.

Apart from the humans themselves the most important harnessed source of power in antiquity was the bullock, and in many developing countries it still is. In India today there are about 70 million bullocks capable of delivering about 24 GW of power – which is almost equal to that country's total electric power capacity (Premi 1979:1). During a six-hour day an average bullock can produce about 340 W of power (Premi 1979:23). The modern harness for a bullock is essentially the same as it has always been – a yoke bearing on the vertical hump – and although the bullock's power is less than that of a modern horse it is probably comparable to that of the earlier breeds. Since the bullock was much less costly to keep than the horse it is not surprising that the horse was reserved for occasions where speed was important.

The camel is more powerful than the horse and, though it was occasionally used for ploughing and drawing water, it served mainly as a pack animal. In Australia, camels (originally imported for the Burke and Wills expedition of 1860) were used well into the twentieth century to draw wagons (Barker 1964). Not only were camels powerful, but they could live off the vegetation of the Australian outback and were thus cheaper than bullocks, which had to carry their own feed. The standard camel wagon was drawn by 14 camels and on reasonable roads was loaded with up to 14 tonnes. Denny Murphy, who carted on contract for the Wiluna goldmines, had the best team and could keep it moving over soft ground until the front wheels had sunk up to the axle (Barker 1964:26). Lesser mortals used 18 camels on more rugged roads and carried a load of up to 10 tonnes. The task of driving a wagon along a road in the outback of Australia at the beginning of this century was probably equal to crossing an English field – for which a draught of about 920 N/tonne load is needed (see Table 8.3). Since the wagons themselves weighed about 4 tonnes,

Fig. 2.7. Second-century relief on a Roman sarcophagus depicting horse-driven grain mills. Now in the Museo Chiaramonti in the Vatican.

a reasonable estimate for the draught force of a camel is 1200 N.
The speed of the camel wagons is not reported, but they were
probably no slower than a bullock wagon whose average speed is
about 0.8 m/s; hence our estimate of the power of a camel is 960
W, or about 1·7 times the power of a horse. A modern collar-
harness was used on the Australian camels, but a yoke secured by
a strap behind the hump would be just as efficient and our
estimate of the capability of the camel would therefore equally
apply in earlier times.

The ass and the mule were also harnessed as draught
animals. The ass' docile nature made it ideal for mill work and it
played a minor role in ploughing. The mule is less amiable and
was mainly used as a pack animal and to pull wagons. The
values quoted for the power of these animals vary considerably
and we have taken the ones given by Rankine (1889:251)
(Table 2.5).

Though draught and pack animals were extensively used in
late antiquity human beings themselves were the most adaptable
and available source of power. Humans, and other vertebrate
animals, possess two kinds of muscle fibre (Alexander 1982).
During long-term effort the muscles are sustained by an aerobic
metabolism in which energy is obtained by oxidation. Therefore a
person's steady-state power output will depend on the rate at
which their bloodsteam can absorb oxygen. Every litre of oxygen
will yield some 4500 J of energy, and since a fit young man can
absorb up to 4 litres of oxygen per minute, his power output for
any length of time is limited to an absolute maximum of 300 W
(Wilkie 1960). In work lasting all day, the average useful power
output is less than half this value because of muscular fatigue. For
effort over short periods, the muscles can use an anaerobic
process in which glucose is converted into lactic acid. The amount
of energy released by this process is limited to a total of about
27000 J, because excessive concentrations of lactic acid cannot be
tolerated (Wilkie 1960). After strenuous exercise we breath
heavily to reconvert the lactic acid to glucose. The oxygen used in

Table 2.5 *Power of various domestic animals over a working day of
six to eight hours (contemporary breeds)*

Draught animal	Draught (N)	Velocity (m/s)	Power (W)	Ratio of power to that of horse
horse	520	1·1	570	1·0
bullock	410	0·8	340	0·6
camel	1200	0·8	960	1·7
mule	260	1·1	290	0·5
ass	130	1·1	140	0·3

Source: Rankine 1889:251

this period of recovery can be thought of as repaying an oxygen debt of some 20 litres. The muscle fibres that work by an aerobic process tend to be red, while those that rely on an anaerobic process are white. So, for example, chickens, who use their ability for semi-flight only when disturbed, have white meat on their breast, and darker red meat on their legs which are used more continuously (Alexander 1982).

The power that champion male athletes can produce for various lengths of time is shown in Table 2.6; a fit average man of today can produce between 70 and 80% of these values. Over a full day five men can therefore perform about the same work as one horse, an estimate that agrees with the eighteenth-century observations of Desaguliers (1734:253).

Because people are no longer a significant source of power there is little contemporary information on human capabilities other than in sporting activities. To find data on man's ability in a work situation we must look to nineteenth-century or earlier sources. For pumping water Desaguliers tells us that 'a man with the best water engine cannot raise above one hogshead of water [250 kg] in a minute 10 feet [3 m] higher to hold it all day, but he can do almost twice as much for a minute or two' (Desaguliers 1743:498). The useful power expended in pumping water throughout the day is, from Desaguliers' data

$$250 \times 9{\cdot}81 \times 3/60 = 120 \ W.$$

This value is high in comparison with data from the nineteenth century, but of course Desaguliers was only giving a rough estimate. John Smeaton[7] gave what is probably a more realistic estimate of 90 W as the power that 'a good English labourer' could develop in pumping water all day, and he added that ordinary people 'promiscuously picked up' were only capable of developing about half this power output (Clark 1878:718).

Treadmills, first employed to grind corn, were also used from Roman times to raise water and to power cranes (Fig. 2.8). The Chinese used treadmills at least as early as the eighth century to power paddlewheels on boats (Needham and Wang 1965:213). In the early nineteenth century the British had treadmills built in some of their colonial prisons for punishment and, inevitably, for profit. Two such mills, popularly known as dancing academies,

Table 2.6 *Maximum useful power of champion athletes*

Duration	Power (W)
< 1s	up to 4500
10 s – 5 min	370–1500
5 min – 150 min	300–370
150 min – 8 h	150

Source: Wilkie 1960

[7] John Smeaton (1724–1792) was the first fully professional English engineer, best known as the designer and builder of the Eddystone Lighthouse. He was also an innovative designer of windmills and watermills.

Fig. 2.8. Roman crane powered by a
treadwheel. Relief on the funerary
monument of the Haterii in the Lateran
Museum of Rome. Dated to about
AD 100.

were installed in Sydney in 1823 for the grinding of grain (Cannon 1971). In the first year they proved to be so profitable, making almost £600, that six more were later built. Assignment to the treadmills was dreaded by the convicts. In 1850 28 prisoners refused to tread the mill, saying that they preferred to be hanged instead. The treadmill was particularly cruel for the women prisoners as local British justice did not consider pregnancy to be of much account and some women miscarried. The prisoners worked the treadmill for about 40 minutes in every hour, from sunrise to sunset, climbing the equivalent of nearly 4.8 km, or about half the height of Mount Everest. A convict weighing 60 kg could exert a maximum force on the treadmill of $60 \times 9.81 = 590$ N. During a twelve-hour day the maximum work a convict could perform would be $590 \times 4800 = 2.8$ MJ, which represents a power output of some 70 W. A compilation of the capabilities of people in work activities, derived largely from nineteenth-century sources, is given in Table 2.7.

Until about the end of the second century BC, apart from wind in the sails of water craft, humans and domesticated beasts were the only sources of power. Although the idea of rotary power is obvious now it must have been thought a novel

Table 2.7 *Useful human power in various activities*

Kind of exertion	Force (N)	Velocity (m/s)	Duration	Power (W)
hauling up weights with rope and lowering rope unloaded	180	0·23	6 h	40
raising a weight 3·4 m and lowering it again, by pulling on a horizontal rope (performed by university students)	270	—	10 min.	120
lifting weights by hand	200	0·17	6 h	30
carrying weights up stairs and returning unloaded	640	0·04	6 h	30
treadmill, 19th-century convicts in Australia	600	—	12 h	70
pushing and pulling capstan or oar	120	0·6	8 h	70
working a pump	—	—	8 h	90
	60	0·8	10 h	50
turning the crank of a crane	160	3·9	2 min.	620
	160	2.1	4 min.	340
	60	1·1	8 h	70

Source: Rankine 1889:251, Clark 1878:718–21, and the authors' experiments

innovation in the second century BC. Before Roman times cereal grinding was done by hand between two reciprocating stones (Moritz 1958:57). The rotary mill was a comparatively late invention that enabled more efficient grinding in larger mills worked by asses (Moritz 1958:62–6). At the beginning of the first century BC it was realised that water-power could be harnessed to turn a millstone. The most primitive watermills had vertical axes, and the millstone was mounted directly to the shaft of the water-wheel[8] (Fig. 2.9). This type of mill was most suited to mountainous or hilly regions where water could be channelled through a chute onto the wheel. The power of these mills could have been no more than about 300 W, which is not very much at all, but they were simple to construct and remained popular in Europe until late Medieval times (Forbes 1956a:590). A more efficient watermill with a horizontal axis is described by Vitruvius (X, 5, 2) and in this type gearing is necessary to convert the rotary motion about a horizontal axis into motion about a vertical axis. Although in later European mills the gearing usually stepped up the speed of the millstone, in Vitruvius' description it is geared down (Landels 1978:24). The first water-wheels with a horizontal

Fig. 2.9. The four types of water-wheel: (*a*) vertical; (*b*) horizontal – undershot; (*c*) horizontal – overshot; (*d*) horizontal – breast.

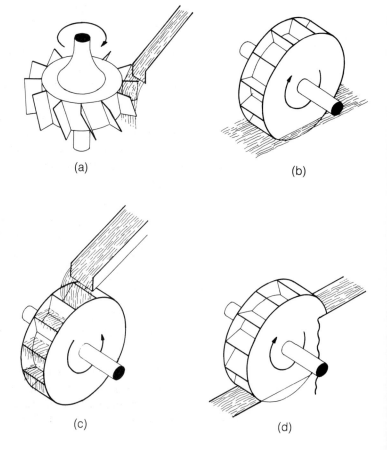

(a)

(b)

(c)

(d)

[8] Whether the horizontal or vertical watermill was invented first has not been resolved. The vertical watermill is simpler in itself since it does not require any gearing. However, whereas the vertical mill requires a specially constructed water shoot with a drop of some 3 m (Landels 1978:18) the horizontal mill could operate directly in a fast-running stream. The *noria*, a horizontal watermill that used the kinetic energy of a stream to lift water in pots attached to the wheel, probably predates the watermill and may be the origin of the horizontal mill (Needham and Wang 1965: 361–2, 405; Reynolds 1983: 24). In this view, the vertical watermill for which there is no Greek or Roman evidence was invented east of the Mediterranean basin (Needham and Wang, 1965: 365; Reynolds 1983: 24).

axis were of the undershot type, where the water impinges on the bottom of the wheel (Fig. 2.9b). With this mill it is the kinetic energy of the stream that is utilised and a relatively fast flowing stream is needed for its efficient generation. Even so, the power of about 1.5 kW attainable from this design was considerably greater than that obtained from the more primitive water-wheel with a vertical shaft (Reynolds 1983:36).

More power can be generated if the water is delivered by chute to the top of the wheel. An overshot mill (Fig. 2.9c) can utilise both the kinetic and potential energy of the water, but there has to be a large difference between the two water levels. In Rome the aqueducts provided a ready source of water for the overshot wheel. If such a supply of water was not available a river or stream would have to be dammed to provide a sufficient head of water. The earliest known overshot wheel was built in the mid-fifth century in the Agora in Athens, but the new design did not become common until late Medieval times. These water-wheels were capable of producing considerably more energy than the undershot type. It has been estimated that the fifth-century Athenian mill, which was geared down because of the high velocity of the water, had a power output of about 3 kW. In their heyday during the Industrial Revolution water-wheels were known to produce up to 30 kW of power, though the average output was still only about 5 kW (Reynolds 1983:38, 183).

The water-mill that most people who live in Europe or North America are familiar with is none of the above varieties of horizontal mill, but the breast wheel (Fig. 2.9d), which utilises only the potential energy of the wheel and has a close-fitting casing to improve efficiency. This last type of wheel was an innovation of the Industrial Revolution and a favourite of John Smeaton (Reynolds 1983:280–2).

Antipater of Thessalonica, writing at the end of the first century BC, greeted the watermill as the end of woman's labour of grinding corn:

> Cease from grinding, O ye toilers; women, slumber still,
> Even if the crowing roosters call the morning star;
> For Demeter has appointed nymphs to turn your mill,
> And upon the water-wheel alighting here they are.
> See, how quick they twirl the axle whose revolving rays,
> Spin the heavy hollow rollers quarried overseas;
> So again we savour the delights of ancient days,
> Taught to eat the fruits of Mother Earth in idle ease.
> (Higham and Bowra 1938:632)

But it was the ass not the water-wheel that first brought women relief from this tiresome task. When the Emperor Caligula commandeered Rome's mill animals to carry his plunder, the city was threatened by a bread shortage (Moritz 1958:99). Rome suffered another bread shortage five centuries later when it was

44   *Basic mechanics*

besieged by the Goths. This time the reason for the shortage was that the Goths had cut the aqueducts leading to the Janiculum, a ridge in the city where the watermills were located (Moritz 1958:139).

Windmills, unknown in the ancient world, were evidently invented in Persia some time during the eighth century. Like the original water-wheel, the first windmills had vertical axes. The origin of the European windmill is obscure, but there is a tradition that the concept was brought back to Europe by the first crusaders at the end of the eleventh century.

For most of human existence people have had to rely on the power of their own muscles. Even after domesticated animals were yoked to carts and wagons, societies still relied mainly on human power. Today, when all but the simplest actions are performed for us by machines, it is difficult to conceive of life without a ready supply of power at the flick of a switch; it is no wonder then that writers who invoke the supernatural to explain the feats of the ancients are so often believed.

Equilibrium and stability

All of us at some time or other have tried to balance a box on its corner (Fig. 2.10). If we are careful, we may succeed, but a gust of air or tremor in the table causes the box to fall back onto a base. The box is now stable, and unless we move the table violently it will remain on its base. The forces acting on the box are in equilibrium, either when it is balanced on one corner so that the box's weight acts through the corner and is in line with the reaction force, or when it rests on its base. However the box is stable only when resting on a base. When balanced on a corner the box is unstable and the smallest tremor makes it fall. If we rotate the box from either position of stable equilibrium we have to raise its centre of gravity, which requires work on our part and increases the potential energy of the box. When it is balanced on

Fig. 2.10. The stability of a matchbox.

a corner the centre of gravity is in its highest position, and hence the potential energy of the box has a maximum value. If we disturb the box either way from this position of unstable equilibrium the potential energy decreases. On the other hand, if we rotate the box from its stable position of resting on a base the potential energy will increase. These results are general. *For stable equilibrium, the potential energy of a mechanical system is a mathematical minimum.* By this we mean that any possible displacement causes the potential energy of the system to increase, which does not necessarily imply that the potential energy is an *absolute* minimum. *A mechanical system is in unstable equilibrium if the potential energy is a mathematical maximum.* In this position any small disturbance causes a decrease in potential energy which can be utilised to do work and equilibrium is not regained.

The concept of stability can be applied to all mechanical systems, not just to rigid bodies. Instead of floating gently to earth, the first parachutes oscillated from side to side in an unstable fashion as air spilled out intermittently over their edges. Robert Cocking, a water-colour painter, observed one of these early parachutes descend over London in 1802, noting also how sick the man had become from the violent motion. Many years later Cocking designed an inverted parachute (Fig. 2.11) which undoubtedly did solve the problem of aerodynamic stability, though unfortunately for Cocking the structure was inherently unstable. Neglecting to do any preliminary tests Cocking jumped from the basket of a hot-air balloon over Vauxhall Gardens in London, his gaily-painted parachute collapsing like an umbrella in a storm and plunging him 1500 metres to his death (Gibbs-Smith 1953:123). It was a considerable time before a simple method of stabilising a parachute's descent was devised. All that was required was a hole cut at the parachute's centre so that air could escape continuously at the crown rather than intermittently around its periphery.

Fig. 2.11. Cocking's inverted parachute.

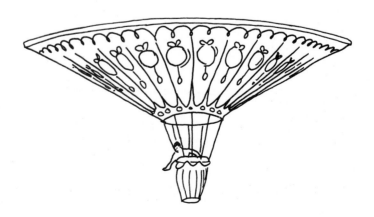

[9] Robert Hooke was one of a group of brilliant scientists who were contemporaries of Newton. The time was right for the arrival of Newton's *Principia* and not surprisingly a number of Newton's colleagues, notably Hooke, were thinking along similar lines. Hooke made headway in the study of gravity and by 1679 had conceived the inverse square law. Eight years later, when Newton published his *Principia* without acknowledging Hooke's work, an acrimonious quarrel ensued which was never settled – Newton's aloofness certainly did not help. As his epitaph in Westminster Abbey says, Newton was 'an ornament to the human race', overshadowing his contemporaries. With the limelight already fully occupied Hooke's individual genius was not adequately recognised.

In this chapter we have briefly summarised the basic tenets of classical mechanics. These tenets have developed out of man's collective empirical experiences. The users of the spear and the bow had to understand dynamics in a practical way, perhaps appreciating inertia better than Aristotle. The great synthesis of mechanics in the *Principia* was Newton's crowning achievement. However, as Newton himself realised, he could not alone have achieved what he did. In a letter to his rival, Robert Hooke[9] (1635–1703), Newton wrote: 'If I have seen further it is by standing upon the shoulders of giants'. Galileo and Kepler provided that strength, and they themselves were supported by many others including the innovators of our remote past who fashioned the first stone tools and discovered the advantage of the spearthrower. Through the basic laws of mechanics we are able to better appreciate these early achievements.

3

Fluids and solids

While some mechanical problems in material culture studies can be solved using rigid body mechanics, others can only be dealt with by considering the way a solid deforms or a fluid flows. The flight of an arrow can be approximately determined through rigid body mechanics alone, but an accurate prediction needs the resistance offered by the air as it flows away from the arrow's path to be considered. Similarly, problems such as the mechanics of the bow can only be solved through an understanding of how a bow deforms when its string is drawn. This chapter provides the basic mechanics for investigating problems such as these.

Fluids

Fluids are incapable of permanently resisting forces that tend to change their shape; they can be liquids, like water, or gases, such as air. Gases can freely expand and will always fill a container, whereas liquids may partially fill a vessel leaving a free surface between it and the air. There is an obvious difference between the compressibilities of gases and liquids – gases are easily compressed, but liquids show little change in volume even under large forces. In the topics studied in this book we can ignore the small changes in volume in liquids and even neglect the compressibility of gases, as for instance when considering the resistance of air to the flight of projectiles. In flight the compressibility of the air only becomes important if the projectile's velocity approaches a third of the speed of sound.

It is the ability to flow that characterises a fluid. If we smash in the side of a water barrel, the water will rush out and spread thinly over the ground. The same will happen if the barrel were filled with treacle, the only difference being that the flow across the ground will occur much more slowly. Fluids that flow slowly are said to be *viscous*. Even if the viscosity of a fluid is small its effect can be important – arrows are slowed by the viscosity of the air; and considerable effort is required to move a ship through the water at speed.

Concept of pressure

When stationary a fluid can only transmit a force perpendicular to a surface. The perpendicular force per unit area of surface, either of the container or of any imagined internal surface, is called the *pressure*. Apart from changes due to the weight of a fluid, the pressure in a stationary fluid is the same everywhere within it. Most people realise that when a car tyre is inflated each part of it will be subjected to the same pressure. If for some reason the tyre is filled with water, differences in the pressure at the top and bottom of the tyre will occur because of the water's weight. Air also has weight, but since it is very light it has no significant effect in a car tyre.

The principle that pressure communicates itself equally to all parts in a stationary fluid may seem self-evident to us now, but before the seventeenth century the idea of uniform pressure was not at all obvious and was not generally accepted by scholars. Although Leonardo da Vinci, along with others, had tried to demonstrate the principle (Rouse and Ince 1963), it was Blaise Pascal (1632–62) who gave the first convincing explanation of the nature of fluid pressure in his book, *Traité de l'equilibré des liquers*, published in 1663 just after his death. In so doing he invented the hydraulic press, though its practical application did not come about until the nineteenth century. In the hydraulic press a small force on a piston overcomes a large force on a bigger piston. Pascal showed that the forces acting on the pistons are in proportion to their areas using as an example a press with two pistons, where the area of the large piston was one hundred times that of the small one. His proposition was that 'if the man who pushes on the small piston moves it forward an inch, he will push out the other one only one-hundredth part of an inch...since this movement occurs because of the continuity of the water' (Magie 1963:76). If there are no losses due to friction, then the work done *on* the small piston must be equal to the work done *by* the large piston. Hence the force on the large piston is one hundred times that exerted on the small piston. Since this is the ratio of the areas of the pistons, the pressure must be the same. Once Pascal had demonstrated this he extended his proposition with the argument that the same pressure must be exerted on every part of the press, not just on the two pistons.

Although we are discussing static fluids, the explanation apparently requires the fluid to move. However in Pascal's imaginary experiment the movement of the pistons can be made as small and as slow as one likes, so that, in effect, it applies to a static fluid. In honour of Pascal's work the unit of pressure in the Système International is the pascal (Pa), which is defined as a newton per square metre (N/m^2).

So far we have paid no attention to the effect of a fluid's weight. When one dives into deep water, or rapidly descends in an aircraft, the increase in pressure that occurs registers on one's eardrums. The pressure of the air around us is due to the weight of the air above and, in the words of Evangelista Torricelli (1608–47), the inventor of the barometer, 'we live immersed at

the bottom of a sea of elemental air' (Magie 1963:71). At a depth
h below the free surface of a fluid of density ρ, the pressure force
acting on an area *A* must support a column of mass $\rho h A$ which
weighs $\rho g h A$, where *g* is the acceleration under free-fall. In
addition, the pressure force must support the atmospheric pressure
acting on the surface of the fluid. If the atmospheric pressure is p_a
then the pressure at depth *h* below the free surface of a fluid is

$$p = p_a + \rho g h. \tag{3.1}$$

This is the *absolute* pressure; that is, the pressure measured above
a perfect vacuum. Since we live in a sea of air, it is often useful to
measure the pressure above atmospheric value rather than above
a vacuum. We call the difference between the *absolute* pressure
and the atmospheric value, the *relative* pressure. Thus in equation
(3.1), $\rho g h$ is the relative pressure. In future when referring to
absolute pressure we will omit the word absolute and only qualify
pressure if it is relative.

　　The relationship between the height of a fluid and its
pressure was utilised by Torricelli in the design of his barometer.
When a tube sealed at one end is filled with mercury (or indeed,
any other liquid) and turned upside-down, its contents will of
course readily flow out. However, if the tube is inverted in a bowl
of mercury with a thumb placed over the open end, no mercury
will run out when the thumb is removed if the tube is less than
about 750 mm long. If the tube is longer, mercury will run out
until its height is reduced to 750 mm above the level of the
mercury in the bowl. In the process of escaping through the
bottom of the tube the drop in the level of mercury creates a
vacuum at its sealed top. This happens because the atmospheric
pressure acting on the free surface in the bowl can only support a
column of about 750 mm of mercury. Since there is a vacuum
above the mercury in the tube, the pressure at the level of the free
surface in the bowl must be $\rho g h$, where *h* is the height of the
column of mercury. The pressure at this point must be
atmospheric, and therefore the atmospheric pressure must be $\rho g h$.
A less dense liquid can be supported to greater heights. For the
same atmospheric pressure, water, which is $1/13 \cdot 6$ as dense as
mercury, can be supported to $13 \cdot 6 \times 750$ mm, or $10 \cdot 2$ m.

　　Since air pressure is due to the weight of the air above,
pressure decreases with height. This effect was demonstrated by
Pascal who, being too ill at the time, persuaded his brother-in-law
Florin Périer to take a Torricellian barometer to the top of an
adjacent mountain (Magie 1963:73–5).

　　At first sight it seems very strange that the pressure in a
fluid depends only upon the depth and not on the weight of
water being supported. Pascal illustrated this hydrostatic paradox
with a set of various vases of different shapes connected at their
base. When this composite vase was filled, the water reached a
common level, showing that despite the different weights of water

the pressure at the base of all the vases was equal. The paradox is
not really very difficult to resolve, though from personal
experience we know that it has eluded even some Australian
plumbers. A few years ago one of us lived on an island where,
because there was no reticulated water, the residents had to rely
on individual tanks that supplied water by gravity. The water was
pumped from a lower collection tank to a higher one so that it
had an adequate head, using the same pipe that supplied water to
the house. In constructing a new tank system for a neighbouring
house the plumber, obviously not understanding the hydrostatic
paradox, thought that it would require more pressure to pump the
water directly into the bottom of the tank. To overcome this
supposed problem, he supplied an unnecessary branch pipe to the
top of the tank. Now, unless the owner climbs the hill to close the
stopcock at the bottom of the tank, the water will never flow
through this extra pipe.

The motion of ideal fluids

People who lived by hunting and gathering would normally
position their base camps adjacent or close to natural bodies of
fresh water. With the advent of farming the number of people
that could be supported on fertile land began to increase and, in
time, populous cities emerged. As a city's survival depended on an
adequate and regular supply of fresh water such provisioning was
a matter of priority, sometimes entailing amazing ingenuity and
engineering skill. For instance Herodotus describes a tunnel more
than a kilometre long that was driven through a hill to supply
water to the island city of Samos (Forbes 1957, I:164). Rome,
which was densely packed with high-rise tenements, was supplied
with water through a vast network of channels and aqueducts
many hundreds of kilometres in length. These remarkable
constructions were by no means unique, and so one would
imagine that the engineers of the Classical World understood at
least the basic principles of fluid flow. Yet apart from the obvious
fact that water flow requires a downhill slope the Greeks and
Romans knew pitifully little. Heron of Alexandria did know that
the quantity of water supplied depended on both the cross-section
of the flow and its velocity, but the Roman engineers seemed
much less clear about the role velocity played (Rouse and Ince
1963:21–2). The quantity of water flowing per unit time is the
product of the mean velocity and the cross-sectional area of the
pipe. Because liquids undergo little change in volume, this flow is
constant at all sections whether the cross-sectional area is
constant or not. This last statement is a particular form of a
general principle for ideal fluids called the *principle of continuity*.

Our best account of Rome's water supply comes from Sextus
Julius Frontinus (*c.* AD 35–103) who was Water Commissioner
during the last eight years of his life. Frontinus took over an office
that had been badly mismanaged, and was confronted with

longstanding corruption and abuse. He was obviously an able administrator and during the term of his office greatly improved Rome's water supply. One of Frontinus' major worries was the apparent discrepancy between the amount of water supplied to Rome by the aqueducts and the evidently lesser amount that was being used. Undoubtedly the records of the previous Commissioners were in poor shape and a good deal of water was being illegally diverted for private use, but the method of accounting was itself deficient. Rome's water supply was continuous; there were no large reservoirs, and stopcocks or taps were almost unknown. Water was metered through standard adjutages which were brass pipes of fixed diameter fitted at the delivery tank. The unit of discharge was the quinaria, which was the cross-sectional area of a pipe $1\frac{1}{4}$ digits in diameter (Frontinus I, 25). The total cross-sectional area of all the water flowing into Rome on the aqueducts was found by Frontinus to be 18 433 quinariae, whereas the sum of all officially recorded outlets was only 14 018 quinariae. Frontinus was right in believing that some water was being illegally diverted, but the actual amount that was being supplied could only be determined if its velocity at each adjutage was known. Like his contemporaries, Frontinus (I, 35) was only vaguely aware that the rate of flow depended upon the height of the pipe and its frictional resistance, and he spent a great deal of time fruitlessly trying to balance his books.

One of the first problems of fluid flow to be studied was the rate of discharge from a tank (Fig. 3.1). This phenomenon could not be properly tackled until Galileo had described the motion of falling bodies. It is not surprising therefore that Leonardo da Vinci should be wrong in his hypothesis that the rate of discharge was proportional to the orifice's depth below the surface of the liquid. Torricelli was deeply impressed by Galileo's *Dialogues* and in 1644 he published *Del moto dei gravi* which extended Galileo's work on gravity. By analogy with falling bodies, Torricelli argued that a jet of liquid would discharge from an orifice with the same velocity as that of a solid body falling from the free surface to the orifice (Rouse and Ince 1963:632–3). He neatly corroborated his hypothesis by observing that if the jet was directed vertically upwards it would almost reach the level of the free surface. As Torricelli realised, the jet would not climb to the exact height of the free surface because the liquid would fall back on itself and the resistance of the surrounding air acted as an impedence.

In arriving at an approximation it is quite often useful to assume that a liquid is 'perfect' in the sense that there is no frictional resistance to its flow. A jet of such a liquid will inevitably return to the height of the free surface and since no energy is lost the principle of conservation of energy will apply. If the cross-sectional area of the tank is large compared with that of the jet, then the velocity of the fluid within the tank is small compared with the velocity of the jet. Therefore the potential

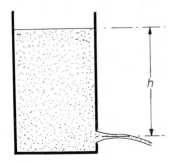

Fig. 3.1. Discharge through an orifice at the bottom of a tank.

energy of the fluid in the tank is converted into the kinetic energy of the jet. If the fluid discharged from the tank during a small time interval is dq, then it will lose potential energy of $\rho g h\, dq$ where h is the height of the free surface above the orifice. The kinetic energy of the jet increases by $\frac{1}{2}\rho v^2\, dq$ during the same interval in time. By the principle of conservation of energy

$$\rho g h\, dq = \tfrac{1}{2}\rho v^2\, dq,$$

and hence

$$v = \sqrt{2gh}, \tag{3.2}$$

which is the same velocity a solid body attains by falling through the height h.

The rate of discharge from the tank is the product of the jet's cross-sectional area (A_j) and the velocity v of the discharge, since in a small time interval dt, a cylinder of liquid with area A_j and length $v\,dt$ issues from the tank. If a tank has a sharp-edged orifice the jet contracts as it passes the orifice, so that the area of the jet is less than that of the orifice A_1. In these instances the rate of discharge will not be the velocity v (given by equation 3.2) multiplied by the area of the orifice. Newton (1686:II §VII) introduced the concept of a coefficient of contraction C_c which is the ratio A_j/A_1. Thus the theoretical rate of discharge Q is given by

$$Q = C_c A_1 \sqrt{2gh} \tag{3.3}$$

where for sharp-edged orifices $C_c \approx 0.7$. In practice, because of frictional resistance, the true rate of discharge Q is slightly less than this and given by

$$Q = C_d A_1 \sqrt{2gh} \tag{3.4}$$

where C_d is the coefficient of discharge.

Fig. 3.2. Demonstration of Bernoulli's equation

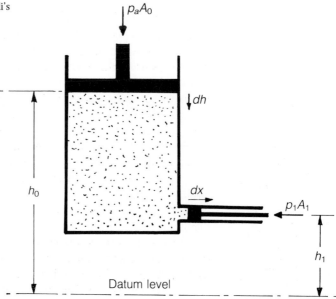

Datum level

If a pipe is fitted to the base of the tank, the pressure is not necessarily atmospheric and equation (3.2) will not apply. Imagine the tank and the pipe fitted with pistons (Fig. 3.2). If in a small time interval the piston on the top of the tank, which is subjected to atmospheric pressure (p_a), moves a distance dh, it does work *on* the liquid equal to $p_a A_0 dh$, where A_0 is the cross-sectional area of the tank. If the piston in the pipe moves a distance dx the work performed is $P_1 A_1 dx$, where P_1 is the pressure and A_1 is the cross-sectional area. The volume of liquid dq flowing from the tank must be equal to the volume flowing into the pipe. Hence

$$dq = A_0 dh = A_1 dx.$$

Therefore the net work done *on* both pistons by the liquid can be written as $(p_1 - p_a)dq$. The potential energy lost by the liquid during the discharge dq is $\rho g(h_0 - h_1)dq$, where the heights are measured from the datum level shown in Fig 3.2. At the same time the kinetic energy gained by the same quantity flowing into the small pipe is $\frac{1}{2}\rho v_1^2 \, dq$. Assuming that the kinetic energy of the fluid in the tank is negligible (that is, $A_0 \gg A_1$) the work done by the fluid is given by

$$(p_1 - p_a)dq = \rho g(h_0 - h_1)dq - \tfrac{1}{2}\rho v_1^2 \, dq,$$

or

$$p_a + \rho g h_0 = p_1 + \rho g h_1 + \tfrac{1}{2}\rho v_1^2.$$

In this problem the pistons were introduced only to aid in understanding the concepts involved. Providing that the pressures are the same, the work performed is identical whether the pistons are there or not. We can perform the same energy balance at any point in the pipe, and therefore for the flow of an ideal frictionless liquid along a pipe

$$p + \rho g h + \tfrac{1}{2}\rho v^2 = \text{a constant.} \tag{3.5}$$

This equation, which is known as Bernoulli's equation,[1] states that the 'total' pressure in a perfect fluid, which is the sum of static pressure p, the gravity pressure $\rho g h$, and the dynamic pressure $\frac{1}{2}\rho v^2$, is constant. In a real fluid there will be losses due to friction in the total pressure as one goes downstream with the flow. However the flow of very low viscosity gases like air can be accurately predicted from Bernoulli's equation provided the flow is steady without any mixing between layers. Under such conditions even the flow of a low viscosity liquid like water can be reasonably predicted from Bernoulli's equation provided the pipe is not too fine or long.

Steady fluid flow without mixing between layers is called laminar, in contrast to turbulent flow where a random motion is superimposed on the average flow thereby causing a good deal of mixing. Smokers can see both types of flow taking place in the column of smoke that rises from their cigarette. Bernoulli's equation cannot be used for turbulent flow.

[1] Daniel Bernoulli (1700–1782) implicitly made use of this important equation in his famous book *Hydrodynamics*, which he published in 1738. Bernoulli came from a remarkably gifted Huguenot family. His father Johann (1667–1748) and his uncle Jakob (1654–1705) were both renowned mathematicians. Daniel Bernoulli never married, but a nephew, Jacques (1759–1789), continued the family tradition, applying his mind to problems in the mechanics of solids.

The siphon

Although an efficient water pump was invented by Ktesibios of
Alexandria in the third century BC (Vitruvius X, 7), the most
common way of making water flow, other than directly downhill,
was by the siphon. It is not difficult to understand how the siphon
was invented. The Egyptians must have sucked liquids through
reeds or straws much in the same way as we do today. If the end
of the reed that is being sucked is taken below the level of the
liquid in the container it will start to siphon automatically. One
presumes that this simple experience led to the use of the siphon
used by the Egyptians to fill small containers from a larger vessel
(Fig. 3.3). During the Ptolemaic period the siphon was used by
the Alexandrian Greeks in the construction of many of their
ingenious automata – which seem to have fascinated them as
much as electronic toys do today's generation. Two books, one
written by Philon of Byzantium in the third century BC, and one
by Heron in the first century AD, describe a remarkable number
of applications of the siphon. In one of the contrivances illustrated
in Heron's *Pneumatica* a satyr empties the water from an upper
tank into a lower one through his wineskin (Fig. 3.4). By making
the tube in the wineskin very fine the flow would have continued
for a long time, no doubt astounding audiences who were
unaware of the siphon arrangement inside the tank.

  While the siphon provided a good deal of entertainment, the
way it worked was little understood. Philon thought that the
existence of cohesion forces between 'particles' of liquid was an
adequate explanation of why the liquid climbed the tube. Heron,
however, had an inkling that pressure acting on the surface of the
liquid in the container forced it up the siphon into the vacuum
created by the initial sucking (Rouse and Ince 1963:21).

  A siphon cannot lift liquid to any height. The pressure in
the siphon above the level of the free surface of the liquid is below

Fig. 3.3. Egyptians siphoning a liquid.

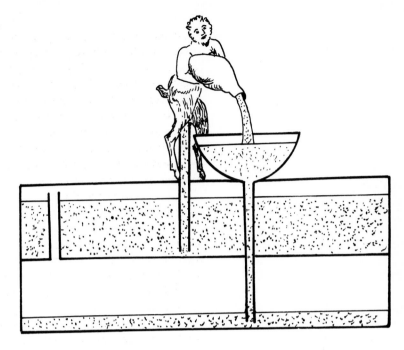

Fig. 3.4. A satyr pouring water from a skin into a full basin without making the contents overflow.

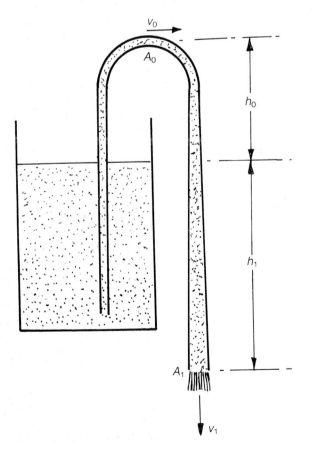

Fig. 3.5. The action of a syphon.

Fluids and solids

atmospheric pressure. If the height of the siphon is too great the pressure will fall to zero and the siphon will cease to function. This in fact is what happened when Galileo tried to lift water more than 18 cubits (10.4 m) with a suction pump.[2] Actually, as one can see from Bernoulli's equation, the maximum height to which a fluid can be lifted depends on its velocity of flow. At the free surface of the liquid in the reservoir and at the discharge outlet of the siphon the pressure in the liquid is atmospheric (p_a). If the pressure at the top of the siphon is p_0 then Bernoulli's equation applied to the free surface of the liquid, the top of the siphon, and the discharge outlet (Fig. 3.5), yields

$$p_a = p_0 + \rho g h_0 + \tfrac{1}{2}\rho v_0^2 = p_a - \rho g h_1 + \tfrac{1}{2}\rho v_1^2.$$

Obviously for the siphon to flow the discharge pipe must be below the free surface of the liquid in the reservoir. Ignoring frictional losses in the pipe, the velocity of discharge is then given by

$$v_1 = \sqrt{2g h_1}$$

(where h_1 is the height of the free surface of the liquid above the discharge) and is identical to the discharge from an orifice. If the diameter of the siphon varies, then the velocity is inversely proportional to the area, that is,

$$v_0 = \frac{A_1}{A_0} v_1.$$

Hence the pressure at the top of the siphon is

$$p_0 = p_a - \rho g \left[h_1 \left(\frac{A_1}{A_0} \right)^2 + h_0 \right].$$

And thus the siphon will operate, provided that

$$h_1 \left(\frac{A_1}{A_0} \right)^2 + h_0 < \frac{p_a}{\rho g}. \tag{3.6}$$

The water wheel
Bernoulli's equation only applies if energy has not been extracted from the fluid. To deal with the performance of water-wheels and similar devices another approach is required. The Parisian scientist, Antoine Parent (1666–1716), argued that no power can be extracted from an undershot water-wheel if the floatboards are either stationary or moving with the same velocity as the water, and that therefore between these two extremes there is a velocity at which the extracted power is at a maximum value (Girard 1810). Although Parent correctly sensed the nature of the problem, the solution eluded him. Newton's second law provides the key to solving the problem. If the area of the floatboard of the water-wheel in contact with the water is A, and the velocity of the mill race is v_w, the mass of water impinging on the floatboard each second must be $\rho v_w A$. The momentum of the water just before impact with the floatboard is $(\rho v_w A) v_w$. After passing

---

[2] Galileo (1638:64) at first thought that something was wrong with his pump, but a workman assured him that all was satisfactory and that it was impossible to lift water more than 18 cubits – an example of the scientist being taught by the artisan.

through the water-wheel, the water is slowed to the velocity of the floatboard (v_m) and has a momentum of $(\rho v_w A)v_m$. Therefore there is a change in momentum of $\rho v_w(v_w - v_m)A$ every second, which, by Newton's second law, must be equal to the impressed force F. The power (P) which the water supplies to the wheel is $F v_m$ and is given by

$$P = Fv_m = \rho v_m v_w(v_w - v_m)A. \tag{3.7}$$

This expression for the power of a water-wheel is at a maximum when the velocity of the floatboards is half the velocity of the stream. We have analysed an ideal water-wheel that fully utilises the momentum of the stream. In practice not all of this momentum can be extracted and the actual power of the mill is a lot less than that given by equation (3.7). Nevertheless the maximum power is attained when the floatboards have about half the velocity of the stream.

Viscous flow
In solving many of the problems in fluid mechanics frictional resistance to flow cannot be ignored. The viscosity of a liquid is a measure of its resistance to flow, a property that finds an obvious expression in its degree of 'stickiness'. The term viscosity derives from the Greek word for mistletoe, a berry which contains a very sticky substance used to trap birds.

If two plates separated by a layer of fluid are sheared relative to one another, a uniform velocity gradient will be established across the fluid (Fig. 3.6). For many fluids, including water, the force necessary to shear the fluid is proportional to this velocity gradient. Such fluids are termed Newtonian, though Newton did not himself perform experiments on real fluids but applied the concept to Descartes' imagined ether to disprove the vortex theory of the universe (Newton 1686:II §IX). We now call the constant of proportionality between the shearing force per unit area (otherwise known as the shear stress $\tau = F/A$) and the velocity gradient dv/dy, the *coefficient of viscosity* μ. Hence

$$\tau = \mu \frac{dv}{dy}. \tag{3.8}$$

The flow of fluids through pipes is governed by viscosity and was first studied by a French physician, Jean Louis Poiseuille (1799–1869), who was primarily concerned with the flow in

Fig. 3.6. Two sheared plates separated by a viscous fluid.

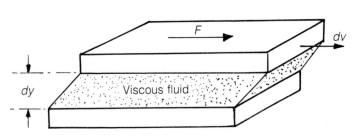

capillary blood vessels (Rouse and Ince 1963:160–1). In the
Système International the Unit of the coefficient, the Ns/m^2 or
Pa s, is sometimes called the poiseuille. The coefficient of viscosity
of water at 25 °C is 8.93×10^{-4} Pa s.

Fluid under a moderate pressure flows steadily in a fine pipe
without any mixing between layers. In such laminar flow through
long pipes a steady velocity gradient is established across the tube.
The velocity of the fluid is zero at the surface of the tube, where it
is trapped, increasing parabolically to a maximum value at the
centre (Fig. 3.7). The maximum velocity of the flow is twice the
average value (v) and the velocity gradient at the surface is $8v/d$,
where d is the diameter of the tube. By substituting this velocity
gradient into equation (3.8) we find the frictional shear stress that
the fluid exerts on the tube to be given by

$$\tau = \frac{8\mu v}{d}. \tag{3.9}$$

The total frictional force resisting flow is the shear stress
multiplied by the surface area of the pipe. A pressure force equal
to this frictional force is necessary to make the fluid flow. Hence
the pressure loss p_μ over a pipe of length l is given by

$$p_\mu = (\pi dl)\left(\frac{8\mu v}{d}\right)\bigg/\left(\frac{\pi d^2}{4}\right).$$

$$= 32 \; \mu v l / d^2 \tag{3.10}$$

This equation, sometimes called *Poiseuille's equation*, is accurate for
long tubes ($l > 50 \, d$), where transition regions are small compared
with the overall length of the pipe.

In experimental fluid mechanics geometrically similar scale
models are often used to predict full-scale behaviour. We can
appreciate how the physical characteristics of the fluid must be
modelled from Poiseuille's equation. Let us recast equation (3.10)

Fig. 3.7. Flow in a pipe.

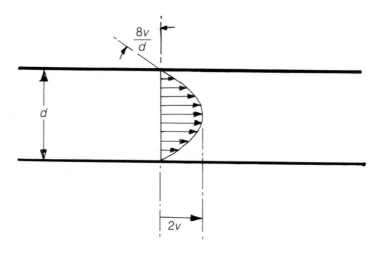

to express the pressure loss p_μ due to viscosity as a fraction of the dynamic pressure $\frac{1}{2}\rho v^2$ to obtain

$$p_\mu/\tfrac{1}{2}\rho v^2 = (64\,l/d)\Big/\left[\frac{\rho v d}{\mu}\right]. \tag{3.11}$$

Here the pressure loss along the tube has been non-dimensionalised by dividing by the dynamic pressure of the fluid flow ($\frac{1}{2}\rho v^2$). We can expect similar behaviour between the model and the full-scale pipe if the non-dimensional pressure loss is the same in both. The first term in equation (3.11) must be the same as that of the full-scale pipe and hence, for complete similarity, the second term $\rho v d/\mu$ must be kept a constant. Therefore if we make the diameter of the model pipe smaller than the one in the full-scale pipe we must either test it at a lower velocity, or change our fluid to obtain true similitude. The term $\rho v d/\mu$ is proportional to the ratio between the dynamic pressure $\frac{1}{2}\rho v^2$ and the viscous shear stress $8\,\mu v/d$. This non-dimensional parameter, which is of great importance, is called the *Reynolds number* (R_e) in honour of Osborne Reynolds (1842–1912), the creator of the science of lubrication. The essential feature of equation (3.11) is that the fluid flow is a function of the Reynolds number for geometrically similar models. This relationship is general, and if there is geometric similarity any characteristic length can be used in place of the diameter d in the expression for Reynolds number. At low Reynolds number the flow is laminar and the pressure loss is inversely proportional to the Reynolds number as shown in equation (3.11). However, at a higher Reynolds number, because the dynamic pressure is larger compared with the viscous shear stress, the flow becomes unsteady and turbulent. In pipes, fluid flow changes to turbulent at a Reynolds number of about 2300 (Francis 1969:211). For turbulent flow the pressure loss for a smooth pipe is approximately given by

$$p_\mu/\tfrac{1}{2}\rho v = 0\cdot316\,l/d\,R_e^{-\frac{1}{4}}. \tag{3.12}$$

Later we will look again at turbulent flow in dealing with projectiles and ships.

Water-clocks

In ancient Egypt the priests needed to tell the time during the night so that the temple rites and sacrifices could be performed at the right hour. On clear nights the Egyptians could use the stars to mark the hours, but they needed a clock when it was cloudy. The Egyptians had a water-clock for this purpose in their temples which made use of the viscous flow of water through a fine orifice for time regulation. The oldest water-clock yet discovered was made during the reign of Amenhotep III (*c.* 1417–1379 BC) and used in the Temple of Amen-Re at Karnak where it was found in fragments in 1905 (Fig. 3.8). In common with all early water-clocks the Karnak clock, as it is now known, was of the outflow

Fluids and solids

type where the hours were gauged by the time taken for a vessel
to empty. With the outflow clock the velocity of the water flow
decreases as the water-level drops. Since the Egyptians used a
linear scale on the inside of their clocks to mark the hours, the
bottom of the vessel had to have a smaller cross-sectional area
than the top. Until the invention of the inflow clock during the
Ptolemaic era, all Egyptian water-clocks were shaped like a
flower-pot – a design that provided remarkable accuracy. According
to his tomb inscription this type of water-clock was invented by
Amenemhet (*c.* 1556–1515 BC), a court official at Thebes, but
could just as well have been the idea of one of his priestly staff. If
indeed it was Amenemhet's own invention then he would have
the honour of being the world's first-known inventor.

The design of Egyptian water-clocks was still further
complicated by their method of time-reckoning which was based
on the rising of a set of decan stars (Neugebauer and Parker
1960). In the Egyptian system the night was divided into twelve
'hours' so that, as the length of the night changed with the
season, so did the length of the hour.[3] Hence the Egyptian water-
clock had twelve different scales, one for each month of the year.
Amenemhet's tomb inscription gave the lengths of the scale
for the midsummer and midwinter, and it was assumed that the
length of the scales varied linearly for the months in between
(Borchardt 1920:10). In the Karnak clock, the scale length for
the shortest night is almost precisely the 12 digits (225 mm)
specified by Amenemhet, and the longest scale is close to 14 digits
(262·5 mm). Unfortunately the part of the tomb inscription
specifying this latter length is missing. An apparent anomaly in
the Karnak clock is that the longest scale is for the fourth month

Fig. 3.8. The Karnak water-clock.

[3] The notion of having *hours* of varying
duration may seem strange to us, but it
was quite common in early times. In
Europe it was not until mechanical
clocks arrived in the fourteenth century
that the old system of varying the
hours according to the season was
abandoned. Turkey kept the old time
system until the First World War.

and the shortest for the tenth month, which at the time of Amenhotep III corresponded to September and March respectively. Naturally we should expect the longest night to occur at the winter solstice and the shortest at the summer one. The apparent anomaly is explained by Egyptian conservatism. The Egyptian civil year had 365 days, as ours does, but they made no provision for a leap year. So every four years the civil year fell behind the solar year by a day. Quite obviously the Karnak clock was made strictly to the rules laid down by Amenemhet, because when he designed the clock the year began in September which, as we should expect, puts the longest scale in December.[4] The correct months for the time of Amenhotep III may have been painted on the rim of the clock or possibly a conversion calendar was used.

It is interesting to speculate on the accuracy obtainable from water-clocks of the Karnak type. We have little idea of the kind of accuracy demanded, but the performance of the nightly rites was especially important to the Egyptian priests as it was their duty to ensure that the Sun-god Horus, who symbolically died each night, was resurrected the following morning. The 'hours' in the Karnak clock are marked by rows of small depressions about 5 mm in diameter that would have made it difficult to read the clock to an accuracy of more than 10 minutes. In later clocks lines replaced the dots, but even so the meniscus on the water surface would have made accurate reading difficult. No orifices of water-clocks have ever been identified in collections of Egyptian antiquities. We know from Vitruvius (IX, 8, 1, 4) that the orifices of Roman water-clocks were made from gold or gemstones. The Egyptians used bow drills to pierce hard gemstone (Lucas 1962) and it would not have been difficult for them to have produced an orifice of about 1 mm diameter required in water-clocks like the Karnak one (Cotterell *et al.* 1986). Alternatively the Egyptians could have cast an orifice in gold using a piece of drawn copper wire as the core. In both cases the length of the orifice could not have been large compared with its diameter. Hence in analysing water-clocks the equations for flow in long pipes cannot be used.

For short orifices entry and exit effects on the flow of water are important and must be added to the Poiseuille pressure loss. We have shown (ibid.) that an appropriate expression for the discharge coefficient (C_d) (see equation 3.4) for water-clock orifices is given by

$$1/C_d^2 = 1{\cdot}15 + 0{\cdot}0201\,(l/d) + \frac{909 + 54{\cdot}4(l/d)}{R_e}. \qquad (3.13)$$

We know that the rate of fall in the water level dh/dt in terms of the velocity of flow (v) in the orifice from the principle of continuity is given by

$$\frac{dh}{dt} = (d/D)^2 v. \qquad (3.14)$$

[4] A similar example of Egyptian conservatism is seen in the calendar ceilings of Seti I and Rameses IV which, although separated by about a century and a half, are basically of the same design (Parker 1950).

Fluids and solids

where D is the internal diameter of the vessel at the water surface. Hence if equation (3.13) is combined with equations (3.12) and (3.4), the rate of fall in water-level dh/dt can be integrated to give the change in height of the water-level with time.

Using the above equations we can examine the performance of the Karnak clock. A remaining problem in the analysis is that the Egyptian definition of night is not known with any certainty. Neugebauer and Parker (1960:101) have deduced from the star charts of the Ninth to Twelfth Dynasties (*c.* 2160–1786 BC) that the Egyptian's definition of night excluded twilight and roughly corresponded to the period of darkness when the sun is more than 18° below the horizon. Such a period of darkness is called *astronomical night*. However the Karnak clock was more suited to *civil night*; that is, the period between sunset and sunrise. We have calculated the dimensions of orifices that would have been suitable for either astronomical or civil night at the time of the spring equinox assuming that the water temperature was 20 °C (Fig. 3.9). It is obvious that the diameter of the orifice for the Karnak clock must have been less than a millimetre. The accuracy of the clock's timekeeping throughout the night is illustrated in Fig. 3.10 where true Egyptian time is plotted against the time indicated by the Karnak clock. The greatest inaccuracy would have occurred at about the ninth hour of the night when

Fig. 3.9. Dimensions of orifices suitable for the Karnak clock.
11:56 hour night: ——
9:19 hour night:----

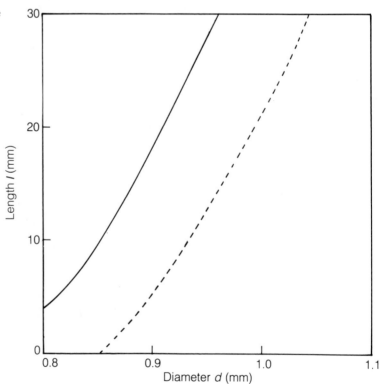

the clock would have been about 15 minutes fast. Because the scales could not have been read to a much greater accuracy, the clock would have been accurate as far as the Egyptians were concerned. Thus Amenemhet's claim that the clock was 'unlike any other ever made' was justified.

The performance of the Karnak clock through the changing seasons is more difficult to assess. Not only does the length of the night vary with the seasons, but also the temperature. There is some evidence that the effect of temperature on the flow from water-clocks was known at quite an early date both in Egypt and China. Huan Tan (about 40 BC – AD 30), who was the Chinese court secretary in charge of water-clocks, mentions both the effects of temperature and humidity, since there would be some loss of water through evaporation (Needham and Wang 1959:321). In the third century AD Athenaeus of Naukratis (II, 16) relates that water 'used in hour glasses does not make the hours in winter the same as those in summer but longer, for the flow is slower on account of the increased density of water'. An increase in water temperature of 1°C will cause the Karnak clock to run fast by about 10 minutes, because the viscosity of water decreases as its temperature rises. Naturally we do not know the exact temperature of the water. However, since the Karnak clock was probably located within the massive temple of Amen-Re, which would tend to maintain an even temperature, we can assume that the water temperature was somewhere between the daily extremes of the air temperature. The ambient temperature

Fig. 3.10. Time as indicated by the Karnak clock (Egyptian hours as a function of adjusted Karnak hours). 0·84 × 3 mm orifice:-—-, theory; ○ experiment. 0·84 × 9 mm orifice:——, theory; + experiment.

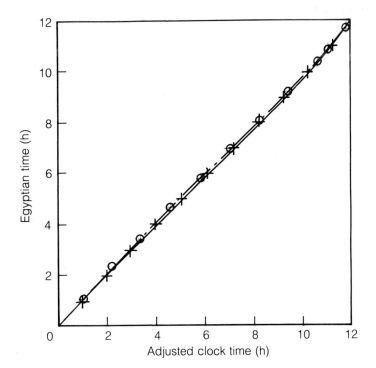

during the second millennium BC is unlikely to have been much different to what it is today. Rather than assume what the water temperature was and calculate the duration of night indicated by the clock throughout the year, we have calculated the water temperature necessary to make it accurate to within ± 10 minutes for each month of the year (Cotterell *et al.* 1986). In Fig. 3.11 the necessary water temperatures if the Karnak clock were adjusted to either civil or astronomical night are compared with the modern day ambient temperature range at Karnak. Clearly the clock would have been more suitable for civil than astronomical night. Analysis of a later clock from the reign of Ptolemy II indicates that it too was more suited to civil than astronomical night (Cotterell *et al.* 1986).

Although by this mechanical analysis we do not prove that the Egyptians used civil night in their ceremonies, the results are highly suggestive and must be considered when describing time-keeping in ancient Eqypt.

Solids

To appreciate the mechanical behaviour of much of early technology requires first an understanding of how solids deform. The reason why we deal with solids in this chapter is because in a mechanical sense they behave in a number of respects very much like liquids. The essential difference between them is that a solid can resist a shearing force without flowing, while a liquid cannot. Except in the simplest of mechanical systems there are

Fig. 3.11. Range in water temperature possible if the Karnak clock were to achieve an accuracy of ± 10 minutes on the duration of night.
Astronomical night (0.90×5.5 mm) ⫶;
civil night (0.83×9.7 mm) I :
temperature extremes ——

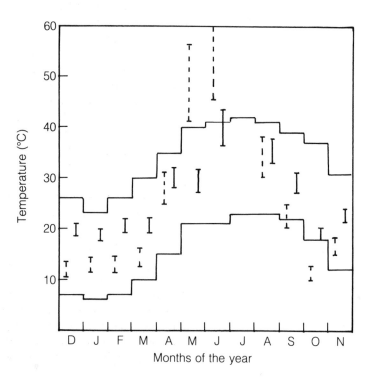

shear as well as compressive and tensile forces. The concept of pressure is generalised to take into account these shear forces. Although the concept of pressure was fairly well understood by the middle of the seventeenth century, the equivalent concept of stress in solids was not wholly formulated until 200 years later.

Stress and strength

All solid materials break. This statement is not profound, but the concept it embodies is evidently one that in the past has been difficult to comprehend. One of the methods early Australian miners used to distinguish small diamonds from similar-looking stones was to strike them with a hammer, and only those stones that did not fracture were considered to be diamonds. However, while diamonds are very hard, they are not tougher than other similar types of stones and will fracture if hit hard enough. Although, as we discuss in Chapter 6, badly flawed diamonds would fracture more easily than near perfect ones, thousands of good quality diamonds must have been smashed to worthless fragments. A major responsibility of engineers and architects is to make sure that the materials they use do not deform excessively or break under load. Until comparatively recently an empirical approach was followed with successful designs being repeatedly copied until an adventurous soul attempted some change. Failure of course meant condemnation for not following ways tried and true. Leonardo da Vinci was the first to describe a method of measuring the strength of a solid (Parsons 1968:72–3). From Leonardo's very practical description of a testing procedure to measure the strength of iron wires it is very likely that he actually performed such tests. Leonardo did not give any results of tests on wires of different diameters, but he did consider columns of different cross-sectional areas. In an analysis that may reveal his arithmetic deficiencies Leonardo considered two columns of equal length, one with a cross-sectional area four times greater than the other that would, he calculated, support eight times the load (Hart 1925:137–8). He also concluded that the strength of columns varied inversely proportional to their lengths. Slender columns will buckle more easily if they are long, but the columns illustrated by Leonardo are very stocky and would not have failed by buckling. The strength of these columns would be proportional to their cross-sectional area and independent of their length. Thus Leonardo had no clear idea about the relative strengths of components of different sizes.

Galileo devoted a considerable part of his book, *Dialogues*, to a discussion on the strength of materials. He recognised that the strength of bars under tension is proportional to their cross-sectional areas, reasoning that the number of 'fibres' binding the parts together is proportional to the area. To Galileo (1638:55) wood was like rope, composed of fibres, each of which would carry a given load. Stone and metal did not have an obvious

fibrous structure and Galileo found their mechanical properties
more puzzling. He discounted the notion that some kind of glue
held the parts together because no known glue could withstand
the heat of a furnace and yet molten metals retained their original
strengths when they resolidified (Galileo 1638:65). He was able to
demonstrate by simple experiments that the fracture of a solid was
clearly different to the rupture of a column of water when a
vacuum was created. From experiments on the strength of copper
wire Galileo (1638:64–5) deduced that, regardless of diameter, the
maximum length of wire that could be supported without
breaking was 4801 cubits (2770 m), whereas water could only
sustain a column 18 cubits (10.4 m) high. If copper ruptured like
water does when a vacuum is produced, then it would only
support a length of 2 cubits (1.16 m) because copper is about
nine times heavier than water. Galileo (1638:66), not being
prepared to abandon entirely the idea that materials failed when a
vacuum was produced, speculated that there might be extremely
small vacua scattered throughout solid bodies and that these
would be more difficult to break than a single vacuum. It is now
known that a solid is composed of atoms bonded together by
electrostatic forces. However the actual strength of a solid cannot
be directly calculated from the strength of the bonds between
atoms because when fracture occurs it is not necessary for all the
bonds to break simultaneously. We consider the strength of brittle
solids like stone in Chapter 6.

In fluids the most important concept is that of pressure – the
force per unit area it exerts either on a surface of the container or
on any imaginary surface within the fluid itself. The same concept
is used in solids, but under a different name. We call the force per
unit area of surface in a solid, *stress*. Solids are more rigid than
fluids and can resist a shearing force without flowing, so that in
general the force acting across a surface can have a component
parallel to the surface as well as perpendicular to it. The
perpendicular component of the force per unit area in a solid is
similar to the pressure in a fluid, and is called the *normal* stress.
Although a solid does not flow like a fluid there is a tendency for
stresses to be uniform in those parts of a body that have no
abrupt change in cross-section. For instance when we take a
standard engineering tensile test piece shaped like the one in
Fig. 3.12a, firmly grip the larger ends and pull, the stress over the
central portion of reduced diameter is uniform and perpendicular
to the cross-section. If the force applied to each end of the
specimen is F and the perpendicular cross-sectional area is A,
then the normal stress σ over the central portion is as given by
Fig 3.12b,

$$\sigma = \frac{F}{A}. \tag{3.15}$$

The pascal, which is the unit of pressure, is also used to denote
stress. However since solids are usually subjected to much larger

stresses than fluids their values are usually given in megapascals (MPa = 10^6 Pa). As an example, if we pull on a test specimen whose cross-sectional area is 100 mm² with a force of 4000 N, the stress is $4000/100 \times 10^6$ Pa, or 40 MPa. If there are notches or defects with sharp internal angles in the solid then the local stress will be much larger than the average stress. The ratio of the local stress at the notch to the average stress is called the *stress concentration factor*.

   If we pull hard enough on any tension specimen we can break it. The stress at which a solid breaks under tension is called its *ultimate tensile strength*. For homogeneous materials tensile strength is reasonably independent of the size of the specimen. Hence if we know the tensile strength of a material we will also

Fig. 3.12. (*a*) Tensile specimen; (*b*) stress acting on a perpendicular section of a tensile specimen; (*c*) stress acting on an oblique section of the tensile specimen.

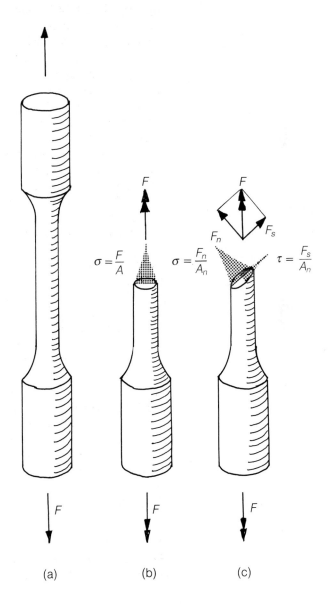

$$\sigma = \frac{F}{A}$$

$$\sigma = \frac{F_n}{A_n}$$

$$\tau = \frac{F_s}{A_n}$$

(a)   (b)   (c)

know what force any component of it can withstand in tension. Approximate tensile strengths for a range of materials are given in Table 3.1.

Before the nineteenth century philosophers and engineers did not use the word stress in a strictly technical sense but to describe the distress experienced by a solid when subjected to load. The comparisons were made between solids that were equally stressed, although the degrees of stress were not quantified. The concept of stress as we know it in a technical sense today was first formulated by Augustin Cauchy (1789–1857), one of the great mathematicians of the nineteenth century (Todhunter and Pearson 1886:321). In a fluid at rest pressure acts equally in all directions, and we obtain the same pressure at a point regardless of the orientation of the surface at that point. Such is not the case in solids. If we consider the stress acting across an oblique section of our tensile specimen (Fig 3.12c) then the force F that must still act across this section can be resolved into a perpendicular component F_n and a tangential component F_s. The stress acting across this oblique

Table 3.1 *Mechanical properties of some typical materials*

Material	Density (kg/m³)	Tensile strength (MPa)	Maximum elastic strain[a] (%)	Young's modulus (GPa)	Resilience per unit volume (kJ/m³)	Resilience per unit mass (J/kg)
Metals						
wrought iron	7800	150	0·04	210	20	3
modern spring steel	7800	2000	0·8	210	6700	860
modern low carbon steel	7800	450	0·15	210	240	30
bronze	8700	120	0·06	120	20	3
Softwoods						
Scots pine	460	90	0·9	10	400	900
yew	630	120	1·2	10	700	1100
Hardwoods						
ash	600	120	1·0	12	600	1000
elm	460	70	1·0	7	350	800
oak	610	90	1·0	11	550	900
hickory	680	100	0·8	13	420	600
Other materials						
sinews	1300	100	8·3	1·2	4100	3200
buffalo horn	1300	120	4·4	2·7	2600	2000
rubber	1200	10	300·0	—	10000	8000
carbon	2200	2000	0·5	410	5000	2000
kevlar	1500	2700	2·0	130	27000	18000

[a] The maximum strain given for wood is after loading. Some inelastic deformation would occur on the first load.

section has a *normal* component σ and a *shear* component τ defined by

$$\sigma = \frac{F_n}{A_n} \quad \text{and} \quad \tau = \frac{F_s}{A_n} \tag{3.16}$$

where A_n is the area of the oblique cross-section. As we change the direction of our section the stresses also change. To fully define the state of stress at a point we need to know the stress acting across three separate planes about the point. In general the stresses acting across a plane comprise of both a shear and a normal component. However Cauchy showed that it is possible always to find three special planes across which only normal stresses act (Todhunter and Pearson 1886:319). These three planes are called *principal planes*, and the normal stresses that act across them, the *principal stresses*. The state of stress at a point is characterised by the principal stresses. In bodies of more complicated geometry than the one shown in Fig. 3.12a the principal stresses vary from point to point, as do the orientations of the principal planes.

Deformation and strain

A solid can only resist a stress by deforming. In a rubber band this deformation is obvious, but what may not be appreciated is that even seemingly rigid materials must deform under load, because all stress is resisted by the forces between atoms. There are two kinds of forces: an attractive electrostatic force, and a repulsive force caused by the interaction between the electrons of adjacent atoms. The repulsive force, which is in some ways similar to a mechanical interaction, has a shorter range than the attractive force. Therefore, when a solid is free from mechanical load, the atoms come into equilibrium at a distance where the repulsive and attractive forces just balance one another. A tensile stress applied to the solid is resisted by the atoms moving further apart so that there is a net attractive force between them which balances the applied stress. Under a compressive stress, the opposite happens: the atoms move together so that there is a net repulsive force between them. If the applied stress is uniform, then the interatomic distance changes by the same amount everywhere, so that the change in length of the solid is proportional to the length over which it is measured. Writing in the nineteenth century Rankine introduced the technical term *strain* for the proportionate change in length (Todhunter and Pearson 1893:288). In everyday usage stress and strain are synonymous, as they were to scientists and engineers before Rankine's day, which of course makes it quite confusing for the layman. Technically these words have separate distinct meanings, though there cannot be one without the other.

Just as there are two kinds of stress, normal and shear, so

similarly there are two kinds of strain. Normal strain ε (Fig. 3.13a) is the proportionate change in length that occurs under a normal stress σ, and is defined by

$$\varepsilon = \frac{u}{x} \tag{3.17}$$

where u is the elongation measured over a length x. If a solid with a square grid on it is sheared, the grid will distort so that its sides are no longer perpendicular (Fig 3.13b). The shear strain is defined by the distortion in the angle γ of the grid. In terms of displacement an expression for the shear strain is

$$\gamma = \frac{v}{x} \tag{3.18}$$

where v is the displacement in the y direction.

Stress–strain relationships

If the stress applied to a solid is relatively small, the atoms will not be permanently displaced and they will be able to move back to their original positions on the release of the stress. Such behaviour is called *elastic*. In the seventeenth century Robert Hooke (1676) recognised that for all materials small elastic deformations were proportional to the applied force. This principle is utilised in the spring balance, which extends in proportion to the load applied. The extension in a spring is relatively large in comparison to the deformation in the steel, which remains small. The large extension comes from the spring's design rather than the material's deformation. In some materials, such as rubber, large elastic deformations are possible, but they are not *linear*; that is to say, the deformation is not proportional to the load.

Hooke had made his discovery of linear elasticity in 1660 when he invented a spring escapement for clocks, but he did not immediately publish the result because he wanted to obtain a patent for a particular application of the principle. When Hooke (1676) finally committed himself to print he did so in the form of a cryptic anagram. It was not until after the death of Henry Oldenburg, the troublemaking Secretary of the Royal Society, that Hooke (1678) felt free to publish the solution, 'ut tensio sic vis', which means, 'as the extension so the force'.

Fig. 3.13. (a) Normal strain; *(b)* shear strain.

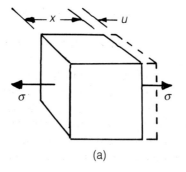
(a)

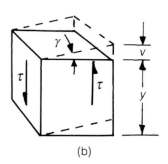
(b)

Hooke's law states that an elastic body extends in proportion to the force applied. As such the law is concerned with the overall behaviour of the body. In fact, not only is the overall extension proportional to the force, but the elastic strain at every point in the body is proportional to the stress. Furthermore the constant of proportionality between the stress and the elastic strain is a material constant. This generalisation of Hooke's law was made by Thomas Young in his 1802 lectures at the Royal Institution (Young 1845, I:106). The constant of elastic proportionality between normal stress and strain has since been named *Young's modulus* (E) in his honour. Thus:

$$E = \frac{\sigma}{\varepsilon}. \tag{3.19}$$

Because strain is non-dimensional the units of Young's modulus are those of stress. Most engineering materials are very stiff, and Young's modulus is therefore usually expressed in gigapascals (GPa = 10^9 Pa). The values of Young's modulus for some common materials are given in Table 3.1.

An elastic rod that is stretched by a tensile stress also contracts laterally in proportion to the axial strain. The constant of proportionality between the lateral and axial strains is called *Poisson's ratio* (v) after the French mathematician Siméon Poisson (1781–1840). If a material were incompressible it would have a Poisson's ratio of a half. Since no material is completely incompressible, Poisson's ratio is always less than a half, and for most rigid materials it is in the range 0·2–0·3. For rubber and rubber-like polymers Poisson's ratio is larger.

Shear stress (τ) is also proportional to shear strain (γ), and the constant of proportionality G, called the shear modulus, is

$$G = \frac{\tau}{\gamma}. \tag{3.20}$$

Cauchy (1829:293–319), in his study of general stress systems, showed that only two constants were necessary to describe the elastic behaviour of an isotropic solid (that is, a solid whose properties are the same in any direction).

Hence the shear modulus G is a function of Young's modulus E and Poisson's ratio v which is

$$G = \frac{E}{2(1+v)}. \tag{3.21}$$

Since v is about 0·25 for many materials, the shear modulus is about 0·4E.

Brittle materials like glass and stone are elastic right up to the point where they break. Other materials such as metals are more ductile. Below a certain stress level ductile materials behave elastically, but at higher stresses they undergo permanent deformation and flow plastically. The level of stress at which the deformation becomes non-elastic is called the *yield strength*.

Fluids and solids

Ductile materials can withstand substantial strains before failure. For example wrought iron can only sustain a stress of about 80 MPa and a strain of 0·04% without yielding, but will elongate in tension by about 30% before failure. The resistance of ductile materials continues to increase with deformation after they yield and the *ultimate tensile strength* can be considerably larger than the *yield strength*.

Resilience and strain energy
The work performed in deforming an elastic solid is recovered when it is unloaded. A hunter, by drawing his bow, stores elastic energy in it. On release this energy is transferred to the arrow, which is propelled forward. Similarly the Greek and Roman catapults could store remarkable amounts of energy in their sinew torsion springs – sufficient to hurl rocks 40 kg or more in weight several hundred metres. The ability of a material to store energy is important in applications like these.

When we stretch an elastic bar we must apply a force that increases in proportion to the degree of elongation (Fig. 3.14). The work done by a force is the product of that force and the distance through which it acts. In stretching a bar the force continuously increases in proportion to the elongation. Since the force applied does not remain constant during the entire elongation, the work done cannot be simply the product of the maximum force applied and the elongation of the bar. To illustrate this point let us examine the increase in work that occurs during a small increment in the elongation du (Fig 3.14). There is little variation of the force during a small extension of the bar and the increment in work dW is simply Fdu. If we sum all the work done during all such small increments in elongation the total work (W) done in stretching a bar an amount u is equal to the area under the force-elongation diagram, that is,

Fig. 3.14. Work done in stretching a bar.

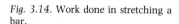

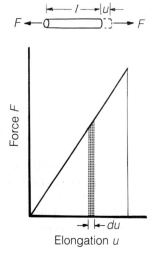

Force F

$\leftarrow$ du
Elongation u

$$W = \frac{1}{2}Fu. \tag{3.22}$$

If the cross-sectional area of the bar is A and its length l, the expression for the work done in terms of the stress σ and the strain ε becomes

$$W = \frac{1}{2}(\sigma A) \times (\varepsilon l) = \frac{1}{2}\sigma\varepsilon \times Al = \frac{1}{2}\sigma\varepsilon \times \text{volume}.$$

This work is stored as elastic energy, which is recoverable on unloading. Therefore, the elastic energy stored per unit volume, which is called the *strain energy density* U, is given by

$$U = \frac{1}{2}\sigma\varepsilon. \tag{3.23}$$

Since the stress can be related to the strain by Young's modulus, alternative expressions for the strain energy density are

$$U = \frac{\sigma^2}{2E} = \frac{E\varepsilon^2}{2}. \tag{3.24}$$

Young (1845 I:110) called the maximum elastic strain energy that a material could store its *resilience*. Table 3.1 shows that some natural materials are very efficient at storing energy. In fact only rubber and modern fibres are more resilient than sinews or horn on a mass basis. The resilience of sinews is quite phenomenal by any measure, and it is therefore not surprising that they were used for the torsion springs of Greek and Roman catapults.

The resilience of a material is also important where there are dynamic loads. In a storm the loads caused by a sudden gust of wind on the sails of a boat have to be resisted by the rigging. It is not the tensile strength of the ropes that matters in this case, but their resilience – how much energy they can absorb. Since the resilience is proportional to the volume, a long rope is capable of absorbing a larger energy than a short one. The rigging on sailing ships was very resilient because most of the ropes were long.

4

Machines

In developed countries people are familiar with an array of complex machines. Just about every home possesses a vacuum cleaner, sewing machine, electric razor and similar labour-saving devices. At work nearly all of us use a machine of some sort in our job. Books and newspapers are printed by presses that would hardly be recognised as such by Caxton. Many people, because they do not understand how machines work, assume that they are intrinsically complex. However, even the most complex machine can be disassembled into quite simple basic elements. The word *machine* was used in English originally only in reference to these basic elements. Before the nineteenth century the much older word *engine*, which now has the specialised meaning of machine capable of generating power, was used to describe the combination of *machine elements*. Thus in the seventeenth century Desaguliers (1743:122) defined an engine as 'the combination of two or more of the simple machines for the uses of life'. Here we are mainly concerned with machines in the original sense of the word.

The purpose of a machine (whether simple or complex) is to perform a particular task in a more convenient way than could be done through muscular power alone. The machine itself cannot make the task easier in the sense that less mechanical work is required, though usually the task is made physiologically more convenient. Sometimes the muscular force required is unaltered by the machine but we find the task easier to perform. For instance water can more readily be drawn from a well by a bucket with a rope that passes over a simple pulley so that the action is to pull down, rather than to haul up the bucket. The *useful* work done – the product of the weight of the bucket full of water and the height it is raised – is the same in both cases. However the *total* mechanical work performed must be slightly greater when a pulley is used because there is some friction to be overcome. As we have emphasised in Chapter 2, it is only *mechanical* work that is relevant in the study of mechanics. This important distinction between physiological effort and mechanical work has not always been appreciated.

In antiquity the major value of machines was their ability to amplify human muscle force. The force amplification of a machine is its *mechanical advantage (MA)*, defined as the ratio of the force applied by the machine to the force required to operate it. If the mechanical advantage is greater than one, then the driving force acting on the machine operates through a larger distance than the output from it. When a lever is used, for instance to move a rock, a far heavier weight can be lifted than can be done unaided, but the lever has to be moved through a larger distance than the rock. The ratio between the velocity of the driving force and the output of a machine (both velocities being measured in the direction of the forces) is called its *velocity ratio (VR)*. If we had a perfect machine that was weightless and did not dissipate any work in friction, the work done *on* it would, by the principle of energy conservation, be equal to the work done *by* it. The ratio of the work done *by* the machine to the work done *on* the machine is equal to *MA/VR*, since

$$\frac{MA}{VR} = \frac{\text{output force}}{\text{input force}} \times \frac{\text{output velocity}}{\text{input velocity}}$$

$$= \frac{\text{work done by the machine}}{\text{work done on the machine}}.$$

So for a perfect machine this ratio is one, and the mechanical advantage is equal to the velocity ratio. As Galileo wrote, 'whatever is gained in force is lost in speed' (Drabkin and Drake 1960:163). For a real machine, the mechanical advantage is always less than the velocity ratio because more work has to be done on it than is obtained from it. The ratio between the input and output of work is called its efficiency (η). Hence

$$\eta = \frac{MA}{VR}. \tag{4.1}$$

In this chapter we will discuss the basic machine elements and their uses in antiquity. There is no single classification of machine elements. The Alexandrian Greek, Heron, described five basic machine elements: the lever, winch, pulley, wedge and screw (Drachmann 1963:21). Heron assumed that the gear wheel belonged theoretically to the winch and did not include the inclined plane as a machine element. Other writers have viewed the screw as an application of the inclined plane rather than an element in itself. Ignoring the quibbles over classification we shall recognise seven machine elements: the lever, inclined plane, pulley, winch and capstan, screw, gear wheel and wedge.

The lever
The most natural of all machines is the lever: every movement of our bodies is facilitated by a system of bone levers. A tree branch used as a lever to move a rock is in one sense an extension of our arms. In this simple but general form the lever must have been the first machine. Needless to say, it is unnecessary to understand the mechanics of levers to be able to

use one for shifting a heavy weight. However from quite early times people have needed a reliable weighing machine for commerce, and the invention of such devices did require at least some understanding of the mechanics of levers. The principle of the equal-arm balance is self-evident. Archimedes embodies it in his first postulate for the theory of levers: namely, that equal weights suspended on a balance of equal arms will be in equilibrium (Clagett 1961:31). That this equilibrium was sometimes quite illusory is shown by the statement 'sellers of purple arrange their scales to deceive, by putting the cord out of true centre, and pouring lead into one arm of the balance' that appears in the *Mechanical problems* (problem 1) written by the followers of Aristotle in about 280 BC. The butcher's leaden thumb is a less ingenious deception.

The first discussion on the mechanics of levers appears in the *Mechanical problems* as do those of many of the simple machines. Although somewhat obscure, the Aristotelian derivation of the lever rule was essentially based on the modern concept of virtual work. A modern version of the Aristotelian argument goes as follows: imagine that a lever assumed to be weightless with two masses m_1 and m_2 attached at either end is displaced from its position of equilibrium through a small angle $d\theta$ (Fig. 4.1a). If there is no friction at the fulcrum, the work done *by* the descending weight must be equal to the work done *on* the ascending weight. The virtual displacements of the two weights ($x_1 d\theta$ and $x_2 d\theta$ respectively) are in proportion to their distances from the fulcrum. The virtual work of each weight is therefore proportional to the product of the weight and its distance from

Fig. 4.1. The lever rule.

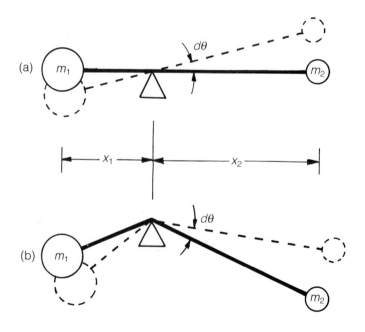

the fulcrum. Equating the virtual works of the two weights we have

$$m_1 g\, x_1 d\theta = m_2 g\, x_2 d\theta$$

or

$$\frac{m_1 g}{m_2 g} = \frac{x_2}{x_1},$$ (4.2)

that is, under equilibrium conditions the weights must be inversely proportional to their distance from the fulcrum. A more rigorous proof of the lever rule was given by Archimedes,[1] who in popular tradition was so impressed by the efficacy of the lever that he boasted that given a place to stand he could move the earth (Drachmann 1958).

In a work *On balances*, that has since been lost, Archimedes almost certainly extended his study on levers to include the case of the bent lever (Fig. 4.1b). For small displacements of the bent lever from its position of equilibrium the virtual vertical displacements of the weights are in proportion to their horizontal distances from the fulcrum. Thus the lever rule (equation 4.2) applies to the bent lever, providing that the distances used are measured horizontally. There is, however, one important difference between the straight and the bent lever – regardless of the orientation, the horizontal distances of the weights on a straight beam are always in the same proportion. Therefore the lever is in equilibrium at any angle to the horizontal. Such a lever would obviously not function as a balance. The bent lever has only one position of equilibrium and if it is displaced will return to that position and forms the basis of the balance.

The moment of a force
The lever rule is only a particular case of a more general principle of mechanics that is concerned with the twisting action of a force. Recall that in Chapter 2 we showed that a body is in equilibrium if the vector sum of the forces acting on it are zero. When a bar is loaded at each end by an equal and opposite force the vector sum of the forces is zero; but there is obviously a twisting action that will cause the bar to rotate. Galileo called the twisting action of a force its *moment* (Drabkin and Drake 1960:151). It is easiest to open a door by pushing on the door knob, because the twisting action of the force is larger the farther away it is from the hinge. The door will also open more easily if one pushes perpendicular to it. Pushing at an oblique angle to the door is less effective, and the door cannot open at all if one pushes towards the hinge. In scalar terms, the moment of a force about an axis is the product of the force F and the perpendicular distance r of its line of action from the axis. Thus the moment M about the hinge of the door illustrated in Fig. 4.2 is given by

$$M = Fr.$$ (4.3)

[1] Ernst Mach (1838–1916) showed that Archimedes' proof was not entirely rigorous because the lever rule was tacitly assumed in its derivation. More sophisticated versions of Archimedes' proof conceived by Galileo and by Huygens have the same defect (Mach 1942:16–26).

Alternatively we can resolve the force F on the door knob into the components F_p perpendicular and F_t tangential to the door. As we have noted, the tangential component does not contribute to the moment opening the door, and

$$M = F_p r^*$$

since $F_p = F \cos \theta$

and $r^* = r / \cos \theta$,

this expression for the moment is identical to that given in equation (4.3).

A moment is a vector quantity similar to force and its unit is the newton metre (Nm).[2] In most of the problems we will consider that moments have common axis and can be added algebraically, taking anti-clockwise moments as positive and clockwise moments as negative. However when we consider the mechanics of boomerangs in Chapter 7 it will be necessary to examine the vectorial nature of a moment more closely. For equilibrium of a body, not only must the vector sum of the forces acting on it be zero but also the vector sum of the moments. Let us see how the principle of moments applies to the lever (Fig. 4.1). If we take moments about the fulcrum for either the straight or bent lever

Fig. 4.2. The moment on a door hinge.

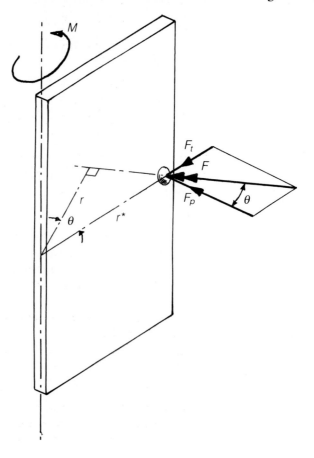

[2] Although the unit of a moment is the same as the unit for work, the newton metre should never be referred to as a joule when it applies to a moment.

we have an anti-clockwise moment $m_1 g x_1$ and a clockwise moment $m_2 g x_2$. The total moment on the beam must be zero for equilibrium, therefore

$$m_1 g x_1 - m_2 g x_2 = 0,$$

and hence the lever rule of equation (4.2). When considering the equilibrium of a body it does not matter where one takes moments. For instance we could have taken moments about either end of the lever instead of at the fulcrum and still have obtained the same result.

The levers in Fig. 4.1 are a particular example of three forces acting on a body. One of the consequences of the principle of moments is that if there are only three forces acting on a body they must act in the same plane and, if not parallel, their lines of action must intersect at one point. There is no similar limitation if there are more than three forces acting on a body.

If we apply a moment $\mathbf{M}$ to the balanced lever of Fig. 4.1a it will start to rotate. Assuming that the lever is light so that its weight can be neglected we can calculate its dynamic behaviour directly from Newton's second law. The effect of the moment $\mathbf{M}$ will be to apply out of balance forces $\mathbf{F}_1$ and $\mathbf{F}_2$ to the two masses on either end of the lever, where

$$\mathbf{M} = \mathbf{x}_1 \times \mathbf{F}_1 + \mathbf{x}_2 \times \mathbf{F}_2.$$

These forces cause the two masses to accelerate so that from equation (2.1)

$$\mathbf{F}_1 = m_1 \mathbf{a}_1 \text{ and } \mathbf{F}_2 = m_2 \mathbf{a}_2$$

where $\mathbf{a}_1$ and $\mathbf{a}_2$ are the two accelerations. If the angular acceleration (rate of change of angular velocity) of the lever is α, these two accelerations are given by

$$\mathbf{a}_1 = \alpha \times \mathbf{x}_1 \text{ and } \mathbf{a}_2 = \alpha \times \mathbf{x}_2.$$

We can obtain an expression for the moment in terms of the angular acceleration it produces

$$\mathbf{M} = I \alpha \qquad (4.4)$$

where $I = m_1 x_1^2 + m_2 x_2^2$ is the *moment of inertia* of the lever about the fulcrum. If the body is free and there is no fixed fulcrum (as will be the case when we study the dynamics of a spear in Chapter 7) then the moment and the moment of inertia are taken

Table 4.1 *Moments of inertia about the centre of gravity of some geometric bodies*

Object	Axis	Moment of inertia
thin rod	perpendicular to length	$\frac{1}{12} m l^2$
rectangular block	perpendicular to plane	$\frac{1}{12} m (a^2 + b^2)$
solid cylinder	axis of cylinder	$\frac{1}{2} m r^2$

about the centre of gravity of the body. In this section we have derived the moment of inertia for a bar with discrete masses. The moment of inertia of real bodies with distributed mass are a little more difficult to calculate and for reference we give values in Table 4.1 for a few of the common shapes. The kinetic energy T of a body of moment of inertia I rotating about its centre of gravity with an angular velocity ω is given by

$$T = \tfrac{1}{2}I\omega^2. \tag{4.5}$$

Lever systems of animals

The physical movement of many forms of animal life is facilitated by a system of levers. The muscles are attached quite close to the joints so that there is a mechanical advantage of less than one. By taking moments about the elbow we can calculate the force F an average person would need to generate in their flexor muscle to lift a rock weighing 8 kg (Fig. 4.3). The bone joints of animals are well lubricated with synovial fluid and are consequently very free. Thus with little approximation we can neglect the friction in the elbow joint. The forearm and hand weigh about 1·6 kg and have a centre of gravity about 170 mm from the elbow joint. For equilibrium the total moment about the elbow must be zero, hence

$$0{\cdot}04\,F - 0{\cdot}17 \times 1{\cdot}6 \times 9{\cdot}81 - 0{\cdot}36 \times 8 \times 9{\cdot}81 = 0.$$

Therefore the flexor muscle must exert a force of 790 N to lift a rock that weighs 8 kg. The mechanical advantage of the arm in this position is $8 \times 9{\cdot}81/790 = 0{\cdot}1$. The contraction of the muscle is much smaller than the movement of the rock and the velocity ratio of the arm is equal to the ratio of the lever arms, $40/360$ or $1/9$. In the natural design of the arm the two opposing requirements of mobility and strength are balanced to give an optimum performance. Different animals, of course, require different solutions. The legs of a horse which are designed for fast movement require a high mobility and hence have a low velocity ratio of about $1/12$. The armadillo on the other hand does not need to run fast but requires strong front legs for digging. Consequently it has a larger velocity ratio of about $1/4$ and hence a larger mechanical advantage.

Lifting with a lever

Before the invention of the pulley there were only two machine elements that could be used for lifting: the lever and the inclined plane. Levers can be used on moderately sized stone blocks to manoeuvre them during placement, and in Egyptian and Greek masonry walls small handing bosses can still be seen on some of the blocks. In lifting a block a person makes use of two 'levers' – one the actual lever, and the other the block itself as it rotates about one edge. Heron of Alexandria attempted to solve the theoretical problem of lifting a block with a lever. While

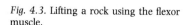

Fig. 4.3. Lifting a rock using the flexor muscle.

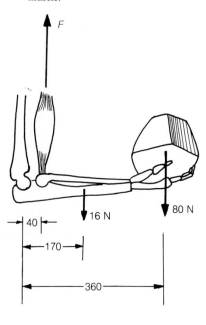

appreciating that only part of the block had to be lifted, Heron
was confused about the application of the lever rule to the block
itself (Drachmann 1963:63–7). Galileo (1638:154–6) gave the
correct solution in his *Dialogues*. Consider the lever and the block
separately (Fig. 4.4). There will be a reaction force R between the
lever and the block. If the block and lever were frictionless this
reaction would be perpendicular to the lever, as shown in Fig. 4.4
Taking moments of the forces on the lever about its fulcrum Q,
neglecting the weight of the lever, we obtain

$$Rb - Fa = 0$$

and moments of the forces on the block about its fulcrum P give
us
$$Rc - mgd = 0.$$

The force F necessary to lift the block can be found by eliminating
the reaction force R between these two equations. Thus

$$F = mg\left(\frac{bd}{ac}\right). \tag{4.6}$$

The direct lift possible with a lever is limited, but an object
can be raised to a considerable height in stages by inserting blocks

Fig. 4.4. Lifting a block with a lever.

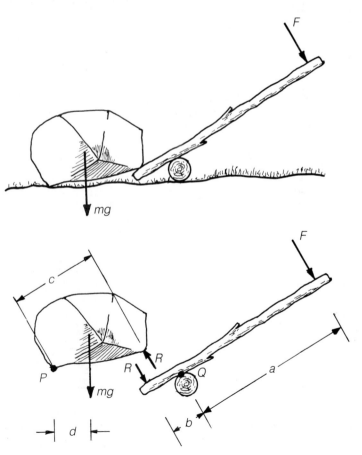

under it after each lift so that a platform is gradually built up. In 1955, the Mayor of Easter Island, Pedro Aten, told Thor Heyerdahl that according to tradition the Easter Island statues had been erected by this means. To demonstrate the method's feasibility Heyerdahl had Aten re-erect a fallen 25-tonne statue. The task required 11 men a total of eighteen days to complete

Fig. 4.5. A traditional Chinese building method for raising heavy weights. A slip-knot hoists the main cable in successive pulls by means of a lever and radiating ropes; a monk directs the operation. Nineteenth-century European lithographic copy of a Chinese drawing.

(Heyerdahl 1958:145–8). It has been suggested by some archaeologists that much the same method was used to lift the lintels into place at Stonehenge. The traditional Chinese method for lifting heavy weights also uses the lever. In this method (Fig. 4.5) the burden was suspended by a rope secured by two or more purchases around one of the beams of the scaffolding, and raised by the successive actions of the lever attached by a slip knot to the main rope.

The beam press

The press for extracting oil from olives, and juices from grapes and other fruits, has always been an important item of farm technology in Mediterranean countries. The simplest form of press, known in Egypt since very early times, is the bag press, where the fruits were placed in a linen bag that was first twisted and then stretched apart to extract the juice. An illustration from the Great Pyramid at Giza (Fig. 4.6) shows the acrobatics that this type of press required for its operation.

In ancient Greece olive oil was an important part of the diet, as it still is today in that country. Considerably higher pressures are necessary to squeeze oil from olives than juice from fruits, and the Greeks developed the beam press which worked on the lever principle. In its simplest form, dating from about 1500 BC, one end of the beam was hinged in a recess in a wall and pre-crushed olives were heaped between a number of wooden boards placed

Fig. 4.6. An Egyptian press.

near the hinge. The other end of the beam was loaded with stones. It must at times have been difficult to obtain the required pressure with these simple presses, and Greek vases depict scenes in which slaves cling to the beam to add their weight to the load. The Greeks and later the Romans made a number of improvements to this simple press. In some versions the beam was drawn down by a windlass rather than heavy weights. This type of press had the disadvantage that the pressure on the crushed olives would relax with time. Other presses used a heavy weight, but lifted it to the beam with a windlass and pulley system, giving a steady pressure and allowing a heavier weight to be employed. The major disadvantage of the beam press was its size. The Roman statesman, Marcus Cato (XVIII, 2), wrote that the beam should be 7·5 m long. Thus a press room containing two presses, four mills for crushing the olives and four vats, measured a capaceous 20 by 15 m. The invention of the much more compact direct-screw press – probably some time in the first century AD – must have had an effect on the design of villas in Greece and other Mediterranean countries.[3]

The balance

Although the basic principle of the equal arm balance (called the *trutina* by the Romans) is obvious, its stability needs some discussion. If a balance is to be stable its potential energy must be at a minimum when the beam is horizontal. Hence the centre of mass of the whole balance including pans, loads, weights and beam, must be below the fulcrum point. However the centre of mass cannot be too far below the fulcrum or it will be insensitive.

The balance illustrated in Fig. 4.7 is based on an early Egyptian design – for the purpose of clarity it is drawn out of proportion. The beam was cylindrical, with its ends in the form of a lotus flower, and the pans were pivoted on its centre line. By hanging the beam on a stand by a loop of cord the fulcrum point O is effectively positioned on its top surface. Let us analyse the balance when one of the pans is a little heavier $d(mg)$ than the other, causing the beam to tilt through a small angle $d\theta$. The sum of all the moments of the forces about the fulcrum O must be zero. If the angle of tilt $d\theta$ is small we can use the approximation $\cos(d\theta) = 1$ and $\sin(d\theta) = d\theta$ to obtain

$$(m+dm)g(l-ad\theta) - mg(l+ad\theta) - m_bgad\theta - m_pgbd\theta = 0,$$

where m_b is the mass of the beam, and m_p is the mass of a plummet suspended from the beam by three strings to indicate precise balance. Neglecting the very small second order quantity $dmd\theta ag$ we find that the inclination $d\theta$ of the beam is given by

$$d\theta = \frac{l\dfrac{dm}{m}}{\left[\left(2+\dfrac{m_b}{m}\right)a+\dfrac{m_p}{m}b\right]}. \tag{4.7}$$

[3] Pliny the Elder (XVIII, 317–19) wrote in about 79 AD that in the 'old days' people used the type of press described by Cato, but that within the last 20 years the direct screw press began to be used (Drachmann 1932:54–60).

For a sensitive balance the inclination $d\theta$ must be large. Therefore if the denominator in equation (4.7) is large the balance will be insensitive. The beam can be made longer to increase the sensitivity. Although some Egyptian balances were small, there are many illustrations of man-sized balances where the length of the beam is greater than 1·5 m. The illustrations of ancient Egyptian balances (other than ones depicting the weighing of the soul) often show cylinders of some kind being weighed.

For accurate weighing it is necessary to have a device that will indicate when the beam is in balance. In most illustrations of Egyptian balances a plummet is shown attached to the beam, usually by three strings. We suspect that the plummet was important because it was often shown being steadied by a weighmaster. Yet we are not certain exactly how this plummet was used. If it was arranged that most of the load was taken on the centre string, with only a very slight tension on the outside two, then one of these would go slack when the beam was out of balance, but this method would not be very sensitive. On the other hand, the plummet lines does not seem long enough for it to indicate only imbalance by its inclination to the vertical.

Fig. 4.7. Sensitivity of a balance (based on an early Egyptian balance).

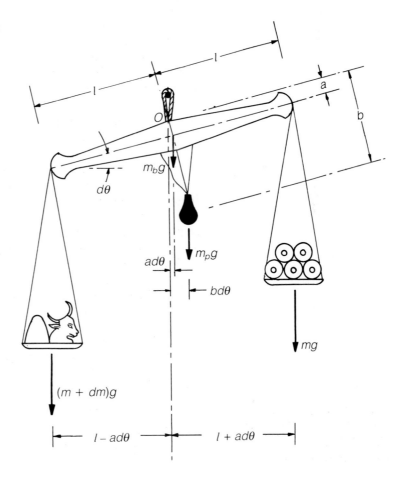

The Egyptians knew only the equal arm balance. The development of an unequal arm balance seems to presuppose knowledge of the lever rule. The first mention in the Western world of this balance is in the Aristotelian *Mechanical problems* (problem 19), where is it called a *phaloggos*. In this version, known as the bismar in Medieval Europe, the counterpoise weight is fixed and balance is achieved by moving the fulcrum, which was normally a simple loop of cord (Kisch 1965:56–66). The more familiar version is now known as the steelyard.[4] In this balance, the fulcrum is fixed and the counterpoise weight moved along the arm. The steelyard was introduced in the West by the Romans, who called it a *statera*. It has also been the most common type of scales in China since the Han dynasty of the second century BC.

The inclined plane

The Egyptians made extensive use of the inclined plane to lift weights. In the tomb of Rekhmara at Thebes there is a painting that Egyptologists believe shows a brick embankment with what may be a roofing block ready to be hauled up (Newberry 1900:pl 19). Embankments were undoubtedly used in the construction of the pyramids. The actual remains of a constructional embankment are evident on the unfinished great pylon of Karnak, dating from the reign of Sheshonq I (*c.* 945–924 BC) (Clarke and Engelbach 1930:93). Embankments were also employed to erect the obelisks – which surely must have been the Egyptians' most difficult feat of lifting. The largest obelisk ever erected in Egypt weighs about 500 tonnes, and now stands in the Piazza di San Giovanni in Rome. After dragging an obelisk up onto an embankment of about two-thirds its own height, the Egyptians lowered it onto its base by allowing sand to gradually run out from a pit in the end of the embankment (Chevrier 1970:33–8). The plinth of the obelisk had a groove which keyed the obelisk into position for the final lift to the vertical by means of ropes.

Heron of Alexandria failed in an attempt to calculate the force necessary to drag a weight up a frictionless incline. The correct solution was not given until the thirteenth century when the monk, Jordanus of Nemore, wrote his treatise *De ratione ponderis*.[5] Jordanus used the principle of virtual work to solve the problem, and it is fitting that we give a similar solution.

In Fig. 4.8 a mass m_1, resting on an inclined plane, is just in equilibrium with a mass m_2 to which it is attached by a string passing over a pulley. Such a system is often used in schools to establish experimentally the inclined plane theory. We assume all parts are frictionless and that the smallest change in either mass will cause movement. If we give mass m_2 a virtual downwards displacement dh, then mass m_1 will move an equal distance dh along the plane. The virtual work performed *by* mass m_2 will be

---

[4] The Hanse merchants used steelyards during the fifteenth century at their establishment on the north bank of the Thames, above London Bridge, which was called the steelyard. The English word steelyard is the result of a mistranslation of stäl (meaning sample) as steel (Little *et al.* 1978:2119).

[5] Although the Renaissance marked a change in the attitude to the study of mechanics, important works on mechanics were published earlier in Medieval times. The most significant writer on mechanical matters was Jordanus of Nemore. Almost nothing is known of his life apart from the fact that he taught at the University of Toulouse in 1229. Leonardo da Vinci certainly knew of Jordanus' work and was greatly influenced by it (Clagett 1961).

m_2gdh. In moving a distance dh along the incline, the mass m_1 rises vertically by $dh \sin \alpha$ and hence the virtual work done *on* it is $m_1gdh \sin \alpha$. For equilibrium the total virtual work is zero, hence

$$m_2g = m_1g \sin \alpha.$$

The tension T in the string must be equal to m_2g, and therefore the force T necessary to drag the burden up a frictionless incline is given by

$$T = m_1g \sin \alpha. \qquad (4.8)$$

Simon Stevin also gave a solution for this same problem and it is worth examining because it not only illustrates the ingenuity of the sixteenth-century thinkers but the range of methods that can be used in mechanics. Suppose we are in a frictionless world and throw an endless chain of uniform mass over a triangular block. The chain will hang stationary (as shown in Fig. 4.9) even though there is a greater weight on the inclined face than on the vertical one, since any movement would be perpetual and therefore impossible. The festoon of chain around the base of the

Fig. 4.8. The inclined plane.

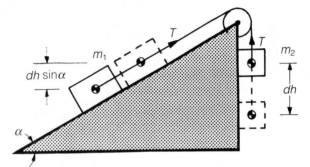

Fig. 4.9. Stevin's analysis of the inclined plane.

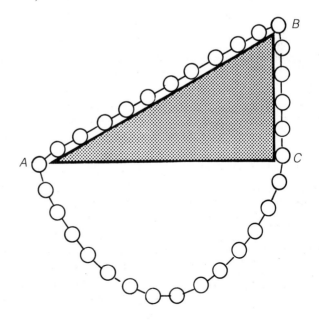

inclined plane is symmetrical and must effect both sides of the plane equally. It can, therefore, be removed without affecting the equilibrium, leaving a weight on the inclined face that is proportional to the length AB in fig. 4.9, and balancing a weight on the vertical face that is proportional to BC. The ratio of these weights, as we have already proved, is $\sin \alpha$.

Let us now examine the practical case of a sledge being hauled up a rough incline with a rope (Fig. 4.10). Because of the roughness of the surface, the reaction between the sledge and the incline is offset from the perpendicular by the friction angle λ. We assume that the rope attached to the sledge makes an angle θ to the incline. The three lines of action of the forces acting on the sledge, the tension in the rope T, the reaction R, and the weight of the sledge mg must all pass through the same point. For equilibrium motion the resultant of the tension T and the weight mg must be equal and opposite to the reaction R. Applying the sine rule we obtain

$$\frac{T}{\sin (\alpha + \lambda)} = \frac{mg}{\sin \left[\dfrac{\pi}{2} + (\theta - \lambda)\right]}.$$

Hence the force necessary to pull the sledge up the incline is

$$T = mg \frac{\sin (\alpha + \lambda)}{\cos (\theta - \lambda)}. \tag{4.9}$$

The force necessary to pull the sledge is at a minimum when $\cos(\theta - \lambda)$ has its largest value which is one, that is, when $\theta = \lambda$. The minimum force necessary to move the sledge is therefore

$$T = mg \sin (\alpha + \lambda). \tag{4.10}$$

The friction effectively increases the angle of the incline α by the friction angle λ.

An alternative method of getting a heavy stone up an embankment is to roll it. Needless to say, this method is easiest

Fig. 4.10. A sledge being hauled up a rough incline.

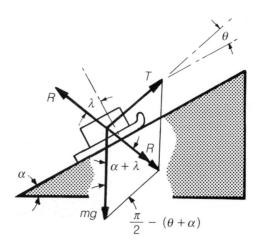

with cylindrically-shaped stones, but a rectangular one can be moved in much the same way by enclosing it in a round timber frame. By taking a number of turns of rope around a cylinder, which unwind as the rope is pulled, it can be moved up an incline in exactly the same manner as barrels of beer are parbuckled into a pub's cellar. It has been suggested that the lintels in Stonehenge may have been parbuckled up an earthen ramp (Thomson 1954:493), though we consider it much more likely that they were lifted by levers. The force necessary to parbuckle a cylinder up an incline can be found by taking moments about the point of contact O (Fig. 4.11). Neglecting the resistance due to rolling (which is a topic dealt with in Chapter 8), we have, for equilibrium,

$$mg(r \sin \alpha) - T(2r) = 0$$

or

$$T = \frac{mg}{2} \sin \alpha \qquad (4.11)$$

If we compare this equation with equation (4.10) then we see that the force necessary to parbuckle a roughly cylindrical block up a slope is only half of what would be required to drag it up a frictionless incline.

The pulley

The first representation of a pulley occurs in an Assyrian relief of the eighth century BC (Burstall 1963:58). The simple pulley provides no mechanical advantage, but does enable a burden to be conveniently lifted with a downward pull by a number of men. As such the simple pulley may have developed from the use of a rope thrown over a tree limb. Strangely, the pulley was unknown to the ancient Egyptians; the sweep (Fig. 4.12) was the Egyptian means of drawing water. In this simple machine a pole with a bucket attached to one end is pivoted near

Fig. 4.11. A cylinder being parbuckled up an incline.

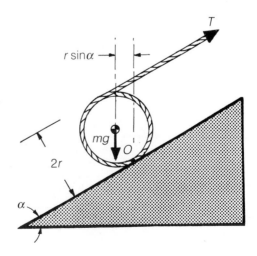

its centre and is counterpoised with a rock or heavy lump of clay at the other end. The empty bucket has to be pulled down into the water, but the counterpoise lifts the full bucket thereby eliminating the more physiologically difficult task of lifting up with the hands. The earliest illustration of a pulley in China appears on a Han Dynasty jar in a scene depicting a well-head. However, because the names of the hand-guard for a sword and other common objects were derived from the pulley, it must have been known at least as early as the fifth century BC (Needham and Wang 1965:96).

The great efficacy of the pulley is in a compound machine where blocks containing a number of pulleys are joined by a rope that passes successively over them. Archimedes is said to have invented the compound pulley, but since it is described in the Aristotelian *Mechanical problems* (problem 18) it must have been an earlier invention. Although Archimedes almost certainly understood the theory of the compound pulley the first record of it is an analysis given by Heron of Alexandria in the first century AD (Drachmann 1963:69–70). Heron showed that the ratio of the weight of the burden lifted to the applied force is equal to the number of ropes supporting the burden. Thus the force necessary to lift a burden with a compound pulley that has two pulleys in the upper block and one in the lower (Fig. 4.13), called a *trispast* by Vitruvius (X, 2, 3), is one-third of its weight. This value is true if the pulleys are frictionless and the rope perfectly flexible because

Fig. 4.12. Egyptian sweep – from a tomb painting at Thebes (*c.* 1300 BC).

the tension in the rope would then be the same in all its parts. Since in the *trispast* the load is supported by three ropes, the free rope could be pulled with one-third the force. Therefore, the mechanical advantage of an ideal *trispast* is 3. The velocity ratio is also 3, because only one-third of the movement of the active rope is communicated to the burden.

In practice, of course, there is friction in all machines, and the mechanical advantage is never as large as the velocity ratio. Heron of Alexandria seems to have recognised this fact, because when he described a series of compound pulleys that together had an ideal mechanical advantage of 200 he added a final remark that the last block would actually need more pulleys than the theoretical number (Drachmann 1963:86). There are two sources of energy loss in pulleys: the friction between the axle and the pulley, and the stiffness and internal friction of the ropes. Both effects cause an increase in the tension of the rope as it goes

Fig. 4.13. Vitruvian crane with trispast and winch.

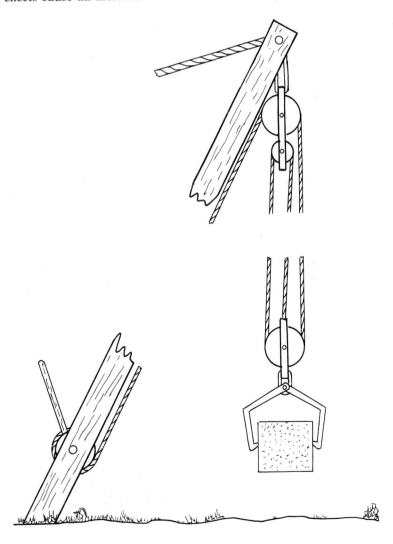

round a pulley. First let us examine the increase in tension caused
by the friction at the pulley's axle. Assuming that the rope makes
a complete half-turn around the pulley (Fig. 4.14), the reaction at
the axle will be twice the tension T in the ropes – neglecting for
the moment the small increase in rope tension dT_a caused by the
friction. If we assume that the bearing is in good condition this
reaction force will create a uniform pressure p between the pulley
and the axle, which is given by

$$p = \frac{2T}{d}.$$

Because friction is present there will be a shear stress μp between
the pulley and the axle which will cause a resisting moment
of $\mu p \, d/2 \times \pi d/2$ about the axle's centre. The moment of the
two ropes about the axle that must overcome this resistance is
$dT_a \, (D+a)/2$. Therefore equating these two moments yields

$$dT_a = \frac{\mu \cdot \pi T d}{(D+a)} \tag{4.12}$$

where a is the thickness of the rope. Ropes are not much used in
engineering today so it is no surprise to find that the major
studies on the effect of their stiffness were performed in the
eighteenth and nineteenth centuries when the sailing ship was
supreme. The most important work on rope friction is that of
Charles Augustin Coulomb (1736–1806), who won the prize
offered by the French Academy of Science for a work on friction
relevant to naval machines. Although Coulomb's classic work on
friction is remembered, his work on the stiffness of ropes in the
same paper is now largely forgotten (Coulomb 1785). Modern
textbooks contain no references to the effect of the stiffness of ropes
on the efficiency of pulleys and we have to turn to a book written
at the very beginning of the twentieth century (Du Bois
1902:235). An empirical expression for the increase in tension
dT_r caused by the stiffness of new hemp rope is given by

$$dT_r = \frac{900 + 3 \cdot 3T}{D+a} \tag{4.13}$$

where T is the tension in newtons, D is the diameter of the pulley,
and a the thickness of the rope in millimetres. The total increase
in tension for the rope as it passes round a pulley is the sum of
the two increments given by equations (4.12) and (4.13). To
give an example let us calculate the increase in tension as a 15
mm diameter rope passes over a 150 mm diameter wooden pulley
running on a 20 mm diameter iron axle. The coefficient of friction
of lubricated wood on iron is about 0·1 (see Table 2.4), and hence
from equation (4.13) the increase in tension caused by the friction
of the axle is 0·038T. The increase in tension due to the stiffness
of the rope is from equation (4.12), 5·5+0·02T. Therefore the
total increase in tension each time the rope passes over one of the
pulleys is 5·5+0·058T.

Fig. 4.14. The effect of friction at the axle of a pulley.

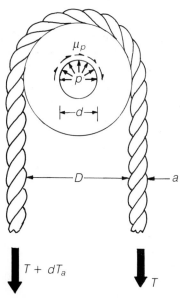

Let us imagine a hypothetical *trispast* constructed from similar pulleys. Ignoring the differences in diameters, the tension in the successive rope drops of the *trispast* will be as shown in Table 4.2. The load carried is the sum of the tension in all of the three rope drops, that is, $16 \cdot 8 + 3 \cdot 18T$ N. Supposing we are lifting a burden that weighs 1000 N, then the tension in the first rope is 309 N and the tension required in the running rope to lift the burden is 384 N. The mechanical advantage of this hypothetical *trispast* will be 1000/384, or 2·61. Since the velocity ratio is 3, the efficiency of the machine can be calculated as $2 \cdot 61/3 \times 100$, or 87%. Each rope drop added to a compound pulley block decreases its efficiency. For example a *pentaspast* (where the load is supported by five ropes) constructed from the same pulleys and lifting 1000 N would only have an efficiency of 79%. This loss of efficiency with the number of rope drops was almost certainly appreciated in a practical fashion by the early engineers. Vitruvius did not describe a compound pulley of more than five sheaves because the Romans probably knew that it was more efficient to place two machines in series. The standard Vitruvian crane employed a winch combined with a *trispast* (Fig. 4.13). Vitruvius (X, 2, 5) also mentioned that if a crane was to lift very heavy burdens, a third machine, the capstan, should be added in series to the winch. In this type of crane two compound pulleys were used side by side in parallel, presumably because it was easier to use double ropes than a single thick one which would be stiff and less efficient. The two ropes were then taken to either side of an axle mounted between the legs of the crane. This axle had a large drum at its centre which was driven by a capstan. Vitruvius (X, 2, 7) also remarked that a treadmill could be fitted to drive the winch and accomplish the work more swiftly (see Fig. 2.8).

The winch and capstan

The winch is probably about as old as the pulley, to which it is closely related. Winches were used by the Greek surgeons of the fifth century BC to set broken limbs (Gille 1956:630). The plays of Euripides, like the *Star Wars* films of today, required special effects, and most probably winches assisted the gods in their descent to the stage. These early winches were not operated by a crank but were turned by radial spokes (Fig. 4.15a). The true crank handle (Fig. 4.15b) is a late innovation and does not

Table 4.2 *Tension in the ropes of a trispast*

Rope drop	Tension
1	T
2	$5 \cdot 5 + 1 \cdot 058T$
3	$11 \cdot 3 + 1 \cdot 119T$
running rope	$17 \cdot 5 + 1 \cdot 184T$

appear in Europe before the ninth century AD (Needham and Wang 1965:111–19). The oblique crank (Fig. 4.15c) was used in ancient Egypt as a drive for a primitive drill. It is still used to this day on winches in some parts of China.

The mechanical advantage of the winch, neglecting losses due to friction in the axle and rope, is the ratio of the radial distance at which the force is applied to the radius of the drum. The capstan is similar to the winch, but it has a vertical axis which enables the radial spokes to be worked horizontally. The spokes of a capstan can be much longer than those of a winch and consequently it can have a larger mechanical advantage. The capstan has extra flexibility in that it can be driven by animals as well as by men.

Fig. 4.15. The three basic drives for a winch: (*a*) radial spokes; (*b*) true crank handle; (*c*) oblique crank.

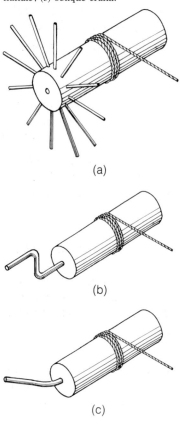

(a)

(b)

(c)

The screw

The screw is perhaps the least natural of the machine elements. As Galileo remarked, 'among all the mechanical instruments devised by human wit for various conveniences, it seems for ingenuity and utility the screw takes first place' (Drabkin and Drake 1960:169). Although the screw is often attributed to Archimedes it was probably invented earlier, perhaps by the Pythagorean philosopher, Archytas of Tarentum, in about 400 BC (Gille 1956:631).

To make a screw a right-angled triangle of soft metal was wound round a cylinder so that one edge formed a circumference and the hypotenuse a spiral along with the thread could be cut. As with the winch one of the screw's first uses was in machines for resetting broken limbs. For these machines the screw-threads were square. At first the screw engaged with a peg rather than a nut, because it was difficult to cut an internal thread, and the load capacity was therefore limited. The application of the screw to the direct olive press described by Heron required a more efficient nut (Drachmann 1932:73–77). The early screw press still used the beam principle and a nut made in two halves was satisfactory.[6] The later designs of olive presses used one or two screws to load the press directly without a beam. The screws for these presses had to carry large loads, and their development was made possible by the invention of a machine for cutting an internal thread. This machine was described and probably invented by Heron of Alexandria (Drachmann 1963:205). Since there were difficulties in cutting a square female thread, a V-shaped form was adopted.

The other application of a screw in a machine is in conjunction with a gear wheel in a worm drive. However, apart from its operation in a limb-setting machine, its use was confined to instruments that did not transmit power. Heron describes two instruments with worm drives – the *hodometer*, for measuring distance, and a surveying instrument that he called the *dioptra* (Drachmann 1963: 22–32).

[6] A recent Australian invention, the split nut, is a worthy successor to these early threaded blocks. The split nut was invented to make easier the task of assembly and removal of pipes in chemical processing plants. The halves of the split nut have a conical end and the nut is fitted with a conical washer so that the halves are forced together when tightened (Cotterell 1978).

The mechanics of the screw, as Heron of Alexandria realised, is similar to that of the inclined plane (Drachmann 1963: 56–8). Let us examine first a screw with a square thread form that requires a moment M applied to the screw's axis to advance it against a force F_l (Fig. 4.16). The thread helix angle α is given in terms of the pitch of l and the mean radius of the thread r by

$$\tan \alpha = \frac{l}{2\pi r}.$$

The frictional force on the screw-thread is very similar whether a peg or nut is used to transmit the load, although a peg will tend to force the screw to one side. Thus the reaction on the thread of the screw can be concentrated into a single force R that is offset from the perpendicular to the thread by the friction angle λ. The force F_m acting at the mean radius of the thread that will just move the burden F_l can be found from the parallogram of forces (Fig. 4.16) to be

$$F_m = F_l \tan (\alpha + \lambda).$$

The moment M that has to be applied to generate the force F_m is given by

$$M = F_m r = F_l r \tan (\alpha + \lambda). \tag{4.14}$$

If the screw is rotated so as to lower the burden, the reaction force R will be inclined at an angle λ on the other side of the perpendicular to the thread, and the moment required to lower the screw will be

$$M = F_l r \tan (\lambda - \alpha). \tag{4.15}$$

If $\alpha > \lambda$ it is necessary to apply a moment to prevent the burden descending.

Let us now calculate the efficiency of the screw. When we rotate the screw through one turn, the work done *on* the screw is the product of the force F_m and the distance $2\pi r$ through which it moves. That is, the work done on the screw is

$$(2\pi r) F_m = 2\pi M.$$

This result is a particular example of a general result, namely, the work done by a moment is the product of the moment M and the angle θ (measured in radians) through which it turns. That is

$$W = M\theta. \tag{4.16}$$

The work done *by* the screw, is the product of the force F_l to be moved and the distance l through which it moves. Thus the efficiency of a screw is given by

$$\eta = \frac{\text{work done by the screw}}{\text{work done on the screw}} = \frac{F_l l}{2\pi M} = \frac{\tan \alpha}{\tan (\alpha + \lambda)}. \tag{4.17}$$

The maximum efficiency occurs when the helix angle $\alpha = 45 - \lambda/2$. However such large helix angles are not normally used because, first, the mechanical advantage would not be very large,

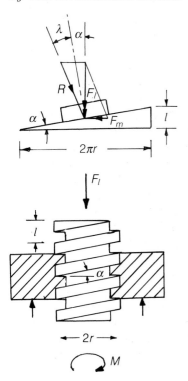

Fig. 4.16. The mechanics of the screw.

Machines

and second, the helix angle α would be greater than the friction angle λ, allowing the burden to descend if a restraining torque were not applied to the screw. A typical helix angle for a wood screw suitable for a press is $5°$; assuming a coefficient of friction of $0·2$ for wood on wood (friction angle $\lambda = \tan^{-1} 0·2 = 11·3°$), the screw's efficiency would be only 30%. It is no wonder that screws were not generally used in ancient machinery.

The gear wheel

Gear wheels enable the drive on an axle to be transmitted to an adjacent one. To be highly efficient the teeth of gear wheels need to be accurately cut to a form that ensures a uniform drive and avoids sliding between the teeth. Not until the seventeenth century was it established that the cycloid was the curve to which gear teeth should be shaped.[7] Even by the beginning of the Industrial Revolution there were few accurately cut gears. Before the seventeenth century power transmission gear wheels had pins and not teeth. There are only three kinds of gear trains with pins that are at all efficient (Fig. 4.17). While gears with pins fixed in the edge of the felloe of the wheel will not mesh if the axes of the

Fig. 4.17. Three practical gear trains that use pegs for teeth: (*a*) right-angled drive using pins perpendicular to the axis of the gear; (*b*) right-angled drive using pins parallel to the axis of the gear; (*c*) parallel drive using a combination of gear wheels.

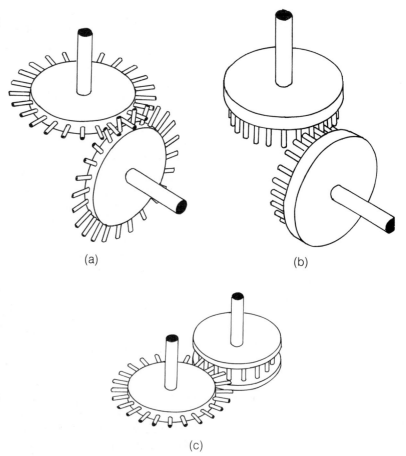

(a)　　　　　　　　　(b)

(c)

------

[7] The tooth form is made up partly by an epicycloid and partly by a hypocycloid. The epicycloid is the curve traced by a point on a circle as it rolls around the outside of a larger circle. If the circle rolls around the inside of the other circle it forms a hypocycloid.

wheels are parallel, they will mesh fairly satisfactorily if their axes are at right-angles, provided the two wheels do not differ greatly in their diameters (Fig. 4.17a). This kind of right-angled drive was employed in the sáqiya (a wheel of pots for drawing water) so that it could be worked by a draught animal turning a capstan (Forbes 1956b:675). This method of irrigation spread throughout the Mediterranean and even today is still used in Egypt. The Vitruvian water-mill with its horizontal axis also needed a right-angled gear train to drive its millstone (Vitruvius X, 5, 2). The right-angled drive already described would not have been very efficient with one wheel much smaller than the other, and so a modification was introduced. Instead of having pins fixed perpendicular to the axis, the pins in this wheel were attached to the face so that they were parallel to the axis (Fig. 4.17b). The smallest, or pinion wheel, was often strengthened from Roman times by having two wheel discs joined by the pins (Landels 1978:24). Because of its appearance this form of gear wheel is known as a lantern pinion. The third possible gear train using pins instead of teeth is a parallel drive that has a lantern pinion engaging a larger wheel that has pins in the edge of its felloe (Fig. 4.17c). This gear train may have been used in Classical times, though there are no clear descriptions of it. The velocity ratio of a gear train is the ratio of the number of pins or teeth on the driving wheel to the number on the driven wheel.

In the ancient world there were gear wheels that did have teeth, but they were mostly confined to use in mechanical instruments. Heron of Alexandria described how in theory a geared machine, which he called a *barulkos*, could have a mechanical advantage of 200 (Drachmann 1963:22–32). It was not, however, a practical device. Only one ancient instrument with gear wheels has been found in the Western world – a planetarium of the second century BC recovered from a shipwreck off the Greek Island of Antikythera (Drachmann 1963:201). In China, on the other hand, there have been many finds of gear wheels, the earliest also dating from about 200 BC. These Chinese gears are small and, except for a few ratchets that may have been used in the arming mechanisms of cross-bows, they most probably came from instruments that did not transmit power.

The wedge

The wedge is one of the five classical machine elements, though differing from the rest in that its mechanics involves dynamic action; that is, since the wedge accelerates when struck it is never in equilibrium as are the other machines we have described. Its mechanical principle eluded even Galileo and was not finally understood until the latter half of the seventeenth century. The newly founded Royal Society had asked for contributions on the subject of impact, and three men, John Wallis, Christopher Wren and Christian Huygens, described by

Newton as 'the greatest geometers of our times', responded to the
invitation (Mach 1942:403). Together they established the laws
of impact.

The question of impact was first posed in the Aristotelian
Mechanical problems (problem 19): 'why is it that if one puts a
large axe on a block of wood and a heavy weight on top of it, it
does not cut the wood to any extent; but if one raises the axe and
strikes with it, it splits it in half, even if the striker has far less
weight than the one placed on it and pressing it down?'. The
question had to wait more than eighteen centuries for an answer.
Until Galileo, all those who attempted to solve the problem vainly
explored the mechanics of static bodies. Galileo recognized the
true nature of the problem and discussed the force of percussion,
but he died before he could complete his study (Drabkin and
Drake 1960:179–82). The decisive factor in impact is *momentum*,
which was shown in Chapter 2 to be the product of the mass of a
body and its velocity.

Let us examine the impact of a cued billiard ball that
squarely hits a stationary ball. During the collision between the
two balls they must impress each other with equal and opposite
forces. These forces cannot be calculated from rigid body
mechanics alone, but we can evaluate what is called the *impulse*
of the forces. The impulse of a force is the product of the force and
the time over which it acts. Newton's second law states that the
rate of change of momentum is proportional to the applied force.
Thus the momentum change is equal to the impulse. This simple
extension of Newton's law is essential in dealing with impact
problems. The impulse on the moving billiard ball tending to stop
it is equal and opposite to the impulse on the stationary one. So
the change in momentum of the cued ball must be equal and
opposite to that of the stationary ball. Taking both balls as a total
mechanical system, there is no change in the total momentum of
the system during the impact. This statement is fundamental to
the impact of bodies. We cannot determine the individual
momenta of the bodies after impact from rigid body mechanics
alone. We know from experience, and can show using elastic
wave theory, that when the two equally-sized billiard balls collide
they exchange momentum, and hence velocities. That is, the cued
ball stops dead and the one that is struck moves off with the same
velocity that the cued ball had previously. If we have a line of
stationary billiard balls just touching each other, and hit the line
squarely with a cued ball, all the balls will remain apparently
motionless, except the ball on the end, which will move off with
the velocity of the cued ball. Although the rest of the balls appear
to be motionless, an elastic wave travels through them to be
completely absorbed in the end ball. An experiment similar to the
one we have just described was first performed by Marcus Marci
(1595–1667) in a more dramatic way (Fig. 4.18) – if he is to be
believed – by firing balls from a cannon (Mach 1942:396–8).

We now have a new principle, the *conservation of momentum* (Mach 1942:377–6). Previously in Chapter 2 we introduced the principle of the conservation of energy. In general, under impact conditions, energy is not conserved. Let us illustrate this principle by a discussion of the ballistic pendulum. Suppose we want to measure the velocity of an arrow; one method is to use today's sophisticated electronic techniques, another is to use the simple ballistic pendulum that was invented by Benjamin Robins in 1742 for measuring the speed of a bullet. A ballistic pendulum is a simple pendulum which has a suspended block of mass m_p in which the bullet or arrow can be embedded. The projectile of mass m_a is fired at the block with a velocity v_a. From the conservation of momentum principle we know that the momentum of the block and projectile after impact must be equal to the momentum of the projectile before impact. Hence the block will have a velocity v immediately after impact defined by

$$(m_p + m_a)\,v = m_a v_a$$

or

$$v = \frac{m_a v_a}{m_p + m_a}.$$

Now, the kinetic energy before impact was $\frac{1}{2}\,m_a v_a^2$ (see equation 2.9) and the kinetic energy after impact will be $\frac{1}{2}\,(m_p + m_a)\,v^2$, which substituting for v is $\frac{1}{2}\,(m_a^2 v_a^2)/(m_p + m_a)$; that is, less than the original kinetic energy. Although energy is not conserved *during* the impact we can apply the principle to the motion of the pendulum *after* impact to determine the initial velocity v of the pendulum. After impact the pendulum will swing to a height h above its stationary position. The kinetic energy of the pendulum block and projectile after impact is converted into an increased potential energy of $(m_p + m_a)\,gh$. Hence

$$v_a = \frac{(m_p + m_a)}{m_a}\sqrt{2gh}. \tag{4.18}$$

We shall now answer the question posed in the Aristotelian *Mechanical problems*. Suppose we swing a 2 kg axe at a log of wood hitting it with a velocity, of say, 10 m/s. The loss in momentum of the axe will be 2×10 kg m/s, which is the impulse the axe delivers to the log. To estimate the force we need to know the duration of the impact. At a guess, the impact might last

Fig. 4.18. The impact experiment of Marcus Marci.

1/500 of a second. Supposing that this was the duration of the impact, then the average force on the log would have been $2 \times 10 \times 500 = 10\,000$ N. Therefore to achieve the same force statically would require a weight of about a tonne. Thus we see that where there is impact loading the dynamic force may momentarily be extremely large.

Wedges as such find little application in machines. One of the important exceptions is the Chinese press operated by hammer-driven wedges. This type of press was able to provide the higher pressures needed to extract oil from rape seeds. Although the pile driver does not operate on the wedge principle the mechanics of its operation are essentially the same. A heavy hammer or 'monkey' is hauled to the top of scaffolding and slipped down a guide onto the top of the pile, where the momentum of the monkey is converted into an impulse. The Romans used piles extensively in marshy regions for foundations, and though Vitruvius (III, 4, 2) did not give an account of the pile driver he gave information about the best woods to use for the piles.

5

Structures

The construction of bridges and roofs of large buildings presented considerable difficulties to the ancient architects. They used three, possibly four, basic methods to span a void (Fig. 5.1). Wide river gorges were bridged by suspension cables under tension. Beams or slabs resisting loads by bending could span moderate distances. Arches and domes of stone in compression were used for larger spans. A possible fourth construction method was the truss, which has members in tension as well as compression. The truss may have been used for the larger roof spans in Greek and Roman architecture.

Materials differ in their ability to resist different kinds of stress (see Table 5.1). Obviously ropes can only be used in tension. Stone and brick easily fracture in tension but are strong in compression. Wood is slightly stronger in tension than compression, because under compression parallel to the grain the wood fibres can kink to form creases at 45°, and can be used in both tension and compression. The Greek column and lintel architecture had its origin in wood, and stone only came into substantial use after 700 BC. The Doric order retained vestiges of the original timber construction – the ends of wooden cross-beams, the roof boards and the pins that secured them being faithfully modelled in stone. In other parts of the world where timber was abundant a full transition to stone did not always

Fig. 5.1. Basic methods of spanning an opening: (*a*) suspension cable; (*b*) column and lintel; (*c*) arch and dome; (*d*) truss.

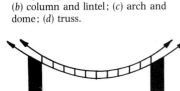

(a)

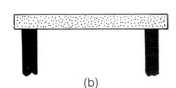

(b)

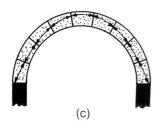

(c)

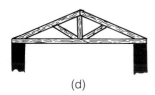

(d)

Table 5.1 *The strength of some building materials*

	Density (kg/m³)	Young's modulus (GPa)	Tensile strength (MPa)	Compressive strength (MPa)	Modulus of rupture (MPa)
sandstone	2 300	30	4	70	8
limestone	2 600	60	5	90	17
marble	2 700	60	7	100	14
granite	2 700	55	20	140	17
brick (baked)	2 000	14	1	30	6
spruce	400	12	100	40	70
oak	680	10	90	50	105
cedar	470	6	—	40	60

occur. The magnificent forests of Japan provided timber for the construction of temples that were no less impressive than those of Greece. Indeed, the Daibutsuden,[1] built in Nara during the eighth century AD, was larger than the Parthenon.

In Mesopotamia, where the earliest city states, arose, timber and stone suitable for building purposes were in scarce supply. Instead, clay was moulded into sun-dried and baked bricks. A brick structure can only take compressive stresses, and to span large open spaces Mesopotamian buildings developed an architecture based on barrel vaults and domes. Stone is even more suitable for structures in compression and it was with this material as well as with brick and concrete that the Romans fully developed the arch and dome.

Suspension bridges

The simplest form of suspension bridge, constructed entirely from rope, is very old and has been used right up to the present in at least three parts of the world – South Asia, Equatorial Africa and South America. Other types of bridges built in ancient times could not span a wide river without the support of numerous piers, and so were liable to be washed way during storms. The 'primitive' suspension bridges on the other hand have spans that are still impressive today. The bridge over the river Brahmaputra (Fig. 5.2), which flows between the Tibetan plateau and the plain of Assam, is 180 m long – nearly the same span as Brunel's famous Clifton suspension bridge.

In Southeast Asia, bamboo was a favourite material for the cables of suspension bridges. Bamboo ropes are made by plaiting strips taken from the outer part of the stem, around straight strands of its inner part. The outer layers of bamboo are the strongest part and have a tensile strength of about 180 MPa (Fugl-Meyer 1937:110). The inner layers, which make up about half the cross-sectional area of a bamboo rope, contribute little to its strength.

In the simplest form of suspension bridge there was no provision for tightening the cables, and consequently they had a large sag which increased with age. The Brahmaputra bridge for example has a sag of 25 m, which not only makes the climb up from its centre tiresome but allows the bridge to swing some 10 m in a high wind, making the crossing a horrendous experience at times. The more developed rope bridges, such as those in West China, had capstans for tightening the cables which enabled them to be built with and maintain a much smaller sag. From the sixth century onwards the Chinese used chains instead of ropes for many of their suspension bridges. In Europe chains did not appear for another thousand years.

A rope hanging under its own weight forms a curve known as a *catenary*. If a deck is suspended below the cable so that the weight is distributed uniformly over the span rather than along

---

[1] The original Daibutsuden, measuring 87 by 51 m, was burned down by a raiding army in the twelfth century and again after reconstruction in the sixteenth century. The present Daibutsuden built in the early eighteenth century is considerably smaller than the original and, though only a clumsy imitation, retains enough of its former grandeur to be very impressive.

Fig. 5.2. Cane suspension bridge over
the Brahmaputra River (from Popper
1948:249).

the rope, then the curve formed by the rope is a *parabola*. In practice there is little difference between a catenary and a parabola and we will illustrate the mechanics of the suspension bridge assuming that the load is distributed uniformly over the span (Fig. 5.3a). Let the proportion of the load carried by one cable be mg. If we consider the equilibrium of half of one cable of span l and sag h, the resultant of the tension T at the support and the tension H at mid-span must balance half of the load mg carried by the cable (Fig. 5.3b). These three forces must pass through the same point (see Chapter 4); hence from similar triangles

$$\frac{2T}{mg} = \frac{[h^2 + (l/4)^2]^{\frac{1}{2}}}{h}$$

or

$$T = \frac{mgl}{8h}\left[1 + 16\left(\frac{h}{l}\right)^2\right]^{\frac{1}{2}}.$$
(5.1)

The maximum tension T in the cable depends upon the sag that is tolerated at the bridge's centre. Obviously the tension T must be at least half the weight of the load carried and be much greater if the sag is to be small.

Column and lintel construction

In column and lintel construction the lintel or architrave acts as a beam to support the roof, and the columns holding up

Fig. 5.3. (*a*) Loads on a suspension bridge; (*b*) equilibrium of one half of a suspension bridge.

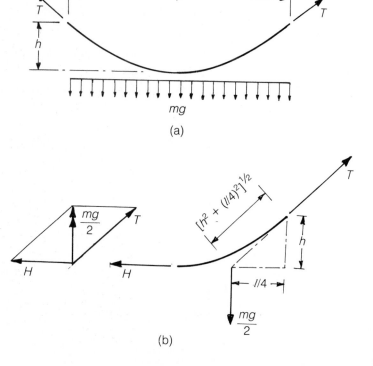

the lintel are in compression. The lintel also had to resist the side thrust of the walls. The columns used in ancient architecture carried very little stress. For instance the limestone columns in the Temple of Aphaia, built on the Greek Island of Aegina in 490 BC, have a base diameter of 0·98 m, and the load carried by each central column was about 20 tonnes (Heyman 1972). The columns themselves weigh about 8 tonnes, making a total compressive force of some 28 tonnes at the foot of the column. Dividing this total force by the area of the column we obtain an average compressive stress of only 0·4 MPa, which is only about a two-hundredth of the compressive strength of limestone. One of these columns would have to be more than 3·5 km high before its base could be crushed by the column's weight, though such a tall column would buckle before it crushed under its own weight. Because the columns of ancient buildings were never very highly stressed they did not present a design problem. It was lintels that were of main concern to the architects. The early architects were often reluctant to place any bending load at all on a lintel, which was used only to resist the side thrust of the walls, placing a corbelled triangular relieving-space above the lintel. This technique was used in Mycenae where it can be seen in the 'Tomb of Agamemnon' (*c.* 1450) shown in Fig. 5.4 and other tombs as well as in the famous Lion Gate.

Fig. 5.4. The so-called Tomb of Agamemnon, or Treasury of Atreus, at Mycenae.

Architects realised that buildings with lintels supporting the roof could not be increased in size simply by scaling up the dimensions. Larger temples meant an increase in the number of columns to keep the inter-columnar distances the same. The Egyptians did build huge temples with column and lintel construction, though in a very timid fashion – the span of the lintels being no more than one-and-a-half times the diameter of the columns (Straub 1952:8). In his book on architecture, Vitruvius (III, 3) discussed the various proportions of inter-columnar spacing in Greek and Roman temples. The safest was the *pyncostyle*, which was the same as the Egyptian spacing. However this style and the *systyle*, where the inter-columnar distance was twice the diameter of the column, had, according to Vitruvius, the disadvantage that matrons could not pass through the inter-columniations with their arms about one another; slim figures were evidently not then the fashion. The *araeostyle*, with an inter-columnar distance of four times the columnar diameter, was considered to be too large to be spanned safely by stone, and wooden beams were recommended. In Vitruvius' opinion the *eustyle* with a general inter-columnar distance of two-and-a-quarter times the columnar diameter and a middle inter-columniation three times the diameter was the best. Through such empirical rules the architects of the Classical world successfully constructed buildings using columns and lintels for many centuries. However, except for a few men of genius, builders understood very little about the strength of beams in earlier times.

Beams

Leonardo da Vinci deduced that the strength of a beam supported at both ends is proportional to its width and inversely proportional to its length (Parsons 1968:9). What he did not fully understand was the effect of the depth of the beam. Galileo (1638:156–90) was able to deduce that the strength of a beam varied in proportion to its width and in proportion to the square of its depth, but was in error in his assumption that the beam was effectively hinged about its lower edge. Like Galileo we shall first consider a cantilever built into a wall at end A and carrying a mass m at end B (Fig. 5.5). Consider a hypothetical cut at section X–X in the beam a distance x from the loaded end. On the hypothetical cut the stresses in the beam are equivalent to a shear force F and a bending moment M_b, which act in opposite directions on each side of the cut to conform with Newton's third law. Each part of the beam must be in equilibrium. Therefore, if the weight of the beam per unit length is w, to satisfy the equilibrium of the forces we must have

$$F = wx + mg$$

and to satisfy the equilibrium of the moments we must have

$$M_b = (wx)\frac{x}{2} + mgx. \tag{5.2}$$

The load-carrying capacity of a beam is primarily determined by the bending moment since the shear stresses which arise from the shear force are generally small compared with the bending stresses. If a beam is of uniform cross-section it will fail where the bending moment is at a maximum. For Galileo's cantilever the maximum bending moment occurs at the abutment where $x = l$.

Galileo (1638:172–4) also considered the important problem of a beam resting on two supports. Let us suppose the beam is loaded by a force W applied somewhere between the two supports (Fig. 5.6) and that in this case the weight of the beam is small compared with W so that it can be neglected. Before we can find the bending moment we have to know the reactions at each support. The sum of the reaction forces R_A and R_B must for equilibrium be equal to the applied load W, that is

$$R_A + R_B = W.$$

The moment of the forces on the beam must also be in equilibrium. Hence, taking moments about the point of application of the force W

$$b R_B - a R_A = 0.$$

Solving these two equations simultaneously we obtain

$$R_A = \frac{b}{a+b} W,$$

$$R_B = \frac{a}{a+b} W.$$

Fig. 5.5. Bending of a cantilever (after Galileo 1638).

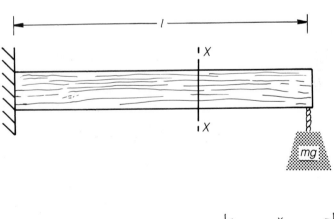

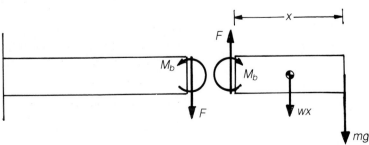

The bending moment in the beam is zero at the supports and increases to a maximum at the point of application of the force. Considering the forces applied to the left of a hypothetical cut XX made just to the left of the force W, we find that this maximum bending is

$$M_b = R_A a = \frac{ab}{a+b} W. \tag{5.3}$$

This bending moment is a maximum if the force is applied at the centre. As Galileo (1638:174) saw, this answers one of the questions posed in the Aristotelian *Mechanical problems* (problem 14), which asked why a stick is more easily broken over the knee when it is centred.

Now let us look at the way the beam resists a bending moment. Galileo (1638:156) argued that failure of a cantilever occurred by the beam hinging about its underside at the abutment. The moment of the stresses at this section must be equal to the bending moment. Galileo assumed that the stress was distributed uniformly over the cross-section, and by taking moments about the bottom of the beam he obtained the expression for the bending moment:

$$M_b = (\sigma bh)\frac{h}{2}, \tag{5.4}$$

where σ is the bending stress and b and h the width and depth of the beam (of course he did not express the result algebraically).

Fig. 5.6. A supported beam.

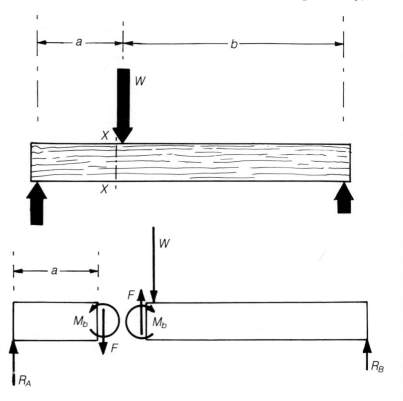

While Galileo was wrong in assuming that the bending stress is uniform over the cross-section, the form of equation (5.4) is correct; it is only the numerical constant that is wrong.

Although the shortcomings of Galileo's theory were recognised in the seventeenth century (Todhunter and Pearson 1886:6), it was not until the nineteenth century that the complete solution was given for elastic stresses in beams. Under pure bending a beam bends into an arc of a circle so that the material is compressed on the concave side and stretched on the convex side. Plane sections perpendicular to the axis of the beam remain plane when the beam is bent (Fig. 5.7). On one axis, called the *neutral axis*, there is neither stretching nor compression. Thus the undeformed length of an element *AB* is equal to *NA*; hence the strain at a distance y from the neutral axis is given by

$$\varepsilon = \frac{AB - NA}{NA} = \frac{(y+R)\theta - R\theta}{R\theta} = \frac{y}{R}, \tag{5.5}$$

where R is the radius to which the neutral axis is bent and θ is the angle subtended by the two plane sections that were originally parallel. For an elastic beam, the stress is given by

$$\sigma = E\varepsilon = \frac{Ey}{R}, \tag{5.6}$$

where E is the Young's modulus. Since no horizontal force is applied, the net horizontal component of the stresses acting on the cross-section must be zero. This condition is met if the neutral axis coincides with the centroid of the section which, for beams whose cross-section is symmetrical about a horizontal axis, is the mid-depth. The bending stresses are then as we have shown in Fig. 5.7. The maximum stresses occur at the top and bottom surfaces of the beam, with tension on the top half and compression on the bottom half of the beam. The bending moment that is resisted by these stresses can be found by taking

Fig. 5.7. Deformation of an elastic beam under pure bending.

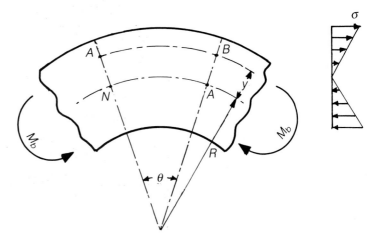

moments about the neutral axis. Without going into the details it can be shown that

$$M_b = \frac{EI}{R},$$ (5.7)

where I is a function of the shape of the cross-section with the dimension of length to the fourth power, called the *second moment of area* (values for some simple shapes are given in Table 5.2). The maximum bending stress on the surface of the beam is obtained from equations (5.6) and (5.7) and is

$$\sigma_{max} = \frac{M_b}{I} y_{max},$$ (5.8)

where y_{max} is the distance from the centroid to the surface of the beam. For a beam of rectangular cross-section, $y_{max} = h/2$ and $I = bh^3/12$; therefore the bending moment is given by

$$M_b = \frac{\sigma_{max} bh^2}{6},$$ (5.9)

which is a third of the value calculated by Galileo (equation 5.4).

Although Galileo's equation for the bending moment was incorrect numerically, it did enable him to use dimensional

Table 5.2 *Second moment of area of some common beam sections*

Section	Area	Second moment of area about X–X
	bh	$\dfrac{bh^3}{12}$
	$\dfrac{\pi(D^2-d^2)}{4}$	$\dfrac{\pi(D^4-d^4)}{64}$
	$\dfrac{\pi D^2}{4}$	$\dfrac{\pi D^4}{64}$
	πab	$\dfrac{\pi a^3 b}{4}$

analysis to show that there was a limit to the maximum size of beams (Galileo 1638:168–73). The maximum bending moment in a beam bent by its own weight is proportional to the product of its weight and length. If we scale up the size of a beam its weight will be in proportion to the cube of its length and hence the maximum bending moment will be proportional to its length raised to the fourth power. However for any particular material of a given strength the maximum bending moment that can be resisted by a beam is only proportional to the cube of its dimension. Therefore there must be a limit to the size of a beam, which for stone is not that large. Galileo (1638:169) saw that this size effect placed a limit on the size of structures, both man-made and natural, which makes it impossible to build 'ships, palaces, or temples of enormous size in such a way that all their oars, yards, beams, iron bolts...will hold together; nor can nature produce trees of extraordinary size because their branches would break down under their own weight; so also it would be impossible to build up the bony structures of men, horses or other animals so as to hold together...if these animals were to be increased in height enormously'. The size limitation for beams is much more severe than for columns. For example a limestone cantilever with a rectangular cross-section whose depth is one tenth its length would break under its own weight if it were longer than about 20 m.

It is more efficient to use a beam so that it will bend about its largest dimension, since the bending moment that can be supported is proportional to the square of the beam's depth. The Greeks must have known that the depth of a beam contributes more to its strength than did its width, but generally the shape of their beams was governed more by considerations of aesthetics than strength. Some stone beams carrying coffered ceilings had ribs that were hidden by the ceiling. In instances where these ribs are only a few centimetres high they probably represent remnants of rough quarry working. In a few cases, however, the height of the rib is appreciable (Fig. 5.8) and may have been a way of intentionally strengthening a beam whose visible dimensions were governed by considerations of the correct proportions. On the other hand wooden roof beams, that were always hidden and therefore were dimensioned without regard for appearance, were as often as not laid so that they were broader than they were high (Coulton 1977:148).

A beam of uniform cross-section is not stressed equally along its length. An economy in material is possible if the depth of the beam is increased where the bending moment is greatest. In general the Greeks only used beams of uniform cross-section. A notable exception to this rule can be found in the fourth century BC Hieron at Samothrace (ibid:147). The beams of the Hieron's vestibule, which carried a marble ceiling across a span of 6 m, all had hidden ribs that tapered from 0·5 m high at the centre, where

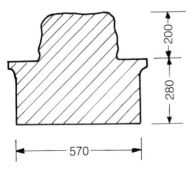

Fig. 5.8. Cross-section of a ceiling beam in the Temple of Ares, Athens.

200

280

570

the bending moment was greatest, to nothing at either end
(Fig. 5.9). It is difficult not to conclude that the architect of the
Hieron had some knowledge of the mechanics of beams and
deliberately tapered the depth of the rib in order to minimise the
weight of the beam while still preserving its strength.

The equations of bending that we have derived give very
accurate predictions of the elastic behaviour of beams. However
wooden and masonry beams are inelastic at high loads. To allow
for this inelastic behaviour engineers use a *modulus of rupture* (σ_B)
to define the strength of a beam. The modulus of rupture is not the
actual stress at the outer surface of the beam at failure, but the
stress that would exist in a perfectly elastic beam of the same
dimensions subjected to the bending moment that just causes
fracture. Table 5.1 lists typical values of the modulus of rupture
for masonry and timber.

When a wooden beam is bent, the fibres on the compression
surface start to kink at high loads.[2] As the bending moment is
increased the kinking progresses towards the centre of the beam
until the stress on the opposite side reaches the tensile strength
(σ_t) of the wood, and the beam fractures. After the fibres in the
beam begin to buckle there is little increase in the compressive
stress (σ_c) and, at fracture, the stress distribution can be idealised
in the form we have shown in Fig 5.10. The bending moment at
the point of fracture can be calculated from the idealised stress
distribution in terms of the compressive (σ_c) and tensile strengths

Fig. 5.9. Ceiling beam from the Hieron
at Samothrace.

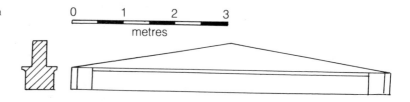

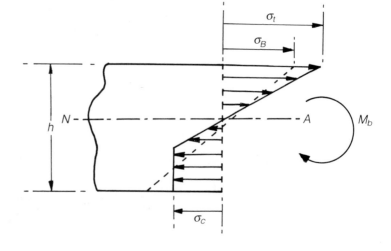

Fig. 5.10. Idealised bending stress in a
wooden beam just before fracture
(——idealised stress; ---equivalent
elastic stress).

_____

[2] Trees compensate for the comparative
weakness of timber in compression by
growing so that their outer layers are
in tension. Hence when trees are bent
by winds the stresses on their
compression sides are reduced (Gordon
1978:282).

(σ_t) of wood, and equation (5.9) can be used to find the modulus of rupture (σ_B) (Fig. 5.11). From this simple theory we find that the modulus of rupture can be up to 1·6 times the compressive strength of the wood. Actually size effect in wood will cause the modulus of rupture to be higher than is predicted from our idealized model but always less than the tensile strength. The strengths given in Table 5.1 are average values, and in normal situations beams are stressed at most to about a quarter of their strength.

The main cause for the enhanced bending strength of stone beams is their *strain-softening* behaviour (Chuang and Mai 1989). When stone is stretched under tension it continues to support a reduced stress after its ultimate tensile strength is reached. This behaviour, caused by the generation of microcracks, is referred to as strain-softening. In bending, the strain-softened region is confined to a narrow zone called the *fracture process zone* which develops into the beam from the tensile side. The beam fractures completely when the fracture process zone has developed to a critical size at which the load sustained by the beam reaches a maximum. It is the gradual development of a fracture process zone that causes the modulus of rupture of a stone beam to be greater than its tensile strength. Another lesser effect also combines to enhance the bending strength of stone beams. Under tension, flaws in the stone can open, whereas under compression the flaws will close at a comparatively low stress. Hence stone under tension has a lower elastic modulus than when under compression. Consequently when a stone beam is bent the maximum tensile stress is less than would occur if the elastic

Fig. 5.11. Theoretical modulus of rupture of wood as a function of the ratio of compressive and tensile strengths.

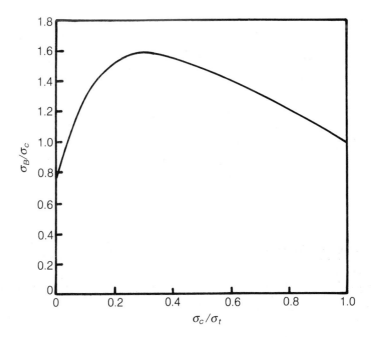

modulus was the same in tension and compression – this effect increases the modulus of rupture. In addition there is a size effect on the strength of stone.

Small stone beams have a larger modulus of rupture than large ones. This size effect is due to the relative size of the critical fracture process zone. In very large stone beams the critical fracture process zone is small compared with the depth of the beam, whereas in small beams this zone can penetrate most of the beam's depth. In stone, size effect is very important. Since the strengths we list in Table 5.1 were determined from relatively small laboratory-sized specimens, a safety factor has to be allowed in calculating the strength of large beams.

The architraves of the Temple of Aphaia spanned a distance of 1·43 m between the columns; two limestone blocks, 0·85 m deep by 0·43 m wide, composed each architrave (Heyman 1972). Estimating that each half of the architrave supported a load of 10 tonnes, the bending moment at their centres would have been 17·5 kNm. The maximum bending stress calculated from equation (5.9) is 0·3 MPa, which is only about a fiftieth of the modulus of rupture of limestone. So it is evident that the architect was well within the limit of the strength of his stone for the architraves. The Greeks were decidedly timid in their approach to stone lintels because they did not understand the mechanics.

The Propylaia in the Acropolis at Athens, built by the famous architect Mnesikles in about 437 BC, illustrates the precautions taken by the Greeks when they thought that the span or the load carried by an architrave was too great for safety (Coulton 1977:148–9). Each architrave was composed of two marble beams, 850 by 500 mm thick, and had a clear span of about 2.5 m. The beams that carried the marble ceiling were arranged with one over each column and one at the mid-span of the architrave (see Fig. 5.12). The weight of each beam of the architrave over the clear span is about 2·9 tonnes, and the weight of half of one of the ceiling beams with its share of the marble ceiling is about 6 tonnes. Treating the load applied by the ceiling beam as a central load, the bending moment at the centre of each

Fig. 5.12. Architrave of the Propylaia at Athens showing iron insets.

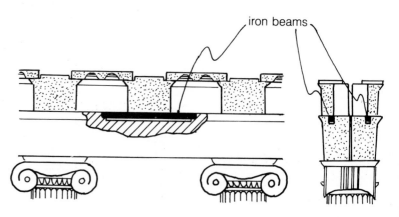

beam will be 46 kNm, and producing a bending stress of 0·7 MPa, which is quite acceptable. However Mnesikles did not trust the strength of his marble beams. Since aesthetic considerations prevented him from increasing the size of the architraves, he resorted to redistributing the load with iron bars. On the top of each beam Mnesikles cut a groove, 140 mm deep and 76 mm wide, for half the length of the architrave. At the ends of the groove there were shoulders, 25 mm above the bottom and 1·6 m apart, on which an iron bar rested. The central ceiling beam sat on the iron bar so that, instead of its weight together with that of the marble ceiling being applied to the centre of the architrave, it was applied equally to the shoulders at the ends of the groove. By adding the iron bars Mnesikles halved the maximum bending moment, thereby reducing the bending stress in the marble to 0·3 MPa. In the course of time the iron bars rusted, allowing the ceiling beams to rest directly on the architraves, some of which are now fractured – not by overload but by an earthquake. The Egyptians were similarly cautious in their use of beams. The blocks placed above the lintels in the great gateway of Nectanebos II at Karnak were recessed so that they bore on the beams over the jamb, and therefore only had to sustain their own weight (Clarke and Engelbach 1930:190).

Trusses

The usual method of supporting the roofs of Greek temples was to use beams and vertical props, like those shown in Fig. 5.13 (Hodge 1960). Such a method was adequate for the normal widths of the cella, or internal colonnade (usually less than about 6·5 m), though even then very heavy timbers were employed. In Sicily, however, temples with much wider inner sanctuaries were built without recourse to an internal colonnade and it has been suggested that a more efficient triangulated truss construction may have been used (see Fig. 5.1) (Hodge 1960:38–44). Some Roman buildings had roof spans of 25 m or more,[3] indicating the probable development of a roofing system more efficient than the prop and beam. However as yet there is no positive evidence that the Romans incorporated the truss in roof constructions. The

Fig. 5.13. The prop and beam roof construction.

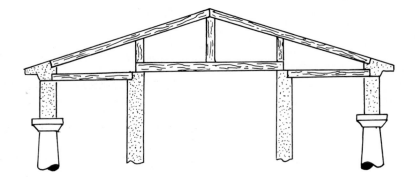

---

[3] The Theatre of Pompeii had a roof span of 27·6 m, while the Basilica Aemilia in the Forum at Rome had a span nearly the same at 27 m.

Structures

earliest suggestion of a structural truss is from a relief on Trajan's column in Rome, depicting a bridge he had built over the river Danube in about AD 99 (Fig. 5.14). Too much has been made of this solitary bit of evidence (Hopkins 1970:109; Hill 1984:62) because it is not at all clear that the supposed truss was a structural part of the bridge. The main supports for the bridge were the timber arches, and we think that the 'truss' was a non-structural parapet. There are a number of other scenes on Trajan's column that show similar lattice-like structures around the upper floors of frontier towers, on the decks of naval vessels (through which oars were inserted) and on a military pontoon bridge (see Richmond 1982). This structure on the pontoon bridge is clearly a parapet, because the lower legs of soldiers are hidden by it; also it would have had no structural purpose as there had to be a degree of flexibility between the boats to allow for the motion of the water.

In bending, the outer parts of beam are highly stressed and the bending moment that can be resisted depends primarily on the depth of the beam, which in timber is rather limited. A truss is like a beam, though instead of the tension and compression both being carried in a single structural unit, the tension is carried by one member and the compression by another. These two members can be spaced far apart, enabling much larger bending moments to be resisted. Diagonal members also have to be added to resist shear loads.

A bridge built in northern Italy by the master architect, Andrea Palladio (1518–1580), provides the first authenticated

Fig. 5.14. Relief on Trajan's column showing a Roman bridge built over the Danube (from Richmond 1982: pl 13).

example of a truss (Parsons 1968:488–9) (Fig. 5.15). Although the mechanical knowledge needed to solve the forces in a truss similar to Palladio's one was sufficient by the time of Newton, it was not until the nineteenth century, when wrought-iron truss bridges were first built, that the theory of trusses was developed. The first book to contain methods of analysis of trusses was published by the builder of early American iron bridges, Squire Whipple (1847). The American iron trusses were pinned together, which made analysis easy if it was assumed that all forces including the bridge's own weight could be concentrated at the nodes, since under these conditions the members can only take axial loads. Even if the joints are not pinned, a safe estimate of the forces in the members can be obtained by neglecting the rigidity of the joints. The forces in a simple truss can be found by writing down the equation of equilibrium for each joint.[4] However in estimating the forces carried by the members over the central section of Palladio's bridge we use another method devised by two German engineers, Schwedler (1851) and Ritter (1879). Imagine a cut or section X–X through the bridge that intersects three of its members (Fig. 5.15a). The two parts of the bridge divided by the hypothetical cut must be in equilibrium. Let us examine that part of the bridge to the left of the cut (Fig. 5.15b). The total forces and moments on the part of the bridge to the left must be zero. Assuming that the loads acting on Palladio's bridge are as shown

Fig. 5.15. Palladio's sixteenth-century bridge over the river Cismone in northern Italy (loads in kN, lengths in m).

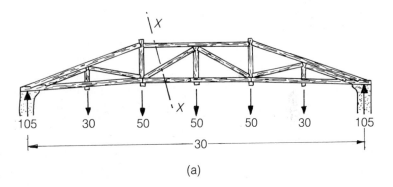

(a)

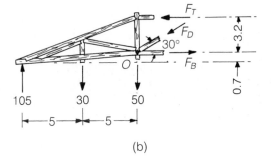

(b)

---

[4] Trusses like those of Palladio can be analysed using only the equations of equilibrium. For more complex frameworks, deformation as well as equilibrium has to be taken into account.

in Fig. 5.15 we can equate the vertical components of the forces to zero to give

$$F_D \sin 30 + 30 + 50 - 105 = 0$$

and, similarly, equilibrium of the horizontal forces yields

$$F_B - F_T - F_D \cos 30 = 0.$$

Taking moments of the forces about O (any other point could have been chosen, but this way the moments of two of the unknown forces are eliminated), and equating them to zero, gives

$$3 \cdot 2\, F_T + 30 \times 5 - 105 \times 10 = 0.$$

Solving these three equations simultaneously we obtain: the compressive force in the top member, $F_T = 281$ kN, the tensile force in the bottom member, $F_B = 324$ kN, and the compressive force in the diagonal member $F_D = 50$ kN.

The main advantage of a truss in building construction is that the timbers used in its construction can be smaller and lighter than a beam carrying the same loads by bending. It is also not necessary for the timbers to be as long as the total span, since it is easy to make a joint that will take a direct force whereas it is much more difficult to make a joint that will take bending. Another important advantage of the truss is that the horizontal tie beam takes the horizontal thrust of the roof away from the walls.

There is no mechanical reason why the Greeks should have used trusses in the roofs of their temples. In Sicily, where the inner sanctuaries of Greek temples were larger than usual, there was an abundant supply of timber, and the prop and beam construction would have presented no difficulties (Coulton 1977:158). The same is also true for the Council Chamber at Miletos (c. 170 BC) which had a span of 16 m; it was built with the assistance of Antiochus IV of Syria who controlled the renowned cedar forests of Lebanon. Large beams were available even in Roman times. Pliny the Elder wrote of seeing a beam that measured about 40 m long and 0·7 m thick (XVI, 76). The Greeks were usually as conservative in their use of timber beams as they were with their stone architraves, and the larger spans may simply indicate the availability of sizeable timbers. In fact the limitation on the load carried by a wooden beam is usually not strength, as it is with stone, but deflection. For example a 900 mm square cedar beam with a 16 m span could safely carry a distributed load of 180 tonnes with a maximum stress of about 30 MPa. However the deflection at the centre of such a beam would be nearly 200 mm, which might not have been appreciated by the aesthetically sensitive Greeks. The larger Roman spans may imply some rudimentary form of truss – if not for strength to at least reduce the sag in the roof.

Arches and domes

The arch and dome are particularly efficient and stable structures which enable the compressive strength of masonry and concrete to be fully utilized. Because they are so stable there are many natural arches formed by erosion. In Utah the world's longest natural arch has a span of nearly 90 m. As an architectural element, the arch goes back to the third millennium BC in Mesopotamia and Egypt where it was built of brick.

Arches

The most primitive arch form is the corbelled arch, in which each course of bricks or stones slightly overlaps the one below it until the two sides meet (Fig 5.16). Corbelled arches were usually built without any centring (temporary support structure) and therefore had to have steep sides to fulfil stability requirements. As an incomplete arch it is very fragile, but when completed the halves press together to form a very stable structure. In fact, provided that sufficient horizontal thrust can be sustained, even a cracked architrave is stable (Heyman 1972). Earthquakes have cracked many architraves of Greek buildings and yet they have not fallen. In the temple of Zeus in Athens an architrave has fractured and sagged slightly, leaving a wedge-shaped crack (Fig. 5.17). The architrave is hinging about the upper point of contact with the moment of the vertical forces balanced by the moment of the horizontal thrust. The horizontal thrust (H) is at a minimum if it is taken through the lower corner. The thrust line and forces on

Fig. 5.17. Temple of Zeus, Athens. ▶

Fig. 5.16. Corbelled roof in the chamber of a Twelfth Dynasty mastaba at Dahshûr (after De Morgan 1894).

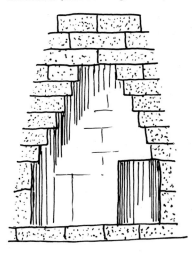

Structures

an architrave are shown in Fig. 5.18. Equating the moment of the horizontal thrust about the hinge point O to the moment of the load and the vertical reaction, we have

$$Hh = \frac{W}{2} \times \frac{l}{2} - \frac{W}{2} \times \frac{l}{4}.$$

or

$$H = \frac{Wl}{8h}.$$

Provided the adjacent architraves can support this horizontal thrust then the cracked architrave will remain stable, as has the architrave shown in Fig. 5.17.

A primitive arch can be formed by leaning a pair of slabs against each other. This construction was often used in the burial chambers of Egyptian pyramids. The core of a pyramid consists of unbonded, roughly-dressed stone blocks, and a burial chamber situated near its base will have considerable pressure on its side as well as on its roof. The danger with this form of construction, as the Egyptians obviously realised, was that too much side pressure would cause the roofing slabs to hinge inward about their lower margins of contact. To avoid such disaster the Egyptians would insert a horizontal stone bridging slab over each chamber. The King's Chamber (Fig. 5.19) in the Great Pyramid of Cheops provides a good example. In this instance, however, there are not one but *five* bridging slabs, which form four low chambers. Although usually described by architectural historians as 'relieving chambers', they do nothing to relieve the load. The main chamber would have been just as strong if the two arching slabs had been laid directly over the top of the first bridging stone. The additional height of the chamber increases the side load on the walls and it is only this additional height that has made the extra bridging stones necessary. The Egyptians were always unsure about spanning spaces and either attempted unnecessarily

Fig. 5.18. Thrust line for minimum horizontal thrust in a cracked architrave.

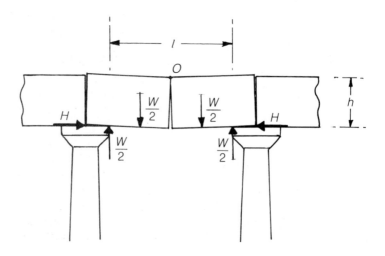

to relieve the load, or made their arches very massive. For instance in the Fifth Dynasty pyramid at Abusir three huge stone blocks were used, one upon the other, for the gable roofing of the burial chamber (Lloyd 1954:482). Only on completion is an arch strong and stable. Failures during construction of arch-like structures may well have given early architects the impression that the completed arch was not a particularly strong construction.

It was the Romans in the West and the Chinese in the East who perfected the true stone arch. To this day many Roman bridges and aqueducts remain standing as testimony to their strength. Roman bridges stood the test of time mainly because they had such good foundations. It was *pozzolana* (volcanic dust) that enabled the Romans to make a natural cement which set underwater and could be used to construct firm foundations in a river (Hopkins 1970:26, 240–2). The Chinese did not possess a hydraulic mortar and so they had to build their foundations without the benefit of a bonding agent (Needham *et al.* 1971:169). Consequently the foundations of Chinese bridges were generally not as permanent as Roman ones and none of the surviving Chinese bridges pre-date the seventh century AD.

In some cultures it was thought necessary to appease the river gods for the presence of a bridge which they might otherwise mischievously destroy. The Pons Sublicius, made famous by the legendary Horatio who defended the earlier wooden bridge against the Etruscans, was the site of an annual ritual in which straw effigies of men were cast into the river – possibly indicating an earlier custom of human sacrifice (Hayden 1976:19). Such ceremonies were not thought necessary for later Roman stone bridges. The Chinese continued sacrificing to the river gods even until the nineteenth century when eight children were sacrificed on the rebuilding of a bridge that had been frequently damaged by floods. There was vigorous resistance by the local population to the building of the bridges for the Shanghai–Hangzhou railway because they feared that a child had to die for every bridge constructed (Fugl-Meyer 1937:129). If the Chinese had possessed a hydraulic cement the dragons would undoubtedly have had much less of an appetite; and some of the earliest Chinese bridges would still be standing.

The shape of a stone arch is not a critical factor in its stability, provided that it is reasonably thick. The Roman arches were usually semi-circular. Arches with rises of less than half the span, called segmental arches, create larger horizontal thrusts on the piers and abutments than do semicircular ones. The Romans were particularly conscious of the horizontal thrust of an arch and to counteract it they built massive piers of between a quarter and a third of the arch's span. It seems that the Romans failed to appreciate that the horizontal thrusts of adjacent arches would balance each other. While segmental bridges, with their larger

Fig. 5.19. The King's Chamber in the Great Pyramid of Giza (after Perrot and Chipiez 1882:127).

horizontal thrusts, were not adopted in the West until the fourteenth century, the Chinese, from a very early date, saw the advantage that this design offered (Needham *et al.* 1971:179). The Zhaozhou bridge (*c.* AD 610) built by Li Chun over the river Jiao Shui in southern Hebei Province, is the oldest segmental bridge in the world and is remarkably similar to many modern railway bridges.

The strength of an arch does not come from the strength of the joints between its stone blocks (called voussoirs). In fact the Chinese seldom used mortar in the construction of their arches (Needham *et al.* 1971:169). For an arch to stand, a thrust must exist between the voussoirs. This thrust creates high frictional forces that prevent any slipping between the voussoirs. If the thrust line touches the outer or inner surfaces of the arch it can hinge open. However the formation of a single hinge does not necessarily mean that the arch is in imminent danger of collapse. Clare bridge, built in Cambridge in the seventeenth century, is a much cited example of an arch where a hinge has formed at its apex due to settlement of the foundations, but which is still quite stable. In order to collapse, at least four hinges must form in the arch to convert the stable structure into a mechanism (Heyman 1969).

An arch of perfect form would have its force, or thrust line, coinciding with its centre line. In 1675 Robert Hooke devised a method of determining this perfect form, but, because of his quarrels with Newton, gave it in the form of a Latin anagram (Hooke 1676), as he did for his more famous law of elasticity. The solution to Hook's anagram, '*ut pendet continuum flexile, sic stabit contiguum rigidum inversum*', was common knowledge by the time of his death in 1703 (Hopkins 1970:47). Translated, Hooke's statement reads: 'as hangs a flexible cable, so inverted stand the contacting voussoirs'. Thus an arch is the inverse of a suspension bridge and the catenary is the perfect form for a free-standing arch of constant thickness. The shape of a stable arch can be considerably different from its perfect form as long as the thrust line lies within the arch.

Modern limit theory has application in the analysis of stone arches and domes (Heyman 1966, 1969). In the limit theory it is assumed that the masonry has no tensile strength, and its so-called *safe theorem* states that an arch or dome is stable if a thrust line can be drawn that is in equilibrium with all the external loads and is wholly contained within the masonry. This line does not have to be the actual thrust line. There is a whole family of thrust lines that satisfy the equations of equilibrium alone and, provided that one of these is within the masonry, the arch will be stable. Thus stability analyses of arches are comparatively unsophisticated. A semicircular free-standing arch needs to have a thickness of only 5·3% of its span in order to be stable (Heyman 1969:368). The advantage offered by the segmental circular arch is that it does not have to be as thick as a semicircular arch. The audacity of an arch design can be assessed by the ratio of its thickness to the theoretical minimum for stability.

The most serious thing that can go wrong in designing an arch is to have loaded the crown too lightly relative to the haunches. This was the cause of not one but three failures of the eighteenth-century minister turned bridge-builder, William Edwards, in attempting to build a bridge over the river Taff at Pont-y-Pridd in Wales (Hopkins 1970:67–70). The failures were due to the ill-disposed load forcing the crown of the bridge upwards, creating the collapse mechanism we have sketched in Fig. 5.20. Both the Chinese and the Romans were apparently well aware of the danger of too heavily loading the haunches of a bridge, and often perforated the spandrels to lighten them. Edwards finally achieved success in his bridge building by increasing the load on the crown and perforating the spandrel-walls. It was not the total load on Edwards' bridges that was the cause of his failures, but the *apportionment* of that load. Arch design is only a question of geometry for most spans. Strength becomes a consideration only for arches like the Gladesville bridge in Sydney, that span more than about 300 m. The compressive stresses in arches of smaller span are far below the crushing strength of stone and, unlike column and lintel construction, a successful arch design can be simply scaled up.

Domes

Domes are even more stable than arches – the Pantheon, erected by the Emperor Hadrian during the second century AD, has a dome 43 m in diameter and is the best-preserved ancient building in Rome. The dome of Santa Sophia, built in Constantinople in the sixth century, has been shaken a number of times by severe earthquakes which, although they have caused partial collapse of the main dome, have never completely destroyed it. The amazing strength of a dome construction can be seen in the hen's egg which, though easily shattered by a chick pecking from within, is quite resistant to external forces.

Fig. 5.20. Collapse mechanism of the bridge at Pont-y-Pridd, Wales.

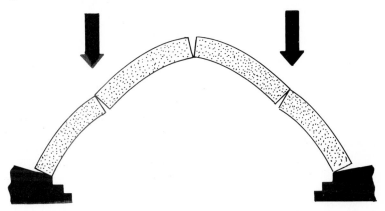

The limit theory applies to domes as well as to arches (Heyman 1966). Stability is assured if a thrust surface can be found that is in equilibrium with the applied loads and is contained within the masonry. For a segmental spherical dome, with a rise of less than about a quarter of its span, a spherical thrust surface is possible and collapse cannot occur by hinging no matter how thin the dome is. Because the circumferential stresses are tensile towards the base or springing of a full hemispherical dome a hemisphere cannot form a thrust surface in equilibrium with the external loads. The presence of iron hoops and chains around the springing of some domes is testimony to the concern that engineers have felt about the possibility of failure under tensile stress, and in fact cracks often do form at the springing of domes. In the eighteenth century the dome of St Peter's in Rome developed alarming cracks which almost divided it into two half-spherical lunes. Giovanni Poleni (1685–1761), the engineer commissioned to report on the problem, while recommending that further ties should be provided, observed that the cracking was not critical. Poleni's argument is in accord with modern limit theory – if an orange slice of the dome is stable on its own, then the whole dome must also be stable (Heyman 1967:234). Because the orange slice tapers to nothing at the crown, a dome can be very thin and yet still stable. A hemispherical dome of constant thickness only needs to be thicker than 2·1% of its diameter to ensure that it is stable (Heyman 1967:235). Both the dome of the Pantheon and that of an earlier Augustan Temple of Mercury at Baiae have minimum thickness that are 2·8% of their diameters, while Santa Sophia has a value of 2·5%. Although these domes are thicker nearer the springings, they are still quite audacious in concept.

6

Stone tools

Tangible evidence of the vast antiquity of the human species was first revealed by a few stone tools. At the close of the eighteenth century an obscure antiquarian from Suffolk, John Frere, argued that some of the pieces of flint he had found 4 m below the ground in a brick-pit near his home had been humanly fashioned and 'belonged to a period even beyond that of the present world' (Frere 1800). The clay of the brick-pit was a Pleistocene deposit, and the flints were hand-axes more than 100 000 years old (Fig. 6.1). Although these implements are called hand-axes they could have been used for a number of activities. The butt ends of many hand-axes are so sharp that they could not have been held in the hand and used in a chopping action. Similar flint implements had been found before, but their true nature was not understood until the eighteenth century. At the time of Frere's discovery the more usual explanations for these chipped flints were like that of the Italian naturalist of the Renaissance, Ulisse Aldrovandi (1520–1605), who described them as 'an admixture of a certain exhilation of thunder and lightning with metallic matter, chiefly in dark clouds, which is coagulated and conglutenated into a mass, and subsequently indurated by heat' (Evans 1897:64). It was not surprising that Frere's observations attracted little attention in a society that had accepted Archbishop Ussher's pronouncement that man was created in the year 4004 BC. Not until the middle of the nineteenth century did it become generally accepted by scholars that hominids had lived as far back as the Pleistocene era.

It was a French customs official and antiquarian, Boucher de Perthes, who perhaps more than any other gave proof of the great antiquity of humanity. De Perthes discovered flint tools similar to ones described by Frere in the ancient gravels of the River Somme near Abbeville. Most authorities were reluctant to accept de Perthes' claims and it was not until a visit to Abbeville by an English geologist and pioneer archaeologist, Sir John Evans, that professional opinion gave Boucher de Perthes his due. The earliest stone artifacts found so far, just fragments of smashed quartz, are from sites in East Africa and date to about 2 million years ago (Isaac 1984:7–9). It is possible that the beginnings of flaked stone technology will be traced back hundreds of thousands of years earlier than this time.

Fig. 6.1. An Acheulian 'hand-axe' from the British Palaeolithic site of Swanscombe.

Because flaked stone artifacts are the most durable prehistoric remains they are the most common artifacts found in early archaeological sites, and are often the only evidence of past human activity. Despite the enormous contribution radiocarbon dating has made to archaeology, stone artifacts are the most important evidence for establishing the age of unstratified Palaeolithic sites. Stone artifacts come in many different shapes and sizes and only a small proportion of them are actually tools; most are the debitage left from tool-making. Some artifacts can be very aesthetically appealing, especially ones from recent prehistoric times such as the projectile point shown in Fig. 1.1. However archaeologists are interested in what an assemblage of stone artifacts as a whole can reveal. Apart from being able to estimate the age of a site from the tool types represented in it, archaeologists also use assemblages of artifacts to obtain information on the behaviour of the people who made the tools and their level of technological development, and even clues about past environments.

Pieces of stone can be fashioned into tools either by chipping flakes from them or by grinding. The oldest method, and the one that has been the most important in tracing early prehistory, is flaking. Ground stone tools (Fig. 6.2) appear much later – in Japan at least 28 000 years ago (Oda and Keally 1973), and in Australia about 25 000 years ago (White 1967). In Europe ground stone axes appear much more recently at about 9000 years ago (Clark and Piggott 1970:147).

Archaeologists study flaking and grinding for two main reasons. First, they need to know how particular stone tools were produced – which provides information about cultural and technological development. Some of the methods are very simple and are common to all stone tool-makers; on the other hand, some are very specialised and sophisticated, with restricted distributions in both place and time. A second aim of research is to identify the uses to which tools were put. Just as kitchen knives become blunt and coated with food residue, so too did the stone knives of our early ancestors. In engineering the study of wear is a field called tribology, which is important because the cost of replacing worn components is an appreciable investment in industrial societies. Archaeologists study the phenomenon of wear for quite different reasons than those of the industrial engineer. Use-wear in the form of flaking or abrasion forms part of the wider field of functional analysis of stone tools. In addition to chipping or abrasion, a stone tool can sustain permanent modification in a number of other ways. For example a stone knife will become brightly polished when used to harvest grasses (Kamminga 1979), and a residue of blood can bond to the surface of the stone when game is butchered (Loy 1983). Functional analysis enables the identification of raw materials that were worked and even some of the objects that were made (Kamminga

Fig. 6.2. Australian Aboriginal ground stone tool.

1982). In this chapter our discussion of use-wear is limited to its purely mechanical aspects. By identifying wear that takes the form of flaking or abrasion, which can be so fine that a scanning electron microscope is needed to study it, archaeologists are able to distinguish very simple stone tools from similar-looking waste pieces that result from tool-making. The problems in making correct identification of tools arises in assemblages that contain few formally shaped tools. Recently an archaeologist was able to identify by use-wear analysis more than 200 tools in an assemblage of nondescript stone artifacts excavated from an Aboriginal rockshelter in Australia where previously only eight tools had been recognized (Fullagar 1982).

The stone materials

The material requirements for flaked and ground stone tools are usually different, though it is possible to use both techniques of shaping on the same stone. Hatchet and axe heads can be ground directly from a suitably shaped pebble that only needs a cutting edge, though frequently a ground stone tool would be first roughly shaped by flaking or hammer dressing before the cutting edge on the faces were ground down (Dickson 1981:33–8). However, in general, a more brittle stone was required for flaking than for grinding.

It is a common misconception that flaked tools were usually made from stones that split along a well-defined cleavage plane. In fact such stones are difficult to flake into successful tools and the materials favoured were the more homogeneous and isotropic stones; that is, those materials that have the least direction-dependent properties. With a homogeneous and isotropic material the shape of the flake to be detached from a nucleus is more predictable. The stone needs to be hard and fine-grained so that the cutting edge of a tool will be sharp and durable. Our hominid ancestors discovered that many of the more finely textured and dense siliceous stone materials had the right properties for flaking. This family of siliceous stone is a large one.

Although they are not the hardest, the natural glasses are the most isotropic and homogeneous of the siliceous stones. Of these natural glasses, obsidian, formed by the rapid cooling of siliceous lava, was the most highly prized for sharp edged light-duty cutting tools. Glasses are amorphous in that they have no crystalline structure, and are isotropic. Apart from small air bubbles and mineral inclusions most obsidians are homogeneous. Because obsidian is brittle, it is easy to flake; its homogeneity and isotropy enable the flake to have an edge that is many times sharper than that of a modern surgical scalpel. In fact obsidian blades have been used in experimental open heart and eye surgery because less tissue damage is caused by their ultrafine edges. Obsidian was so desirable for tool-making that prehistoric people exploited all accessible exposures. Trace element and density analyses reveal that obsidian from some quarries was transported or exchanged over land and water for many hundreds of kilometres (*cf.* Ambrose 1973; Perlès 1979; Willms 1983). Flakes of obsidian from the quarries on the Willaumez Peninsula in northern New Britain have been found on islands up to 2600 km away (Ambrose and Green 1972).

While obsidian was very desirable because of the sharpness of its flakes, it is one of the scarcest of the stone types suitable for flaking. In Europe obsidian outcrops occur only in a few places, such as at Tokai in Hungary and on the Mediterranean islands of Lipari and Melos. The next most homogeneous and isotropic siliceous stone is chert, which includes the well-known variety flint. Chert is considerably tougher than obsidian and can keep a sharp edge for a longer time, and was therefore competitive for many tool-use activities. Because flint is widely distributed in Europe it was the most common material in this region for flaked stone tools. Hence in textbooks on European prehistory stone tools are often referred to as 'flint implements'. The cherts used for tool-making were mostly formed from dissolved silica which concentrated in layers or as nodules under the ocean bed. In time these ocean sediments were uplifted to form dry land and erosion exposed the chert. Like obsidian, chert was highly valued where it was scarce and was traded over long distances (e.g. Butler and May 1984). In the nineteenth century the desert Aborigines living along the route of the South Australian overland telegraph line discovered that porcelain insulators were an excellent substitute for chert. To stop the continual theft of insulators, caches of gin, beer and sauce bottles were deposited at intervals along the line. The desert Aborigines, discovering that glass was sharper and more easily shaped than porcelain, henceforth left the insulators alone (Spencer 1928:510–11).

In many parts of the world the flaking qualities of chert and chalcedony were intentionally improved by heat treatment. The process entailed burying the stone core in sand and building a fire on the ground above it so that it would be slowly heated to at least 250°C. After heating, the core was allowed to slowly cool. In natural chert the fracture is largely intergranular. Heat treatment of chert causes dehydration which creates numerous microvoids and increases the bonding between the grains so that the fracture is transgranular (Mandeville 1973; Rick and Chappell 1983; Schindler *et al.* 1982). The fracture surface of heat-treated chert is smoother, has a more lustrous appearance and absorbs less energy. Because heat-treated chert is more brittle flakes can be detached with less force, allowing much finer pressure flaking to be done.

It was only in fortunate regions of the world, like Western Europe, that chert and, to a lesser degree, obsidian were readily available. More often prehistoric people had to contend with coarse-grained or crystalline materials like quartz, quartzite and silcrete. Quartz is a crystalline form of silica, usually occurring in its massive form as veins or geodes. Although quartz has a crystalline structure, its cleavage planes are ill-defined and therefore do not significantly affect the path of the fracture (Hartley and Wilshaw 1973). However in polycrystalline quartz there are often abundant flaws that can have a significant influence on the path of the fracture. The fracture path in polycrystalline quartz is less predictable and the flaws cause small cracks to form on either side of the main fracture, and these can often be seen beneath the surface. Quartzite is an altered sandstone that has been either recrystallised by the heat of volcanic activity occurring near the sediment or strengthened by silica filling the small spaces between grains. All the varieties of quartzite have a granular texture. Silcrete, which is often similar in mechanical properties and appearance to quartzite and, on the other end of its scale of variability, to chert, is formed by silica solution over a very long time replacing the original minerals in a geological layer to form a matrix of fine-grained quartz and amorphous silica (Langford-Smith 1978). While coarse granular types of siliceous stone provide cutting edges that are less keen than finer siliceous stone, they can be preferable in activities like chopping wood because of their general toughness (Hayden 1977:183; Kamminga 1982:62).

For ground stone tools the tougher stones were preferred, especially for chopping tools where a greater resistance to fracture damage was desirable (Dickson 1981; Kamminga 1982). Hardness was another desirable property but, since hardness is associated with brittleness, a compromise between the two properties was necessary. There is also a conflict between the requirement of hardness and ease in grinding. Hence the prime quality for ground stone tools was their toughness. Certain of the fine-grained varieties of igneous and metamorphic stones that had

Table 6.1 *Some results of the Los Angeles Abrasion Test modified for small samples*

The values are for single sources of stone types suitable for stone tool-making and do not represent the range of variability that occurs within these groupings.

Stone type	Test value	
andesitic basalt	7	↑
volcanic tuff	8	
rhyodacitic volcanic	8	
chalcedony	13	
chert	13	
quartz	25	increasing
obsidian	30	toughness

Source: Kamminga and Hudson 1982

little in the way of glassy phases were preferred for making ground stone tools (Dickson 1981:24). Stone types of the basalt family have a low silica content and some are particularly suitable for making chopping tools because of their toughness (Kamminga 1982:25). Basalts and other volcanics can also be easily ground, for example Semenov (1964:69) had estimated that diorite can be ground two or three times faster than flint. The Los Angeles Abrasion Test (Minty 1961), designed for determining the suitability of different basalts for road aggregate, is also a useful means of quantifying the toughness of stone used for making ground stone tools. The comparative toughness of a range of stone types as measured by the Los Angeles test is given in Table 6.1, where the difference between those types suitable for either flaked or ground tools is clearly evident.

Flaked stone tools

The first accounts of how prehistoric and ethnographic flaked stone artifacts were made were based on observation of the nineteenth-century manufacture of gun-flints at Brandon in England (Evans 1872:17, 246). The gun-flints were segments of blades struck off a prepared piece of flint, called a nucleus or core, with a metal hammer. This indeed was one of the earliest methods of flaking, though in prehistoric times a round or often elongated pebble, and later sometimes a billet of wood or bone, was used (Fig. 6.3). The fracture surface of a flake struck from a nucleus by a stone hammer (called free-hand hard-hammer percussion) has a unionid shell-like appearance which gave rise to the name conchoidal flake (Fig. 6.4).

Fig. 6.3. Percussion flaking with a hammerstone.

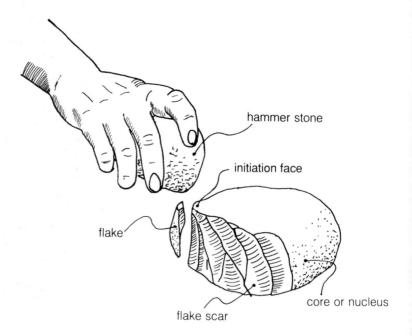

hammer stone

initiation face

flake

flake scar

core or nucleus

In the nineteenth and early twentieth century the characteristic form and the fracture markings on conchoidal flakes were used as evidence to counter the claims of the proponents of an 'Eolithic Age' which was believed to have preceded the Palaeolithic Age. It is now known that our hominid ancestors flaked stone in East Africa during the Pliocene (Isaac 1984:7–8). It is ironic that many of the pieces of stone thought to be humanly worked during the supposed 'Eolithic Age' also came from Pliocene gravel deposits in Europe. As we have already mentioned, simple stone tools can now frequently be identifed by their edge wear and what has also been recognised is that not all flakes produced by humans or their hominid ancestors are conchoidal.

In general, conchoidal flakes are initiated near the edge of a nucleus and detach part of its side. Another flaking technique at least as old as free-hand hard-hammer percussion is bipolar flaking. The method of bipolar flaking is much like cracking a nut with a hammer. A pebble or similarly shaped nucleus is placed on a hard surface that serves as an anvil and is struck with a hammerstone until the nucleus splits longitudinally into a number

Fig. 6.4. A conchoidal flake (the obsidian flake has been sprayed with a flat paint to prevent glare).

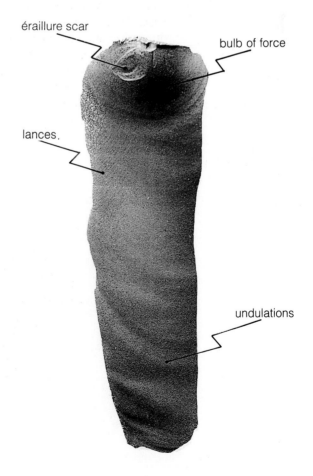

éraillure scar

bulb of force

lances.

undulations

of flakes. These flakes (Fig. 6.5) are usually not conchoidal,
though conchoidal flakes can occur in the early stages of
fragmenting a small nucleus by the bipolar technique. The typical
bipolar flake is chunky with a not very distinctive fracture
surface. While there is little control over the shape of the resultant
flakes, bipolar flaking is often the only effective way of utilising
small nuclei that are too small and light to be flaked by free-hand
percussion. In many parts of the world there is only poor-quality
flaking stone available (such as quartz, which is difficult to flake
by other methods), and this is undoubtedly the reason why
bipolar flaking was practiced until recent years by a variety of
different groups (Kosambi 1967:109; MacCalman and Grobbelaar
1965:23; White 1968). Bipolar flaking is an expedient means
of producing small flakes with straight sharp edges that are
useful for a wide range of light-duty cutting activities–such
as butchering game and resharpening wooden spear points
(*cf.* Hayden 1980).

It is difficult to control accurately the detachment of fine
flakes by free-hand stone percussion (hard-hammer), and the later
and finer Acheulian 'hand-axes' were probably finished by using
a billet of wood or bone as a soft hammer. Finishing the fine
bifacial projectile points of Late Pleistocene Europe and North
America required even tighter control than is possible with billet
flaking. The finer work on these points was performed not by
percussion but by pressure. Flakes can be removed from a nucleus
by a more or less impulsive application of force with a tool of
stone, wood or bone (Fig. 6.6). Australian Aborigines have even

Fig. 6.5. A bipolar flake.

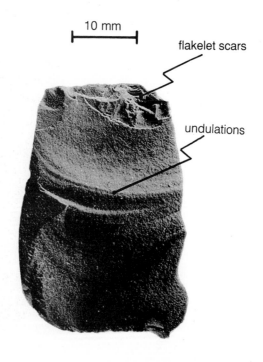

10 mm

flakelet scars

undulations

been observed to use their teeth in resharpening dulled cutting edges of flakes (Horne and Aiston 1924:91; Tindale 1965:149). If the flaking tool is soft, whether it is used for percussion or pressure flaking, there is high probability that a bending flake will be detached (Fig. 6.7). The bending flake, which has only recently been recognised as a distinct flake type, is initiated by bending stresses at a flaw some distance from the point of application of load (Cotterell and Kamminga 1979, 1987; Lawrence 1979; Tsirk 1979). In contrast, conchoidal and bipolar flakes are initiated immediately under the point of impact or pressure. The bending flake has a characteristic segment-shaped top surface (which can be very small) and, if detached from a flattish side of the nucleus, has a typically waisted planform (Fig. 6.7).

Fig. 6.6. Fine pressure flaking to make a spear point.

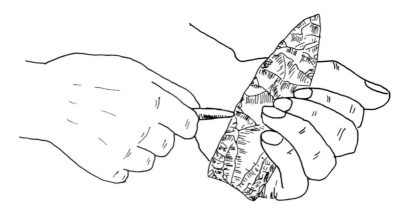

Fig. 6.7. A bending flake.

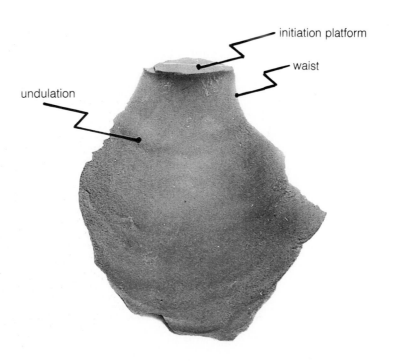

Fig. 6.8. The phases of flake formation
(the drawings are not to scale).

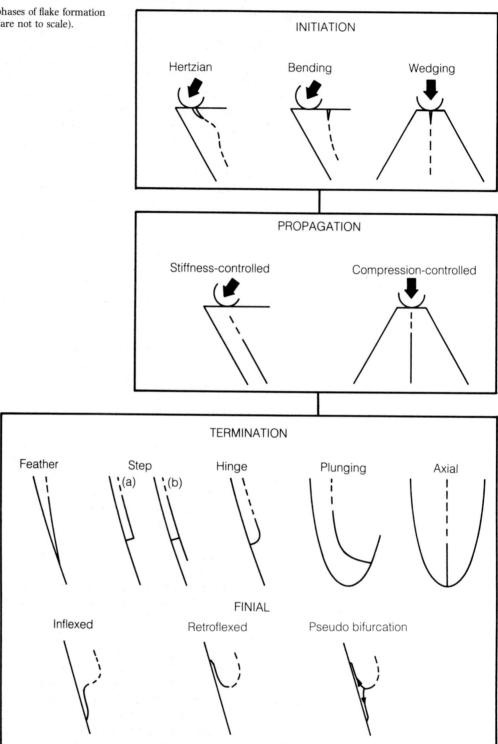

The conchoidal, bipolar and bending flakes form the three major types of flakes and flake scars to be found in stone technology. However flakes can be usefully categorised at a more detailed level. There are three distinct phases of initiation, propagation and termination in the formation of a flake, and within each of these phases there are a number of alternative mechanisms that can operate (Cotterell and Kamminga 1987). This scheme for flake formation is illustrated in Fig. 6.8. An understanding of basic fracture mechanics is necessary for the details of phases in the formation of a flake to be appreciated.

Fracture mechanics

Fracture mechanics is the study of fracture in solid materials. The body of theory has been essential in the development and use of materials in advanced technology, but it can also help the archaeologist understand flaking. The modern theory of fracture begins with Alan A. Griffith (1893–1963), who as a young man was a scientist at the Royal Aircraft Establishment in Farnborough. In the course of an investigation on the effect of scratches on the fatigue strength of metals he wrote two papers that form the foundation of fracture mechanics (Griffith 1920, 1921). Griffith sought a simpler material than metal to develop his theory of fracture. The material he chose was glass, which is almost an ideal brittle elastic solid. Obsidian is, of course, a natural glass, and its fracture mechanics is the same as that of man-made glass. The other materials used for stone tools are brittle and in many ways behave like glass. Griffith's superiors viewed his work on glass with some disfavour; after all, at that time aeroplanes were not made from glass (glass and other fibres are now incorporated as reinforcement in plastics for many aircraft components). Although Griffith's work has been developed to explain the fracture behaviour of all solid materials its fundamental importance was not appreciated in the 1920s and, after his assistant Ben Lockspeiser (afterwards Sir Ben) left alight a gas torch causing a small fire in the laboratory, Griffith was told to cease his work on glass (Gordon 1968:71). For some years very little attention was paid to Griffith's innovative approach to fracture, and it was not until the 1950s boom in the aerospace industry that any renewed interest was shown in his ideas.

The theoretical strength of all solid materials, including those used for flaked stone tools, is high. For example the theoretical strength of glass is about 20 000 MPa (Lawn and Wilshaw 1975a:31). However only solids in the form of fine fibres or whiskers approach their theoretical strengths. Brittle materials are particularly weak; for example the bulk strength of glass is only about 100 MPa. What Griffith did was to explain why the actual strength of brittle materials is so much less than their theoretical strength. The atoms on the surface of a solid are in a higher energy state than those inside it, and the theoretical strength is calculated by equating the work required to separate two rows of atoms to this increase in energy. This model of the fracture process fails to predict the actual strength of materials because it assumes the material to be perfect and that all bonds break simultaneously. Flaws in brittle materials like glass reduce the strength of those materials because they cause a high stress concentration and allow the bonds to be broken sequentially. Glass and the siliceous stones used in making flakes are elastic, and the stress concentrations at flaws cannot be relieved by significant non-elastic flow. Paradoxically, it is this resistance to plastic flow that makes these materials comparatively weak. Ductile metals are also weaker than their theoretical strengths because there are inherent flaws in their crystal structures, called dislocations, which enable plastic flow to take place in a sequential manner. The concept of dislocations was proposed later than Griffith's theory of fracture, and at the time the basic link between the two theories was not appreciated.

Griffith realised that the energy required for fracture could come from the elastic potential energy released as a flaw grows to become a crack. The classic configuration considered by Griffith was a crack of length $2c$ in a very large plate, growing under a tensile stress σ that is perpendicular to the crack. It can be shown that the elastic potential energy (G) released per unit area of crack growth is proportional to the crack length and is given by

$$G = \frac{\sigma^2 \pi c}{E} \qquad\qquad (6.1)$$

where E is the Young's modulus of the material. If this energy released is greater than that needed to create fracture then the crack keeps propagating until the specimen breaks, because the rate of release of energy increases with the crack size c. For a perfectly elastic-brittle material the energy required for fracture is the excess energy of the surface atoms. However no material is perfectly elastic-brittle, and the actual fracture surface energy of a solid has to be obtained from a fracture experiment. The critical value of the potential energy release rate or specific work of facture G_{Ic} (where the I indicates plane strain conditions) is a material property. For soda-lime glass G_{Ic} is about 8 J/m² (Lawn and Wilshaw 1975a:77). The criterion for brittle fracture is then

$$G \geqq G_{Ic} \qquad\qquad (6.2)$$

where G is the potential energy release rate appropriate to the specimen geometry. The specific work of fracture for siliceous stone should preferably be obtained in an inert atmosphere because water present as vapour in air hydrolyses the silicon–oxygen bridging bonds at a crack tip, enabling it to grow under the combined action of chemical attack and stress (Lawn and Wilshaw 1975a:165). Hence the specific work of fracture is less in air than in an inert atmosphere. Flaking takes place very quickly, especially percussion flaking, and therefore the inert value of the specific work of fracture is most appropriate.

The toughness tests that have been developed for metals are not suitable for the siliceous stones used to make flaked tools because these tests require that a standard size specimen be machined from the material, which for hard siliceous stone is expensive and difficult to do. However a technique that has been developed for ceramic materials can be used for many stone materials. In this test all that is needed is a small sample with one flat polished surface on which a standard Vickers hardness indentation test can be applied (Lawn *et al.* 1980). The Vickers hardness test, which was not developed as a fracture test and is used to measure the hardness of metals, is performed by pressing a diamond pyramid indenter (with an angle of 136° between opposite faces) into a flat surface with a known force. In brittle materials, such as siliceous stones, the force causes a pyramidal indentation with radial cracks running from the corners (Fig. 6.9). On the release of the force lateral vent cracks will also form, and we will discuss these later. The specific work of fracture G_{Ic} (J/m²) can be calculated from the applied force P (N), the half length c (mm) of the radial cracks and the half length a (mm) of

Fig. 6.9. Pyramidal indentation and associated cracks in glass.

the diagonals of the identation, from the following expression (Lawn *et al.* 1980)

$$G_{Ic} = (0{\cdot}37 \pm 0{\cdot}06)\frac{Pa^2}{c^3}. \qquad (6.3)$$

Although fracture mechanics was originally developed in terms of the potential energy release rate and its critical value, it is more usual today to use the *stress intensity factor K*. The stresses ahead of the propagating crack during the formation of a flake are tensile even when the predominant stress field is compressive, as it is in bipolar flaking. Outside a small fracture process zone where the stone deforms inelastically, the stress σ near the crack tip can be described in terms of the mode I stress intensity factor K_I by

$$\sigma = K_I/(2\pi r)^{\frac{1}{2}} \qquad (6.4)$$

where r is the distance from the crack tip (Lawn and Wilshaw 1975a:52). The stress intensity factor itself is proportional to the general level of stress and a function of the crack length. For the Griffith crack (Fig. 6.9) the stress intensity factor K_I is given by

$$K_I = \sigma\sqrt{\pi c}. \qquad (6.5)$$

There are engineering handbooks that give the stress intensity factors for other geometries (Rooke and Cartwright 1976; Tada *et al.* 1973), some of which are useful for modelling the phenomenon of flaking. Values are also available for a number of specific flaking situations (Cotterell *et al.* 1985; Cotterell and Kamminga 1986). The criterion for the initiation and propagation of a brittle fracture can be posed in terms of the stress intensity factor K and a critical value K_{Ic} (called the plane strain fracture toughness and measured in units of MPa$\sqrt{m}$) by a similar expression to equation (6.2); namely, that a crack will propagate if

$$K_I \geqq K_{Ic}. \qquad (6.6)$$

Under plane strain conditions, which normally prevail in a flaking situation, the fracture toughness is related to the specific work of fracture by the equation

$$K_{Ic} = \left(\frac{EG_{Ic}}{1-v^2}\right)^{\frac{1}{2}} \qquad (6.7)$$

where v is the Poisson's ratio for the stone, which is about $0{\cdot}2$ for most stone materials (Lawn and Wilshaw 1975a:56–7).

The concept of the stress intensity factor is important to the understanding of the fracture path during the formation of a flake. In a brittle isotropic and homogeneous material a crack will grow so that it maintains local symmetry in the stress field about the crack at its tip (Gol'dstein and Salganik 1974). Inhomogeneities in the stone can cause the path of a crack to deviate from the ideal so that the stress field no longer has true symmetry. When this occurs the stress intensity factor at the tip of the crack has two components: K_I, which is the symmetrical mode I stress intensity factor that causes the crack surfaces to open perpendicularly to one another; and K_{II}, the antisymmetrical mode II stress intensity factor that causes the crack surfaces to slide over one another (Lawn and Wilshaw 1975a:52). Cracks in a brittle isotropic and homogeneous material propagate so that the mode II stress intensity factor is zero and the stress field symmetrical about the crack (Cotterell and Rice 1980). After a small disturbance caused by a local inhomogeneity in the material a crack either returns to propagate stably along its original path, or continues to deviate, in which case its path is unstable. The stability of a crack path depends upon the variation in stress in the neighbourhood of the tip of the crack. The stress distribution given by equation (6.4) is only valid very close to the crack tip. At larger distances the stress field has an additional component which represents a constant stress T parallel to the crack surface (Williams 1957). This constant stress component determines the stability of a crack path (Cotterell 1966; Cotterell and Rice 1980). If T is negative, so that the constant stress term is compressive, the crack path is stable. However a positive or tensile stress promotes instability in the crack path, causing it to curve away from its ideal path with a radius of curvature that is inversely proportional to $(T/K_I)^2$.

So far we have not discussed the possibility of velocity effects on fracture. Cracks can propagate at very high velocities comparable to the velocity of wave propagation. The theoretical limit is the velocity of Rayleigh waves, which are surface waves similar to those that occur in earthquakes. However crack branching effectively limits the velocity of crack propagation to less than half of the velocity of Rayleigh waves (Kerkhof 1962). In flaking, the velocity of crack propagation is significantly less than the maximum. The maximum velocity that we have recorded in hard-hammer percussion of glass is 1100 m/s, and for lithic materials the maximum is even less – 630 m/s for quartzite, 670 m/s for a chert-like volcanic tuff and 800 m/s for chalcedony (Cotterell and Kamminga 1987). The maximum velocity of crack propagation in percussion flaking is therefore about 0·3 of the velocity of shear waves. Cracks propagate more slowly in pressure flaking. The maximum velocity of crack propagation recorded for pressure flaking glass is 280 m/s (Faulkner 1972:121) and for obsidian is 190 m/s (Crabtree 1968:472). Velocity has little effect on the stress field and on the mechanics of fracture at the comparatively low velocities of crack propagation recorded for pressure or percussion flaking and we need not consider velocity effects further (Cotterell and Kamminga 1987).

In this section we have provided the bare essentials of fracture mechanics needed to follow the mechanical aspects of our discussion of the formation of flakes that is to follow. A more comprehensive account of the fracture mechanics of brittle materials is given by Lawn and Wilshaw (1975a).

The initiation phase of flake formation

A flake can be initiated directly under the flaking tool to form a
conchoidal or a bipolar flake or by bending stresses at some
distance from the point of application of the force. If the flaking
tool is hard, the contact stresses between it and the nucleus can
be very high. Immediately under the flaking tool the radial
stresses are compressive but become tensile near the edge of the
contact area. These tensile stresses are enhanced if the flaking tool
is applied with an outwards component near to the side of a
nucleus, as is usual in free-hand flaking, and cause a fracture to
initiate at a flaw in this region (Cotterell and Kamminga
1987).
Sometimes the top of a nucleus was intentionally abraded to
ensure a good purchase for the flaking tool. This abrasion also
had the effect of reducing the force necessary to detach a flake
because the stress intensity factor increases with flaw size. On the
top of the nucleus a partial ring crack forms and develops into a
partial cone before curving outwards to form the 'bulb of force' so
characteristic of a conchoidal flake (see Fig. 6.4).

Information on this mode of flake initiation can be gained
from Hertzian cone fractures. When a spherical indenter is pressed
into a flat surface of a brittle solid a complete cone fracture
develops, which carries the name of the German physicist,
Heinrich Hertz, who first investigated its formation (Hertz 1896).
A Hertzian cone fracture formed by percussion with a ball-headed
steel hammer is shown in Fig. 6.10. There are two excellent
modern reviews of Hertzian and other indentation fractures by
Lawn and his co-workers (Lawn and Wilshaw 1975b; Lawn and
Marshall 1979).

A blow with a hard hammer can often cause a number of
concentric partial Hertzian cone cracks to form on the platform of
the nucleus. One of these cracks will dominate and grow to form
the flake. The others often form separate flakelets. These secondary

Fig. 6.10. A Hertzian cone formed in a
nucleus of flint by hard-hammer
percussion.

detachments are diagnostic of hard-hammer percussion (Cotterell and Kamminga 1987).

Another form of fracture initiation which is similar to Hertzian is wedging. There are two possible wedging mechanisms that can occur. Detrital particles can be wedged into a pre-existing flaw or crack caused by a prior blow (as in bipolar flaking) and cause the nucleus to fracture. An alternative self-wedging mechanism can occur if the contact area of the hammerstone is sharp. In this mechanism, described by Lawn and Swain (1975), the stone flows plastically under the sharp indenter. This plastic deformation has a wedging action that can cause cracks to be initiated at its tip. It is this mechanism that is used in the test we have described to measure the specific work of fracture, and we will return to it again when we describe abrasion. Wedging initiation is more likely than Hertzian initiation if the initiation takes place away from the side of a nucleus or if the angle of the nearby edge is greater than 90°. In bipolar flaking it is wedging initiation that predominates.

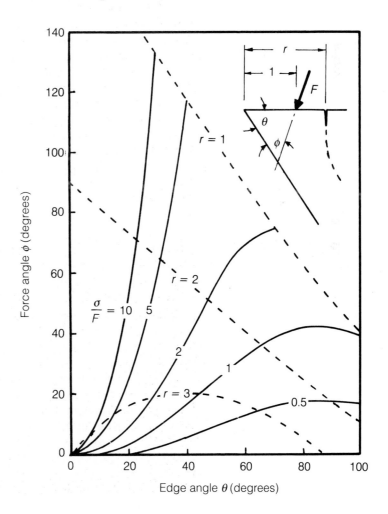

Fig. 6.11. Maximum bending stress as a function of force and edge angles.

If the flaking tool is soft the contact stresses even with percussion can be too small to initiate a fracture by partial Hertzian cone or wedging action. Instead, if the edge angle is reasonably small, a fracture can initiate under bending stress. A two-dimensional model can be used to assess the likely magnitude of any bending stresses (Tsirk 1979). Assuming that the initiation force acts at a unit distance from the side of an idealised nucleus, the maximum will occur away from the point of application of the force. In Fig. 6.11 the contours of the non-dimensionalised maximum stress (σ/F) are shown as a function of force angle and edge angle. Obviously the highest bending stresses occur on edges that have small angles when even hard-hammer percussion can cause bending initiation. As we have already described, flakes initiated by bending have a characteristic form. Bending flakes do not have a bulb of force, though the profile of the flake during the transition from initiation to propagation can superficially look like a diffuse bulb of force (Cotterell and Kamminga 1987; Tsirk 1979:85) and has been often mistaken as such in the past. No secondary flaklets are detached from the initiation region when a bending flake is formed and, though the absence of such flaklets or scars does not exclude the possibility that the initiation is Hertzian, it is one of the indications of a bending initiation.

The propagation phase of flake formation
We have identified two possible modes of crack propagation that occur once the fracture that will form the flake has passed out of the region dominated by initiation. A stiffness-controlled propagation that is responsible for the formation of flakes of high aspect ratio detached from the side of a nucleus (Cotterell *et al.* 1985). Compression-controlled propagation predominates in bipolar flaking (Cotterell and Kamminga 1987).

To the fracture mechanist the long, thin flakes that can be detached from the side of a nucleus are very interesting. If we try to simulate the formation of a flake on the side of a nucleus by using a device that can apply a force at a constant angle to a two-dimensional glass model that has an initial slot sawn along one edge to represent a developing flake, we find the subsequent fracture path to be highly dependent on the angle of force (Cotterell *et al.* 1985). Fig. 6.12 shows the fracture paths obtained when the force angle varies between 5° and 15°. For the particular initial slot length the force angle has to be very close to about 10° to enable the flake to develop parallel to the side of the nucleus. The actual fracture paths agree well with the predicted paths on the assumption that the crack propagates so that $K_{II} = 0$. The results of this simple test tend to suggest that very close control is needed on the force angle used in flaking and that it must change as the flake develops. However in use-wear high aspect ratio microflakes are detached where there is obviously no control over the force angle. Even in tool-making the time taken to detach a flake is so short, less than a millisecond (Cotterell and Kamminga 1987), that it is impossible for anyone to vary the force angle in any controlled manner. How then are long, thin flakes produced? We know that flake production is simple because hominids with limited mental abilities could produce quite usable

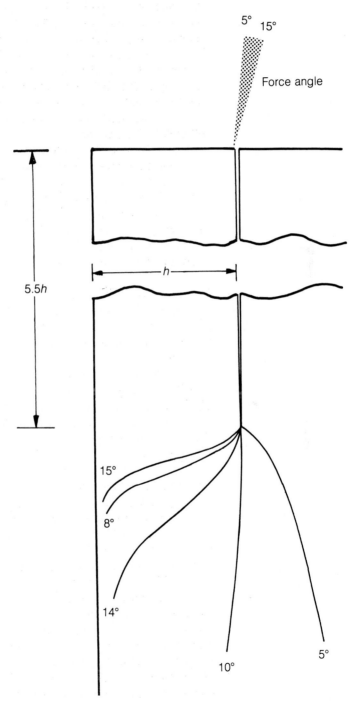

Fig. 6.12. Crack paths obtained from controlled force angles.

flakes. Even an orang-outang can be taught to produce reasonable
flakes (Wright 1972). The answer is that in flaking, whether by
pressure or percussion, one does not actually control the angle at
which the force is applied. What is controlled is the direction of
motion of the flaking tool. Newton's third law of motion – that
action and reaction are equal and opposite – provides the answer
to the question of how long, thin flakes can be formed. As the
flake develops, its bending and compressional stiffness, together
with the angle of motion of the flaking tool, determine the flake
angle. Long, thin flakes are detached because, over a wide range
in direction of the motions of the flaking tool, the actual direction
of the flaking force determined by the developing flake's stiffness is
almost precisely that required to maintain a mode I crack opening
at the top of a crack that is propagating parallel to the side of a
nucleus (Cotterell *et al.* 1985). In Fig. 6.13 we plot the force angle
φ for various angles of flaking tool motion α against a non-
dimensional measure of the length of the developing flake.
Superimposed in Fig. 6.13 is the force angle necessary to keep the
fracture propagating parallel to the side face. For the range of

Fig. 6.13. Stiffness-controlled crack
propagation.

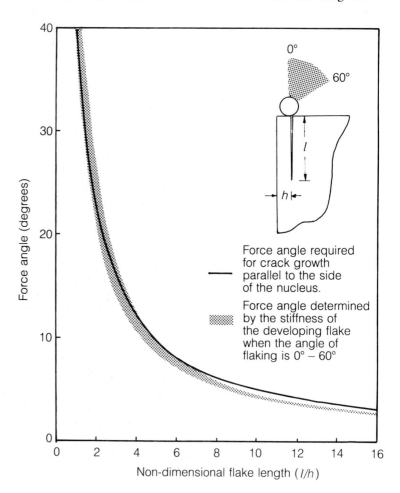

Force angle required
for crack growth
parallel to the side
of the nucleus.

Force angle determined
by the stiffness of
the developing flake
when the angle of
flaking is 0° – 60°

striking angles commonly used in flaking, the force angle necessary to produce a long, thin flake corresponds to that obtained as a consequence of the flake's stiffness. Hence we call this mode of propagation stiffness-controlled. If stiffness-control did not exist, then it would be impossible to detach long, thin flakes from the side of a nucleus.

Flakes formed by bipolar flaking, where a nucleus splits into two or three roughly equal parts, propagate essentially in the direction of the compressive force. The stresses at the crack tip itself are tensile due to the wedging action of the flaking tool and secondary stresses created by the shape of the nucleus. Under an essentially compressive stress field the constant stress term T, in the expression for the stresses near the crack tip, is compressive. Hence a fracture path parallel to the applied compressive force is highly stable. We call this type of propagation compression-controlled (Cotterell and Kamminga 1987). Compression tests on single crystals of rock salt that have highly preferred cleavage planes illustrate the dominance of compression-controlled propagation in bipolar flaking. In such tests cracks will propagate parallel to the applied compressive force even when the preferred cleavage planes are orientated at an angle of 36° to the compressive direction (Gramberg 1965:47–8). Compression-controlled propagation is unlikely to occur in other than bipolar flaking.

The termination phase of flake formation
A flake can terminate in a variety of modes. Feather and axial terminations are simply continuations of the propagation phase, but the other terminations, step, hinge and plunging, are distinct phases (see Fig. 6.8). A feather termination is the natural termination of the stiffness-controlled propagation phase where the fracture meets the side face of the nucleus at a very acute angle. Likewise, an axial termination is the continuation of a compression-controlled propagation where the fracture meets the opposite face of the nucleus at almost a right-angle. Axial terminations can also occur on bending fractures initiated at very acute edges where the crack propagates straight from one face to the other, producing a fracture much the same as one that occurs when a block is broken off a chocolate bar. These transverse breaks are termed snap fractures (Ho Ho Committee Report 1979).

Step terminations leave a step on the nucleus and represent an abrupt change in direction of the crack caused by the arrest of the fracture propagation for at least a split second of time. There are two varieties: either (a), where the flake detaches completely or (b), where part of the flake remains attached to the nucleus. With use-scars on semi-translucent stone like obsidian or flint the continuation of crack beyond the step in a type (b) termination can often be seen highlighted by the reflection of light.

The crack forming a flake near the surface of a nucleus can turn to approach the side of the nucleus roughly at right-angles to form a hinge termination. A flake with a hinge termination has a blunt, rounded end. It has been observed in experiments on blade flaking in obsidian that hinge terminations were formed when there was more outwards pressure applied (Crabtree 1968:466). Our own calculations have shown that an increase in the bending component of the force will cause the crack path to be deflected outwards towards the side of the nucleus (Cotterell *et al.* 1985). Experiments have shown that there is a sharp drop in the velocity of crack propagation immediately prior to the formation of a hinge termination. This drop in crack propagation velocity can provide the necessary time for the development of an outwards force component. In tool-making, hinged flakes are usually undesirable. However the Australian pirri graver, an Aboriginal stone tool used in the arid region for cutting flutes on

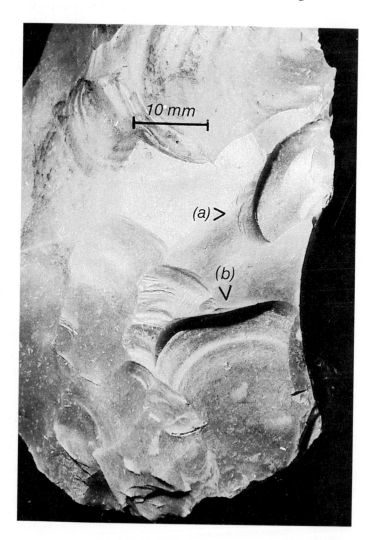

Fig. 6.14. Enlarged portion of the Acheulian 'hand-axe' (Fig. 6.1). Finials on two hinge terminations: (a) inflexed; (b) retroflexed.

wooden artifacts such as boomerangs, was made from the hinge end of a large flake (Kamminga 1985).

The last variety of flake termination is the plunging, or outrépasse termination (Crabtree 1968:466; Tixier 1974:19). In this termination a crack running near the side face of a nucleus plunges into the distal end, detaching part of it with the flake. Plunging terminations are caused by a stiffness-controlled propagating fracture approaching the end of a nucleus. The stress at an external corner must be zero (Timoshenko and Goodier 1951:28) and a crack must veer away to produce a plunging termination.

During the last stages in the formation of hinge and step terminations the crack propagates roughly at right-angles to the side face of the nucleus under a bending force that causes the stress term T, parallel to the crack, to be tensile and large. The crack is unstable, and curves sharply away to run parallel to the side of the nucleus and forms a finial on the termination (Cotterell and Kamminga 1986). The crack can either retroflex back towards the initiation face, or inflex so that it propagates away from the platform of the nucleus to create a thin, fragile extension. These two types of finials on hinge terminations can be seen on the enlarged portion of the Acheulian 'hand-axe' (Fig 6.14).

Flake surface markings

So far we have discussed the gross features of flakes. However the surface of a flake contains finer features that can help identify how it was formed and the use to which it was put. The surfaces of fine-grained stone flakes are usually quite smooth, apart from well-defined features that we shall discuss below. Smooth surfaces are a characteristic of fractures where the crack propagation velocity is low (Cotterell 1965, 1968: Ravi-Chandar and Knauss 1984). The fracture surface becomes rough only at very high velocities greater than that observed in flaking. For example, in glass, the roughening of the surface is first observed as a misting of the mirror-like surface at a crack velocity of about 1500 m/s (Holloway 1973:185).

The commonest, as well as the most noticeable features on the surface of flakes and flake scars are undulations (Bordaz 1970:25; Crabtree 1968:458; Faulkner 1972:152). These markings, seen on the conchoidal flake shown in Fig. 6.4, indicate the shape of the fracture front, and they are caused by either the passage of a shear wave or the fracture passing by an irregularity on the surface of the nucleus. In both cases undulations are caused by a momentary rotation in the principal stress field about an axis parallel to the fracture front (Faulkner 1972:153). The beginning of an undulation is schematically illustrated in Fig. 6.15a, where rotation of the stress about the Y–Y axis has caused the fracture plane to rotate in a similar fashion. After the

Stone tools

Fig. 6.15. (a) The initial stages in the
formation of an undulation; (b) the
initial stages in the formation of three
lances.

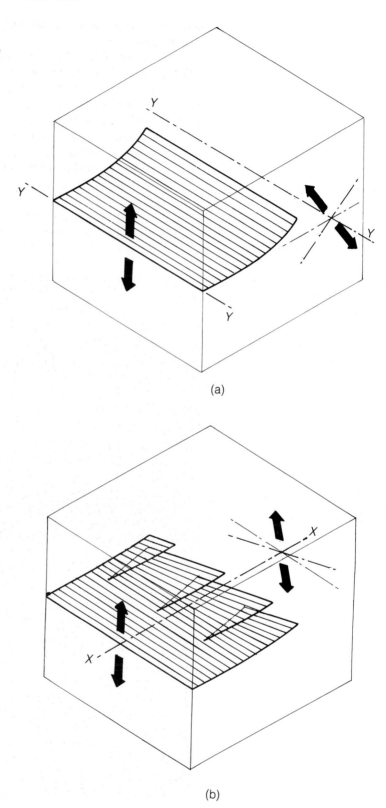

(a)

(b)

passage of the disturbing stress field, the fracture reverts to its
original plane.

Lances (Bordes 1968:3; Crabtree 1968:468; Faulkner
1972:148–51; Kerkhof and Müller-Beck 1969:446) can be seen
on the conchoidal flake shown in Fig. 6.4, and are so-called
because of their resemblance to medieval war-lances. These
markings, which indicate the direction of fracture propagation
and so lie at right-angles to the undulations, are caused by a
rotation of the stress field in the direction of fracture propagation
and perpendicular to the fracture front (Sommer 1969), as
schematically illustrated in Fig. 6.15b. When the stress field
rotates about the axis X–X, a continuous adjustment in the plane
of the fracture is impossible and the fracture breaks up into a
number of separate fronts, each oriented to the new stress
direction. These individual fracture fronts tunnel slightly sideways

Fig. 6.16. The surface of a blade from
Lipari showing Wallner lines.

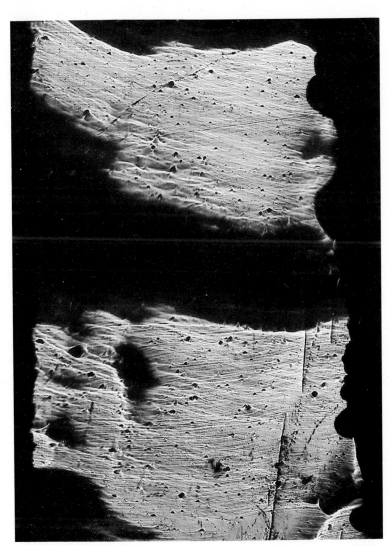

under one another. As the fracture surfaces separate, the small tongues that are left tear apart to form lances.

The éraillure scar on the bulb of force (see Fig. 6.4) is a special lance formation (Faulkner 1972:159, 1974). Lances form on the margin of the bulb of applied force where the change in fracture plane is greatest. The tongue of one of these lances extends sideways crossing the curved face of the bulb to form the éraillure flake. Often the éraillure flake remains delicately attached to the core.

One other distinctive surface marking, Wallner lines (Wallner 1939; Kerkhof and Müller-Beck 1969), are so delicate that they can only be seen on the finest stone flaking material,

Fig. 6.17. Schematic development of Wallner lines on a flake's surface.

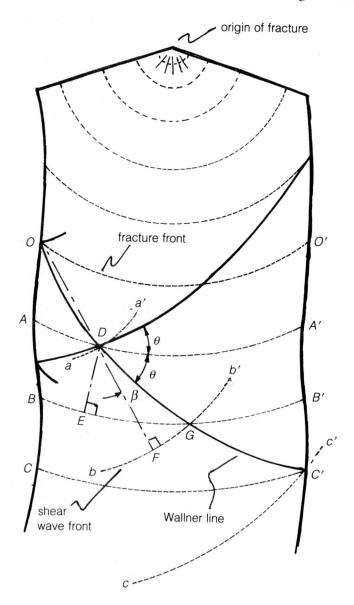

obsidian. Wallner lines are formed by the interaction of the fracture front with a shear wave generated when the fracture front encounters an irregularity in the obsidian. With flakes there are usually two intersecting sets of Wallner lines, because the shear waves are reflected from the edges of the flake. In Fig. 6.16 Wallner lines can be seen on the surface of an obsidian blade flake found on the Mediterranean island of Lipari, and which is at least 3000 years old. The formation of Wallner lines is illustrated schematically in Fig. 6.17. It is assumed that a shear wave is generated at the front when it interacts with the edge of the flake at O. The shear waves propagate radially from O at velocity c_2 and travel faster than the fracture front. When the fracture front reaches AA', the shear wave has reached aa', and it reaches bb' by the time the front is at BB'. The shear wave is reflected from the free surface at C' and forms the complementary Wallner line. Because the fracture front approximately bisects the angle between the two sets of Wallner lines, it is comparatively easy to estimate the velocity of fracture propagation. During a small interval of time dt the crack front advances from AA' to BB' with velocity v_f; hence $DE = v_f dt$. The shear wave emanating from O travels to bb during the same time interval so that $DF = c_2 dt$. Therefore $DG = c_2 dt / \cos \beta$ and $DG = DE \sin \theta$. Hence

$$v_f = \frac{c_2 \sin \theta}{\cos \beta}. \tag{6.8}$$

The Wallner lines on the blade from Lipari illustrated in Fig. 6.17 are almost straight, which implies that the fractures front was also straight. In this particular case $\beta = 0$, and the velocity of the fracture front is simply $c_2 \sin \theta$. The Wallner lines in Fig. 6.16 intersect at an angle of about 21° and, therefore, we can estimate that the velocity of the fracture was 0·18 times the velocity of shear wave propagation. Assuming that the velocity of wave propagation in obsidian is similar to that in soda lime glass, which is about 3500 m/s (Ravi-Chandar and Knauss 1984), the fracture that detached the flake some 3000 years ago must have propagated at a velocity of about 630 m/s. Hence the flake was probably detached by percussion, because its velocity is significantly higher than that observed in pressure flaking.

Ground stone tools

Ground stone tools are most often made from either waterworn cobbles or pieces of stone quarried from massive rock. A hatchet head can be fashioned from a suitably sized cobble by simply grinding an edge on one end. Quarried stone needed to be shaped into a preform blank before grinding. If the stone was amenable it would be shaped by flaking but, because the tougher lithic materials were generally favoured for ground tools, flaking could not be done on all stone materials. The method adopted for the tougher stones was hammer dressing. In this process the blank is battered with a hammerstone, not to remove a flake, but to pulverise small areas of the blank. Hammer dressing can only be used on tough stones, because with a more brittle stone a blow sufficient to pulverise to any extent would fracture the blank.

An edge was ground on a stone blank by abrading the blank against sandstone using water to carry away the detritus. A friable clay-bonded sandstone is very suitable for grinding, because fresh grains continually break out of the sandstone creating fresh cutting edges (Semenov 1964:69). The grinding was accomplished by applying pressure during the forward stroke; on the return stroke, always along the same line, the pressure was relaxed (Dickson 1981:41–4). For hatchets made from basalt cobbles the grinding takes an hour or two using the best

Fig. 6.18. Abrasive wear on glass caused by 220 grit silicon carbide particles: (*a*) free blunt particles (width of field 0·15 mm); (*b*) fixed blunt particles (width of field 0·3 mm); (*c*) free sharp particles (width of field 0·15 mm); (*d*) fixed sharp particles (width of field 0·3 mm).

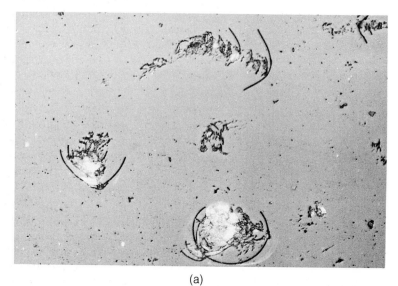

(a)

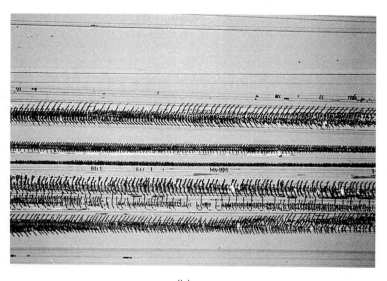

(b)

sandstone (Dickson 1972, 1981:152). The repeated linear action eventually forms a groove in the sandstone, and in many areas of eastern Australia clusters of such grinding grooves can be found in stream beds and around shallow rain-water pools. In Australia the Aborigines often only ground the cutting edges of their hatchets (Dickson 1981:45). Elsewhere the tools were often completely ground and polished on all surfaces, as for example were the greenstone ceremonial axes of New Guinea and the stone imitations of bronze axes in Europe.

The mechanics of abrasion

In grinding, the rate of wear depends on the hardness of both the abrasive particles and the stone being abraded. The simplest

Fig. 6.18.

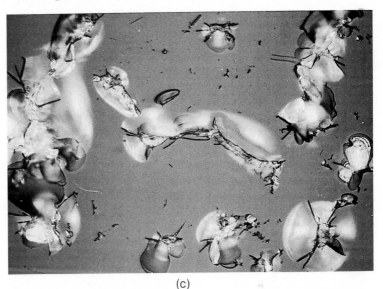

(c)

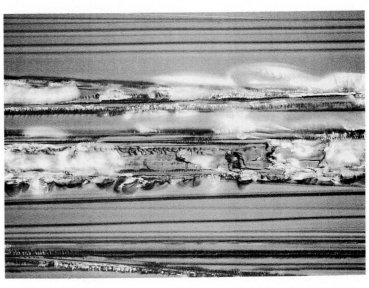

(d)

measure of hardness is the Mohs scratch hardness test. In this test
10 minerals ranging from diamond (hardness 10) and talc
(hardness 1) are used to try to scratch the test material. The
hardness number is chosen on the basis that a specimen of a
higher number will scratch one of a lower number; for example
diamond (10) scratches sapphire (alumina 9). However a more
quantitative method of measuring the hardness of a stone is the
microhardness test, where a diamond pyramid indenter is pressed
into a flat surface on the stone with a light force. Provided the
force is small enough, even the most brittle stone will yield
without cracking to leave a permanent pyramid-shaped
impression. In the standard test developed for metal, the hardness
is expressed as the force per unit area of the pyramidal impression
in the non-standard units of kg/mm². For brittle materials like
stone and ceramics it is more useful to express the hardness H as
the force per unit projected area rather than actual area and to
use the standard SI units of pascals. Khruschov (1974) has
established that the wear rate is inversely proportional to the
hardness of the stone provided the abrasive particles are hard. For
such hard abrasive wear the hardness H_i of the abrasive particle
needs to be about 2·5 times greater than the hardness of the stone
H_s to ensure that the stone is indented (Atkins and Felbeck 1974).
The silica particles in sandstone are more than 2·5 times as
hard as most basalts, so that grinding implements made from
basalt is not too laborious. Some abrasive wear will occur if
$H_s < H_i < 2·5H_s$ but the rate will be much less than that of hard
abrasive wear.

Abrasion of the hard siliceous stone used for flaking occurs
by microfracture. When a blunt, hard particle is pressed into a
brittle surface it creates a Hertzian cone crack. If a blunt particle
is dragged across a surface a series of partial cones are formed,
but there is little chipping leading to loss of material (Lawn
1967). There is a difference in the crack pattern depending upon
whether the abrasive particle is fixed or free (Lawn and Wilshaw
1975b:1076). If it is free, the partial cone cracks will form in
isolated groups (Fig. 6.18a), and if the particle is fixed, they will
form along the whole of its track (Fig. 6.18b). Sharp, abrasive
particles produce a different crack pattern (Lawn and Wilshaw
1975b; Lawn and Swain 1975; Lawn and Marshall 1979). When
a sharp, hard particle is pressed into a brittle surface the material
immediately under the particle undergoes inelastic deformation
followed by the formation of median cracks. After the load is
removed, or the particle has passed on, lateral cracks form under
the residual stresses caused by the inelastic deformation. The
lateral cracks vent to the surface freeing small chips of stone. A
schematic diagram of this mode of crack formation is shown in
Fig. 6.19. Free, sharp, abrasive particles will roll, leaving a
damage pattern of lateral cracks which appear as discrete surface
scars (Fig. 6.18c). If the particles are fixed, a furrow-like striation

consisting of a complex system of median and lateral venting cracks is formed (Fig. 6.18d). When a plate of glass is scored by a diamond cutter a similar but more-defined striation is produced, with the median crack marking the path of the cutter. When a surface is abraded with sharp particles there is considerable material loss due to the lateral vent cracks.

Our description of crack patterns that occur during abrasion is, of course, for ideal conditions on flat and homogeneous surfaces, and these classic patterns may be difficult to distinguish on the more inhomogeneous stone materials. If the abrasive particles are subjected to only light pressure, the material may only deform inelastically without cracking. In these circumstances a fixed particle dragged across a surface produces a smooth-sided indentation line called a *sleek* (Kamminga 1979:148). These microscopic abrasion and plastic flow patterns can reveal the function of a stone tool.

Use-wear on stone tools

The recognition of regular wear-scar patterns on stone tools has allowed archaeologists to identify some of the natural resources exploited in the past. The use-wear seen on stone tools takes such forms as microflaking, scratching, fine abrasion, polishing and rounding of cutting edges (Fig. 6.20). However the most common type of use-wear is micro-flaking of the cutting edge. These wear scars are often the only obvious traces of wear. The difference between wear scars and scars from flake removal during stone tool manufacture is essentially only one of scale, and our description of bending and conchoidal flakes therefore applies to wear scars.

Because most materials worked with stone tools are much softer than stone, and because the edge angles of these tools are often acute, use-flakes are frequently of the bending type (*cf.* Cotterell and Kamminga 1979:102, 1987; Kamminga 1982:65; Keeley 1980:44; Lawrence 1979:119; Odell 1981:99). While bending initiations are not usually diagnostic of particular tool-use activities by themselves, they are essential or important

Fig. 6.19. Formation of cracks under a sharp indenter: (*a*) inelastic deformation under low load; (*b*) median crack formation under high load; (*c*) lateral crack formation on the release of the load.

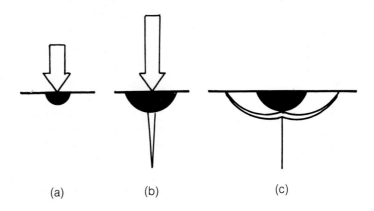

(a) (b) (c)

Fig. 6.20. Use-wear on stone tools. (*a*)
Fine abrasive smoothing on a stone
chisel. This tool was used by Aborigines
to work very light wood (width of field
5 mm). (*b*) A stone drill used on bone
(width of field 5 mm). The use-wear
comprises apex rounding and large use-
scars down the sides. (*c*) Two
conchoidal use scars on the edge of an
obsidian chisel (width of field 2·5 mm):
left, a step fracture; *right*, a feather
fracture, within which can be seen
undulations, lances and the negative
impression of a bulb of force. (*d*) Use-
striations on an obsidian tool used to
slice sweet potato (width of field 1 mm).
In the centre there is a furrow-like
striation, similar to that shown in
Fig. 6.19d caused by a sand grain or
particle from the tool's edge. The finer,
smoother lines are sleeks caused by
plastic deformation of the surface of the
obsidian.

(a)

(b)

Fig. 6.20.

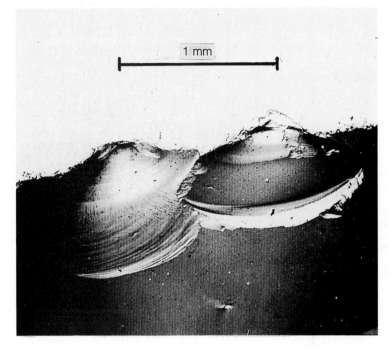

(c)

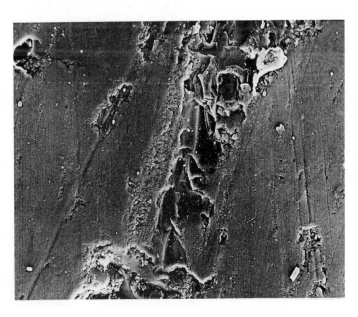

(d)

components in a number of use-wear patterns such as those from adzing wood, sawing bone, and any cutting activity that required thin-edged stone tools. Although the material being worked is softer than the stone tool, frequently hard particles such as silica grains are present embedded in the material. For example sand grains become bonded onto dried skin, and sand or tiny fragments broken from the tool's edge lodge in wood. In such cases Hertzian initiated use-flakes can be detached (Kamminga 1979:152, 1982:11).

The purposeful use of a stone tool is not the only cause of small flake scars appearing on the working edge. Retouch scarring is usually readily identifiable, but a more difficult issue can be the casual handling of a tool either during its use-life or even after its recovery by an archaeologist. Damage to the edges of stone tools sometimes results from improper museum storage. The use-wear analyst must be able to distinguish edge flaking that occurs in these circumstances as well as that which results from a tool's use. The small scars created accidently by rough handling or by the artifact being trodden on as it lay on the floor of a cave are predominantly of the snap variety. The common occurrence of such scars is unsurprising because bending stresses will readily develop when pressure is applied to a tool supported along a thin edge.

Mechanical abrasion is also an important form of use-wear. Abrasion caused by dust or sand on a worked material can cause a cutting edge to become rounded or faceted on a microscopic scale or it can have markings on the surfaces that were in contact with the worked material. The furrow-like striation on the obsidian tool used to slice sweet potato shown in Fig. 6.20d was caused by a hard-embedded particle. Even in today's clean work environments dust and grit are the cause of considerable wear in machinery – a car engine would not last very long without its air filter. Hunter-gatherers often camped on the sandy banks of streams or in the shelter of sand dunes behind sea beaches. Sand and dust were so ubiquitous in the living environment of hunter-gatherers that not only tools but even that people's teeth were worn down. In some tool-use activities, like sawing and drilling, auto-abrasion is the most important mechanism of wear. Particles of stone broken from the tool's contact surfaces lodge themselves in the material being worked and act as fixed abraders, which can do more damage than if the particles rolled freely.

The first recognition of use-wear on stone tools goes back to the mid-nineteenth century when William Greenwell, Canon of Durham, observed that the working edges of some of the Palaeolithic end scrapers he had found on the Yorkshire wolds were smoothed and rounded (Greenwell 1865:101). It is now known that this wear had resulted from the preparation of animals skins in the production of leather. In fact some of the most extreme example of abrasive wear can be seen on skin-working tools (Hayden 1979). Auto-abrasion is the cause of wear on stone tools used to prepare mammal skins. The intensive abrasion on stone scrapers used to clean marsupial skins, which are anatomically different from other mammal skins, appears to come from another cause (Kamminga 1982: 38–40). Marsupial skins are often best worked dry. When the skins were stretched to dry, sand, ash and dust particles would adhere to their sticky inside surface making the surface of the dried skin somewhat like sandpaper.

When abrasive particles are dragged across a stone tool, crack patterns of the types we described can occur. However these classic patterns are more difficult to identify on stone other than natural glass. On granular materials all that usually can be identifed is intense abrasion and scratching. As well as forming a scratch on a smooth surface an abrasive particle can detach poorly bonded constituents and small surface projections on the tool, such as lances, may be torn away. Lances make very suitable bench marks for assessing the abrasion of flaked stone tools. Sleeks (see Fig. 6.20d), formed without any cracking, are only readily detectable on obsidian tools or on surfaces use-polished by the opaline particles contained in such plants as cereal grasses, bamboo and palms. The importance of use-scratching, whether of the brittle or ductile variety, is that it provides evidence of how the tool was oriented during use as well as about the nature of the material worked. This information can go a long way towards achieving a specific identification of a tool's function.

Stone tools that have a granular texture tend to become smoothed by fine abrasion. A true polish, called silica polish, which occurs through combined chemical and mechanical processes, can appear on stone tools such as pounders used in the Pacific region to extract starch from sago palms, Indian hoes from the North American grasslands, and sickle blades from the Middle East – which provides important evidence for tracing the development of farming. Silica polish, which is sometimes known as 'sickle sheen', is strikingly lustrous and is thought to be formed in the same way as polish on gemstones and glass (Kamminga 1979:147–51).

The analysis of use-wear is a field that is in its infancy and much more fundamental research needs to be done to develop the techniques (Hayden and Kamminga 1979). This research field is an important new direction in archaeology and it promises to reveal the functions of stone tools that could formerly have only been guessed at.

7

Projectiles

Human ability in casting projectiles is without parallel in the animal world. Other primates, such as chimpanzees, throw things in displays of excitement or aggression but they cannot do so with the speed, distance or precision that humans can achieve. While the higher primates have a similar anatomical structure of the shoulder girdle which permits powerful thrusting, it is the superior manipulative ability of the human hand that enhances the throw. The design of projectiles, and of the devices from which they are launched, were of fundamental importance in the development of hunting and fighting technology. Skill in casting a spear or a sling stone is no longer required for survival. However skill in controlling the velocity and path of a projectile is still much enjoyed and admired, hence the immense popularity of ball sports.

It is usually through experience that we learn about the behaviour of projectiles; a golfer does not consult ballistic tables before teeing off, but simply knows the right way to hit the ball. However to understand fully the sophistication behind many seemingly simple projectiles one needs to understand their mechanics. In this chapter we draw on the basic dynamics we have already discussed to explain the projection and flight of some of mankind's earlier missiles.

The motion of projectiles

One of the significant achievements of Galileo (1638:268–74) was his demonstration that the path of a projectile in a vacuum is parabolic.[1] Before Galileo published his *Dialogues* the conception of a projectile's motion was based on the Aristotelian idea of *violent* and *natural* motion (*Physics* V, 6). Violent motion was imparted to the projectile which required a continuing force. When this force ceased, the projectile fell in natural earth-seeking motion. Aristotle assumed that when a projectile was thrown, the air was also moved and, due to its special nature, it could in some way communicate this motion to the air ahead (*Physics* VIII 10). So it was thought that air was the continuous mover of the projectile, whereas in reality the air resists its motion. Commitment to this dogma led early philosophers to further believe that the last part of the projectile's

---

[1] The parabola is one of Euclid's *conic sections*. It is the curve obtained by the intersection of a symmetrical cone with a circular cross-section, by a plane, parallel to one side of the cone. In Cartesian coordinates, a parabola is defined by the equation $y = ax^2$.

trajectory was vertical, despite what they must have seen with their own eyes – that arrows strike the ground at an angle.

Galileo observed that the motion of a projectile could be separated into horizontal and vertical components (Galileo 1638:268). Horizontal motion, Galileo asserted, was uniform and unchanging except as influenced by air resistance.[2] This hypothesis, which was revolutionary at the time, is an example of Newton's first law of motion, though Galileo never saw its wider implication. Galileo realised that the vertical motion of a projectile was similar to the free fall of an object and that therefore the vertical motion suffers a constant acceleration towards the ground.

If a projectile is propelled at an angle φ_0 to the horizontal and at a velocity v_0 its initial horizontal and vertical components are $v_0 \cos \varphi_0$ and $v_0 \sin \varphi_0$ (Fig. 7.1). In a vacuum the projectile would reach its zenith at half of the duration of its flight. During the second half of its flight the vertical component of velocity would increase from zero under constant gravitational acceleration g, until the projectile hit the ground at the same speed at which it was launched. Thus if we measure time t from the moment the projectile reaches its zenith, the vertical component of velocity v_v is given by

$$v_v = gt$$

and the distance y fallen can be obtained from equation (2.5), and is

$$y = \tfrac{1}{2}gt^2.$$

Throughout its flight in a vacuum the horizontal component of the projectile's velocity is constant, so that the horizontal distance moved from the zenith position is given by

$$x = (v_0 \cos \varphi_0)t.$$

If we eliminate the time t between these two equations we obtain

$$y = \frac{g}{2(v_0 \cos \varphi_0)^2}x^2,\qquad(7.1)$$

which demonstrates that the path of a projectile is parabolic. Since the vertical component of velocity $v_0 \sin \varphi_0$ with which the

Fig. 7.1. Path of a projectile in a vacuum.

[2] John Buridan (1300–1358), a rector of the University of Paris, had earlier recognised that air, far from aiding the motion of a projectile, resisted its motion, though he believed the impetus imparted to the projectile provided a motive 'force' that continued its motion (Clagett 1961:505–40).

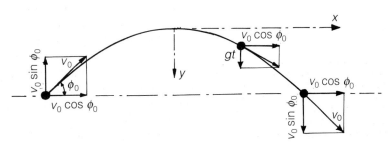

projectile is both launched and hits the ground is the same, the duration of the flight (T) is given by

$$T = \frac{2v_0 \sin \varphi_0}{g}. \tag{7.2}$$

Hence the distance R travelled by a projectile (over level ground) is given by

$$R = \frac{2v_0^2 \sin \varphi_0 \cos \varphi_0}{g} = \frac{v_0^2 \sin 2\varphi_0}{g}. \tag{7.3}$$

In a vacuum a projectile will attain the maximum range if it is launched at an angle of 45° to the horizontal, because $\sin 2\varphi_0$ has a maximum value of one when $\varphi_0 = 45°$. The maximum range of the projectile is therefore given by

$$R_{\max} = v_0^2/g. \tag{7.4}$$

In his discourse on projectiles Galileo attempted to explain the nature of air resistance, which he recognized would increase with velocity. Galileo knew that the air resistance to a ball fired from a gun was considerable and described a simple yet effective experiment that could demonstrate this resistance. In the experiment, Galileo suggested a comparison of the flattening effect on a lead ball fired at a stone pavement from a height of a metre or so to the deformation that would result if the ball were fired from 70 m (Galileo 1638:279). As with so many of Galileo's 'experiments' he probably never actually performed it, and nor have we, though we are as confident as Galileo was that the ball fired from a metre away would be the most flattened. The muzzle velocity of a ball is greater than its terminal velocity under free fall, and a bullet fired downwards is slowed by air resistance rather than accelerated by the force of gravity. So it is no use trying to kill someone by dropping a bullet on the person's head, no matter from what height it is released. Although Galileo appreciated that air did have resistance he underestimated how much and thought that the flight of an arrow would be little affected (Gallileo 1638:276). In fact the range of an arrow in air varies from 60% to 90% of its theoretical range in a vacuum (Pratt 1976:203).

The resistance of the air on a projectile, often called in aerodynamics its *drag* (D), is, like the pressure loss in pipes, proportional to the dynamic pressure $\frac{1}{2}\rho v^2$ where ρ is the density of air (1·23 kg/m³). The drag is also proportional to the projectile's surface area S and can be expressed in terms of a coefficient C_D which depends on the Reynolds number of the flow. Therefore we can write

$$D = \tfrac{1}{2}\rho v^2 S C_D. \tag{7.5}$$

The drag on a projectile, like the resistance to flow in pipes, is caused by the viscosity μ of the fluid, despite its low value for air

(1·79 × 10⁻⁵ Pa s, or about one-fifth that of water). Only a thin layer of air adjacent to the projectile, called the *boundary layer*, is disturbed by its passage. In pipes the boundary layer quickly thickens to fill them, so that all the flow is affected by the friction along the surface of the pipe. The drag of slim projectiles, such as spears and arrows with small fletchings, is nearly all due to skin friction. Because of their shapes other projectiles, such as catapult stones, will also experience significant form drag which occurs when the boundary layer breaks away from projectiles over its rear surface. The boundary layer is turbulent over the major portion of a spear or arrow since the Reynolds number of the flow[3] is in the range $5 \times 10^5 - 10^7$, and the skin friction drag coefficient (Hoerner 1965:2–5) is given by

$$C_F = 0 \cdot 074 \, R_e^{-0 \cdot 2}. \tag{7.6}$$

The true trajectory of a spear or arrow can be found from its equations of motion. Resolving the drag force into horizontal and vertical components (Fig. 7.2) one can apply Newton's second law (equation 2.1) to the motions in these two directions and obtain

$$D \cos \varphi = m a_x, \tag{7.7}$$

$$mg + D \sin \varphi = -m a_y, \tag{7.8}$$

where m is the mass of the spear, and a_x and a_y are the accelerations of the projectile in the horizontal and vertical directions. These equations do not have a simple solution, but they can be solved numerically on a computer with comparative ease. The elevation to obtain the maximum range with an arrow is slightly less than the theoretical value of 45° for flight in a vacuum.

The spear

There can be no doubt that one of the earliest weapons fashioned by man was the spear: fragments of Palaeolithic spears have been unearthed from caves in Europe and East Africa.

Fig. 7.2. Drag on a spear.

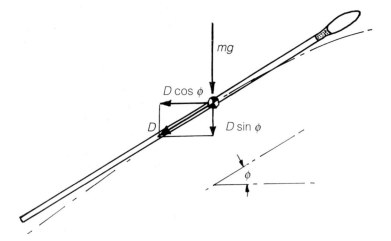

---

[3] The Reynolds number of a spear is $\rho v l / \mu$ where l is its length. For a boomerang l is the width of its arm.

Although these actual pieces are few, the widespread occurrence of stone spokeshaves with concave cutting edges are testimony to the importance of the spear. Some of these spokeshaves are small and it can be presumed that many served to sharpen the dense-wood tips of spears. In fact concave spokeshaves were used in this manner by groups of Australian Aborigines even into the twentieth century (Roth 1904:20; Aiston 1922).

Skill and a good deal of muscular effort are required to fell a relatively distant and fast-moving target with a spear. By the end of the Palaeolithic period the advantage of throwing a spear with a hooked stick, or spearthrower, was much exploited. One part of the world where the spearthrower was not adopted was Tasmania, which was cut off from the Australian mainland by the rise in sea level at the end of the last Ice Age. In most societies the hand-thrown spear was retained only as a weapon of war. For instance in ancient Greece the hand-thrown spear was used by lightly-armed soldiers, called *peltasts*. The early Roman infantry, modelled on the Greek pattern, used a heavy hand-thrown spear called the *pilum*, which weighed about 2 kg. These heavy spears were difficult to throw and, with the decline in military skill during the last centuries of the Roman Empire, the *pilum* was replaced by a lighter spear (Hall 1956:696, 704–5).

While light spears can be thrown faster and more easily than heavy ones, their mechanical efficiency is less. In all actions of throwing, kinetic energy is unavoidably imparted to the thrower's body as well as to the projectile. The efficiency of throwing a spear is most easily assessed by employing the concept of the *virtual mass* (m_v) of the thrower's body (Klopsteg 1943). Such a hypothetical mass moving with the same velocity (v) as the spear has a kinetic energy equal to that of the thrower's body at the moment the spear leaves the hand. The mechanical efficiency η of the throw is the ratio of the kinetic energy of the spear, $\frac{1}{2} mv^2$ (where m is the mass of the spear) and the total kinetic energy of the spear and the body of the thrower $\frac{1}{2}(m+m_v)v^2$. Hence, in terms of the virtual mass, the efficiency of throwing can be expressed as

$$\eta = \frac{m}{m+m_v}. \tag{7.9}$$

When a spear is thrown by hand about half its velocity comes from a final wrist flick (Cooper and Glassow 1968:122). At the moment of release there is little angular velocity in the upper arm, though it does contribute to the early stages of the throw, and the shoulder velocity is less than 15% of the spear's velocity (O'Connell and Gardner 1972:70). For a simplified analysis we shall assume that the final velocity of a spear comes from forearm and wrist rotation, with the hand rotating at five times the speed of the arm (Cundy 1980:67–9). At the moment the spear leaves the hand the velocity of the finger tips in the direction of flight must be equal to the spear's velocity. Assuming that the geometry at the moment of release is as we have illustrated in Fig. 7.3, we can calculate the velocity of the spear v from the angular velocities of the arm ω_a and hand ω_h to be

$$v = 0.29\,\omega_a + 0.09\,\omega_h \text{ m/s,}$$

and assuming that $\omega_h = 5\,\omega_a$ we find that ω_a is $1.4v$ rad/s and ω_h is $6.8v$ rad/s. The velocities of the centre of gravity of the hand and forearm are therefore $0.80v$ and $0.14v$ m/s respectively. The kinetic energies of rotation of the hand and forearm are small and we will neglect them. Hence the kinetic energy of the body during hand-throwing, assuming that the masses of the hand and forearm are 0.6 kg and 1.5 kg respectively (Woodson 1981:710), is approximately $0.21v^2$ J. The virtual mass of the body is therefore about 0.4 kg.

Fig. 7.3. Throwing a spear (lengths in mm).

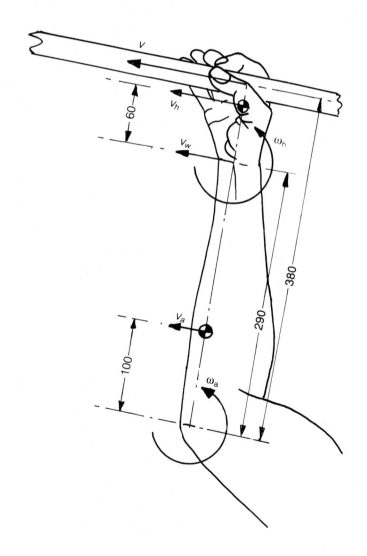

Projectiles

Since the average mass of a Tasmanian hand-thrown spear was about 0·6 kg (Noetling 1911), they could have been thrown with an efficiency of about 60%. The Tasmanians were capable of throwing their spears from between 35 and 60 m (Roth 1899:71), though normally in hunting the range would have been much less. The Olympic record for the javelin, which weighs 200 g more than the average Tasmanian spear, is 104·8 m (Russell and McWhirter 1987:298). To cast a spear 50 m requires a velocity of more than 22 m/s. The total energy required to throw a 0·6 kg spear at this velocity is about 240 J.

The spearthrower

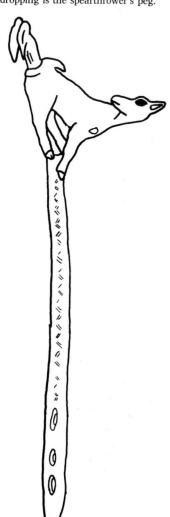

Fig. 7.4. Magdalenian spearthrower of reindeer antler carved in the form of an ibex defecating. A bird feeding on the dropping is the spearthrower's peg.

The invention of the spearthrower considerably lessened the amount of strength and skill needed to cast a spear. The spearthrower was known in Europe by at least the end of the Palaeolithic Age. We illustrate an especially magnificent example recovered from a cave in France (Fig. 7.4). While the spearthrower was used widely in the Palaeolithic world, it reached its most developed form in Australia, where it is called a *woomera*. The antiquity of the woomera in Australia is not known, but present evidence indicates at least a few thousand years (Flood 1983:199). The spearthrower is basically a stick of, at most, a metre in length, provided at its end with a peg that engages a concavity in the butt end of the spear. Because it lengthens the throwing lever, casting a spear with a spearthrower requires less wrist action than if it were done by hand. Measurements taken from films of Australian Aborigines casting spears show that the angular velocity of the wrist when a spearthrower is used is only about a fifth of that needed in hand-throwing (Cundy 1980:63–71). Because the velocity of the body is reduced, a spearthrower increases the efficiency of the cast. We now calculate the virtual mass of a person casting a spear with a spearthrower. As in our previous calculation we assume that only the kinetic energy of the hand and forearm is significant, but now we must also consider the kinetic energy of the spearthrower. If the configuration of the arm and spearthrower at the moment of release is as shown in Fig. 7.5 we can calculate the angular velocity of the hand and spearthrower ω_h, on the assumption that the angular velocity of the wrist is five times faster than that of the forearm, to be

$$\omega_h = 1\cdot43v \text{ rad/s}.$$

The velocities of the centres of gravity of the spearthrower (v_t), hand (v_h) and forearm (v_a) can then be calculated to be

$$v_a = 0\cdot03v \text{ m/s},$$

$$v_h = 0\cdot17v \text{ m/s},$$

$$v_t = 0\cdot51v \text{ m/s}.$$

Assuming that the mass of the spearthrower is 0·33 kg, its linear kinetic energy is $0·044v^2$ J and its angular kinetic energy (see equation 4.5), assuming that the moment of inertia of the spear is given approximately by the formula for a long thin rod (see Table 4.1), is $0·013v^2$ J. The total kinetic energy of the spearthrower is then about $0·06v^2$ J, as compared with only $0·009v^2$ J for the hand and forearm. Hence the virtual mass for casting a spear with a spearthrower is about 0·13 kg, or about a third of that when throwing a spear by hand alone.

Fig. 7.5. Casting a spear with a spearthrower (lengths in mm).

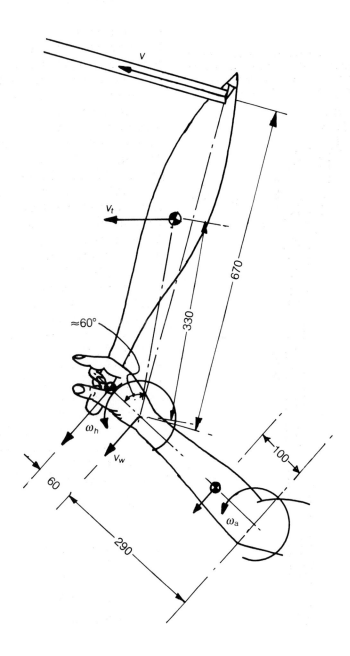

In hunting or fighting, a spear has to be thrown with accuracy and it has to have enough kinetic energy to kill or wound the victim. For accuracy a low trajectory is preferable, although this necessitates a high velocity. Experiments in throwing balls of different weights have shown, as one might expect, that light balls can be thrown faster than heavy ones. However the heavier balls have greater kinetic energy (Toyoshima and Miyashita 1973). It is necessary, therefore, for the hunter to compromise between the competing needs of high velocity and high kinetic energy. The Tasmanians, who were highly proficient with the hand-thrown spear, favoured ones weighing about 0·6 kg (Noetling 1911). Spears three times heavier could be thrown by the Melville Islanders distances of between 32 and 44 m (Spencer 1928:690). The spearthrower eases the wrist action and makes it possible to cast a lighter spear at higher velocity, thereby achieving both a low trajectory and high kinetic energy. In Australia the mechanical efficiency of a woomera used to cast a matching spear, which on average weighed about 0·25 kg (Palter 1977:163), is from our calculation about 70%. Thus the light woomera-thrown spear is more efficient than a heavier one thrown by hand. With the aid of a woomera the Australian Aborigine could cast a spear from 90 to 125 m – an exceptional cast of 180 m is recorded (Falkenberg 1968:34). To cast a spear 100 m requires a velocity greater than 31 m/s. The total energy needed to throw a 0·25 kg spear at this velocity with a woomera is about 170 J, significantly less than the 240 J needed to cast a 0·6 kg spear at 22 m/s by hand, though the kinetic energies of the two spears are comparable (120 J by spearthrower and 140 J by hand).

A spearthrower can take any one of a number of forms. From a mechanical point of view its mass should be as small as possible, consistent with the need to maintain its stiffness so that little energy is lost in bending the spearthrower. The stiffest and hence the most efficient spearthrower has a circular cross-section tapering from the hand-hold (where the bending moment has its maximum value) to the hook. Some Australian spearthrowers, such as the Central Australian type, differ considerably from this ideal mechanical form. The Aborigines of the Central Desert had to be highly mobile and were therefore lightly equipped. Their spearthrower was a multi-purpose tool which, in addition to its main function, was also a handle for a stone chisel blade, a shallow container for pigments and blood used during ceremonies, fire-stick, a digging implement, a spear deflector and even a musical instrument (Cundy 1980:147, 148). An American curiosity is the bannerstone, a weight that was slipped over the spearthrower (or *atatl*, which is its American Indian name). The occurrence of these stones has led some archaeologists to believe that the efficiency of a spearthrower can be increased by adding to its mass. Whatever purpose the bannerstone served it had nothing to do with mechanical advantage. As can be seen from our analysis, a heavy spearthrower is inefficient.

When casting with a spearthrower the butt end of the spear has to deflect sideways from its intended flight path. The

Fig. 7.6. Spears bending during a demonstration throw by two Australian Aborigines (from Herrmann 1967:111).

Fig. 7.7. The deflection of a spear during throwing.

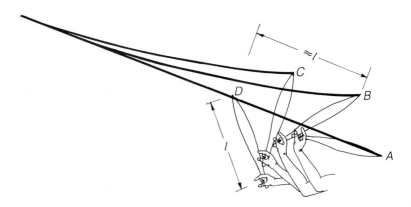

spearthrower's maximum length is governed by the need to limit this sideways deflection.[4] It is also essential that the spear is flexible enough to accommodate the deflection by bending (Fig. 7.6). A schematic representation of the successive positions of spearthrower and spear are shown in Fig. 7.7. If the spear were rigid, a high angular velocity would be imparted to it during the final phase when its butt end is pulled downwards. Many Australian spears were only marginally stable. Any angular velocity imparted to these spears would cause them to tumble in flight. Such an effect, which is called *hooking*, can occur if the spear does not have the right flexibility. With a flexible spear the butt end is bent away from the flight path during the initial stages of the throw: the stored elastic energy in the spear is then recovered as it straightens. On release the spear vibrates, but these vibrations are damped by hysteresis effects in the wood and should not greatly affect the accuracy of the throw. To achieve a perfect throw the spear's dynamic flexibility or *spine* must be matched to the spearthrower. Ideally there should be no transverse force imposed on the butt of the spear. This condition can be achieved if the spine of the spear is such that in free vibration the butt end returns in the same time that the spearthrower moves from *B* to *D*. If we assume that the average velocity of the spear is about half its final velocity *v*, then the time taken for the spearthrower to move from *B* to *D* is about $2l/v$ where *l* is approximately the length of the spearthrower. A perfectly matched spear would complete a quarter of a full vibration in this time. Therefore a spear cast with a Central Australian spearthrower of length 0·67 m at a velocity of 30 m/s should have a period of free vibration of about 0·18 s. The period of free vibration of a uniform rod with mass m, length l_s, second moment of area of the cross-section $I = \pi d^4/64$, and Young's modulus E is given by

$$T = 0.25 \left[\frac{m l_s^3}{EI}\right]^{\frac{1}{2}}.$$ (7.10)

For an average Central Australian spear of mass 0·42 kg, length 2·7 m, average diameter 15 mm and Young's modulus 14 000 MPa, the period of free oscillation is about 0·12 s. Thus, though our calculation is only approximate, it does suggest that the spine of a spear roughly matches the spearthrower and the velocity of the cast.

The stability of a spear

Once the spear disengages from the spearthrower or the hand its centre of gravity will describe a parabolic-like trajectory determined by equation (7·9). Of course it is essential that the spear remains roughly tangential to the flight path so that its point will hit the target. The way a spear's attitude changes during flight depends on relative positions of its centre of gravity and the point through which the resultant aerodynamic forces

---

[4] The length of a spearthrower is not limited by the strength of the user's wrist. Because a long spearthrower will remain in contact with a spear for a longer time, the acceleration needed to achieve a given spear velocity is inversely proportional to the length of the spearthrower. The force on a spear is, therefore, inversely proportional to the length of the spearthrower. Consequently the wrist moment (the product of the force and the length of the spearthrower) is independent of the length.

act, which is called the *centre of pressure*. If the centre of gravity
(CG) is ahead of the centre of pressure (CP) (Fig. 7.8a) then the
moment of the aerodynamic forces about the centre of gravity
tends to align the spear with the flight path. On the other hand, if
the centre of gravity is behind the centre of pressure (Fig. 7.8b),
the aerodynamic forces will tend to increase the angle of
incidence, and the spear may be unstable.

A spear's centre of pressure is not a fixed point, but moves
backwards with increasing angle of incidence. We can estimate
the centre of pressure for a spear that has a streamlined wooden
point. There are three forces acting on an ideal slender body like a
spear when it is at a small angle of incidence. We have already
mentioned the drag force D resulting from the skin friction,
though now we must use the tangential component of velocity v
$\cos \theta$ in equation (7.5). This force acts along the centre line of the
spear. In addition there is a lift force L that acts near to the point
of the spear due to air flow circulation and, because of the cross-
flow component of velocity $v \sin \theta$, a force N perpendicular to the
spear acting at its centre point (Fig. 7.9). These forces are
approximately given by:

$$L = \tfrac{1}{2}\rho\, v^2 S_c \sin 2\theta,$$

$$N = \tfrac{1}{2}\rho(v \sin \theta)^2 S_l,$$

Fig. 7.8. The stability of a spear:
(*a*) stable flight; (*b*) unstable flight.

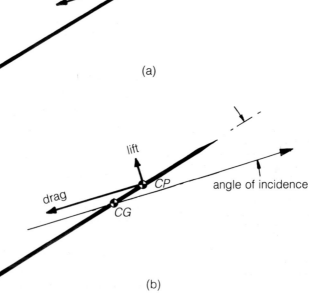

(a)

(b)

where $S_c = \pi d^2/4$ is the cross-sectional area, $S_l = dl$ the lateral area and d and l the diameter and length of the spear respectively (Hoerner and Borst 1975:ch19). The line of action of the resultant of these forces passes through the centre of pressure. Hence the moment of the three forces about the centre of pressure must be zero. The drag force D passes through the centre of pressure so that its moment is zero, and we are left with

$$L l_p = N(l/2 - l_p)$$

which gives the distance of the centre of pressure from the tip of the spear as a function of the angle of incidence

$$l_p = \frac{l}{2\left[1 + \dfrac{\pi}{2}\left(\dfrac{d}{l}\right)\cot\theta\right]}. \tag{7.11}$$

For very small angles of incidence the centre of pressure is close to the point of the spear, but will move quickly back towards the midpoint of the spear as the angle of incidence increases. A spear is in equilibrium with zero angle of incidence, but it is unstable. In stable equilibrium flight the angle of incidence is such that the centre of pressure coincides with the centre of gravity (Fig. 7.10). Obviously if the centre of gravity is behind the midpoint of the spear, equilibrium flight is impossible and the spear would eventually turn through roughly 180°.

To penetrate the prey a spear must hit at small angle of incidence, probably less than 5°. The angle of incidence at which the spear hits the prey is not necessarily its equilibrium value. In fact it is possible to throw even an unstable spear ($l_g/l > 0.5$) successfully over a short distance. The control over the angle of incidence at which the spear is launched depends upon the person's skill. Olympic javelin throwers need very close control on the angle of incidence they use so that the javelin develops the maximum lift drag ratio and hence the longest flight (Dyson 1962). The variation in the angle of incidence of a spear during

Fig. 7.9. Forces acting on a spear inclined to its flight path.

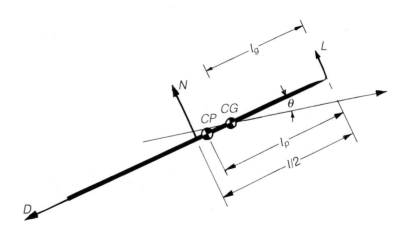

flight depends upon the moment of the forces acting on the spear
and its moment of inertia I which is $ml^2/12$ (Table 4.1).

Taking moments about the centre of gravity we have from
equation (4.4)

$$I\alpha = Ll_g - N(l/2 - l_g) \tag{7.12}$$

where α is the spear's angular acceleration. In hunting, a spear
will be cast on a low trajectory and to a first approximation we
can neglect the curvature of the flight path. Hence we have
solved equation (7.12) by computer for a spear travelling on an
artificial straight flight path to find the variation in incidence with
time. To enable graphs indicating the change in attitude of the
spear to be universal for spears with the same l_g/l and d/l ratios
we have introduced a non-dimensional time defined by

$$\tau = \left(\frac{6\rho v^2 d}{m}\right)^{\frac{1}{2}} t.$$

A typical d/l ratio for both Tasmanian hand-thrown spears (Noetling
1911) and Central Australian spears used with a spearthrower
(Cundy 1980: appendix C) is about 0·006, and we have used this
value to construct the variation in angle of incidence of three
spears where l_g/l ratio varies from 0·04 to 0·5 cast at three
different initial angles of incidence 1°, 5°, and 10° (Fig. 7.11). If
the l_g/l ratio is less than 0·45 the spear reaches equilibrium in a
non-dimensional time of not much more than 20. The spear with
a l_g/l ratio of 0·5 is of course unstable but, if cast at a small

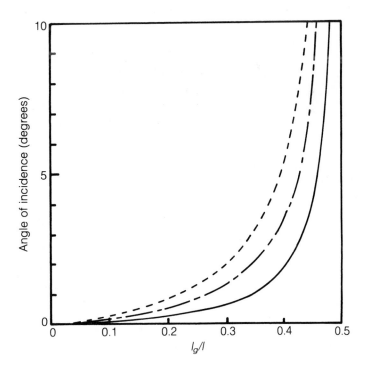

Fig. 7.10. The equilibrium angle
of incidence for a spear's flight.
——$d/l = 0·005$; ---$d/l = 0·010$;
---$d/l = 0·015$.

enough angle of incidence, could still effectively hit its prey
provided the non-dimensional flight time is less than about 10.
The mean mass of the Tasmanian spears held in the Tasmanian
Museum is about 0·6 kg and their mean diameter is about 18 mm
(Noetling 1911). Assuming that such a spear was thrown with a
velocity of about 20 m/s at prey at a distance of 20 m the flight
time would be about one second and the corresponding non-
dimensional flight time from equation (7.13) is about 10. Hence
an exceptionally skilled hunter can use a spear with its centre of
gravity at its midpoint provided the person can cast it at a very
small angle of incidence. The nearer the centre of gravity is to the
tip of the spear the more rapidly the spear will achieve its
equilibrium attitude. From Fig. 7.11 we can see that if the spear
were cast with an initial angle of incidence of 10° it would be
necessary for the centre of gravity to be within about the first
40% of the spear's length if it is to hit its prey with an angle of
incidence less than 5° after a non-dimensional flight time of 10. It
is not therefore surprising to find that hand-thrown Tasmanian
spears had their centres of gravity closer to their points than 40%
of their length.[5]

There is less control on the angles of incidence of spears
thrown with a woomera, and their *non-dimensional* flight times are
longer. As a consequence it would be extremely difficult to cast a
spear that has its centre of gravity halfway or more from its
point. On the other hand it is not necessary for the spear to be
especially stable. The average mass of the Australian spear used
with a woomera was about 0·25 kg (Palter 1977:163). Assuming
that the spear was cast with a velocity of 30 m/s over a distance

Fig. 7.11. Variation in the angle of
incidence during flight for three spears.
——$l_g/l = 0·04$; ---$l_g/l = 0·45$;
---$l_g/l = 0·5$.

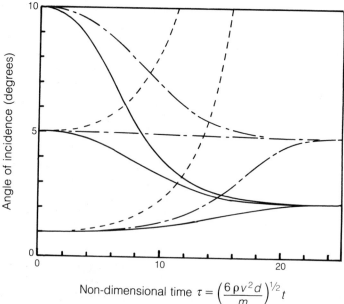

Angle of incidence (degrees)

Non-dimensional time $\tau = \left(\dfrac{6\rho v^2 d}{m}\right)^{1/2} t$

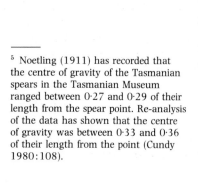

[5] Noetling (1911) has recorded that
the centre of gravity of the Tasmanian
spears in the Tasmanian Museum
ranged between 0·27 and 0·29 of their
length from the spear point. Re-analysis
of the data has shown that the centre
of gravity was between 0·33 and 0·36
of their length from the point (Cundy
1980:108).

of 20 m, the non-dimensional flight time would be about 30.
Obviously the longer non-dimensional flight times make unstable
spears ($l_g/l > 0.5$) impossible. However, provided the l_g/l ratio is
less than about 0·45, the spear should be sufficiently stable even if
the initial angle of incidence is considerably larger than the
equilibrium value. Palter (ibid.:168) has measured the position of
the centre of gravity of 293 spearthrower projectiles and found
that they were between 26 and 48% of the spear's length from
the point. Our mechanical considerations clearly show that some
spearthrower projectiles could have had a centre of gravity far
back and yet still be serviceable.

The boomerang

A short stick is most successfully thrown with rotation as
well as translation. Just about everyone has thrown a stick in this
manner for a dog to fetch. Essentially the same action is used to
throw a stick to stun birds and other small game. Compared with
a stone or a spear, a thrown stick has the advantage of covering a
relatively large area, though because of its high resistance it tends
to have a very limited range. If a suitably bent stick is trimmed so
that it has a lenticular cross-section it is no longer a crude
throwing-stick, but a sophisticated boomerang. Because the
lenticular section provides lift, just as an aeroplane's wing does,
the distance over which such a projectile can be thrown is
increased to about 100 m. The *true* boomerang is very much an
Australian weapon, having been used on that continent for at
least the last 10000 years (Luebbers 1975).

Throwing-sticks in their infinite variety are known from
around the world, but it seems that very few would have had
sufficient aerodynamic lift to be classed as boomerangs. The
throwing-sticks that Carter (1933:142) found in Tutankhamun's
tomb may not be true boomerangs (Hess 1975:72, 73). What
appears to be a non-returning boomerang, made from mammoth
tusk and dating to the last Ice Age, has recently been unearthed
in Poland (Valde-Nowak *et al.* 1987). The only prehistoric
boomerang outside Australia that has been positively identified
so far is one found in Holland, which has been dated to about
300 BC, and is of the returning type (Hess 1973). In Australia the
returning boomerang was as much a plaything as it was a
weapon, and the Aborigines used it in competitive sport as well as
for fowling (Hess 1975:52–3). The white settlers were likewise
entertained by the returning boomerang and its popularity quickly
spread to the home country where, early in the nineteenth
century, an undergraduate wag at the University of Dublin
wrote:

> Of all the advantages we have derived from our Australian
> settlements none seems to have given more universal
> satisfaction than the introduction of some crooked pieces of
> wood shaped like a horse's shoe, or the crescent moon; and

called boomerang, waumerang, or kilee. Ever since their
structure has been fully understood, carpenters appear to
have ceased from all other work; the windows of toy shops
exhibit little else; walking sticks and umbrellas have gone
out of fashion, and even in this rainy season no man carried
anything but a boomerang; nor does this species of madness
appear to be abating. (Anon. 1838)

The returning boomerang still retains its popularity with all
races.

Although most Australian boomerangs were designed to be
effective in hunting or fighting, and were non-returning, it is
easiest to explain first the mechanics of the returning type. The
most significant, though frequently the least-mentioned, feature of
the boomerang is its cross-section which is lenticular, with one
side less convex than the other (or even flat), usually with a front
to back symmetry. This cross-section will generate a lifting force,
even when there is no angle of incidence, though the tips of the
boomerang's arms are frequently twisted so that the angle of
incidence is increased. This twist, which is not essential, makes
the boomerang suitable for either a right-handed or left-handed
thrower, depending on its direction. The arms of the boomerang
must be slightly bent in planform for stability, though the
planform is really not critical and a wide range of variation is
permissible for effective flight.

To throw a right-handed boomerang the end of one arm is
gripped so that the flatter side is to the right of the thrower. The
boomerang is thrown towards the horizon with the plane of
rotation nearly vertical. Australian Aborigines invariably throw a
bomerang so that its free-end points forward, but it can be
thrown equally well with the free-end pointing backwards. When
thrown correctly the boomerang will follow a roughly circular
path about 30 m in diameter. At first the boomerang flies level,
but as it *lies down* (that is to say, as its plane of rotation becomes
more horizontal) it rises to a height of about 15 m and then
descends to fall at the thrower's feet. Hess (1968, 1973:379–86)
has taken spectacular night-time photographs of the flights of
experimental boomerangs by attaching a small light-bulb on the
end of one of the arms (Fig. 7.12).

Since the boomerang has both a forward speed v and spins
about its centre of gravity with an angular velocity ω, the
velocities at corresponding points a distance r from the centre of
rotation on its two arms are not the same (Fig. 7.13). The
velocity of the uppermost arm is always greater than that of the
lower one. Consequently, more lift is generated on the upper arm,
creating an anti-clockwise moment M as viewed by a right-handed
thrower. If the boomerang were not spinning it would turn over
on its back. However the effect of a moment on a spinning body is
not quite that simple and to understand the flight of a boomerang

one first has to understand the precessional motion of a gyroscope.

Moments and angular velocities are vector quantities similar to forces and linear velocity. Both need a direction as well as a magnitude to describe them. Usually the vectorial direction of a moment is defined by what is called the *right-hand rule*. If the right hand is clenched so that the fingers curl in the direction of

Fig. 7.12. Boomerang in flight. The photograph was taken by Hess at night, with the camera's shutter left open during the flight. The path of the boomerang was illuminated by a light built into the end of one of its arms.

Fig. 7.13. Moment generated because of unequal lift on the two arms of the boomerang.

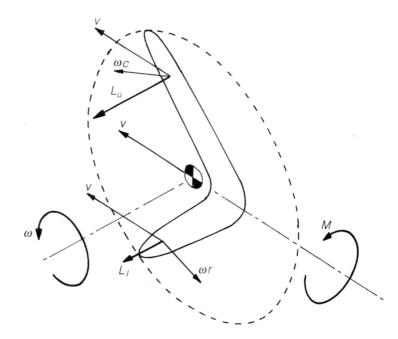

the moment, the vectorial direction is indicated by the thumb (Fig. 7.14). The vectorial direction of rotation, angular velocity and acceleration are similarly defined. When a moment is applied to a spinning disc or boomerang, the change in *angular momentum* (the product of the moment of inertia of the body and its angular velocity) is in the direction of the moment vector. Therefore if we apply a moment **M** about a horizontal axis to a disc spinning in a vertical plane (Fig. 7.15a) it cannot turn about that horizontal axis, as would seem to be natural, because such a motion would cause a vertical change in the angular momentum (Fig. 7.15b). To produce change in the angular momentum (that is, in the direction of the applied moment) it is necessary for the plane of the disc to precess about a vertical axis (Fig. 7.15c). If the rate of precessional rotation is Ω, then the change in angular momentum $d(I\omega)$ during a short time dt is given by

$$d(I\omega) = \Omega dt \times I\omega.$$

The rate of change of angular momentum is equal to the applied moment **M** and is therefore given by

$$\mathbf{M} = \Omega \times I\omega. \tag{7.14}$$

It follows then that the circular path of the returning bomerang is due to precession. The moment **M**, caused by the

Fig. 7.14. The right-hand rule for the direction of a moment.

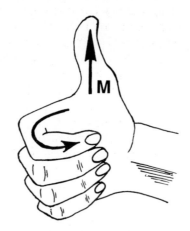

Fig. 7.15. Precessional motion of a spinning disc: (a) moment *m* applied at right-angles to spin axis; (b) disc precessing in an 'apparently' natural way; (c) disc precessing in actual way.

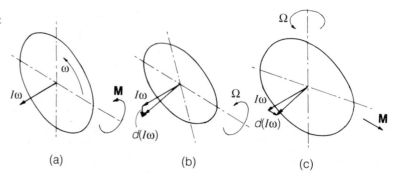

(a)   (b)   (c)

asymmetrical lift on the arms, makes the boomerang precess in an anti-clockwise direction rather than turn over on its back. The boomerang's plane of rotation cannot be exactly vertical, because the lift must have a vertical component to counteract the force of gravity and keep the boomerang in the air. The horizontal component of the lift L_h provides the centripetal force that keeps the boomerang on a circular path of radius r. Equating this force to the centripetal acceleration v^2/r (equation 2.7) we obtain

$$L_h = \frac{mv^2}{r} \qquad (7.15)$$

where m is the mass of the boomerang. Since the horizontal component of lift is proportional to the square of the velocity, the size of the circular path of the boomerang is independent of the speed with which it is thrown. Heavy boomerangs will take a wider circular path than light ones, and simply to keep them airborne will require a greater velocity.

The phenomenon of lying down (Hess 1973:111–12) is important in maintaining the boomerang's flight. As its speed drops due to the resistance of the air, the weight of the boomerang can only be balanced if the plane of its rotation becomes more horizontal to compensate for the loss of lift. The moment that is responsible for the boomerang precessing about a horizontal axis so that it lies down results from a number of factors, the most important of which is wake effect. When a boomerang is in flight its leading arm cuts through undisturbed air, whereas its trailing arm moves through the wake created by the leading arm. A small velocity is imparted by the leading arm to the air in the opposite direction to the lift force, which reduces the effective angle of incidence of the trailing arm. Consequently the trailing arm creates less lift and there is a moment about the vertical axis in an anti-clockwise direction when viewed from above. This moment causes the boomerang to precess about a horizontal axis and produces the phenomenon of 'lying down'.

Although the planform of the boomerang is relatively unimportant, a boomerang cannot be straight. While a ruler has an adequate cross-section for a boomerang, if it is thrown it will twist about its longitudinal axis. However if two rulers are joined at their middle to form a cross they will make a satisfactory boomerang.[6] A rigid body possesses three principal axes of rotation mutually at right-angles to each other; about two of these axes the moments of inertia have their maximum and minimum values. The principal axes of a book are the three axes of symmetry. If a book, held closed with a rubber band, is flipped, it will spin easily about axes perpendicular to its cover or parallel to its spine – the moments of inertia of a book about these two axes are its maximum and minimum respectively. However if one tries to spin a book about an axis perpendicular to the spine it will tumble. Bodies are stable when spun about their maximum or

[6] The cross-boomerang was used as a toy by children in North Queensland and in the Indonesian island of Sulawesi (Hess 1973:29–31).

minimum principal axes, provided that the axis of the intermediate principal moment of inertia is not too close to either of these. With a ruler there is not enough difference between the maximum and intermediate principal moments of inertia to enable it to spin in a stable fashion the way a boomerang does. Therefore a boomerang cannot have a straight planform, though the arms only need to be slightly at an angle to make the difference between the two moments of inertia significant and to give the boomerang stability in flight.

So far our discussion has been about the interesting but relatively unimportant returning boomerang. We now need to explain the flight of the more commonly used hunting boomerang that has a straight path. If a boomerang is thrown so that it spins in a horizontal plane it will require less lift to maintain it in the air. By giving the tips of the boomerang's arms a negative twist, the lift generated can be somewhat reduced. In fact the lift force at the tips can even be reversed and the precessional moment about the horizontal axis caused by the asymmetry we discussed earlier can be almost eliminated. Because the non-returning boomerang is thrown in such a way that its plane of rotation is horizontal, the small precessional moment remaining only causes the front of the boomerang to lift slightly. Paradoxically, it is more difficult to make a good non-returning boomerang that flies on a straight path than a returning one. A left-handed returning boomerang, when thrown in a horizontal plane by a right-handed person, will have a reasonably straight flight path.

The bow and arrow

The bow differs from other early weapons in being able to store the energy of the human muscles. On release, the energy of the bow is quickly transferred to a comparatively light arrow which is projected at a much higher speed than can be achieved by hand-throwing. Consequently the flight trajectories of arrows are flatter than those of spears, so that the bow is more accurate at longer distances. The kinetic energy of a hunting arrow is usually no more than 60 J (Klopsteg 1943:190), which is less than the energy of a well-thrown spear. The great penetrating ability of an arrow is due to its slender shaft and sharp tip. American Indians were able to fell bison with stone-tipped arrows shot from a relatively weak bow. If the arrow did not hit bone it would sometimes penetrate right through the bison's body. The Spanish conquistadors at first underestimated the penetration power of the Indian stone-tipped arrow and thought that their coats of chain mail would be adequate protection. In Florida the Spaniards, wishing to test the effectiveness of the native archery, offered a captive Indian his freedom if he could shoot an arrow through a coat of mail. The captive's arrow penetrated not one but two coats of mail. After experiences such as these, the Spaniards exchanged their heavy mail for padded cloth armour that proved more effective (Pope 1909:40-1).

The energy that can be stored in a bow is limited by the archer's arm length and physical strength. In some parts of the world, and in times past, bows of impressive size have been made. An example worthy of mention is the bow of the Liangulu, a Kenyan tribe, which required a drawforce (called by archers the bow's 'weight') of about 450 N (Hardy 1976:26). Most bows were much lighter – for instance, the average 'weight' of bows used by the American Indians was around 200 N (Pope 1909). If a bow is drawn to the ear the maximum draw is about 900 mm, the more usual draw for hunting bows being about 700 mm (Pratt 1976:199). Disregarding the characteristics of the bow, the maximum energy that can be stored is the product of the 'weight' of the bow and its draw. However the draw force of a longbow increases roughly in proportion to its draw, so that the actual energy stored is approximately half the maximum possible value (equation 3.23). Therefore the average amount of energy stored in a hunting longbow is about 70 J. Not all this energy can be transferred to the arrow.

When an arrow is released some of the bow's energy is retained as kinetic energy by the limbs of the bow. The efficiency of the bow can be most easily assessed by the concept of its *virtual mass* (Klopsteg 1943). In a similar fashion to spearthrowers, the virtual mass of a bow is defined as that mass which, moving with the velocity of the arrow, would have the same kinetic energy as that retained by the bow. The efficiency of a bow is therefore given by equation (7.9) if we substitute the mass of the arrow for the mass of the spear. The efficiency of a bow increases with the mass of the arrow. It has to follow that, while a heavy arrow cannot be shot with as high a velocity as a light one, it has more energy and hence greater penetrating power. The English medieval war arrows were heavy (weighing about 60 g) and had bodkin points that could pierce plate armour (Hardy 1976:53–5; Pratt 1976:203). In hunting, provided the arrow has a sharp head, the impact energy is not quite so important, though for accuracy reasonably high velocity is. Consequently a lighter arrow was employed in hunting; for instance, the average weight of the American Indian arrow was around 30 g (Pope 1909:44). Likewise, when adversaries were not heavily armoured, a lighter war arrow could be used to effect, as the bodies of some 60 Egyptian soldiers of the Eleventh Dynasty, found in a communal grave at Deir el Bahari, grimly testify. The foreshafts of arrows still remain in some of the bodies – the arrows, tipped only with dense-wood points, probably weighed no more than 15 g apiece (Hardy 1976:23). Surprisingly, apart from shields of leather, the Egyptian soldiers wore no defensive armour at all until the New Kingdom (James 1979:224).

The maximum range of an arrow depends on its velocity and so it is the lighter arrow that is used in distance shooting. Yet in a mechanical sense a bow is not efficient with light arrows. An increase in the 'weight' of a bow does not produce a corresponding increase in the distance an arrow can be shot, because a stronger bow means a heavier one with a larger virtual mass. Hence the distance record of 358 m for a massive longbow that 'weighed' 769 N was not a tremendous improvement over the distance of 311 m set at the turn of the century with a bow that was only a third as strong (Hardy 1976:155, 171).

The efficiency of a bow depends on its design and the materials of its construction. The bow material must be light and resilient so that the bow has as small a mass as possible. In Europe, yew, which has the highest resilience per unit mass (Table 3.1) was esteemed above all other bow-woods (Clark 1963:51; Rausing 1967:35–47, 153; Hardy 1976:17–20). In terms of its resilience, ash appears from Table 3.1 to be a close rival to yew, but it is inferior because it creeps under load to take on a permanent set and has a high hysteresis loss (Klopsteg 1943:185). The next best European bow-wood after yew is shade elm with its fine growth rings (Hardy 1976:17). In Medieval England the supply of yew from the churchyards was inadequate and bow-staves had to be imported. King Edward IV enacted a statute requiring merchants to import four yew bow-staves for every ton weight of goods – default meant a fine of six shillings and eightpence, quite a penalty in those days (Hardy 1976:128). In an effort to get the most out of a longbow it was usually stressed somewhat past its elastic limit, until small compression ridges were formed on the bow's belly (Hardy 1976:136, 168; Blyth 1976:196; Gordon 1978:284). Although a loss in energy would occur during initial use of the bow, there would be very little further permanent deformation as hardening would take place and allow the bow to deform elastically at the higher stresses (Blyth 1976:196). The maximum working strain for bow-wood, allowing for some permanent deformation, is about 1·2% (Blyth 1976:195).

When we draw a bow it bends so that its back is in tension and its belly is in compression. An efficient bow is equally stressed along its length. Since at least as early as the Mesolithic period efficient *flat* bows (where cross-sectional width exceeds thickness) have been made in Europe by tapering the sides of the bow almost to a point at its tips (Clark 1963). High-stacked bows (where cross-section thickness exceeds width) were usually tapered in thickness to achieve the same purpose. When drawn, a flat bow deforms roughly into an arc of a circle. Assuming that the bow-stave is initially straight, the maximum strain ε_m in the back and belly is given by equation (5·5) and becomes

$$\varepsilon_m = \frac{t}{2R} \tag{7.16}$$

where t is the thickness of the bow, and R the radius of curvature of the bow when drawn. If we assume that the maximum strain for a wooden bow is $1 \cdot 2\%$, then the maximum thickness t_m for any given radius of curvature is

$$t_m = 0 \cdot 024\, R.$$

The relationship between the radius of curvature R and the draw D can be found from the geometry of the bow (Fig. 7.16) and is given by

$$R = \frac{D - S/2 \cos \theta}{1 - \cos (l/2R)}, \tag{7.17}$$

where $\sin \theta = 2R/S \sin l/2R$, l is the length of the stave and S is the length of the bow string.

Assuming that the distance between the handle and bowstring when braced (called in archery the *fistmele*) is about 150 mm, we can calculate the maximum thickness of the bow. In Fig. 7.17 we show the maximum thickness of a bow as a function of its length for draw lengths ranging between 600 and 900 mm, which represent the practical limits of the draw as a dotted band; we also give the dimensions of a number of European and American bows. It makes sense that most bow thicknesses fall within the range that utilises the bow wood to its maximum potential.

We can calculate the draw force P of a longbow using the geometry of the deformed bow shown in Fig. 7.16. As we draw

Fig. 7.16. Geometry of a drawn bow.

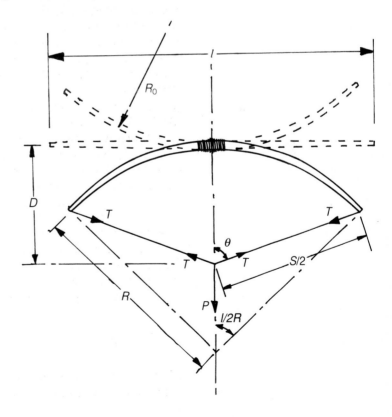

the bow, the draw force P must remain in equilibrium with the bow-string tension T, and hence

$$P = 2T\cos\theta.$$

The bending moment M at the handle of the bow is given by

$$M = TD\sin\theta = \frac{PD}{2}\tan\theta.$$

The bending moment required to bend the bow to a radius of curvature R is given by equation (5·7) and therefore

$$P = \frac{2EI}{DR\tan\theta},\qquad(7.18)$$

Fig. 7.17. Bow-limb thickness and stave length (data from Clark 1963; Pope 1909; Rausing 1967). European high stacked bows: pre-Iron Age ● ; post-Iron Age ○. Flat bows: European pre-Iron Age + ; American Indian ×.

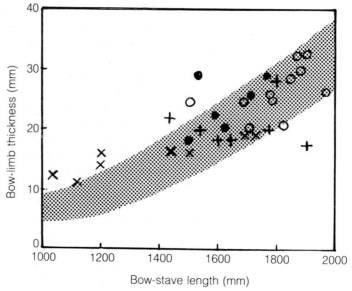

Fig. 7.18. Force-draw curves of bows. ——1200 mm stave; ---2000 mm stave; ---reflex bow, 2000 mm stave with 300 mm reflex.

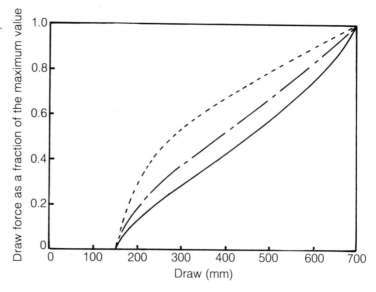

where I is the second moment of area of the bow's cross-section near to the handle. Curves of the draw force against the draw are given for two stave lengths in Fig. 7.18 assuming that the fistmele distance is 150 mm in each case. As we have already mentioned, the draw force of a longbow is roughly proportional to the draw. More energy is stored in bows with long staves. A more exact method of calculation of the dynamics of simple segment bows is given by Hickman (1937).

The composite bow

About two thousand years ago bow-makers in northern Europe realised that yew bow-staves could, with profit, be made thicker if they were cut so that the white sapwood formed the back of the bow and the red heartwood the belly (Rausing 1967:132,133). The heartwood of yew has a significantly higher Young's modulus than the sapwood, but is comparatively brittle (Pope 1909:37, 38). In this natural composite bow-stave the heartwood, which forms roughly three-quarters of the thickness, is used because of its high resilience. The more ductile sapwood on the back prevents premature fracture. The use of natural composites for bow-staves are recorded from other parts of the world but they have not been the subject of systematic study. In eastern Brazil staves were made from *pao d'arco* ('bow-wood') which has dense black growth rings encasing a softer white heartwood (Métraux 1963:230; Heath and Chiara 1977:35–6). Similarly, over much of Southeast Asia and the Pacific, palm or bamboo staves were cut in such a way that the skin formed the belly of the bow (Simmonds 1959). The American Indians frequently glued sinews to the back of their bows, even when using high grade timber such as yew, so that these can be considered truly composite (Pope 1909; Rausing 1967:19). An extremely efficient composite bow was developed as early as the fourth millennium BC in the region east of the Caspian Sea (Rausing 1967:138).

The most sophisticated ancient design of a composite bow incorporated two of the most resilient natural materials – sinews for its back and horn for its belly (Table 3.1). Since these materials were much more capable than wood at storing energy the wood component was reduced to a mere skeleton on which the sinews and horn were glued. The large working strain of the materials in the developed composite bow enabled it to be short and reflexed; that is, when unstrung the bow bends away from the archer (Fig. 7.19). Reflexing the bow enables the draw force characteristic of the bow to be improved so that more energy is stored for the same bow weight. The addition of rigid ears to the tips of the bow-stave lessens the draw force over the final part of the draw and makes the bow even more efficient. A good reflexed bow can store about 50% more energy than a simple longbow of the same weight (Klopsteg 1947:147).

The deformation of a reflexed bow is complex, but the

increased energy storage capabilities can be seen qualitatively from a simple extension of our analysis of the longbow. Let us assume that the bow-stave, instead of being straight when unstrung, is reflexed so that it curves away from the archer on an arc with a radius of R_0 (Fig. 7.16). When drawn the change in effective curvature $1/R_E$ of the reflexed bow is given by

$$1/R_E = 1/R_0 + 1/R.$$

The draw force of the reflexed bow is then given by equation (7.18), but with the radius of curvature R of the drawn bow replaced by the effective value R_E. The effect of reflexing is illustrated in Fig. 7.18, where the draw-force characteristic is shown for a 2 m bow reflexed so that the tips of the stave are 300 mm beyond the handle. A more sophisticated analysis of the reflexed bow analysis is given by Schuster (1969).

While the simple longbow was more than adequate for the chase the reflexed composite bow was superior in warfare. Hardly any armour could stop an arrow fired from the more efficient composite bow (Klopsteg 1947:3) and since the bow was short it could be easily used on horseback. The Parthian mounted archers were formidable enough to halt the eastwards expansion of Imperial Rome – for successful combat just about all that they needed was a sufficient supply of arrows (Hall 1956:706). Despite its obvious advantages some historians and archaeologists have believed that the composite bow was developed because suitable

Fig. 7.19. A reflex bow (after Rausing 1967).

rigid ear

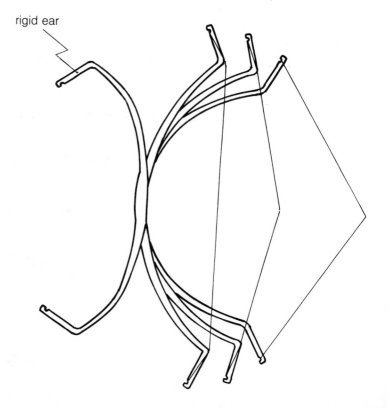

bow-woods were not available and that it has no technological
advantages over the longbow (Balfour 1890; Clark 1963). In the
English-speaking world the tradition of Crécy is strong and the
myth of the supremacy of the longbow takes a long time to die.

In Turkey the bow was abandoned as a weapon of war
during the seventeenth century but archery continued as a
popular sport under the patronge of the sultans who, more often
than not, were themselves the best archers (Klopsteg 1947). The
most popular form of archery among the Turks was distance
shooting. In 1794 a Turkish diplomat, Mahmoud Effendi,
astounded members of the Toxophilite Society of London by
shooting an arrow 379 m against the wind and 440 m with the
wind (Klopsteg 1947:17). By his own testimony Mahmoud was
not considered a first-class bowman in Turkey. The Sultan Selim
shot an arrow the incredible distance of 1400 gez (about 880 m)
at the famous Ok Meydan butts at Istanbul in 1798 (Klopsteg
1947:24). Such a distance was only recently surpassed with a
modern bow. The record for a modern composite bow made from
synthetic fibres is 1126 m, set in 1982 by Alan Webster of
England (Russell and McWhirter 1987:224).

The Archer's Paradox
To conclude our discussion on the bow and arrow we will
examine the Archer's Paradox (Klopsteg 1943: 186–9). If an
arrow were rigid it would be deflected away from its mark during
its release (Fig. 7.20a). Of course an arrow is not absolutely rigid,

Fig. 7.20. The Archer's Paradox:
(*a*) flight of a rigid arrow; (*b*) flight
of a flexible arrow that has the
correct spine.

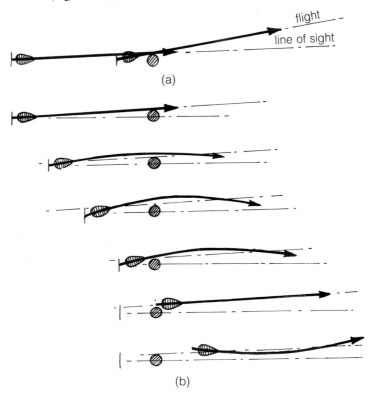

and if its flexibility or *spine* is matched to the bow it will snake around the bowgrip without actually touching it (Fig. 7.20b). To achieve the correct motion, the arrow must complete about half a full vibration by the time it passes the bow's handle. Provided that its head is relatively light, the period of vibration of an arrow will be given approximately by equation (7.10), and it is fairly simple to show that the diameter of the arrow should be proportional to $(\eta UL/E)^{\frac{1}{4}}$ where η is the efficiency of the bow, U is the energy stored and L the length of the arrow.

Torsion catapults

The energy stored in a hand bow is limited by the strength of the arm muscles, and once drawn the bow-string has to be released almost immediately. The invention of the crossbow, which has a lock to hold the bow-string back, enabled archers to use different and more powerful muscles to draw the bow. The earliest form of crossbow, in use from about 400 BC, was the *gastraphetes*, or belly-bow, so-called because it was drawn with both hands while braced against the archer's belly (Marsden 1969:5–13, 48–9). Not long after the invention of the belly-bow, much bigger artillery versions using a winch to draw the bow-string were being made (Marsden 1969:13–16). These early artillery pieces were antipersonnel weapons, but there was a strong incentive to develop catapults capable of breaching fortifications. The crossbow cannot be efficiently increased in size, as Heron noted in his artillery manual (Marsden 1971:18–60). However a much more efficient catapult using a torsion spring of sinews or hair (Fig. 7.21) was developed in about 340 BC, probably under the patronage of Philip of Macedonia, the father of Alexander the Great (Marsden 1969:60). Some of these machines were immense and could hurl boulders of up to $1\frac{1}{2}$ talents (40 kg) in weight some hundreds of metres (Marsden

Fig. 7.21. A torsion catapult (after Soedel and Foley 1979).

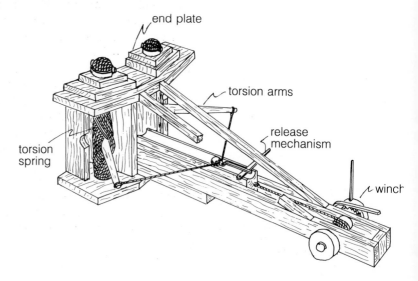

1969:81). Vitruvius (X, 11, 3) gives the dimensions of even larger machines suitable for 100 kg shot or more, but it is likely that these were just theoretically possible dimensions and that catapults of this size were actually never built. Even so, torsion catapults required huge quantities of sinews and horse hair – a surviving document states that in about 220 BC the island of Rhodes shipped 100 talents (2·6 tonnes) of sinews and 300 talents (7·9 tonnes) of hair to Sinope, a Greek city on the southern shore of the Black Sea (Marsden 1969:75).

The improvement of torsion catapults led to a revolution in warfare. They were not only used on land but were mounted on immense war-galleys. For instance, in 332 BC, Alexander the Great used ship-borne catapults to breach the harbour walls of Tyre; some 250 years earlier Nebuchadnezzar, who did not have the benefit of artillery, unsuccessfully besieged the same city for 13 years. After the invention of the torsion catapult, tower walls had to be made thicker to withstand the destructive power of artillery. Philon of Byzantium advised that fortification walls should be at least 10 cubits (4·6 m) thick to give adequate protection from bombardment. This value seems unnecessarily large and, in practice, walls were thinner (Marsden 1969:151).

The most crucial element in the catapult was of course the torsion spring, which was made from plaited cords of sinews or hair.[7] Stringing the torsion spring was a difficult task. Each cord had to be threaded through the end plates and be stretched with a special winch-operated device until its diameter was reduced by a third. As many cords as possible were squeezed through the holes and, with the early machines, the last few strands were drawn through with iron needles, which sometimes damaged the cords. Even so, the tension in the springs relaxed after use and it was necessary to tighten them by twisting their ends. Philon pointed out in his criticism of this method of retensioning that 'the engine loses its springiness because the strands are huddled up in to a thick spiral and the spring, becoming askew, is robbed of its natural force and liveliness' (Marsden 1971:121). The extra twisting created higher frictional forces between the strands and this would have reduced their efficiency. Not only was the method of retensioning poor, but the cords passing around the thin iron bar would suffer wear. Philon suggested an improved method of tightening, in which wedges under the end plates could apply both some of the initial tension and any subsequent retensioning that might become necessary in the field (Marsden 1971:125, 169).

The Greek engineers who introduced science into the design of torsion catapults based the catapult's proportions on the diameter D of the torsion spring. They gave a formula for the size of the torsion spring required for any mass m of the shot, which was

$$D = 1 \cdot 1 \, m^{\frac{1}{3}}, \tag{7.19}$$

[7] Sinews were regarded as the strongest and were therefore normally preferred. However, in times of emergency, horses' hair could be used and even the tresses of the women of a besieged populace (Marsden 1969:87–8).

where m is measured in drachmas and D in dactyls (Marsden 1969:25). In more familiar SI units this formula becomes

$$D = 130\, m^{\frac{1}{3}} \tag{7.19}$$

where D is given in millimetres and m in kilograms. We shall now show that the Alexandrian formula was mechanically accurate and did give the correct size of torsion springs.

The torsion on the arms of the catapult is derived from the tension in the cords (Fig. 7.22). By pulling back the catapult's arms the spring will twist and the cords will form a helix whose angle φ is given by the angle of twist θ and the radial position r of any particular cord, according to the expression

$$\varphi \approx \frac{2\theta r}{l}$$

where l is the length of the torsion spring. If the cords were stressed to a working stress, σ, and it is assumed that the stress increases only slightly during further stretching, each cord would

Fig. 7.22. The torsion spring.

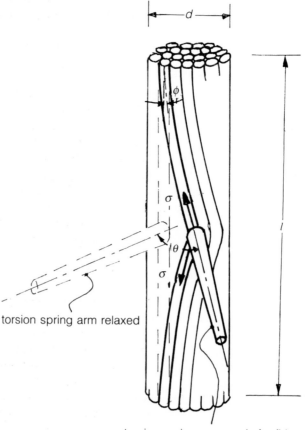

torsion spring arm relaxed

torsion spring arm ready for firing

create a twisting moment dM on the torsion arms for small angles φ of

$$dM = 2\sigma r\varphi dA$$

where dA is the area of the cords. The total twisting moment on each arm is the sum of the moments of all the cords

$$M = \sum dM = 2\sigma r \sum r\varphi dA = \frac{4\sigma\theta}{l} \sum r^2 dA.$$

If there is a large number of cords

$$\sum r^2 dA = \frac{\pi D^4}{32}$$

where D is the diameter of the torsion spring. Thus the total twisting moment is given by

$$M = \frac{\sigma\pi D^4\theta}{8l}. \tag{7.21}$$

The energy stored in each spring (U_S) is

$$U_S = \tfrac{1}{2}M\theta = \frac{\sigma\pi D^4\theta^2}{16l}.$$

The standard spring length was nine times its diameter, and hence the total energy stored (U_T) in both springs of a standard catapult was

$$U_T = \frac{\sigma\pi D^3\theta^2}{72}.$$

Just like the crossbow the torsion catapult possesses a virtual mass, but because the springs themselves move very little, the catapult is more efficient. So if the efficiency of a catapult is η, then the kinetic energy available for the shot is $\eta\, U_T$ and the velocity will be given by

$$v = \left(\eta \frac{\sigma\pi D^3\theta^2}{36m}\right)^{\frac{1}{2}}$$

where m is the mass of the shot. The theoretical maximum range $R_{\max}$ would then be given by equation (7.4) as

$$R_{\max} = \eta \frac{\sigma\pi D^3\theta^2}{36mg}. \tag{7.22}$$

If the catapult was built to the standard formula (equation 7.19), then the range would be independent of the mass of the shot.

We can get some idea of the tremendous power of the torsion catapult by estimating its maximum range. In the best torsion catapults of the ancient world the arms could move through as much as 50° (0·87 rads) (Marsden 1969:22). If we assume that the sinews were strained to a working stress of about 60 MPa, and that the diameter of the springs was standard, then for a 70% efficient catapult the maximum theoretical range is

Projectiles

about 600 m. The actual range would be less than the theoretical maximum, and so the distance of two or more stades (approximately 400 m) that Josephus said one talent (26 kg) stone balls were hurled by Titus' artillery during the siege of Jerusalem in AD 69 (Marsden 1969:90) is in line with our calculation (Josephus V: 240). The ability to construct powerfully efficient catapults declined in the late Roman period. Although catapults were still being made during the Middle Ages, they were merely poor imitations of the earlier artillery pieces.

8

Land transport

Most people in today's affluent societies would find that carrying a
load of 25 kg for any distance was quite an arduous task. Until
recently, in Europe, labourers were expected to carry much
heavier loads (see Table 8.1). In the eighteenth century, John
Desaguliers (1734) observed that the coal porters of Custom
House Quay in London regularly bore loads of about 90 kg:
'running all the way at every turn they go up two ladders and
often the length of St. Dunstan's Hill, which is a street pretty
steep and ill-paved, and perhaps climb up a staircase or two before
they shoot their coals, and this most of them will do above sixty
times a day'. The notion of what constitutes a reasonable load is
a very flexible one. In the First World War the British High
Command insisted that infantrymen carry 30 kg kits on their
backs, even when charging into machinegun fire. Army mules
were treated better; they only had to carry a third of their body
weight compared with nearly half for the infantryman (Liddell
Hart 1970:240). Today, in developing countries, some people
carry loads that are even heavier than their bodyweight. For
example Bhutanese porters carry 100 kg sacks of potatoes along
tracks in the thin air of the Himalayan mountains (Scofield
1976:680).

    Humans have the ability to move about efficiently in an
upright posture with the arms and upper torso free to support a
heavy burden, either individually or in a team. Evidence of the
long antiquity of bipedal gait is seen in the Pliocene hominid
bones found in Ethiopia (Johanson *et al.* 1982) and the hominid
footprints preserved in volcanic ashfall at Laetoli in northern
Tanzania (Leakey and Hay 1979; White 1980). Significantly,
man is the only fully bipedal mammal, and it has long been
argued that bipedalism was a crucial factor in our evolution
(Carrier 1984). Even after the power of animals was harnessed,
human muscle power remained important in transportation. It is
therefore appropriate that we begin this chapter with a review of
the mechanics of walking.

The mechanics of walking

    A person expends very little mechanical work in walking
along a level surface. Mechanical work has to be done to raise

one's centre of gravity with each step taken, but it is recovered when the centre of gravity falls again. A mechanical robot could be made that would store most of the potential energy recovered as its centre of gravity fell. Such a robot would only need to supply the energy to overcome the friction in its joints and the slight air resistance to its motion. However people can only store a small amount of the potential energy gained at mid-stride as elastic energy in the tendons and muscles of the legs,[1] and must expend metabolic energy even when mechanical work is being done on them. The body also experiences changes in kinetic energy, but these can be neglected when calculating the energy balance for walking at a moderate pace. Thus in walking we do an equal amount of positive and negative work in raising and lowering our centre of gravity. It has been estimated that we perform equal amounts of positive and negative mechanical work

[1] Quite a lot more energy is stored when the foot strikes the ground in running. The kangaroo has an exceptional ability to store energy in its tendons (Proske 1980) and with its efficient bounding locomotion is able to reach speeds of up to 60 km/hr (Frith and Calaby 1969:64).

Table 8.1 *Loads carried by man and beast*

	Load (kg)	Distance travelled per day km	Velocity km/h	Transportation per day (kg km)
Man				
18th-century London porter	90–150	—	—	—
18th-century London sedan chairman	70	—	2·5	—
19th-century Englishman travelling with a burden	40	20	2·7	800
19th-century Englishman carrying burden and returning unloaded	60	11	—	660
19th-century Englishman carrying bricks	50	9	—	450
Horse				
Walking	100–120	40	4·0	4000–4800
Trotting	80	60	8·0	4800
Mule				
European	150–180	20–24	3·0–5·0	3600–3900
British and US Army	70–80	30–48	—	2500–3500
Ass				
British Army	80–100	24–30	—	2400
Dromedary				
Middle East (normal march)	230	40	—	9200
Middle East (short march)	450	—	—	—
British Army in Egypt	170	—	—	—
India	320–300	32	3·0–4·5	8300
Australia	400	—	—	—
Bactrian camel				
Middle East	250	48	—	12 000
China	120–140	40	3·0	5000
Llama	30–50	25–45	—	800–2000
Reindeer	70	80	—	5200

Source: Based on data or figures given in Barker 1964, Clark 1878, Desaguliers 1734 and Zeuner 1963

with an efficiency η, which is about 0·2 (Margaria 1968). In other words to provide 1 J of positive and 1 J of negative work we expend about 5 J of metabolic energy.

In estimating energy expenditure for a person walking at moderate pace a stiff-legged model can be used (Bekker 1956:21–4; Alexander 1976). Consider the man shown in Fig. 8.1. When he is in full stride his centre of gravity is at its lowest position. As he moves forward, his centre of gravity rises in height by h and the work done for every pace (p) taken is

$$W = mgh$$

where m is the mass. The increase in height of the centre of gravity can be calculated as a function of the man's leg length l, and his pace p from the theorem of intersecting chords (see Appendix III), and is given by

$$h = \frac{p^2}{8l}$$

and the work done for each pace taken is $mgp^2/8l$. This is the maximum work that is done, because it is possible for some of the potential energy to come from the kinetic energy of forward motion. That is, the forward velocity of a man increases as his centre of gravity falls and decreases as it rises again (Alexander 1976). Thus the maximum metabolic energy expended for every step taken is $mgp^2/8l\eta$. If a man is walking with a speed v the

Fig. 8.1. Increase in the height of centre of gravity during walking.

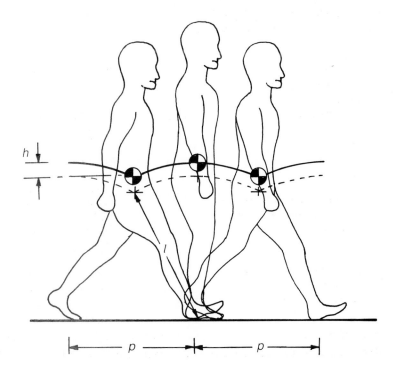

time taken for each pace is p/v and therefore the extra metabolic power (P) expended in walking over standing still is

$$P = \frac{mgpv}{8l\eta}. \tag{8.1}$$

Measurements of the actual metabolic power (in watts) expended in walking for men weighing between 60 and 75 kg can be expressed by

$$P = 200v + 35 \tag{8.2}$$

for speeds between 1–1·8 m/s (Durnin and Passmore 1967:40). The average ratio of leg to pace length (l/p) for a man is 1·65 (Bekker 1956:23). Therefore our maximum estimate of the excess of metabolic power required for the average man from which the data of equation (8.2) was obtained (assuming $\eta = 0·2$) is $250v$. This estimate agrees well with the value given in equation (8.2). A burden of up to about 15 kg can be carried at low speed with similar efficiency as body weight (Durnin and Passmore 1967:44).

There is a limit to the speed at which one can walk before having to break into a run, because in walking it is necessary to keep one foot on the ground at all times (Alexander 1982:88–9). A person's centre of gravity roughly follows an arc of a circle of radius l, and hence has a centrifugal acceleration (equation 2.7) of v^2/l. When a person is at mid-stride this acceleration is directly vertical, and if it is greater than the acceleration due to gravity, it will require a downward force on the centre of gravity. Unless there is adhesion between the foot and the ground it is impossible to provide such a downward force. At speeds greater than

$$v = \sqrt{gl} \tag{8.3}$$

the foot would leave the ground and the person would have to break into a run. Hence in walking the parameter v^2/lg is important. This parameter, which is called the *Froude number*, will be met with again in Chapter 9. It represents the ratio of kinetic to potential energy in wave-like motions such as walking and ocean waves. Modern European adult men have legs that are about 0·9 m long, and hence our estimate of the maximum walking speed is 3 m/s, only a little higher than the speed at which men do break into a run. Athletes do walk faster in races, but they use a special technique which minimises the variation in height of their centre of gravity (Alexander 1982:89).

Pack transport

During the last few thousand years man has domesticated and bred a number of animals that have been used for carrying loads (see Table 8.1). The main advantage pack animals offer over vehicles is that they do not need roads. This point is clearly made in the scene depicted in Fig. 8.2. where the heavily laden camels pass the mule cart which is attempting to traverse the churned mud of the road. On good roads, of course, the wheeled vehicle is far more efficient than pack transport. The most enthusiastic road builders of the ancient world were the Chinese and the Romans who both needed good communications to maintain their rule over large populous empires. When the Roman Empire distintegrated so did most of its roads. In England roads remained poor until well after the first Turnpike Act in 1663, and even in the eighteenth century strings of 30 to 40 pack-horses were a common sight on the London to Glasgow highway (Boulton n.d.:10).

After the decline of the Roman roads in the Near East the most remarkable of pack animals, the camel, replaced the wheeled vehicle entirely in that part of the world. When the famous nineteenth-century archaeologist, Sir Henry Layard, built a heavy cart to move the human-headed winged lions from the doorway in the palace of Ashurnasirpal II (883–859 BC) for the first part of their journey to the British Museum, he created a local sensation. It was such a novelty that soldiers from the Turkish garrison lectured the throng on the topic of carts and their uses (Layard 1850:75–6). Even today on Teheran construction sites the two-man hod serves in place of a wheelbarrow (Bulliet 1975:226).

Wheeled vehicles

Archaeological evidence suggests that wheeled vehicles originated somewhere in the region north of the early

Fig. 8.2. The advantage of the pack animal in Western China.

Mesopotamian civilisations, between the Caucasus Mountains and the upper reaches of the Euphrates (Piggott 1979). Their occurrence in this region and spread to the settled communities of Mesopotamia in the third millennium BC is attested by finds of at least 50 complete or fragmentary wagons and carts as well as more than 40 metal and clay miniatures. The wheels on the oldest of these vehicles were solid discs of wood cut from logs up to a metre in diameter. In the Near East only the deciduous forests of the north could have provided suitable trees – those no less than two and a half centuries in age. The scarcity and expense of timber for single disc wheels was undoubtedly a direct impetus to the development of the three-piece disc wheel which did not require such large trees. These tripartite wheels were in fact no larger than the single piece ones they replaced, since weight is a limiting factor in determining the maximum size of any solid wheel no matter how many pieces it might be made from.

Friction of rollers and wheels

The frictional resistance of large rollers or wheels is less than for smaller ones. By overcoming the problem of weight, the spoked wheel, which appeared in China and Mesopotamia during the second millennium BC, ultimately made possible the construction of much larger wheels (Piggott 1979:11). But spokes not only offered lightness, they also offered resilience.[2] It would have been difficult to cross rough ground at speed in an unsprung chariot that had solid wheels. The four-spoked wheel, while being no larger than the solid disc wheels, permitted the development of a new lightweight chariot that in essence comprised only a thin shell on a bent-wood frame. The springiness of the spoked wheel gave this new chariot greater stability when driven at high speed.

In time the size of wheels increased, especially with the heavier carts and wagons. The wheels on Chinese carts of the Han Dynasty were invariably large and up to 2 m in diameter (Lu *et al.* 1959a:109), and the magnificent Celtic wagon of Dejbjerg (Fig. 8.3), from the same period, had similarly sized wheels. The mechanical efficiency of large wheels was known in Classical Greece and is mentioned in the Aristotelian *Mechanical problems*. In the seventeenth century Desaguliers (1734) performed experiments which showed that large wheels were better than small ones. However the first truly controlled experiments were performed by Charles Coulomb (1785) at the end of the eighteenth century and described in his prize-winning essay, *Théorie des machines simples*. From his experiments Coulomb deduced that the resistance to rolling varied directly with the load and was inversely proportional to the radius of the roller. A half century later, in 1835, Arthur-Jules Morin (1795–1880), an artillery officer teaching at the Metz Ecole d'Application, published evidence in support of Coulomb's conclusions. However only a few

[2] Some later Greek chariot wheels were so light and springy that they would distort like a strung bow if left under load for a long time. A chariot not in use would normally be leaned against a wall so that the weight was taken off the wheels (Gordon 1978:146).

years afterwards Arséne Dupuit reported the results of experiments which showed that the rolling resistance was inversely proportional to the square root of the roller's radius. For the next three years a fierce debate ensued between Morin and Dupuit. Because Morin had the ear of the French Academy, a commission set up to decide the matter ruled in his favour (Dowson 1979:230–3). In fact Morin and Dupuit were both right, because the rolling resistance depends on the nature of the surface on which the rolling takes place – there is no single correct answer.

If the surface over which a roller moved was perfectly elastic there would be no friction at all. Modern ball or roller bearings have an extremely low friction because they are made of hardened steel and are designed so that the stresses remain essentially elastic. However even modern bearings are not perfectly elastic and there is still a very small hysteresis loss because the elastic strain energy stored as the roller passes is not fully recovered. Timber rollers transporting a sledge on a wooden track behave somewhat like modern roller bearings. Even if the rollers initially deformed non-elastically during the first few metres of rolling, they would afterwards deform essentially in an elastic manner. Continuous use of the same timbers for the track would cause them to behave elastically as well. An elastic roller of radius

Fig. 8.3. One of the wagons found in a bog near Dejbjerg, Denmark (first century BC). Courtesy of the National Museum, Copenhagen.

R pressed into a flat elastic surface with a force P makes contact over a length $2l$ where l is given by

$$l = \left[\frac{8PR(1-v^2)}{\pi EW} \right]^{\frac{1}{2}}$$

and W is the width of the track (Bowden and Tabor 1964:296). The pressure between the roller and its contact surface supports the load. If the elasticity were perfect, the pressure would be symmetrical so that it neither impeded nor aided the motion. However, because of hysteresis effects, the pressure is slightly asymmetric and there is a moment M that resists the turning of the roller (Fig. 8.4). This moment is given by

$$M = \frac{4Pl\alpha}{3\pi}$$

where α depends upon the degree of hysteresis and is less than one. In the absence of any other information a reasonable value of α for a timber roller would be about 0·55 (ibid.:252). During one complete revolution of the roller the work done against the resisting moment (equation 4·16) is $2\pi M$. On the level the traction force is equal to the rolling resistance F_R and since the sledge moves forwards twice as fast as the roller, the work done is $4\pi R F_R$ and hence

$$F_R = \frac{M}{2R} = \frac{2Pl\alpha}{3\pi R}.$$

Fig. 8.4. Rolling friction (elastic deformation) of a wooden roller on a wooden track.

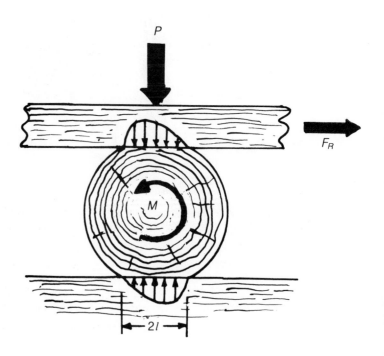

On substitution for the contact length l we obtain

$$F_R = \alpha \left[\frac{32P^3(1-v^2)}{9\pi^3 WRE} \right]^{\frac{1}{2}}. \tag{8.4}$$

The effective coefficient of rolling friction on an elastic surface is then

$$\mu_R = \frac{F_R}{P} = \alpha \left[\frac{32P(1-v^2)}{9\pi^3 WRE} \right]^{\frac{1}{2}}. \tag{8.5}$$

Notice that, in rolling, the coefficient of friction depends upon the load between the two surfaces, unlike sliding friction where the coefficient is a constant. Because of its dependence on load the concept of a coefficient of rolling friction is not especially useful in itself, but it does enable a comparison to be made with sliding friction.

On less rigid surfaces, like an unmade road or a field, a wheel or roller can cause plastic deformation of the surface. In such cases we can treat a wheel or roller as though it were rigid. Some kind of indication of the compressive stress σ_c at which ground will yield is given in Table 8.2. A wheel or roller under a load P will sink into the ground until the contact surface is sufficiently large to support the load. Unlike an elastic surface, the ground does not recover after the passage of the wheel or roller, and contact is only made by the front part of the wheel (Fig. 8.3). The contact length l is given by

$$l = \frac{P}{W\sigma_c}$$

where W is the width of the wheel or roller. Since the pressure is reasonably uniform, the reaction force acts at the centre of the contact surface. This reaction force must pass through the axle of a wheel (Fig. 8.5a). For a free roller, however, the reaction force must pass through the point of contact of the sledge and roller

Table 8.2 *Compressive yield strength of ground of various hardness*

Consistency	Identification	Compressive strength (kPa)
soft	Easily penetrated 50 mm by thumb	< 100
medium	Can be penetrated 50 mm by thumb with moderate effort	100–250
stiff	Readily indented by thumb but penetrated only with great effort	250–500
very stiff	Readily indented by thumbnail	500–1 000
hard	Indented with difficulty by thumbnail	> 1 000

Source: Based on data in Spangler 1966: table 6-2

Fig. 8.5. Rolling friction (plastic
deformation) of (*a*) wheels and
(*b*) rollers, on road or field.

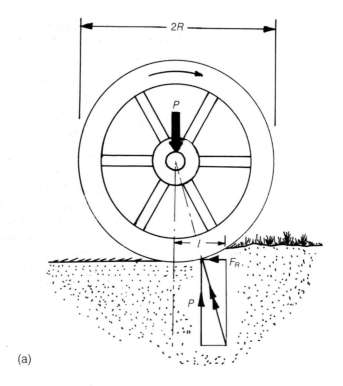

(a)

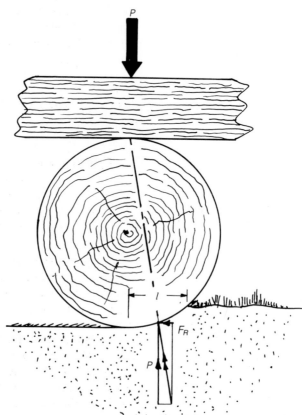

(b)

(Fig. 8.4). The rolling resistance of the wheel or roller is simply a geometric fraction of the load. Hence for a wheel

$$F_R = \frac{l}{2R}P = \frac{P^2}{2WR\sigma_c} \tag{8.6}$$

and

$$\mu_R = \frac{F_R}{P} = \frac{P}{2WR\sigma_c}. \tag{8.7}$$

For a free roller the rolling resistance and effective coefficient of friction are half these values.

So, recalling the French debate of the last century on rolling resistance, it can now be seen that for a constant load Dupuit was right for elastic surfaces, whereas Morin was right for plastic ones.

Wheels also have an additional resistance because of friction at their axles. Since the rolling resistance of a wheel is small compared with the load that it carries, the reaction force at the axle is approximately equal to the load P. Therefore if μ is the coefficient of sliding friction of the axle bearing, the frictional force on the axle is μP. We can calculate the resistance this friction causes to the wheel's motion by estimating the amount of power dissipated there. This power must be supplied by the traction. Since the tractive force on a level surface is equal to the resistance of the wheel F_A, the power dissipated must be a product of F_A and the velocity v of the wheel. The velocity of sliding at the axle is, by simple proportions, r/Rv, where r is the radius of the axle; therefore the power dissipated is $\mu Prv/R$ and hence

$$F_A = \frac{\mu Pr}{R}, \tag{8.8}$$

and the effective coefficient of friction due to friction at the axle is

$$\mu_A = \frac{\mu r}{R}. \tag{8.9}$$

Since the minimum size of the axle is governed by the load the wheel takes, the resistance caused by axle friction is inversely proportional to the wheel size.

On hard ground, carts and wagons with large wheels are relatively easy to move. In Table 8.3 we give the results of some nineteenth-century experiments on the resistance of carts and wagons. The coefficient of friction was less than 0·1 even when the wagon was driven across a hard field. On a gravel road it is the axle that causes most resistance. Specific dimensions of the axles are not given, but their diameters were probably close to about 75 mm. If we assume that the coefficient of friction on the axles was 0·2, then, from (equation 8.9), the effective coefficient of friction due to the axle resistance is 0·011 for the cart and 0·013 for the wagon. If we subtract this estimate from the total coefficient of friction for travel across a field, given in Table 8.3, we obtain the effective coefficients for the rolling resistance on

Land transport

hard earth of 0·052 and 0·083 for the cart and wagon
respectively. Let us now compare these values with estimates
obtained from the theory of rolling. Assuming that the
compressive yield strength of the hard arable field was 1000 kPa
(Table 8.2) we can calculate the coefficient of rolling resistance
from equation (8.5) to be 0·06 and 0·07, which are comparable
values to those quoted above.

The dished wheel
Spoked wheels are efficient at resisting radial loads. However, on
rough ground, wheels are subjected to considerable side loads. If
the wheel is flat with all its spokes lying in a plane perpendicular
to its axis, then any side load must be resisted by the
comparatively small bending stiffness of the spokes. Consequently
large, flat, spoked wheels were heavy. The Chinese wheelwrights
of the fourth century BC discovered that a wheel's resistance to a
side load could be greatly increased by dishing, so that the spokes
formed a shallow cone rather than a flat plane (Lu *et al.* 1959a).
By dishing their spoked wheels the Chinese were able to build
large and elegant chariot wheels such as those found in the royal
tomb at Hui-Xian (Fig. 8.6). Dishing was not known in Europe
until the fifteenth century.

Most of the side load in a dished wheel is taken as a direct
force on the spokes. Since a bar is far stiffer under a direct load, a
dished wheel is stiffer than a plain flat one of similar dimensions.
When a dished wheel is loaded on its convex side, the spokes are
forced more firmly into the rim. Conversely loads on the wheel's
concave side tend to pull on the spokes. Ancient Chinese dished
wheels would not have been successful without iron tyres. Apart
from the general strengthening of the wheel against radial loads,
the iron tyre enabled a dished wheel to take load on the concave
side without the danger of the spokes working loose. The
technology of iron-working at the time was sufficiently advanced

Table 8.3 *Rolling Resistance of Carts and Wagons*

	Cart without springs drawn by a single horse	Wagon without springs drawn by a pair of horses
diameter of wheel	1·37 m	front 0·99 m back 1·45 m
width of tyres	95 mm	83 mm
gross weight (approx.)	1530 kg	3260 kg
effective coefficient of friction on hard gravel road	0·013	0·019
effective coefficient of friction on hard arable field	0·063	0·094

Source: Based on Clark 1878

for the production and fitting of iron tyres to have presented little difficulty. Although there is no historical or archaeological evidence for the use of iron tyres, it is believed that they were probably used in the Han period (Lu *et al.* 1959b:201). The modern bicycle wheel is the culmination of the principle of dishing; the spokes are angled both ways so that side loads can be resisted in either direction by tension alone.

One can gauge the sideways stiffness of a wheel by supporting it around its rim and measuring the deflection produced when the hub is loaded in the direction of its axle. In this symmetrical arrangement each spoke carries a proportion of the side load. In a plain wheel the spokes bend under the side load, and the sideways stiffness of the wheel, defined as the force required to produce a unit deflection, is given by

$$k_p = \frac{12NEI}{l^3} \tag{8.10}$$

where N is the number, l the length, E the Young's modulus and I the second moment of area of the cross-section of the spokes. Dished wheels can be analysed on the assumption that a spoke's bending stiffness is negligible compared with its stiffness under direct load. The sideways stiffness of a dished wheel is approximately given by the expression

$$k_d = \frac{EA_sN\cos^2\alpha}{l\left[1 + \frac{N}{2\pi}\frac{A_s}{A_r}\right]} \tag{8.11}$$

where α is the semi-angle of the cone, A_s the cross-sectional area of the spokes, and A_r the cross-sectional area of the rim. For

Fig. 8.6. One of the wheels of the Hui-Xian chariots (after Lu *et al.* 1959a).

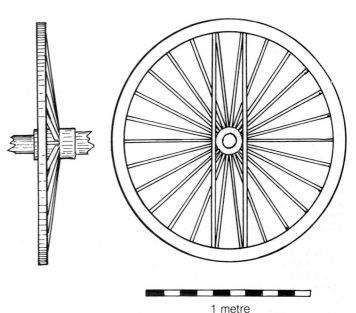

1 metre

spokes with a circular cross-section the ratio of the stiffnesses of a
dished and flat spoked wheel is given by

$$k_d/k_p = \frac{4l^2\cos^2\alpha}{3d^2\left[1+\dfrac{Nd^2}{8A_r}\right]}.$$

(8.12)

Equation (8.12) can be used to demonstrate how the Chinese
were able to build strong and light dished wheels. For instance
the sideways stiffness of the chariot wheel illustrated in Fig. 8.6
was increased forty times by making it dished, even without the
aid of the additional diametral struts. In fact such a light wheel
would not be possible without a dished form.

Animal Ability and Harness

Provided that serviceable roads exist, a cart or wagon is an
efficient means of transport. A comparison of the performances of
modern domestic animals in pulling heavy wheeled vehicles is
given in Table 8.4. It is seen that the camel is not only the
strongest animal for pack transport but for draught work as well.
Unlike the horse, the camel has probably changed little since
Classical times.[3] However, after the Roman roads in the near East
deteriorated, the camel was only used for pack transport.
Illustrations show that camel-drawn carts were occasionally used
in China during the seventh century and in Siberia during the
ninth or tenth century (Needham and Wang 1965:326), but it is
only in recent times that the camel has seen regular employment
as a draught animal. In Australia the camel's ability to live off the
land made it particularly valuable in the outback, and wagons
drawn by teams of as many as 14 camels were quite common
during the early part of the twentieth century.

The original draught animal was the bullock, a beast still
used in many parts of the world. The earliest wheeled vehicles
were drawn by two bullocks yoked on either side of a central pole,
the prominence of their withers permitting quite simple
harnessing. A wooden yoke was placed on the neck in front of the
withers and held down with rods or straps. Although the bullock
is a fairly slow animal, and on good roads cannot do as much
useful work as one of the heavy breeds of modern horse, it is
superior on poor roads or rough ground – especially when
conditions are muddy.[4] In outback Australia bullocks were a
major means of transport until the early twentieth century, and a
notable feature of many of Australia's inland cities, like Ballarat
and Bendigo, is that their main streets were made wide enough to
turn a team of 24 beasts. Until as recently as 1980 a bullock
team was still in operation hauling timber in the forests near Eden
in New South Wales.

The earliest Sumerian chariots (technically battle-carts) were
drawn by asses (Ducos 1975). The domestication of the horse, a
more nervous and sensitive animal, appears to have occurred first

[3] The exception is perhaps Australia
where the camel has thrived and is
generally larger than its Middle Eastern
forebear (Barker 1964).

[4] The difference was brought home to
Daniel Defoe while he was touring
Sussex in 1772. Defoe wrote: 'Here I
had a sight, which indeed I never saw
in any other part of England: namely,
that going to church at a country
village, not far from Lewes, I saw an
ancient lady, and a lady of very good
quality, I assure you, drawn to church
in her coach with six oxen; nor was it
done in frolic or humour, but meer
necessity, the way being so stiff and
deep that no horses could go in it'
(Defoe 1772:129).

on the southern Russian steppes a little over 5000 years ago. When the horse first began to replace its slower cousin the ass in pulling Sumerian chariots sometime during the third millennium BC, it was given the name *anše.kur.ra*, which means 'foreign ass' (Littauer and Crouwel 1979:43). The military role of the early domesticated horse was much enhanced by the redesigning of the chariot from a heavy compressive structure to a light tension one capable of achieving speeds that must have been astonishing at the time. In the second millennium BC, Hyxos immigrants brought the horse and the lightweight chariot to Egypt. At about the same time the horse-drawn chariot was emerging as the basis of military strength in China, and for many centuries afterwards the power of a state was gauged by its war chariots. Amongst agriculturally-based societies the horse's expensive upkeep made it an item of great value and prestige, and therefore a prerogative of the elite. For instance it was customary for Egyptian and Hittite rulers when writing letters to each other to express concern for the health of not only the royal family but also the royal horses!

In drawing carts and wagons modern heavy breeds of horse rival the camel in ability. However the early domesticated horse was only a pony by today's standards and was not generally used for heavy transport in antiquity (Burford 1960). Only in Medieval northern Europe was the horse employed to do agricultural work, because in this region the growing of oats as a fodder crop had become economically feasible. Elsewhere in the world the bullock is still used for heavy work because it can be fed with coarse fodder (Duby 1969). Even so, the horses used were still comparatively small. In the seventeenth century, Surirey de Saint

Table 8.4 *Transportation by modern carts and wagons*

Vehicle and motive power	Total load per animal (kg)	Useful load per animal (kg)	Distance travelled per day (km)	Velocity (km/hr)	Transportation per animal per day (kg km)
two horses (throat & girth harness), light carriage	430	250	43 (?)	—	11 000 (?)
horse and cart (modern harness), walking	—	680	43	4·3	29 000
horse and cart (modern harness), trotting	—	340	36	7·9	12 000
bullock wagon	—	680	29	2·9	20 000
mule (modern harness)	—	340	43	4·3	15 000
mule, US Army (modern harness)					
two mule wagon	600	500	—	—	—
four mule wagon	430	550	—	—	—
ass (modern harness)	—	170	43	4·3	7 000
camel 14-team wagon, Australia	1210	1000	38–48	—	43 000

Source: Based on Barker 1964, Rankine 1898 and Tegetmeier and Sutherland 1895

Rémy (1745) gave the size of the French artillery horse as four (old French) feet seven inches, which corresponds to a height of about 1·39 m.[5] The modern heavy breeds of horse such as the Shires and Clydesdales were not developed until the eighteenth century, and even then they were uncommon (Chives 1976). The Theodosian Code enacted in 438 AD gave the maximum loads to be carried by different state wheeled vehicles, though it is not at all clear about the type or number of draught animals involved. The lightest vehicle, the *birota*, drawn by two mules or horses, was allowed to carry two passengers along with 66 kg of baggage (in all about 180 kg). The heaviest vehicle, the *angaria*, carried a load of 500 kg (Jope 1956). It must be emphasised that these regulations in the Theodosian Code were aimed at conserving the vehicles and roads and may not represent the loads carried privately.

There has been much debate about the efficiency of harness systems since Lefebvre des Noëttes (1931), in 1910, performed his experiments with a throat-and-girth harness. A draught animal can only perform efficiently in a harness system that suits its anatomy. The earliest form of harness – a central pole and yoke fitted to paired animals – was ideal for bullocks pulling a plough or cart because they have prominent withers on which the yoke can bear. No doubt asses were first harnessed in exactly the same way as bullocks. However equids do not have prominent withers and most load would have been taken on the throat strap attached to the yoke. The more the ass pulled, the tighter the throat strap became, restricting the poor animal's breathing. Although experiments in England with a replica of a Sumerian battle wagon have shown that the choking effect was not as severe as thought earlier, this harness system was not efficient (Littauer and Crouwel 1979:29).

Horses are more sensitive animals than asses and it is unlikely that an unsuitable harness system would have been used on them for long. The best places for the load to be taken on a horse are the shoulders or the breast (Spruytte 1983:13). Certainly the yoke was used on the horse, but it could not have been placed on the withers themselves where it would certainly quickly have produced sores. The only practical places for a yoke on a horse are either its neck ahead of the withers or its back behind them. With a simple yoke placed ahead of the withers it is difficult to arrange the strap other than around the throat. The disadvantages of such a system must have been readily apparent.

By the middle of the second millennium BC the domesticated horse was known from Egypt to China. With the horse came the lightweight centre-pole chariot and a significant improvement in harness, both in Egypt and China (Fig. 8.7). Instead of the yoke bearing directly on the horse a separate wishbone-shaped fork[6] was lashed or pinned to the yoke, which sat on a pad placed over the neck (Littauer 1968). A strap attached to the ends of the fork,

---

[5] A simple metrical conversion gives a height of 1·49 m, but in the seventeenth century the height of a horse was measured with a strap that followed the contours of the body. The modern definition is the vertical height of the horse, which is some 0·10 m less than its contour height (Spruytte 1983:109).

[6] Harness forks have been found along with chariots of marvellous workmanship in the tombs of Thutmosis IV (Carter and Newberry 1904) and Tutankhamun (Carter 1927:63, 223). Standing aloft his chariot in ceremonial processions Tutankhamun must have been an impressive sight. The harness forks, although most likely lost among the horses' more sumptuous trappings, were in themselves intricate works of art.

which now being lower passes more nearly around the horse's breast than throat, holds it in place. A girth strap, also attached to the ends of the fork, passed under the horse. In the numerous New Kingdom Egyptian reliefs and paintings of chariots this girth strap is invariably shown loose. While undoubtedly its looseness could have been accentuated by artistic convention, it is almost certain that this strap was not used to hold down the ends of the fork. A horse would not tolerate a tight girth strap which, because of its point of attachment, would bear directly behind its forelegs. Instead of using a tight girth strap on the horses the Egyptians fixed the axle at the rear of the chariot so that the weight of the charioteer would normally keep the fork bearing on the horse's neck. It is quite apparent that the yoke and fork harness system requires a chariot with its axle located at the rear. The loose girth strap was used simply as a backing element to prevent the chariot from running into the horses when slowing down, and made no contribution to the draught system (Spruytte 1983:28).

The fork was designed to transmit a significant proportion $_f$ of the load to the horse's neck where it could be taken reasonably well. To be effective, the ends of the fork, which tend to rotate under the draught force F_d on the yoke, must be held back. There are two basic methods of achieving this objective. Ideally the fork should be lashed rigidly to the yoke so that the moment of the forces F_d could be resisted by a moment M_y supplied by the lashings (Fig. 8.8a). In this case all the load is taken on the shoulders of the horse which is an ideal location. If the fork lashing were loose, then much of the load F_t would be taken on the forward strap (Fig. 8.8b) which would work up towards the throat, and the fork would serve little purpose. Fig. 8.8a and 8.8b represent the extremes of the possible mechanical systems. With an actual harness, properly adjusted, most load would be taken on the neck; some load would also be taken on the forward strap, but because the fork is not free to rotate the strap would lie around the breast rather than the throat. Spruytte (1983)

Fig. 8.7. A chariot discovered in a tomb in Thebes (No. 2678, Museo Archaeologico, Florence).

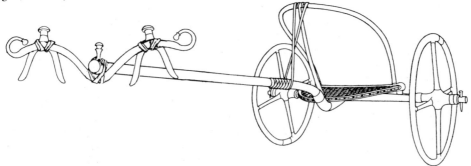

Fig. 8.8. Centre pole, yoke and fork harness (solid lines represent major force-carrying straps, and dotted lines minor ones): (*a*) rigidly lashed fork; (*b*) loose fork.

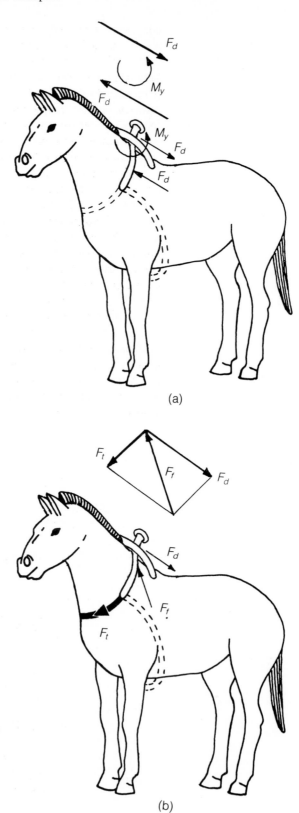

conducted a number of experiments with this harness system and found that it functioned well even at the gallop.

Although the Mycenaeans used a fork and yoke harness very similar to that of the Egyptians, and had the wheel positioned at the rear of their chariot (Littauer 1972), the Classical Greeks used a different system, placing the yoke behind the withers on the back of the horse. The yoke was held in position by a breast strap and a girth strap (Fig. 8.9). Our understanding of Greek harness comes from the numerous paintings on sixth- and fifth-century BC Greek pottery. The Greeks usually illustrate four horses harnessed to a chariot with only two directly under the yoke, the two outspanners being harnessed simply with a breast strap and attached to the chariot by a single trace. The outspanners obscure the detail of the harnessing of the inner two under the yoke. However some scenes show the horses being harnessed, and on these the positions of the yoke and the girth straps are clearly visible. Since the yoke sits behind the withers, the forward strap must lie across the breast. With the Greek chariot the girth strap can be tight because it does not bear behind the horses' forelegs. Hence the chariot's axle did not need to be fixed at the rear, and was more usually at the centre of the chariot. With such an arrangement the weight of the charioteer was balanced and the load carried by the horses' backs was less than that obtained with the yoke and fork system. In experiments with the Greek harness, Spruytte (1983) found that there was no

Fig. 8.9. Centre pole, yoke and breast-strap harness (solid lines represent major force-carrying straps).

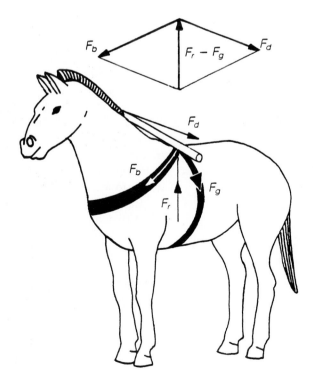

tendency for the breast strap to ride up and constrict the horse's breathing.

The Greek harness does not seem to have been used in the Near East where the Egyptians, Assyrians and Persians all favoured the positioning of the yoke on the neck. A scene depicted in the reliefs on the eastern staircase of the Apadana in Persepolis does depict a Greek harness on some horses in a procession of vassals from throughout the Persian Empire bearing tribute to the king: however the men leading the chariot have been identified as Greek subjects (Schmidt 1953).

Spruytte (1983) suggests that a completely different type of harness was in use in the Sahara at about 1000 BC. A large number of rock paintings with depictions of chariots have been discovered in the Tassili n'Ajjer plateau in Algeria (Lhote 1953). Since savanna-land fauna is also depicted – such as elephants, giraffes and antelope – the rock paintings must date to before the second half of the third millennium when the Sahara climate approached its present level of hyperaridity (Butzer 1976; Frenzel 1973). The rock paintings are found in areas that could have accommodated a road, and Lhote (1966) has suggested that one formerly stretched from Tripoli to Gao on the Niger River in Mali, near Timbuktu. The details of the Saharan harness in the stylised paintings are not at all clear to us. However the harness suggested by Spruytte, with the centre pole of the chariot ending in a cross-bar which fitted not behind the horse's neck but in front, is not inconsistent with the rock paintings. This traction bar clearly could not bear directly on the horses' throats. Spruytte (1983) demonstrated that a traction bar can be fixed rigidly beneath the throat of the horse so that it does not bang into the neck if the draught load is taken on a band that goes around the horse's forehead. Such a harness could pull a chariot containing two riders with no difficulty.

The main problem encountered by the designers of ancient chariot harness, with the exception of the conjectured Saharan harness, was how to get the effective load point low enough so that the draught force could be taken on the animal's shoulders or breast. The centre pole and yoke is not the ideal system with which to achieve this objective. Sometime during the early part of the Han Dynasty the Chinese revolutionised their chariot design when they abandoned the centre pole with its paired draught and adopted double shafts about a single horse (Needham and Lu 1960:127). With shafts, the fork on the horse's neck can be used more efficiently (Fig. 8.10). The ends of the shafts, which were deeply curved to shoulder height, were joined by a yoke with a fork fixed at its centre. The ends of the fork were attached to the shafts by a shoulder strap, while a strap from the shafts went around the horse's breast (supporting straps, which we have not shown in Fig. 8.10, stopped the breast strap slipping down). Judging from drawings of the Han Dynasty period a girth strap

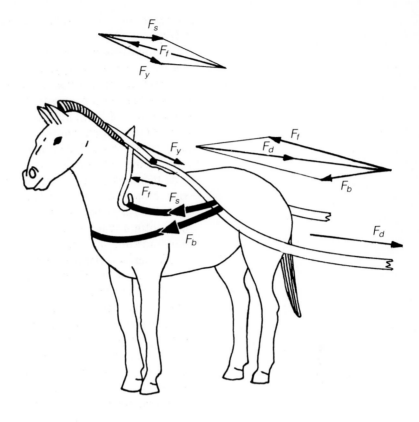

Fig. 8.10. Shaft, yoke and fork harness (only major force-carrying straps are shown).

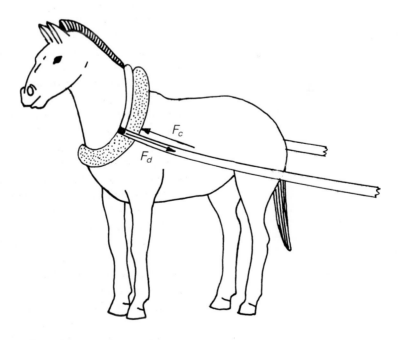

Fig. 8.11. Shaft, fork and soft-collar harness.

was not often used. Instructions that the charioteer should stand
well forward (Needham and Wang 1965:310) suggest that the
Han Chinese, like the Egyptians of the New Kingdom, relied upon
body weight to hold the fork down.

The main advantage of the Han harness system was that it
was no longer necessary to rely on an extremely rigid fixing
between the yoke and neck fork. The load on the fork could be
taken almost equally from the forces at the top (F_y) and ends of
the fork (F_s). In this balanced system the force (F_f) between the
neck and the fork would be more uniformly distributed and there
would be no tendency for the fork to rotate on the yoke while the
breast strap, with its low point of attachment, is more ideally
situated to take some of the draught force. Perhaps, more
importantly, the adoption of shafts led the way to the modern
collar harness.

As early as the first century BC the Chinese may have
dispensed with the yoke and attached the shafts to the ends of the
forks. Although this system has the advantage of taking the
draught from the middle of the horse's neck where it is easiest to
bear, like the earlier fork with a centre pole there was still a
tendency for the fork to rotate. The subsequent addition of a soft
collar behind the fork eliminated this problem and provided a
harness system which took all the load on the horse's neck,
where it can be most easily borne (Fig. 8.11). The fork and soft
collar was practically as efficient as the modern semi-rigid collar
which was developed in China perhaps in the third century AD
(Needham and Wang 1965:324). Vestiges of the fork still persist
in the designs of collar harnesses in countries as far apart as
China and Portugal (Needham and Wang 1965:322).

All modern harness systems have a low draught point. The
key to this development was the change from the centre pole and
paired draught to a single horse between shafts. For some reason
this changeover was delayed outside China. The first evidence of
shafts in the West comes from late Roman times; collar harnesses
were unknown in Europe until the ninth century (Needham and
Wang 1965:327).

The wheelbarrow
As we emphasised at the beginning of this chapter, manpower is
often considered more economical than the power provided by
beasts of burden, and indeed even today people as well as animals
are used to pull heavily loaded carts in many developing
countries. One of the most useful man-powered vehicles is the
wheelbarrow. As with many other simple but efficient devices, the
wheelbarrow seems so obvious that one would naturally suppose
it to have great antiquity; yet its earliest documented appearance
dates back only to the second century AD in China (Needham and
Wang 1965:14, 258). The wheelbarrow was certainly not used
in the Roman world, an absence that we find inexplicable, and

did not appear in Europe until late Medieval times. The earliest form of wheelbarrow (Fig. 8.12), and one that is still in common use, is worthy of close examination. Its wheel, typically about a metre in diameter, has its axis only slightly more distant from the handles than the centre of gravity of the barrow; so that, although there was a small positive downwards load on the handles which is essential for control, the porter did not have to support much load. One of the earliest references to this type of wheelbarrow is attributed to the great Chinese general of the third century AD, Zhuge Liang, who recognised the value of the 'wooden bullock', as he called it, for moving army supplies across rough country. Zhuge Liang claimed in his military manual that a year's rice supply for a soldier (about 180 kg) could be carried more than 10 km in a day (Needham and Wang 1965:260).

Today in China there occurs a variety of wheelbarrows. Those with a central wheel (as illustrated in Fig. 8.12) are common in Jiangxi and in a number of other provinces,[7] but the Chinese also use wheelbarrows similar in design to the European type with the wheel fitted at the front. There is some difference in the use of wheelbarrows in the West and in China. While in the Western world the wheelbarrow is a device used in agriculture and for construction, the Chinese frequently used theirs for general transportation. The wheelbarrow illustrated in Fig. 8.12 would have been employed only for transport of goods and perhaps passengers, though ones with central wheels are also used on construction sites in China.

If the barrow's wheel is fitted at the front, the vehicle constitutes a simple lever system and the porter must support a third or so of the load. English labourers in the nineteenth century were expected to push wheelbarrows containing a load of 60 kg a total distance of 18 km during a ten-hour day, as well as an equivalent distance unladen (Rankine 1889:85). Therefore, with a European-style wheelbarrow, a man experienced in such labour could transport about 1100 kg km. If our estimate of the load carried by General Zhuge Liang's soldiers is correct, they carried the equivalent of 1800 kg km.

Fig. 8.12. A wheelbarrow from Jiangxi Province, China (based on a photograph in Needham and Wang 1965).

---

[7] When the Chinese arrived on the Australian goldfields in the nineteenth century they brought with them the Jiangxi wheelbarrow. It was not long before diggers of all nationalities could be seen wheeling barrows, heaped high with their belongings, from one gold field to another (Cannon 1971).

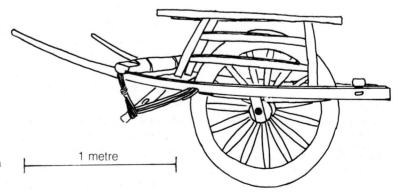

1 metre

Obviously the Chinese wheelbarrow of the Jiangxi type is the most efficient at carrying a load, because with the weight over the wheel the maximum load is limited only by the frictional resistance of the barrow and the need to keep it balanced. It is of interest to examine the record set in 1979 of just over a tonne for a load of bricks carried in a wheelbarrow (McWhirter 1982:182). Although the contestant used a European-stype wheelbarrow, the bricks were stacked high and secured by straps so that, owing to the natural slope of the barrow, their centre of gravity was over the axle. Thus, although a European-style wheelbarrow was used to set this record, the load was arranged in such a way that mechanically the barrow behaved like the more efficient Jiangxi one.

Moving the Colossi

Many civilisations have left records of their passing in the form of great monuments that required enormous loads to be transported by manpower with the aid of only simple technology. The obsession with monolithic statues and memorials reached its zenith in Egypt. Although the largest of the ancient monuments, the Great Pyramid of Cheops, commands most attention, the blocks with which it has been built are not at all large, on average weighing a comparatively modest 2·5 tonnes. Individually such blocks presented no difficulties in transportion but, of course, one can only wonder at the organisational skill needed to handle over 2 000 000 of them. Some of the heaviest stone monuments were the obelisks erected in honour of the sun-god Aten (Dibner 1970; Heizer 1966). The obelisks were much admired by successive conquerors of Egypt, at least 15 having been taken by the Romans to adorn their 'eternal city'. In the nineteenth century three more obelisks were shipped to the cities of London, New York and Paris. There are now more large obelisks outside Egypt than are known to be left within it. The largest obelisk planned by the Egyptians would have weighed about 1200 tonnes (Engelbach 1922). This monolith, which remains attached to the parent rock at the Aswan quarry, was not completed because a serious flaw was discovered, though obviously the Egyptians had felt capable of transporting it. The largest monoliths actually transported by the ancient Egyptians weighed about 1000 tonnes. Of these monoliths perhaps the most impressive are the so-called Colossi of Memnon (Fig. 8.13).[8]

The transportation of huge stones, sometimes over long distances, occurred in a number of places around the world before the Industrial Age. The largest ancient monolith in Europe is the 380-tonne Grand Menhir Brusé in Brittany. In the Americas there are some masonry blocks in Inca fortresses and the Teotihuacá Idol of Coatlinchán which weigh over 200 tonnes (Heizer 1966). And on remote Easter Island hundreds of giant statues carved from volcanic tuff, and weighing up to 82 tonnes, were

---

[8] The Colossi of Memnon are statues of Amenhotep III. Their popular name comes from the Greek historians muddling the name of Amenhotep with the Memnon of their own tradition who was the son of a Nubian god and the beautiful dawn-goddess Eos.

transported up to 10 km from the Rano Raraku quarry in the interior of the island to be erected on low stone platforms facing the villages along the coast. Even as late as the early twentieth century in the mountains of Assam and on some of the Indonesian Islands (Fig. 8.14) stones of enormous size were being transported by tribal groups (Bellwood 1978:255–8).

Given sufficient manpower, and strong enough ropes, large weights can be dragged by using a sledge of very simple design and construction. Evidence for the number of men required comes from two field experiments – the first done in Britain for a BBC television programme on Stonehenge (Atkinson 1956:108–9), and the second on Easter Island during Thor Heyerdahl's expedition (Heyerdahl 1958:151–2; Skjölsvold 1961:371). In the Stonehenge experiment it was demonstrated that 32 'sturdy' British youths could just pull a burden of 1600 kg up a grassed slope that had an inclination of 1 in 15. A fairly efficient way of hauling was devised with the youths arranged in ranks of four along a single rope. Each rank pushed on a wooden bar fastened at its centre to the rope. Assuming that the rope was parallel to the ground, we can use equation (4.9) to calculate the force each

Fig. 8.13. The Colossi of Memnon. These colossi were hewn from single blocks of sandstone. However the colossus in the right of the picture was badly damaged during an earthquake in 27 BC and restored with separate blocks of stone by the Roman Emperor Septimus Severus more than 200 years later (from a lithograph of a drawing made during Napoleon's invasion of Egypt in 1798: Lepsius 1859.)

youth must have exerted. The coefficient of static and dynamic friction of wood on green grass is about 0·5 and 0·35 respectively (Table 2.5), and from these values we can calculate that each youth must have exerted a force of about 280 N to get the sledge started, and 200 N to keep it moving. From the result of the Stonehenge experiment, one can say that it would require about 18 youths to move a sledge over grassed level ground.

The result of the Easter Island experiment is in agreement with the Stonehenge experiment. Pedro Atan, the mayor of Easter Island, having re-erected one of the giant statues, offered to show Thor Heyerdahl how they could have been moved on a Y-sledge.[9] After being feasted by Heyerdahl, 150 to 180 villagers[10] easily moved one of the smaller statues, which weighed some 10 tonnes (Skjölsvold 1961:370). From these experiments it can be assumed that roughly 18 people per tonne would be needed to drag a sledge on level ground.

The number of men that would actually be needed to pull a sledge depends to some extent on the method of hauling. Invariably, in Egyptian wall paintings and reliefs showing the transportation of statues, the men are depicted grasping and pulling the rope in a forward-facing stance, a method that is hardly efficient. The attachment of shoulder harness to the ropes permitted the application of greater force by the labourers; these are shown in some Egyptian tomb paintings that have scenes of fishing nets being hauled in, and we think it is quite possible that men would have also worn harnesses for pulling large statues on sledges. It could well be that the Egyptian illustrations depict a

Fig. 8.14. Transporting a monolith in South Nias, Sumatra (from Schnitger 1964).

[9] The Y-sledge is cut from a suitably forked tree trunk or limb, the two prongs forming the runners. The design is so basic that its occurrence in different areas does not necessarily imply historical contact.

[10] Although in ancient Egypt, with its strict division of labour, the evidence suggests that only men pulled heavy sledges, in the Easter Island experiment the women joined in, as they might well have done in earlier times.

ceremonial stage in the transport of the statues which required the priests and the sons of noble families to pull the sledge for only a very short distance. It may have been thought inappropriate to show men of rank harnessed like common labourers.

Whatever the situation may have been with the Egyptians, harnesses certainly were used by the Assyrians. The bas-reliefs from Nineveh show men in harness dragging a human-headed winged-bull from the banks of the Tigris past the Kouyunjik mounds to the palace (Layard 1850, 1853) (Fig. 8.15). The men were prisoners of war – in some reliefs they are shown being urged on with sticks by the Assyrian overseers. While the stance of the anchorman in a tug-of-war utilises the bodyweight and enables the largest force to be exerted, it could be an awkward position in trying to pull a sledge any distance. In short-term work, using the anchor stance, we found that young Australian men can exert a force of between 325 and 590 N (see Chapter 2). We shall take 300 N as the absolute maximum force that can be exerted by a man for any reasonable length of time. The value of 535 N used by Davison (1961) is too high.

Using the results of the Heyerdahl and Stonehenge experiments one can conclude that to drag the largest of the Egyptian monoliths on simple sledges over the bare ground would have required an enormous number of labourers. For instance 18 000 men would have been needed to move the 1000-tonne Colossi of Memnon. While Egyptian rulers were undoubtedly able

Fig. 8.15 Assyrian transportation of a huge human-headed bull statue for the Palace of Sennacherib (*c.* 704–681 BC). A bas-relief at Kouyunjik (from a lithograph in Layard 1853).

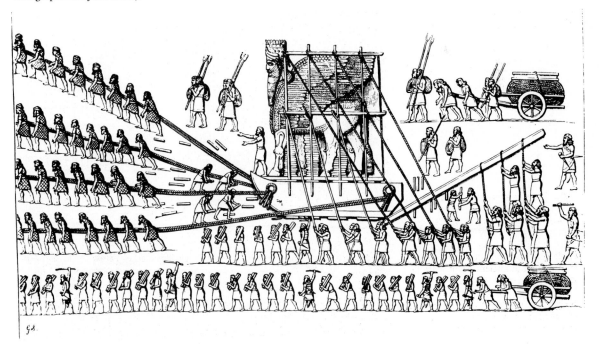

to assemble endless ranks of men, any attempt to make them all pull together would have been extremely difficult. The Egyptians must surely have employed a more efficient method.

Lubrication

There is evidence that the Egyptians understood lubrication, in that they smeared animal fat on their chariot axles to reduce the friction (Parish 1929). It has frequently been suggested that they also used lubricants to reduce the friction on sledges bearing monolithic statues (Davison 1961; Dowson 1979:35–6; Layard 1853;115). The wall in the tomb of Djehutihotep at Gebel el Bersha (Fig. 8.16), in which a man pours water in front of the sledge, has often been cited as evidence of lubrication. It is thought that the sledge ran on a wooden track made of timbers like the one the three men below the statues are shown carrying, and that the water is meant to lubricate the wood (Davison 1961). While we are prepared to accept that the Egyptians may have used lubricants to ease the task of pulling sledges, we do not believe that the man shown in the wall-painting is actually lubricating the track. A man pouring water is almost always shown in Egyptian scenes depicting the transport of life-sized statues of rulers or high officials, but significantly this activity is never shown when the load on the sledge is other than a statue. We believe that the pouring of water before sledges bearing statues is part of a purification ritual. A similar scene is depicted on another wall of the Tomb of Djehutihotep (Newberry 1897), where a man is shown pouring water at the feet of Djehutihotep himself. The inscription in front of the man reads 'the priest cleanses'. The idea of water being a lubricant appears to have arisen from a misunderstanding about the effect of water on wood. Water can significantly reduce the high friction between clean, freshly sanded, dry wooden surfaces, but if the wooden

Fig. 8.16. Egyptian transportation of a statue of Djehutihotep. A wall painting (now destroyed) in the tomb of Djehutihotep, dated to about 1880 BC (from a lithograph in Layard 1853).

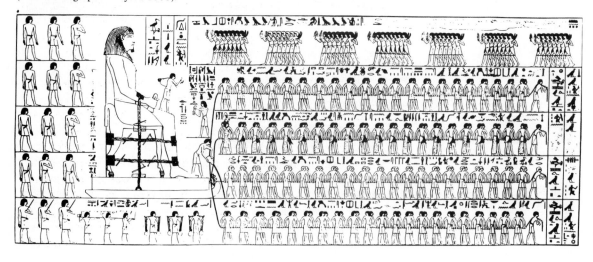

surfaces are slightly greasy – even just from handling – then the friction between dry wooden surfaces is much lower (the coefficient of friction being 0·2–0·25) and wetting will cause an increase in friction. Desaguliers (1734) was the first to observe that water could cause an increase in friction. A likely explanation is that Desaguliers took no particular care in the preparation of his specimens and that they were slightly greasy. Caution should be exercised when using modern data on the friction of wood for modelling ancient or ethnographic situations. For example, in technical works dry wood is defined as clean wood free from grease and containing less than 30–40 per cent moisture, while wet wood does not necessarily mean wood that is wet to the touch (Bowden and Tabor 1964:243–61). Wet wood is reported as having less frictional resistance than dry wood, but this does not mean that water will effectively lubricate wood that is not clean and dry.

Grease or fat can greatly reduce the friction between wooden surfaces. In 1833 a greased track and a wooden cradle were used by Jean Baptiste Le Bas to move the 230-tonne Luxor obelisk up a slight incline to its final resting place in the Palace de la Concorde (Gorringe 1885:89). The force required for this operation was calculated by Le Bas to be 520 kN; that is, he assumed the coefficient of friction to be about 0·2. In the laboratory a well-greased wooden surface can have a coefficient of friction as low as 0·1, but Le Bas wisely chose a larger value where the surfaces might not be especially flat and true. The steam engine Le Bas originally intended to use failed during preliminary tests, and he resorted to the oldest form of power to replace it. Le Bas used five six-fold compound pulley blocks, each drawn by a capstan manned by 48 soldiers, to pull the obelisk up on its cradle. It is interesting to note that Le Bas assumed that each man could exert only 98 N, and, showing particular caution, used almost twice as many men than his calculations called for. From practical experience the Egyptian engineers were probably more sure of the numbers of men required to move a monolith than was Le Bas.

In Malaysia greased wooden sledges running on timber tracks (Fig. 8.17), called a *panglong* or *kuda-kuda*, were used for logging operations until comparatively recently (Arnot 1928; Oliphant 1937; Smythies 1952). The *panglong* consisted of two parallel timbers about 1·5 m apart with round wooden ties laid across them at intervals of about 0·5 m. The sledges, which carried a log of up to 4 tonnes, ran on the cross-members. To pull the sledge on the level or on a gentle downwards slope required six men per tonne load, with an additional two men to steer the sledge from behind. If we assume that 300 N was the maximum pull that each man could exert, then the coefficient of friction would have been no more than about 0·18.

There are natural products other than fat that could easily have been used to reduce the friction of sledges. The Egyptians must have been as aware as any of us that wet clay is slippery and realised its potential as a lubricant; wood can slide over a smooth surface of wet clay or a wooden surface lubricated with a thick clay slurry almost as easily as over a well-greased surface. An oral tradition recorded on Easter Island asserts that mashed yams and sweet potatoes served as lubricants for moving the island's giant statues (Métraux 1940:304). We have discovered from model experiments that baked sweet potato mixed with a little water can reduce the coefficient of friction between wooden surfaces to as little as 0·15. Sweet potato is only one of many vegetable substances that could have helped in reducing friction. One can only conclude that an engineer of the ancient world would have had no problems reducing the coefficient of friction between sliding surfaces to about 0·15–0·20.

If the sledge is lubricated the number of men required to move a 1000-tonne monolith can be reduced to a minimum of between 5000 to 6000, assuming that each could pull with a force of 300 N. Although this number of men is still very large, it is much more acceptable than our estimate of 18 000 for an unlubricated sledge. The largest number of men recorded as working in unison is 900, assembled together with 74 horses by Domeninco Fontana in the sixteenth century to lower the 350-tonne Vatican obelisk (Dibner 1970:33). The operation was a spectacle for Rome's populace. Because so many men were involved orders had to be given by trumpet calls, and the huge crowd of onlookers were constrained to silence under pain of death.

Fig. 8.17. A Malayan *panglong* or sledge-way used for transporting logs (from Oliphant 1937).

Rollers

Another possible means of reducing the number of men needed to pull a sledge is to employ rollers. To be really efficient rollers must be reasonably true and must run on a well-constructed track. Fairly crude rollers were used in the modern experiments on their performance because these investigations concerned far less-sophisticated technologies than that of the Egyptians. In the Stonehenge experiment of 1954 the rollers were logs that had not been specially selected for their roundness, and they were laid directly on the ground. Even so, the number of youths needed to pull the 1600 kg sledge up a 1 in 15 slope was reduced from 32 to 14, although a further 10 were required to shift the rollers and to prevent the sledge from slipping sideways (Atkinson 1956:108–9). If on the basis of our previous calculations we assume that to shift the sledge the youths exerted between 200 and 300 N, then we calculate that the effective coefficient of friction must have been between 0·11 and 0·20.

To move a similar sledge on the level with rollers would require about six youths per tonne load, as well as the necessary helpers. In a recent French experiment on moving a megalith (Mohen 1980) segments of unbarked tree trunks, approximately 400 mm in diameter, were laid as rollers on a rough wooden track. Despite the crudeness of this arrangement some 200 men could drag a 32-tonne stone block; that is to say, it required some six or seven men per tonne load to drag the stone on rollers, which is about the same number that was required in the Stonehenge experiment. On roughly made tracks rollers can jam, and with larger loads it might not be so easy to overcome the problem with levers, as was done in the French experiment. Nevertheless, providing that the load per unit area of roller is not increased, there seems no reason to doubt that even the largest monoliths could have been transported with rollers by about six men per tonne. Therefore it would have been possible to transport a 1000-tonne colossus on rollers with about 6000 men, even on a comparatively rough track. A well-made wooden track would reduce the number of men required still further.

To move the Vatican obelisk 250 m to its final position in the centre of St Peter's Square, Fontana placed his rollers on a wooden track laid upon an earthen causeway. The diameter of the rollers was about 150 mm, and the four runners of the track had a combined width of about 1·5 m. On a hard surface all rollers may not take equal weight. Nevertheless we can estimate the range of possible coefficients of friction from two extreme assumptions: first, all the weight was taken on only two rollers (which is not actually possible because they would deform so much that other rollers would have to bear some load); and, second, that the weight was equally distributed over all the rollers, which numbered about 40. Using equation (8.5) and

taking the Young's modulus of wood as 10 GPa, we calculate that
the range of possible coefficient of friction to move the Vatican
obelisk (which weighed some 380 tonnes with its protective case
of wood planking and iron bars) is between 0·002 and 0·008. In
other words, to pull a monolith on perfect rollers over a dead
level, well-made wooden track would require no more than about
one man for every 4 tonnes.[11] The number of men required to
pull a sledge on a well-made track depends mainly on how level it
is. For example, even if there was no friction at all, it would take
more than one man to pull a tonne up a slope of 1 in 30. One
man can easily push a car weighing a tonne on the level, and it
would not have been beyond the technology of the Egyptians to
have constructed a track on which rollers could have been used
that required no more relative effort to pull a monolith. Hence the
minimum number of men actually required to move a 1000-
tonne monolith would have been no more than about 6000.
However, such a track would have been expensive, even if it was
only a short section that was continually relaid, as Howard Carter
had to do with the steel rails which were used to move the
treasures of Tutankhamun from the Valley of the Kings to the
bank of the Nile.

    There is little direct evidence indicating that rollers were
used prior to Classical Greek times. The set of bas-reliefs at
Kouyunjik was believed by their discoverer, Sir Henry Layard, to
prove that the Assyrians used rollers to move large statues in the
seventh century BC (Layard 1853:106) (Fig. 8.15). However
these 'rollers' are depicted as short, roughly trimmed tree trunks
that would not have been very effective as rollers (Davison 1961).
It must be assumed therefore that the logs were used to make a
relayed track. If this is the case they are too short to be placed
longitudinally as illustrated, and we believe that they must have
been placed transversely to the sledge. While the use of rollers in
antiquity for moving heavy monoliths is in doubt, it is known
that they served for shifting smaller loads. Two short granite
rollers were found in the burial chamber of the Pyramid at Nuri
in the Sudan, and one can presume that they were used to move
the 8-tonne granite sarcophagus into the tomb; in any event, the
archaeologist George Reisner found them indispensable in moving
the sarcophagus out again (Engelbach 1922). The first literary
evidence of rollers is provided by Herodotus (*c.* 484–424 BC) who
wrote that they were employed for transporting boats on land.
There is no reason to believe, as Davison (1961) apparently did,
that these ancient Greek rollers were mounted in a fixed frame as
rollers are today, because the advantages of free rollers over cart
wheels with axles were certainly appreciated by the Aristotelian
writer of the *Mechanical problems*. The extent to which rollers
were used in the ancient world is an issue that will no doubt be
debated for a number of years to come.

[11] If this figure seems an exaggeration
consider the case of John Massis of
Belgium who in 1974 pulled two Long
Island Railroad passenger cars
weighing 80 tonnes along the rails
with his teeth (McWhirter and
McWhirter 1974:466)!

Ropes

One line of investigation into ancient methods of transporting monoliths which has not been pursued before is the strength of the ropes. The Egyptians commonly made rope from halfa grass, palm fibre or papyrus (Lucas 1962:135). While papyrus no longer grows in Egypt, handmade palm-fibre ropes are still used in the villages. Tests which we have carried out on samples of such handmade rope from Egypt show that its tensile strength is about 16 MPa, which is comparable to the strength of modern coir rope manufactured from the fibre of coconut husks (BS 2052:1953). Although we have not carried out tests on ropes of different fibres it is unlikely that ropes were made of significantly weaker fibres. In recent French experiments it was found that suitable rope could also be made from ivy. The strength of cords made from such fibres was about 12 MPa (Eluere 1980).

The force required to move the sledge and its burden must be less than the tensile strength of the ropes attached to it and, if we know the size of the ropes, we will also know the maximum force that could have been applied. The hieroglyphic inscription on the wall-painting depicting the transport of Djehutihotep's statue (Fig. 8.16) shows four ropes being used and the accompanying hieroglyphic inscription confirms that only four lines of men pulled the statue (Newberry 1897). If the ropes were directly grasped, as shown in the painting, then they could have been no more than about 65 mm in diameter.[12] Thus the force required to pull this statue must have been less than about 200 kN. Obviously the Egyptian engineers would have made sure that the rope would not break, so we can assume that the actual force was significantly less than this figure. It has been estimated that Djehutihotep's statue weighed 60 tonnes (Davison 1961), and if we allow another 5 tonnes for the sledge, the maximum possible coefficient of friction would have been about 0·33. The actual coefficient of friction would have been significantly less than 0·33, which suggests that at least some form of timber way, probably greased or otherwise lubricated, was employed by the Egyptians.

We can learn more about the force required to pull the Assyrian winged-bull statue because the bas-relief indicates that four double ropes were used (Fig. 8.15). One can infer that four single ropes would not have been sufficient, and so we can put bounds on the coefficient of friction. Assuming the ropes were about the thickness of a man's wrist (65 mm in diameter), then the force needed to move the sledge must have been between 200 and 400 kN. The weight of the statue has been estimated as between 40 and 50 tonnes (Layard 1853:110), and the sledge itself may have weighed 5 tonnes. Assuming the maximum slope from the Tigris to the Kouyunjik mound was between 1 in 20 and 1 in 10, we can calculate that the coefficient of friction (equation 4.9), (with $\theta = 0$) was probably greater than 0·27–0·40

[12] Ropes of this thickness have been found in the Tura quarries just outside Cairo, where the limestone for the facing of Cheop's Pyramid was obtained.

and less than 0·65 to 0·86. Since we have seen that a coefficient
as least as low as 0·2 can be achieved even with crude rollers, we
have some mechanical evidence suggesting that the logs portrayed
in the relief were not rollers.

Easter Island statues

How the megalithic statues on Easter Island were transported is
an issue that archaeologists have not yet addressed adequately,
which is curious because the public's appetite for anything to do
with the statues is seemingly insatiable. In all there may be more
than 1000 statues on Easter Island, some of them still hidden
under slopewash and quarrying debris (Mulloy 1968; Skjölsvold
1961:369–71). The original Polynesian settlers probably arrived
between AD 400 to 500 from an island in the eastern Pacific
(McCoy 1979:145). They had no metal, and their tools were
made of natural materials such as stone, shell, bone, wood and
bamboo. No doubt they had come with a tradition of wood-
carving, and presumably they made small wooden sculptures. At
about AD 1000 their descendants began fashioning large stone
statues, which they called *moai*, and erected many of them on
enlarged and strengthened *ahu* platforms, which is the common
form of shrine found in Polynesia. In a highly stylised form the
figures represented honoured lineage ancestors, and intense status
competition between kin groups must have been the reason for
the more impressive ones. Towards the end of the statue-building
period the Islanders began adding large cylindrical topknots of red
scoria, thereby increasing the statues' heights and giving them a
more striking appearance. For some reason – and many have been
suggested – megalithic statue building ceased in about 1680
(McCoy 1979; Mulloy and Figueroa 1978). A few decades later,
on Easter Sunday, 1722, the Dutch admiral Jacob Roggeveen
anchored his three ships off the eastern side of the island,
probably in La Perouse Bay where he would have seen the largest
statue (nearly 10 m tall) to have been moved from the quarry.
This was Paro, on *Ahu Te-pito-te-kura*, which belonged to the
Tupahotu-oone lineage (Fig. 8.18). Paro was reputedly the last
statue to be overthrown during the internal war that raged on the
island later that century.

 Traditional Polynesian societies were relatively small with
little or no contact outside their Oceanic culture area. Easter
Island is the most isolated inhabited island in the world. It is
nearly 4000 km from the coast of South America, and is
Polynesia's most eastern island. The population of Easter Island
was reduced considerably by warfare in the early 1770s. Before
their culture could be recorded in any detail the population was
further decimated by the diseases brought by the visitors and by
the appalling depredations of Peruvian slavers. In the late
nineteenth century the island's population numbered a bare
handful. Because there were no safe anchorages for sailing ships

visitors had stayed only for short periods, some – like La Pérouse – for only a matter of hours, and consequently very little was seen or was understood. The outcome is that there are almost no *reliable* observations or oral traditions about the technology of statue building, despite its comparatively recent origin, and we are left with a 'mystery', heightened by the island's remoteness.

Some bizarre explanations have been suggested as to how the Easter Island statues were made and transported. Jacob Roggeveen (1722:15–16) believed that the statues were moulded *in situ* out of some clay-like material, an idea recently resurrected by a polymer chemist and reported in a popular-science magazine (Starr 1983). The statues are actually made of volcanic tuff outcropping at the Rano Raraku volcano – a volcanic ash cemented by calcium and the whole seeded with basalt xenoliths of pebble size (Baker *et al.* 1974:91); the stone is highly susceptible to natural weathering. Although incorrect, Roggeveen's speculation was far more reasonable than a number that have followed. A psychologist, Werner Wolff (1949),

Fig. 8.18. Paro, the largest statue erected on Easter Island.

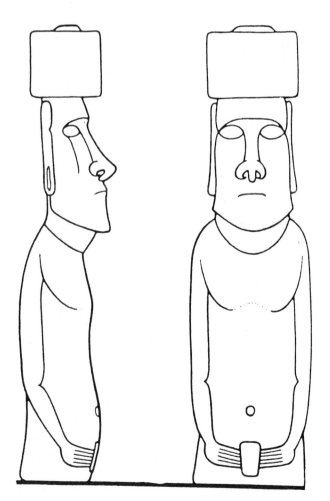

proposed that the statues may have been roughly carved in the quarry, transported by volcanic eruptions, and given their finishing touches in the places where they fell. This extraordinary hypothesis has to compete with electromagnetic forces (Mazière 1969:135), and stranded extra-terrestrials who wanted to attract passing spacecraft (Von Däniken 1970:131). The supposed 'enigma of the statues' remains the fancy of the popular press.

The majority of the Easter Island statues are not very large and, on average, their weight is only about 18 tonnes (Skjölsvold 1961:370). The smaller statues could easily have been transported on a simple sledge over a rough track, as was done by the islanders during Thor Heyerdahl's expedition in 1955. To move one of the larger statues in the same way would have required a sizable workforce. The weight of the giant Paro has been estimated to be about 82 tonnes (Smith 1961:203). To move this colossus on a simple sledge, which itself might have weighed 5 tonnes, would require in the vicinity of 1500 people. Taro or sweet potato used as lubricants (Métraux 1940:304) or, as suggested by Mulloy (1970:12), *totora* reeds which grew abundantly in the caldera lakes on the island, could have reduced the required number of people to 1000 if the sledge with its burden were dragged over the ground. A lubricated timber track would still further have reduced the number to perhaps 600. The population of Easter Island at the time the large statues were being made numbered in the thousands (McCall 1979:134). The labour needed to transport and erect the statues was presumably drawn mainly from the kin groups with assistance from people linked by obligations to the group. It is possible, therefore, that a thousand or more able bodied people could have been assembled to work co-operatively. It is logical that the islanders would have sought the most economical method of transporting a very heavy load, within the bounds of their labour and material resources.

William Mulloy, an American archaeologist and a member of Heyerdahl's expedition, has made the suggestion that the statues could have been transported economically with a curved Y-shaped sledge, made from the fork of a large tree, and a pair of shear legs (Mulloy 1970) (Fig. 8.19). When the shear legs are pulled forward the rope partially lifts the statue, taking some of the weight off the sledge. The action not only reduces the frictional force but also provides a mechanical advantage. Mulloy's estimate of the number of men required to move Paro from the Rano Raraku quarry to La Perouse Bay, some 5 km away, was 90. As Mulloy's hypothesis is widely accepted as an indication of a sophisticated prehistoric technology (cf. Bellwood 1978:369; McCoy 1979:159), we will examine its viability.

Following Mulloy, we assume that Paro was mounted on a curved Y-sledge, although our calculations show that a flat-bottomed sledge is just as good. The curved sledge would have balanced with the statue's back almost horizontal. As the load was taken by the rope, Paro's head would rise until the frictional force reached its limiting value. As the sledge moved forward, the frictional force would fall to its dynamic value, and the head would dip to ensure that the three forces acting on the sledge (the weight mg, the reaction force F_r and the tension in the cable P) all passed through the same point so that the equilibrium was maintained. We can use the sine rule (see Appendix III) to obtain

$$\frac{P}{\sin \lambda} = \frac{F_r}{\sin \alpha} = \frac{mg}{\sin (\alpha + \lambda)}$$

for steady sliding, where λ is the friction angle. Acting on the top of the shear legs we have the tensions P and T in the two parts of the cable which must be in equilibrium with the thrust S delivered by the shear legs. Again, the sine rule gives us

$$\frac{T}{\sin (\alpha + \beta)} = \frac{S}{\cos \alpha} = \frac{P}{\cos \beta}.$$

Solving these two equations of equilibrium simultaneously we obtain the ratio of the force necessary to drag the sledge using shear legs to that required if the statue was dragged on the sledge without using the shear legs

$$\frac{T}{\mu mg} = \left[\frac{\tan \alpha + \tan \beta}{\tan \alpha + \tan \lambda} \right]. \tag{8.13}$$

Provided the angle β is less than the friction angle λ the shear legs enable the friction force to be reduced. In other words, the shear legs must not lean too far towards the sledge or the mechanical advantage will be lost. As the sledge moves, the inclination of the shear legs and the rope will change and the force will vary. With the curved sledge some of the motion is due to slight rolling, but this movement provides no advantage

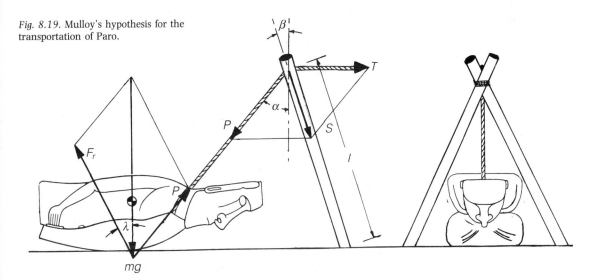

Fig. 8.19. Mulloy's hypothesis for the transportation of Paro.

because when the tension is released the sledge will take up its final balanced attitude. The force needed to move the sledge as a function of the distance slipped for a curved Y-sledge of radius 7·7 m is shown in Fig. 8.20 for two possible shear leg lengths. In each case the length of the rope from the shear legs to Paro's neck has been chosen to be the projected length *l* of the shear legs less the height of Paro's neck from the ground, which is about 3 m. With a rope of this length there is little unnecessary lifting of the statue's head and the traction force is minimised. Once the sledge starts moving the force needed to keep it moving drops until the last stages when it suddenly increases again. Obviously the distance that the statue can be moved each step is greater for the long shear legs. Even with 600 people and shear legs 10 m long, the maximum distance that the statue could have been moved each step is less than 4 m. Our mechanical analysis on Paro indicates that, while Mulloy's method of transporting the Easter Island statues is possible, it is no more efficient than other methods. In fact the average-sized statue could have been easily transported on a rudimentary sledge without the use of shear legs. Mulloy's estimate of only 90 men for the task of transporting Paro is simply not possible.

An issue of more importance than the labour requirements is whether there was suitable timber for making the devices Mulloy envisaged. Mulloy proposed that the Easter Islanders made their sledges from the forked trunk of a large tree; and of course there were also the shear legs of up to 10 m long. We estimate that trunk diameters of about 300 mm would have been needed to prevent these long shear legs buckling under the high compressive loads, even if they had been cut from good quality timber with a Young's modulus of, say, 10 GPa (see Table 5.1). Since the late eighteenth century it has been assumed that a forest with tall timber must have existed on the island during the

Fig. 8.20. Force necessary to move Paro by Mulloy's hypothesis (length of shear legs:——8 m; --- 10 m).

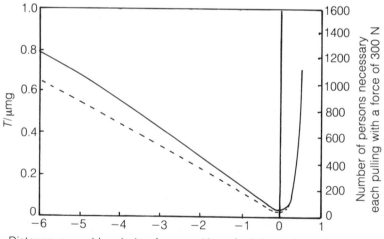

Distance moved by sledge from position of minimum force (m)

statue-building period (Heyerdahl 1957; La Pérouse 1797; Mulloy 1970). However, at best, the evidence for this is equivocal. The archaeological evidence indicates that the largest statues were probably erected in the fifteenth century, and one might assume that there was a progressive increase in size of statues up to these final years. Statues were still placed on *ahu* after the fifteenth century, but only a small one has been identified (Mulloy and Figueroa 1978). Whatever the prehistoric vegetation may have looked like, by the time Europeans arrived the only trees left to see were small cultigens and some patches of twisted toromiro trees (*Sophora toromiro*). The houses were made of reed-thatch over a framework of poles; the seats and pillows inside them were of stone. And while the original inhabitants must have come in substantial voyaging canoes, the few canoes that were seen in the eighteenth century were only about 3 m long and of 'poor and flimsy construction' (Roggeveen 1722:19).

Botanical studies have shown that because of the island's great isolation the few plants that made their way there during its two to three million years of existence before the arrival of people were but 'waifs and strays' (Skottsberg 1956; Flenley and King 1984). While the pollen record may not register every plant that grew on the island, the scene it gives is one of copses and grassland, with the latter especially in the drier interior where the soil layer is thin and the ground porous. Significantly, a palm tree is indicated, but the value of palm wood in making shear legs is limited – its modulus of elasticity is low so that it can survive cyclonic forces. The pollen does not clearly indicate a former tall forest (Flenley and King 1984; Kamminga and Cotterell 1984). Since some timber must have been used in transporting and erecting the statues the islanders must have had a source of dense wood of at least a few metres length. The trunk of a healthy *Sophora* tree would probably have been quite serviceable (though evidently few survived into historic times), or the trunk of *Thespesia populnea*, a tree brought from the Islanders' eastern Pacific homeland.

The palm indicated by the pollen in the lake sediments and by seed casings that have recently been found in rock crevices was probably an extinct species of the family *Jubea*, which is now represented by only a single species that grows in Chile (Dransfield *et al.* 1984). The Chilean *Jubea* is large, and exceptional specimens can have a trunk diameter of nearly a metre. However it is not very strong (with palms a thicker trunk generally means one that is softer), and it is not used structurally, but valued for its high sugar content. If the palm was strong and large enough to use for sledges and runners we expect that it must have been plentiful during the statue-building period, because palm wood is not very durable. The trunks of nearly all species of palm split on drying, without preservatives tend to rot in a damp environment and probably could not be stored for repeated use over a long time. If palm wood was used in any quantity for statue building then it is possible that this activity eventually depleted the island's reserve.

While palm trunks might not be suitable for shear legs they could have been used for a rudimentary sledge or trackway. Palm trunks may also have been used as rollers. Provided the trunks were no less than about 200 mm in diameter they would probably be as efficient as the rollers used in the French experiments if they were used on a trackway. Hence to drag Paro on palm rollers would require between 500 and 600 people.

It is interesting to consider why statue building ceased. Exhaustion of the island's timber is a possible cause. An adequate supply of rope is at least as important for statue building as timber. Consider how much rope would have been needed to drag Paro on a simple sledge over the ground. Let us assume that the people pulled on 10 ropes. Each rope would have to resist the combined force of 150 people, or about 45 kN. Using our value of 16 Mpa for their strength, the diameter of the ropes would need to be about 60 mm. Assuming that the people were arranged on both sides of the rope in pairs separated by a metre, each rope would have to be some 80 m long (allowing 5 m for attachment to the sledge). Hence, 800 m of at least 60 mm diameter rope would be required; that is, a minimum of 2 tonnes of rope. Using the most efficient means of moving available to the Easter Islanders would have required some 600 people. If these people were arranged in six lines, then a minimum of about 300 m of 50 mm diameter rope weighing about 0·5 tonnes would be required. A more efficient means of transportation greatly reduces the quantity of rope needed. It is conceivable that the scarcity of rope may have forced the Islanders to improve on a simple sledge. The only economical rope-making material on the island was the inner bark of a tiliaceous shrub (*Triumfetta semitrolaba*), called *hau* by the Easter Islanders (Métraux 1940:210), and, in earlier times, the crowns of the now-extinct palm. Rope will deteriorate at a much faster rate than palm wood or other timber, and over the years large stores of rope would have had to be constantly replenished. While timber was probably recycled, the demand for heavy-duty rope may have been a limiting factor in statue building.

Classical Greece and Rome

The invention of the capstan and the compound pulley by the Greeks (Drachmann 1963) made the transport of massive loads considerably less of a feat. The Romans employed the machines, in conjunction with a cradle-like sledge drawn over a greased runway, to ship ancient Egyptian obelisks back to the 'eternal city' (Dibner 1970:17). Perhaps significantly, a runway was chosen in preference to free rollers. Not until Fontana moved the Vatican obelisk were rollers known for certain to have been used in such tasks. The principle of rollers, however, was applied in

Classical times, and Vitruvius (X, 2, 11–14) has given us some details. The earlier Greek architect, Chersiphron, made the columns for the Temple of Artemis into giant garden rollers and pulled them to the temple site with bullocks. Chersiphron's son, Metagenes, following his father's example, moved the capitals for the columns by embedding their square ends into huge wheels. Paconius tried to go one better when moving the 40-tonne base of a statue – by enclosing it in wheels joined by longitudinal timbers to make a massive roller. Instead of fitting sockets in the end of the stone and providing a frame which could be pulled, Paconius wound a rope around the cylinder and had the bullocks pull that. The massive roller would not run true and Paconius went bankrupt.

9

Water transport

Rudimentary watercraft must have preceded the development of
even the most basic land vehicles. More than 40 000 years ago
the ancestors of the Australian Aborigines crossed the deep-sea
strait that separated the vast island continent from the mainland
of Southeast Asia. With the lowest possible sea-level, which
occurred about 50 000 years ago, the narrowest crossing would
have been at least 90 km wide (Birdsell 1977). Sea crossings from
Asia were also made before about 20 000 years ago to the deep-
sea island of Okinawa (Kamminga and Wright 1988), and
perhaps a few millennia later across the Bering Strait to North
America. While the earliest sea journeys may not have been
intentional, they would have required at least a raft of some kind.

There is considerable evidence that people were putting to
sea in boats in Europe by early Neolithic times. Obsidian flakes
found in a level of the Franchthi caves in Greece that date to the
middle of the seventh millennium BC have been identified as
coming from the island of Melos, some 120 kilometres from the
caves by sea (Durrani et al. 1971:242; Renfrew and Cann 1966).
The type of watercraft used in the eastern Mediterranean for these
and other voyages is not known, but there is some evidence that
they were either reed-bundle craft or logboats (Johnstone
1980:56–66). In northern Europe it is more likely that the first
boats sufficiently seaworthy to make deliberate voyages were
made from skin (Clark and Piggott 1970:104; Hornell
1970:111–47; Johnstone 1980:26–9). Boats of this type were
probably used in the fourth millennium BC to transport stone axes
from Northern Ireland to the Mersey, Scotland, and the Hebrides,
as well as from the Norwegian island of Bømlo to the mainland
(Clark 1965).

The Nile has always been the natural highway of Egypt, and
much is known about the ancient Egyptian watercraft that sailed
upon it. The earliest watercraft were simple rafts made from
bundles of reeds lashed together (Boreux 1925:3). By the middle
of the fourth millennium BC the Egyptians were forming their
reed bundles into long slender boat-like shapes (Bass 1972).
Planked boats were introduced during the third millennium,
probably in response to the need to ferry massive blocks of stone
(Casson 1971:13). The only timber locally available was short

lengths of acacia (Hornell 1970:215) with which the Egyptians built boats using a construction that Herodotus (II, 96) likened to the laying of bricks. Because of a dearth of good timber the Egyptians imported cedar and other conifers from the Syrian and Lebanese coasts for their larger ships, like the 100-cubit (52 m) vessels built by Sneferu (*c.* 2600 BC) that are mentioned on the Palermo Stone (Jenkins 1980:114). The Egyptian planked boats copied the earlier reed ones, and their hulls were long compared to their depth. Such hulls are not efficient at resisting the bending moments imposed by waves and other unequally distributed loads. In ships, the most severe condition is usually 'hogging' when the ends of the hull are bent downwards. To resist the hogging moments the Egyptian shipwrights stretched a heavy rope supported on props between the bow and the stern (Fig. 9.1). This rope was tightened by twisting the strands of rope with a bar.[1] The Egyptian ships at the end of the second millennium had dispensed with the rope stiffening because their hulls were improved structurally by making them deeper (Casson 1971:35).

Rope stiffening of a hull does reappear briefly a number of times in maritime history. The Athenian triremes were slender war-galleys. The depth of the trireme was only one-thirteenth of its waterline length, and the hull had insufficient strength on its own to resist the hogging moments that it could be expected to encounter (Morrison and Coates 1986:197). Consequently the hull of the trireme was stiffened by a rope called the *hypozōmata* in a similar fashion to the early Egyptian planked vessels (Morrison and Coates 1986:70–2). There has been considerable

Fig. 9.1. An Egyptian sea-going vessel (*c.* 2500 BC) based on a relief in Sahure's mortuary temple at Abusir.

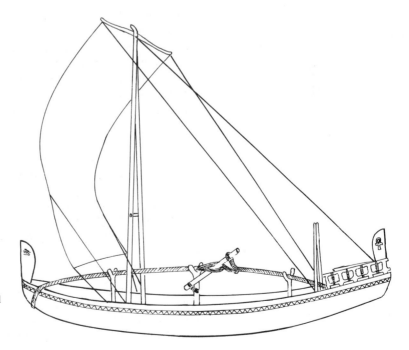

[1] The Egyptians used the same method of tightening ropes to fasten the statue of Djehutihotep to the sledge (Fig. 8.16).

debate in the past about the exact nature of the *hypozōmata*. However the recent reconstruction of a full-size trireme has convincingly demonstrated that the hull needs to be strengthened by a tensioned rope fixed above the neutral axis of the hull section to resist hogging moments (Morrison and Coates 1986:197–200). Much later, in China (*c.* 1300 AD), bamboo cables were used to prevent hogging in the long, narrow, dragon-boats used for ritual races during the Fifth Month Festival (Needham *et al.* 1971:436–7). The structural design of hulls is an important aspect of water transport.

The merchant vessels of the Classical Age, especially the grain carriers, were by no means small; in the third century BC the port regulations of the Greek island of Thasos prohibited vessels of under 80 tonnes burden from using its facilities, and reserved part of the harbour for vessels of 130 tonnes burden or more (Casson 1971:171). Even larger vessels of up to 350 tonnes were not extraordinary. In about 240 BC Hieron of Syracuse had Archimedes supervise the construction of a superfreighter of 1700 tonnes burden for shipping Sicilian wheat to the cities of Greece (Gasson 1971:194–200). The vessel, the biggest in the ancient world, had three decks and luxurious amenities for its crew – such as a shrine, a library and a bath. Like the Boeing 747 when it first flew the air routes, Hieron's superfreighter caused a great deal of public curiosity and people travelled many kilometres to see it.

The Romans also built a few superfreighters. These round ships of the Mediterranean were very sturdy. The beam and depth of the 1300-tonne *Isis* used on the Alexandria–Rome run in the second century AD were about a quarter of her overall length (Casson 1971:187). Such ships were normally able to resist the bending moments imposed by the waves. However even the round ships occasionally needed strengthening with cables during storms, as occurred during St Paul's voyage to Italy. After the collapse of the Roman Empire ships became quite small again, and not until the Chinese junks of the fourteenth century AD were such large vessels constructed again anywhere in the world (Needham *et al.* 1971:479–82). The Chinese ships came 'sailing like mountains with the wings of wind on the surface of the water' was how one impressed Arab writer, Wassaf, described them (Mookerji 1912:185).

The Chinese junk had its origin in the raft (Needham *et al.* 1971:395–6; Hornell 1970:86–90). They were more or less flat-bottomed, built without a keel, a stem or a stern post. In the classic design of junk both the bow and the stern were square in shape. The hull had a very sturdy construction based on solid transverse bulkheads rather than ribs that divided the ship into a number of watertight compartments (Needham *et al.* 1971:390–2). Although social and political circumstances somewhat inhibited long sea voyages the Chinese were certainly trading with East Africa by the eighth century AD (Needham *et al.* 1971:494–503). However long before, sometime between 1500 and 1000 BC, the ancestors of the Polynesians sailed from eastern Melanesia to the uninhabited islands of Tonga and Samoa to accomplish the longest voyages in prehistoric times (Finney 1977:1277). From these islands the Polynesians moved eastward to the Marquesas and the Society Islands. The final stage of the settlement of the Pacific, which was completed by at least 1200 AD, saw voyages of thousands of kilometres to Hawaii, Easter Island and, last of all, to New Zealand.

While it is not known what type of boats were used in the early phases of the settlement of the Pacific, nineteenth-century Polynesian boats were mostly based on the logboat (dugout). The true logboat has a very limited stability and capacity. In northwest Europe, in India, and in the Americas, logboats have been expanded by heat treatment and the gunwale built up with added washstrakes to increase their stability and size. This technique of expanding the logboat is only suitable for certain types of timber which were not available in the Pacific (Johnstone 1980:49–50). The Polynesians could only increase the size of their logboats by adding washstrakes and using outriggers or a second hull to increase the stability. The double-hulled canoe was favoured for long-range voyages because they had greater carrying capacity (Finney 1977:1277). However the Polynesian logboats were much smaller than the single-hulled plank boats of the Mediterranean in the second millennium BC. The boats used for the long voyages of the Polynesians were probably not much larger than the 11-tonne *Hokule'a*, built in 1975 to replicate as near as possible the type of vessel used by the Polynesians some 600 to 1000 years ago (Finney 1977:1278). The advantage offered by the double-hulled canoe was that while it was not large it was stable and, most importantly, fast. The top speed of the *Hokule'a* is about 18·5 km/hr (Finney 1977:1280). Hawaiian legends tell of long voyages between Hawaii and Tahiti. In 1976 the *Hokule'a* sailed the 5370 km from Hawaii to Tahiti using only the navigation methods of the Polynesians in $33\frac{1}{2}$ days – including $1\frac{1}{2}$ days stay at Mataiva. The average speed on the best day's run was 11·1 km/hr (Finney 1977:1281–3). Such fast voyages made up for the lack of carrying capacity.

Whatever the design of vessel used in ancient or modern times, obviously the prime requirement is that it has enough buoyancy to stay afloat.

Buoyancy

There is a well known but fanciful story about the discovery of the principle of buoyancy (Vitruvius IX, 9–12). Hieron of Syracuse, believing that the gold in his crown was debased, asked Archimedes to determine its purity. While thinking over the problem in the public baths, Archimedes observed that the more his body sank the more the water spilled over the edge of the bath. In a flash of inspiration he realised that here was a way of assessing the purity of the gold. Leaping from the bath Archimedes rushed home, completely forgetting to dress, shouting 'eureka' ('I have it'). What Archimedes realised was that if the crown were immersed in a container filled to the brim with water, the volume of the displaced water would be equal to the volume of the crown. If an amount of pure gold equal in weight to the crown displaced less water than the crown, then the latter had to be an alloy because the alloying metals were lighter than gold. Archimedes continued to think about the problem and deduced that if a body floated, the weight of the displaced water would be equal to the weight of the body. From here it was a small step to the more general principle of buoyancy – that the weight of liquid displaced by a body is equal to the upwards buoyancy force. In his discourse on hydrostatics Archimedes gave a rigorous proof of this principle; we shall give a simpler one.

Imagine that we possess an extremely thin, strong and weightless material from which we fashion a boat. If the boat is flooded to any level then it must float at that level. Suppose now that the water is pumped out of the boat and a downward force is applied so that the boat does not rise. When the boat is empty a weight equal to that of the displaced water will have been removed. No change has occurred outside the boat, so that the force required to hold down the empty boat is equal to the weight of the displaced water, and it must therefore be the buoyancy force. When it was flooded, the weight of the boat must have acted through the centre of gravity of the enclosed water. Clearly the buoyancy force has to act through the same point. Therefore, the buoyancy force of a boat, which is equal to the weight of the displaced water, acts through the centre of volume of the boat's immersed part.

When in equilibrium, the buoyancy force must equal the weight of the vessel. For simple floats it is only necessary to ensure that they are sufficiently buoyant; stability is guaranteed if the centre of gravity of any person hanging onto it is far below the centre of buoyancy. If a person climbs onto a floating log its centre of gravity will be shifted to well above the centre of buoyancy, the log will be unstable, and the person will only be able to stay upright precariously. For boats lateral stability is essential.

Lateral stability

In a calm sea, and in the absence of wind, the centre of buoyancy B and the centre of gravity CG of a boat must lie on the same vertical line or else there will be a moment acting to change the boat's lateral orientation (Fig. 9.2). Except in a heavily ballasted keel boat the centre of gravity will be above the centre of buoyancy. If the boat heels over through a small angle θ, the centre of buoyancy will shift towards the side that is heeling over. The buoyancy force must be equal to the weight of the boat *mg* and, provided the centre of gravity is not too high, there will be a righting moment *mga* where *a* is the horizontal distance between the centres of gravity and buoyancy (Fig. 9.2). Such a boat is stable. If the centre of gravity is too high there will be a capsizing moment instead of a righting moment and the boat will be unstable. Clearly no boat that is completely unstable can function. However the seaworthiness of a boat depends not only on its initial stability but also on the variation in righting moment *M* with the angle of heel. As a boat continues to heel over, the horizontal distance *a* between the centres of gravity and buoyancy

Fig. 9.2. Schematic variation of righting moment with angle of heel for a monohull (——righting moment; ------dynamic stability).

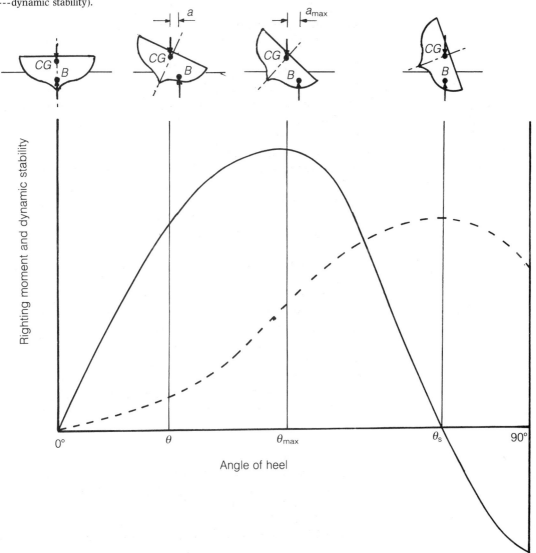

will increase until it reaches a maximum value a_{max} when the boat has heeled over to some angle θ_{max}. If the boat heels over past this angle the centre of buoyancy shifts back towards the centre of gravity and at some angle of heel θ_s will again lie vertically under the centre of gravity. For larger angles of heel the boat is unstable. The variation in righting moment M with angle of heel is shown schematically in Fig. 9.2. The more heavily ballasted the boat or the broader the beam the larger the angle of heel θ_s at which the boat becomes unstable. Ballast was essential in most of the ancient merchant ships. In the ports of Rome, the *saburrarii* were a professional trade guild that specialised in the ballasting of ships (Rougé 1981:68–9). Only a heavily ballasted modern keel yacht with the centre of gravity below the centre of buoyancy is completely stable and self-righting even if capsized by a big wave.

In the presence of a cross-wind the pressure on the sail or superstructure will cause a boat to heel over until the heeling moment caused by the wind pressure is balanced by the righting moment caused by the hydrostatic forces. A sudden gust of wind, or the action of the waves, can cause the boat to heel over further, and to be seaworthy a boat must have sufficient stability to right itself after encountering such a sudden disturbance. A better measure of the behaviour of a boat under such conditions is its dynamic stability. The dynamic stability is defined as the work done in heeling the boat to a particular angle θ. Hence the dynamic stability of a boat heeled over to an angle θ is the area of the righting moment diagram up to that angle. The dynamic stability is shown schematically in Fig. 9.2. The dynamic stability curve enables an assessment to be made of the ability of a boat to resist a sudden gust or wave without capsizing.

The calculation of a full righting moment diagram for a single-hull boat is beyond the scope of this book. However the initial stability of a slab-sided boat can be determined comparatively easily. In Fig. 9.3 we show a slab-sided boat that is heeled over through a small angle θ. As before, the righting moment is mga. However for a small angle of heel a is small and the initial stability of a boat is assessed not from its righting moment directly. A vertical line through the centre of buoyancy intersects the centre line of the boat at a point M called the *metacentre*. For small angles of heel θ the metacentre is virtually fixed and the righting moment M is given by

$$M = mga \approx mgh\theta \qquad (9.1)$$

where h, the height of the metacentre above the centre of gravity, is called the *metacentric height*. Hence the metacentric height can be used as a measure of the initial stability of a boat. However it should be emphasised that the metacentric height only cannot be used to judge the full stability of a boat. When a boat heels over, the wedge of water OCC' shown in Fig. 9.3 is transferred to ODD'.

It is the transference of this wedge of water that causes the centre of buoyancy to move from B_0 to B, and in doing so creates a moment equal to the buoyancy force ρVg (where V is the immersed volume of the hull) multiplied by the shift in the centre of buoyancy b. Let us consider the righting moment of a small length of the hull dx that has the cross-section shown in Fig. 9.3. The weight of the elemental wedge of water is $\rho g W^2 \theta dx/8$ and its moment caused by its transfer is $\rho g W^2 \theta dx/8 \times 2W/3$. The total righting moment is the sum of the moments of all similar cross-sections and is

$$\sum \frac{\rho g W^3 dx}{12}\theta = \rho g I \theta$$

where I is the second moment of area of the water-plane about the boat's centre line. Since, as we have already seen, this righting moment is equal to ρVgb, we have

$$b = \frac{I\theta}{V}$$

and

$$BM = \frac{I}{V}. \tag{9.2}$$

The metacentric height h can be obtained from equation (9.2) if we know the position of the boat's centre of gravity. The recent reconstruction of the Athenian trireme was designed so that it had a metacentric height of 0·5–0·7 m which ensured adequate stability for sailing across a wind of about 15 knots (≈ 28 km/h) (Morrison and Coates 1986:195).

Fig. 9.3. The forces on a slab-sided hull heeled through a small angle.

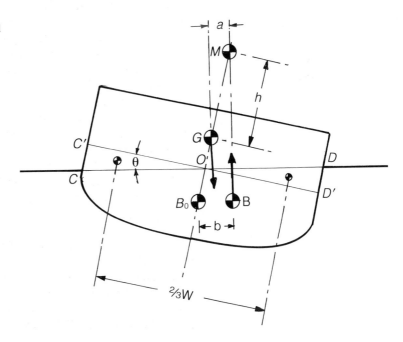

So far we have only considered the stability of a boat with a single hull. Multi-hulled boats behave somewhat differently. We illustrate the stability of double-hulled canoes with an analysis of the *Nalehia* (Fig. 9.4) built in 1966 on the basis of plans of early-nineteenth-century Hawaiian vessels drawn by Admiral Paris in 1839 (Doran 1981:24). The hulls of the 2.3-tonne *Nalehia* had a U-shaped cross-section and floated with the waterline roughly level with the top of the semicircular part. A double-hulled canoe reaches its maximum righting moment when one of the hulls lifts clear from the water. When one hull of a boat like the *Nalehia* lifts clear, the other hull must increase its cross-sectional area of the immersed part by $\pi/8 \; w^2$, where w is the hull's beam (Fig. 9.5). Hence the average waterline rises by $\pi/8 \; w$ and the angle of heel θ_{max} is given by

$$\tan \theta_{max} \approx \left(\frac{\pi}{8} + \frac{1}{2}\right) \frac{w}{W}. \tag{9.3}$$

For the *Nalehia*, whose data is given in Table 9.1, $\theta_{max} \approx 18°$. When sailing, some of the crew members would have positioned themselves on the gunwale of the windward hull to increase the stability of the boat by displacing the centre of gravity from the

Fig. 9.4. The *Nalehia* – a Hawaiian double-hulled canoe (after Finney 1977).

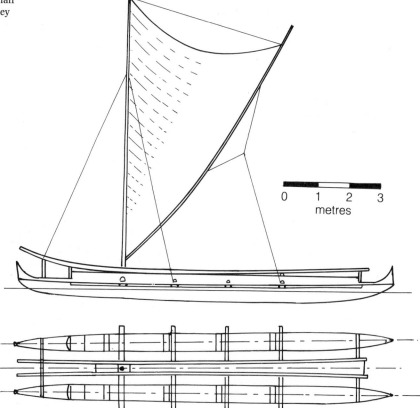

centre line as shown in Fig. 9.5. We have calculated the position
of the centre of gravity shown in Table 9.1 from the data of
Doran (1981:63) assuming that six out of a crew of nine are
sitting on the windward gunwale. For angles of heel sufficient to
lift one hull clear of the water, the righting moment M is given by

$$M = mg\left[\frac{W}{2}\cos\theta + d\sin(\alpha-\theta)\right] \tag{9.4}$$

where it is assumed that the buoyancy force acts through the
centre of the semicircular part of the hull's cross-section. A
stability curve for the *Nahelia* is shown in Fig. 9.6. The righting
moment drops to zero when the angle of heel is about 69°.

Table 9.1 *Dimensions and data for the* Nalehia

overall length	12·9 m
waterline length	11·5 m
beam $(W+w)$	2·3 m
hull beam (w)	0·6 m
distance of centre of gravity (CG) from waterline (d)	0·5 m
angular position of CG (α)	30°
sail area	19·5 m²
height to centre of effort from waterline	6·25 m
weight with 9 crew	2·3 tonne

Source: Based on data given in Doran 1981:63

Fig. 9.5. A double-hulled canoe heeled over so that one hull just lifts clear of the water.

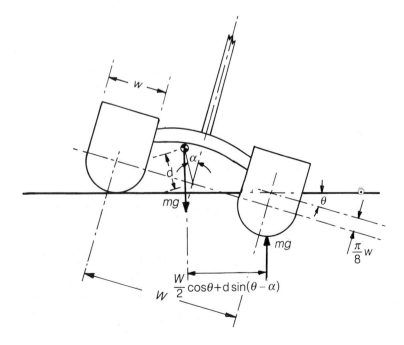

Because some of the crew are sitting on the gunwale there is a positive moment for zero angle of heel given by

$$M = mgd \sin \alpha. \tag{9.5}$$

We have not calculated the righting moment for angles of heel less than θ_{max} and in Fig. 9.6 have simply joined the value at zero angle of heel to the maximum value by a straight line.

The difference between a Polynesian double-hulled canoe and a heavily ballasted Mediterranean round boat is that while the double canoe has a large righting moment for small angles of heel, it reaches its maximum value at a comparatively small angle and for larger angles of heel the righting moment drops quickly. The dynamic stability of a double-hulled canoe is therefore not that impressive. The two hulls of a Polynesian double canoe are much closer together than those of a modern catamaran. A greater width between the hulls would not only improve the double canoe's stability but also increase its maximum speed because the interaction of the bow waves between the hulls is a source of considerable drag. However the strength of the timber crosspieces and the rope lashings limited the spacing of the hulls. Finney (1977:1281) remarks that though generally seaworthy, the traditional double-hull design was vulnerable to breaking apart and swamping in heavy seas – a good number of Polynesian seafarers must have perished in storms.

Having reviewed the necessary requirements for a watercraft to stay afloat and upright we now turn to the methods by which it is propelled.

Fig. 9.6. A stability curve for the Nalehia.

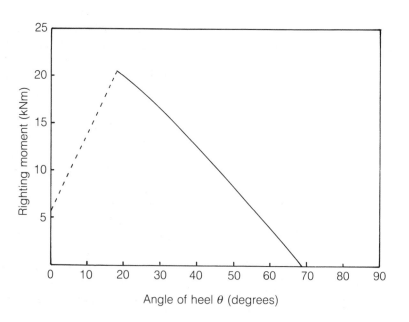

Propulsion

The oldest way of propelling a vessel in deep water is by
paddling. The power that can be obtained from paddling,
however, is very limited because only the muscle of the upper
body can be utilised. In Egypt the oar had replaced the paddle on
larger vessels by about 2400 BC (Boreaux 1925:314). Rowlocks
on these Egyptian craft were of the most basic form – a piece of
rope passed through holes in the gunwale. In ancient Greece the
oar was held against a vertical pin (*skalmos*) with a leather strap
(Casson 1971:46).

Oars

The ancient warships of the Mediterranean were oared galleys. In
The Iliad Homer describes the 'swift' ships in which the Greek
heroes were transported to Troy. One squadron of seven ships
(*The Iliad* II, 719–20) had 50 oarsmen to each vessel and the
Boeotians had 50 ships each with 120 young men (*The Iliad* II,
509–10). Those with 50 oarsmen were probably similar to later
pentecontors and had a single bank of 25 men on each side of the
galley. Such a galley would have been about 35 m long. Probably
at least 100 of the Boeotians were oarsmen.[2] On grounds of hull
strength it is inconceivable that the galleys were some 60 m
long to enable a single bank of 50 men to be accommodated. The
Boeotian galleys were most likely biremes, that is, they had two
banks of oars (Casson 1971:59). Though the galleys described by
Homer were primarily for transport they were probably no
different to the warships. The introduction of the ram changed sea
warfare and placed emphasis on galleys that were fast and
manoeuvrable. The most developed of these new warships was the
trireme – a galley with 170 oars arranged in three banks
(Fig. 9.7). A fleet of such galleys defeated the much larger Persian
navy at Salamis in 480 BC, bringing to an end a war that had
gone on for ten years (Morrison and Coates 1986:49–60).

There has been considerable debate about the exact form of
the trireme, which has culminated in a reconstruction of a full-
sized vessel (ibid.). Using what is known historically about the
trireme and the dimensions of the ship sheds in the harbour at
Piraeus that housed them, it has been estimated that the trireme
had an overall length of 37 m with a waterline length of 32 m
and a maximum beam of 5·5 m (3·8 m at the waterline). The
total weight of the galley in battle condition, including oarsmen,
was probably about 43 tonnes. In order to keep the centre of
gravity low, the three banks of oars were staggered and the
oarsmen packed into the galley like sardines in a can. The bottom
bank of oars (thalamite) were set so low that the oarports had to
be fitted with leather gaskets to keep the water out (Morrison and
Williams 1968:283–4). We learn from a bawdy joke in
Aristophanes' play, *Frogs*, that the next bank of oarsmen (zygite)

[2] Thucydides (I, X, 4) makes it clear
that he believes that most of the 120
were oarsmen.

sat with their buttocks level with the noses of the lower-most men
(Anderson 1962:7). The oars on the top bank (thranite) were
worked from an outrigger so that their length was the same as
that of the oars on the other banks. This arrangement enables the
whole array of oars to be as near the water and as vertically
compact as possible so that they could be worked easily in unison
enabling a high speed to be achieved. The reconstructed
arrangement of the oarsmen is shown in Fig. 9.8.

   A change in battle tactics in the fourth century BC placed
greater emphasis on boarding over ramming. To enable the
weight of soldiers moving about high in the ship to be carried, the
polyremes which were wider than the triremes, were developed

Fig. 9.7. A reconstructed trireme (from
Morrison and Coates 1986: fig. 62).

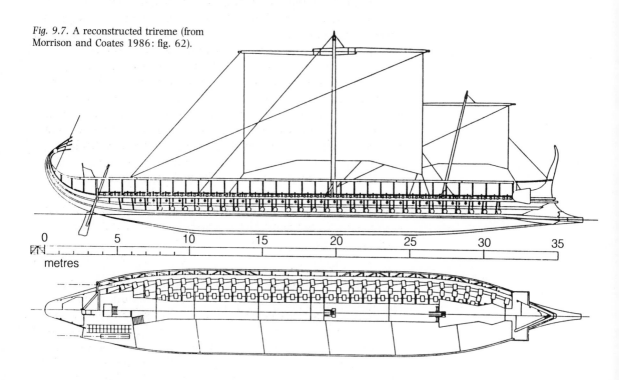

Fig. 9.8. The arrangement of oarsmen
in the reconstructed trireme (after
Morrison and Coates 1986) (*M*,
metacentre; *CG*, centre of gravity;
B, centre of buoyancy).

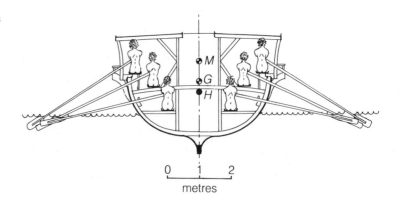

(Casson 1971:97–140; Morrison 1980:320–46). From the first half of the fourth century the polyreme developed from the trireme to the gigantic but unwieldy 'forty' of Ptolemy IV (221–204 BC).[3] The polyremes had more than one man to each oar as well as more than one bank of oars; the numerical denominator referred to the number of fore-and-aft, horizontal files of oarsmen. For example Demetrius' great 'sixteen' had either two banks of eight-man sweeps or three banks with 16 men distributed over thranite-zygite-thalamite positions. With the earlier polyremes which had one or two-man oars the rowers could sit on a bench, whereas, if there were more men to an oar, they would have to rise to their feet to dip the blade, and fall back on the bench for the pull. It is difficult to believe that such a technique was efficient, but it did have the advantage of requiring fewer skilled men, since the oarsmen at the end of the oar had full control while the rest merely added muscle power (Casson 1971:104). In the Western world rowing is performed facing backwards; it was quite the opposite in China where the rower faced forwards (Needham *et al.* 1971:621). Although the Chinese stance is a natural development from paddling it does not call into action as many muscles as the Western style of rowing. We shall confine our discussion to the single-manned oar rowed facing backwards.

The oar creates a thrust on the boat from the drag force that arises when it slips through the water. This drag force D, which is proportional to the dynamic pressure $\frac{1}{2}\rho_w v_0^2$ and the area of the blade S_o, is given in terms of a non-dimensional drag coefficient C_D by

$$D = \frac{1}{2}\rho_w v_0^2 S_0 C_D \tag{9.6}$$

where v_0 is the velocity of the oar relative to the water, and ρ_w the density of the water (1025 kg/m³ for sea water). The non-dimensional drag coefficient depends on the length–breadth ratio of the oar, which in fluid mechanics is called the *aspect ratio*. For an aspect ratio of 5 the drag coefficient is about 1.2. Since the tip of the blade moves through the water with a higher velocity than the inboard part, it seems reasonable to take the effective drag coefficient as 1.0 and to use the blade tip velocity in equation (9.6). If during the stroke the oar has an angular velocity of Ω and the outboard oar length is b, the relative velocity of the tip of the blade through the water is $(\Omega b - v_b)$ where v_b is the velocity of the boat (Fig. 9.9). Therefore the drag force on the oar is given by

$$D = \frac{1}{2}\rho_w(\Omega b - v_b)^2 S_0. \tag{9.7}$$

By the level rule the force exerted by the oarsman is Db/a. The power supplied to the oar (P_0) is the product of the force exerted by the oarsman, and the velocity of the loom end of the oar, relative to the boat. Hence

$$P_0 = \frac{Db}{a}\Omega a = D\Omega b. \tag{9.8}$$

[3] It is believed that the 'forty' of Ptolemy IV was twin-hulled. This ship, the largest of the polyremes, was only used for prestige purposes. The largest fighting ship was the 'thirty' (Morrison 1980:45–46).

The useful power supplied to the boat (P_b) is the propulsive force (equal to the drag D) multiplied by the boat's velocity v_b, which gives

$$P_b = Dv_b. \tag{9.9}$$

Therefore the efficiency η of the oar is given by

$$\eta = \frac{P_b}{P_0} = \frac{Dv_b}{D\Omega b} = \frac{v_b}{\Omega b}. \tag{9.10}$$

A typical value for the efficiency is 0.75.

The effective power of an oarsman has been estimated in a Yale University study on the performance of one of its racing

Fig. 9.9. The forces on an oar.

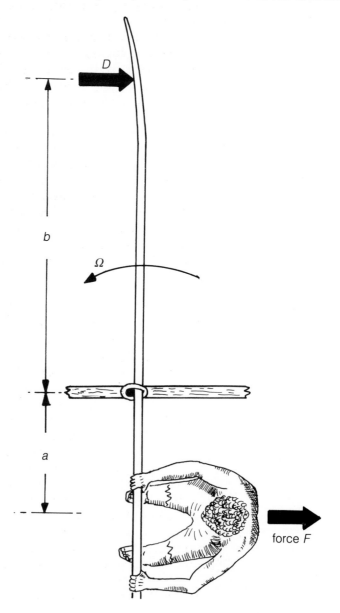

eights (Henderson and Haggard 1925). The Yale crew achieved a speed of 17·6 km/hr (9·5 knots) over a 6·4 km course. By towing their racing boat behind a motor launch and measuring the towing force, which was 436 N, they were able to calculate the propulsive effort of the eight oarsmen. At a speed of 4·88 m/s the total power driving the boat was $4·88 \times 436 = 2130$ W. Each oarsman would therefore have supplied a power of 266 W to the boat. The Yale students were very fit and their boat was equipped with modern sliding racing seats, which allow the muscles to be used more efficiently. Well-trained oarsmen of the Classical world would perhaps have been able to supply about 70% of the power provided by the Yale students, which would be in the order of 190 W.

The propelling force on the racing eight can also be estimated from the mechanics of the oar. If we assume that the area of the oar's blade was 0·12 m² and that the outboard length was 2·5 m, then the maximum force exerted by each oar was

$$\tfrac{1}{2} 1000 \times 0·12 \, (2·5\Omega - 4·88)^2.$$

This force is only exerted during the power stroke, no force being exerted while the oar is returned. Therefore, to calculate the power, we must find the work done during the power stroke and divide it by the duration of a complete stroke (power and return). If we assume that the angular movement of the oar during the power stroke is about $80° = 1·4$ rads, then the time taken is $1·4/\Omega$ and the distance travelled by the boat in this time (neglecting the acceleration of the boat) is $1·4 \times 4·88/\Omega$ m, so that the work done by each stroke is

$$\frac{1·4 \times 4·88}{\Omega} [\tfrac{1}{2} 1000 \times 0·12(2·5 - 4·88)^2].$$

The rowing rate for the course would probably have been about 32 strokes/min giving a time for each stroke of 60/32 s. If the average power developed is equated to the previous estimate of 266 W, we can find the angular velocity Ω of the oar. Hence

$$1·4 \times 4·88/\Omega \, [\tfrac{1}{2} 1000 \times 0·12 \, (2·5\,\Omega - 4·88)^2] \times 32/60 = 266$$

and Ω is 2·7 rad/s. The time of the power stroke is therefore about half a second and the ratio of the power to the total stroke $1:3·5$, which is a reasonable value. The efficiency of the oars from equation (9.10) is found to be 0·73. Therefore the actual power developed by the oarsmen was $266/0·73 = 365$ W, which agrees with the values given in Table 2·6 for the performances of athletes.

Over short-distance races the rowing rate can increase to as much as 40 strokes/min. However rowing becomes less efficient at high ratings because oarsman have to accelerate their body as well as the oar. Consequently it is better to keep the rating down by matching blade area to the steady power output of the crew.

Sails

The earliest representation of a boat with a sail occurs on an Egyptian pot dated to about 3200 BC (Bowen 1960). The early Egyptian boats had lofty masts with tall sails. Such a rig may have developed because the Nile boats needed to catch the breeze in places where the river flows between cliffs, but it was also used on the sea-going ships of the third millennium BC (Casson 1971:19, 21). However, by the middle of the second millennium BC, the tall sails of Egyptian ships had been replaced by broad low ones like those portrayed in the relief at Deir el-Bahri showing the fleet of Queen Hatsheput (*c*. 1503–1482 BC) loading exotic merchandise in the fabled land of Punt (Casson 1971:21).

A square sail is unsurpassed when running with the wind or on a broad reach. The nineteenth-century square-rigged clippers at times achieved speeds comparable to modern ships. The *Sovereign of the Seas*, a nineteenth-century clipper, holds the record time of 68 days for the passage by sail between Melbourne and Liverpool and once reached 19 knots (35 km/h) while running for the Horn (Lubbock 1975:17–20). However a square-rigged ship cannot sail close to the wind. In order to make much headway against a wind a sail must be able to develop lift. The sail needs a high aspect ratio and preferably a tight leading edge so that it can develop an aerofoil section. Such a sail set at an acute angle to the wind generates as much lift from the reduction in pressure as the air accelerates around the leeward side (*cf*. Bernoulli's equation 3·5) as it does by the increase due to its deceleration on the windward side. The lifting force L can produce a driving force R, providing the drag force D on the sail is small

Fig. 9.10. The driving and heeling forces acting on a sail.

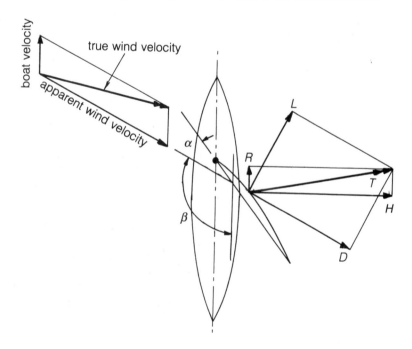

enough, and enable the boat to make some headway against a
wind (Fig. 9.10). How close a boat can sail into the wind depends
as much on the ability of the hull to resist the heeling force *H* as
on the sail's efficiency. It must also be remembered that the
course of the boat to the true wind direction is always less than
its course to the apparent wind direction observed by a sailor on
the boat (see Fig. 9.10).

The principal sail types are shown in Fig. 9.11. The oldest
sailing ships, those of ancient Egypt, were undoubtedly square-
rigged (Fig. 9.11a), but there is much argument over the
subsequent development of sail. Sailors must have experimented
to get the best out of their sails when the wind was unfavourable.
The seventh problem in the Aristotelian *Mechanical problems* asks
'Why is it that, when the wind is unfavourable...they reef the sail
in the direction of the helmsman and slacken the part of the sheet
towards the bow?' This passage has been interpreted to mean
that Greek ships managed to get nearer to the wind by reefing-in
a square sail in such a way that it serves somewhat like a fore-
and-aft rig. However the true fore-and-aft rig may have been
developed first in Southeast Asia. The great sea voyages of the
Polynesians were almost certainly made with some form of sprit-
sail. There are many varieties of sprit-sail and we have only
illustrated the main ones (Doran 1981; Haddon and Hornell
1936, 1937, 1938). The double sprit-sail (Fig. 9.11b 1), also
called the proto-Oceanic sprit-sail, may be the precursor of all the
sprit-sails in the Pacific region (Bowen 1953:84; Doran

Fig. 9.11. Sail types: (*a*) square rig;
(*b*) sprit-sails *1:* double sprit-sail, *2:*
Oceanic sprit-sail, *3:* crane sprit-sail, *4:*
common sprit-sail; (*c*) Lug sails *1:*
rectangular lug, *2:* Vietnamese lug, *3:*
Chinese lug, *4:* lateen.

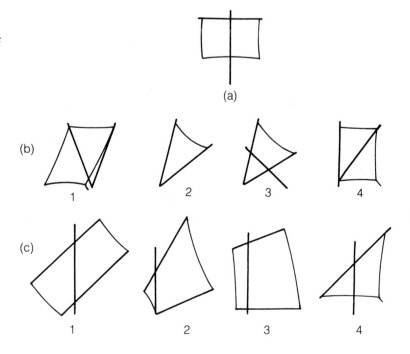

1981:39). In the Oceanic sprit-sail (Fig. 9.11b 2), so
characteristic of the Pacific, the upper sprit is used like an aft-
raking mast. The crane sprit-sail (Fig. 9.11b 3) is a variety of
Oceanic sprit-sail that enables an outrigger to perform a shunting
manoeuvre (see below and Doran 1981:41–3). The common
sprit-sail (Fig. 9.12b 4) is so-called because it occurs not only in
the Pacific region but also in China and Western Europe
(Doran 1981:39). The first record of the common sprit-sail in
Western Europe is on a second century BC relief; it is still
favoured by fishermen in the North Aegean Sea (Casson
1971:244). There is no reason to believe that the common
sprit-sail was not independently invented in Southeast Asia or the
Pacific and Western Europe. On the other hand, the lateen
(Fig. 9.11c 3), which was the most prominent Western fore-and-aft
sail, may be an example of diffusion from Southeast Asia. The
lateen is a type of lug sail.

   In a lug rig a significant portion of the sail is ahead of the
mast. The rectangular lug sail (Fig. 9.11c 1) probably originated
in Indonesia and may be the prototype of all the lug rigs
(Needham *et al.* 1971:608). From Indonesia the lug rig may
have spread north to China where it has been known since the
third century AD in the form of the typical Chinese lug sail
(Fig. 9.11c 3) (Needham *et al.* 1971:601). Certainly the
Vietnamese lug sail (Fig. 9.11c 2) looks as if it is intermediate
between a rectangular and a Chinese lug sail. The Chinese lug sail
is stiffened by battens which serve a number of useful functions. A
stiffened sail is aerodynamically more efficient than a limp sail and
it is for this reason that the sails of modern yachts are stiffened
with battens. Battens also allow simple step-wise reefing of the sail
in high winds and almost eliminate the possibility of a sail being
torn away (Needham *et al* 1971:597). The rectangular lug sail
also spread westwards when the Indonesian seafarers crossed the
Indian Ocean to trade with East Africa and to inhabit the island of
Madagascar. The rectangular lug sail used today on the Nile boats
between the fourth and the second cataract may be a survival of
the rig introduced by the Indonesian seafarers (Hornell
1970:215). It is probable that the rectangular lug sail evolved
into the lateen (Fig. 9.11c 4) in the Indian Ocean or the Arabian
Sea. In the Mediterranean the earliest representation of a lateen
rig is on a second century AD gravestone in Greece (Casson
1971:244), though Rougé (1981:51) believes that the sails may
be square sails partly folded back. Casson (1971:268–9) also
argues that Synesius, who was later Bishop of Ptolemais, travelled
in a ship with a lateen rig from Alexandria to Cyrene in 404 AD.
The lateen sail was only ever used on the mizzen mast in
northern Europe, and even in the Mediterranean the square sail
eventually again replaced the lateen on large ships where the
square sail allowed the provision of more canvas.

   The aerodynamic force F_T on a sail can be given by a non-dimensional force coefficient C_T, the dynamic pressure acting on the sail $\frac{1}{2}\rho_a v_a^2$, and its area S_s by

$$F_T = \tfrac{1}{2}\rho_a v_a^2 S_s C_T \qquad (9.11)$$

where v_a is the *apparent* wind velocity. The force coefficient C_T depends on the sail's shape and its angle of incidence. The force coefficients for a square and a fore-and-aft sail are shown in a polar diagram where the lift coefficient C_L is plotted against the drag coefficient C_D (Fig. 9.12). The total force coefficient C_T is the vector that joins the origin to the point on the polar diagram for any particular angle of incidence of the sail, and the driving force coefficient C_R can be obtained by resolving this coefficient along the course the boat is sailing. The heeling force coefficient C_H is obtained by resolving C_T perpendicularly to the course of the boat. It can be seen that the square sail is superior on broad reaches where the course is more than about 135° off the apparent wind direction. However the higher aspect ratio (defined as height divided by mean width) for-and-aft sail is more efficient on closer reaches.

It is of course impossible to sail directly into the wind. The clippers of the nineteenth century could sail about 70° off the true wind direction; Polynesian sailing canoes could do better, but even they could not sail much closer than about 60° off the wind (Doran 1981:36). By sailing a zig-zag course a boat can make headway against a wind provided it can sail better than 90° off the wind. At the end of each leg of the zig-zag course the boat has

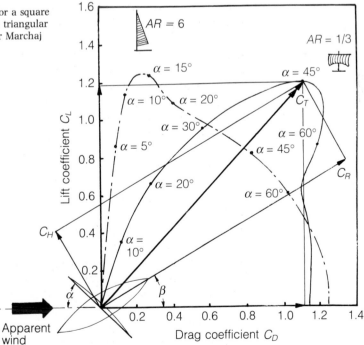

Fig. 9.12. Force coefficients for a square sail of low aspect ratio and a triangular sail of high aspect ratio (after Marchaj 1964: fig. 99).

to change direction, and the way in which it does this depends upon the type of boat. Most people are familiar with the technique of *tacking* adopted by yachts. As the yacht turns into the wind the sail goes slack, and as the yacht turns into its new course the wind is allowed to fall on the opposite side of the sail (Fig. 9.13a). When tacking is performed efficiently, the change in course can be undertaken with little loss in speed. However a square-rigged ship cannot tack, because the wind would fall on the wrong side of the sail, and has to go about in a manoeuvre known as *wearing* (Fig. 9.13b). Since it was difficult to execute a change in trim of a lateen rig quickly and tack without losing too much speed, wearing was also the usual means of working to windward with that rig, though tacking was occasionally performed (Bowen 1949). The Polynesians developed a completely different manoeuvre, known as *shunting*, for outriggers that had a crane

Fig. 9.13. Methods of changing course: (*a*) tacking; (*b*) wearing; (*c*) shunting.

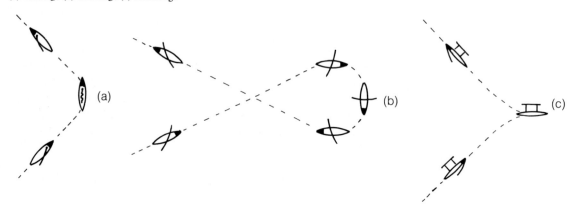

Fig. 9.14. Waves generated by a boat.

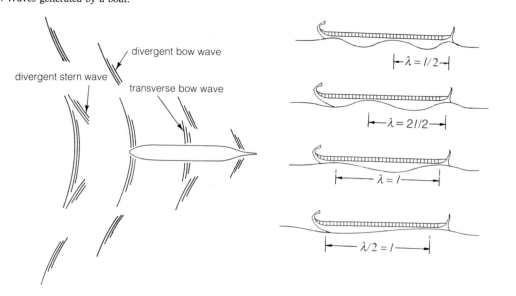

divergent stern wave

divergent bow wave

transverse bow wave

$\lambda = l/2$

$\lambda = 2l/2$

$\lambda = l$

$\lambda/2 = l$

sprit-sail (Doran 1981:36–8) (Fig. 9.11b 3). A single-outrigger canoe is more stable if the outrigger float is on the windward side. Sailing with the float on the leeward side is difficult because the float tends to submerge and can dig into the water, causing the canoe to capsize. The technique of shunting kept the float on the windward side of the canoe (Fig. 9.13c). The outrigger canoe is symmetrical, the bow being identical to the stern, and to change course the direction of the boat is reversed. The sails are hauled in slightly to turn the canoe out of the wind. As soon as this is done the sails are slacked completely and the rig shifted to the opposite end of the canoe. The sail is hauled in and the canoe takes off in the opposite direction on the next leg off the course. Such a manoeuvre is impossible without the crane mast. Clearly Doran (1981:41–3) is correct in categorising this rig as a form of sprit-sail rather than a lateen.

Water resistance

The speed of a boat is limited by the resistance of the water. The most-readily discernible form of resistance and the most important at high speed, is the creation of waves by the boat. Resistance is also offered by the friction of the water over a boat's surface. Only a thin boundary layer of water adjacent to the surface of the boat is affected, and this skin friction resistance is similar to that experienced by an arrow or spear in flight. Other less important forms of resistance are *form drag*, caused by the water breaking away from the boat's hull, and *eddy drag*, resulting from the eddies that form towards the stern.

The skin friction F_F of a boat's hull can be expressed in terms of a drag coefficient C_F and the dynamic force on the hull $\frac{1}{2}\rho_w v_b^2 S_b$ (where S_b is the wetted surface area). Thus

$$F_f = \tfrac{1}{2}\rho_w v_b^2 S_b C_F. \tag{9.12}$$

For all but the smoothest hulls[4] the boundary layer of water is almost entirely turbulent and the drag coefficient can be given as a function of the Reynolds number $R_e = v_b \rho_w L/\mu$, where L is the length of the waterline, μ the coefficient of viscosity of water ($1\cdot22 \times 10^{-3}$ kg m/s), and ρ_w its density (1025 kg/m³ for sea water). An accepted expression for the drag coefficient as a function of the Reynolds number (Barnaby 1969:200) is given by

$$C_f = \frac{0\cdot075}{(\log R_e - 2)^2}. \tag{9.13}$$

As a boat moves through the water energy-consuming waves are created just behind the bow and to a lesser extent behind the stern (Fig. 9·14). There are two systems of waves: short divergent ones with their centres lying on straight lines inclined at about 20° to the boat, and waves transverse to the boat. The short divergent waves are most noticeable after the passage of a boat because they decay slowly under the viscous

[4] The hull of a racing yacht is polished so that the transition from laminar to turbulent flow is delayed, thereby increasing the critical Reynolds number from about 10^6 to 5×10^6.

forces of the water. The transverse waves spread out behind the boat and decrease in height, so that the total energy of the wave remains constant. There is no interference between the two divergent waves at the bow and stern. The transverse waves however do interfere, and they have a marked effect on the resistance to the boat.

Because the wave system travels with the boat it appears stationary to an observer on board. The velocity of the wave propagation therefore must be equal to that of the boat. The velocity of propagation c of the waves generated by the boat depends upon their wave length λ and is given by

$$c = \sqrt{\frac{g\lambda}{2\pi}}. \tag{9.14}$$

Since the waves keep up with the boat and $c = v_b$ the length of the waves is given by

$$\lambda = \frac{2\pi v_b^2}{g}. \tag{9.15}$$

The characteristics of the waves and their resistance depends on the ratio of the wave length (λ) to the water-line length (l) of the boat. This ratio is expressed by the *Froude number*[5]

$$F = \left(\frac{\lambda}{2\pi l}\right)^{\frac{1}{2}} = \frac{v_b}{(lg)^{\frac{1}{2}}}. \tag{9.16}$$

If there were no interaction between the bow and stern transverse waves the wave-making resistance would steadily increase with the Froude number. However the trim of the boat depends on whether a crest or trough from the bow waves coincides with the stern wave's smaller crest. If a trough from the bow waves forms at the stern, the boat's stern will drop and the bow will rise, causing an increase in the resistance to the boat. This effect is most marked when the half-wave length is about equal to the waterline length of the boat (Rawson and Tupper 1968:347–9) which occurs when the boat's speed is given by

$$v_b = \left(\frac{lg}{2\pi}\right)^{\frac{1}{2}} = \begin{array}{l} 1 \cdot 25 \ \sqrt{l}\,(\text{m/s}) \\ 4 \cdot 5 \ \sqrt{l}\,(\text{km/h}). \end{array} \tag{9.17}$$

At this speed the change in trim causes such an increase in resistance that it represents the normal sailing limit even of modern heavy-displacement yachts.[6] The maximum probable speed for the clipper *Sovereign of the Seas*, whose waterline length was 79 m, is estimated from equation (9.17) to be 40 km/hr, which is almost the speed she attained on her record run. Equation (9.17) therefore provides a quick and easy check of the maximum speed possible by mono-hulled ships of the ancient world. The average speed during a voyage would probably be about half the maximum. During the first and second centuries BC the average length of a freighter was 28 m (Casson 1971:190) so we can estimate that their average speed under

[5] Named after William Froude who, in the 1870s, performed the first scientific experiments on a ship's resistance.
[6] Greater speeds can be achieved by yachts with planing hulls that use dynamic lift to rise out of the water.

favourable conditions was of the order of 12 km/hr (6 knots).
This speed corresponds to that recorded by Philostratus (VII, 10)
for a journey of 1240 km undertaken by Apollonius from Corinth
to Pateoli that took just under five days.

For practical evaluation of a ship's resistance it is usual to
add the minor forms of resistance, such as form and eddy drag, to
the wave-making resistance. Collectively they are called the
residual resistance. The most useful compilation of graphs of
residual resistance are those known as Taylor's Standard Series,
that were obtained by Admiral D. W. Taylor from tests performed
in 1910. A tabulation of these series is presented in terms of the
residual resistance per ton of displacement as a function of $v_b l^{-\frac{1}{2}}$
beam to draught ratio, and a coefficient that expresses the hull
shape (Barnaby 1969:219, 220). As an example we estimate the
performance of the trireme.

The performance of the trireme

There is no direct evidence available about the battle speeds
of the Greek triremes though there is an account by Thucydides
(III, IX, 49) of a famous dash of 345 km from Athens to the
island of Lesbos, when the city of Mytilene revolted against
Athenian rule and the public assembly of Athens, swayed by the
demagogue Cleon, decreed that all the male citizens of that city
were to be put to death and the women and children sold into
slavery. A trireme was despatched to carry the order to the
Athenian garrison, probably on the afternoon of the day the
assembly had voted. Thucydides, who was living in Athens at the
time, recorded that because of the dreadful nature of its mission
the trireme made no haste, which was fortunate because the next
day the assembly met again and repealed its harsh edict. A second
trireme was despatched with the countermanding order about 24
hours after the first trireme. The anxious envoys from Mytilene
encouraged the crew to row hard by promising a large reward if
the crossing was made in time. The men rowed and slept in turn
and so reached Mytilene at noon on the second day, shortly after
the arrival of the first trireme, and in time to save the populace. It
can be deduced from this account that the second trireme took
about 24 hours for the journey, from which can be calculated an
average speed of about 14 km/hr (7·5 knots). Let us look at how
reasonable this figure is for the maximum speed of a trireme.

To examine the performance of the trireme we must first
estimate its resistance as a function of its velocity. The skin
friction can be calculated from equations (9.12) and (9.13) using
the wetted surface area, 118 m², of the trireme reconstruction
(J. Coates pers. comm.). The residual resistance of the trireme can
be obtained from Taylor's Standard Series (Barnaby 1969:220).
Using these values we have drawn the total resistance curve
shown in Fig. 9.15.

If we assume that each oarsman contributed an effective

power of 190 W when making an all-out effort during ramming,
then the maximum power available from the 170 men would
have been about 32 kW. The driving force under oars can be
obtained by dividing the boat's power by its velocity (in m/s) and
is shown in Fig. 9.15. The maximum possible speed under oars of
about 20 km/hr (10.5 knots) is given by the intersection of the
driving force curve with the total resistance curve. Landels
(1978:167) obtained a very similar estimate of maximum speed.
The absolute speed of a trireme would be limited by the wave
resistance. Using equation (9.7), the maximum possible speed for
a trireme is found to be about 25 km/hr (13.7 knots) so there
would not be any point in cramming more oarsmen aboard a
trireme even if it were physically possible. The 170 oarsmen are

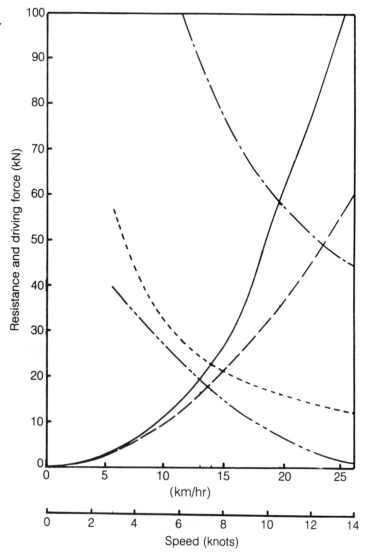

Fig. 9.15. Performance of a trireme
(——total resistance, ——skin friction,
—·—maximum oar driving force, ----
cruising oar driving force, ———sail
force in a 30 km/hr following wind).

about the optimum number for a trireme with a waterline length
of 32 m. It would have been impossible for the oarsmen to keep
up the maximum speed for very long. For periods of up to 8 hours
men can develop a continuous power of about 70 W (see Table
2.7). Assuming that the oars were 75% efficient, the effective
long-term power of 170 men would have been about 9 kW. Using
this value we estimate that the maximum cruising speed of the
trireme under oars was about 14 km/hr, a result that
corroborates Thucydides' account of the dash to Mytilene.

A trireme cruising with a favourable wind would hoist a
sail. Triremes probably carried two sails with a combined area of
about 120 m² (J. Coates pers. comm.). Even with sails of this
combined area, the yard would probably have been lowered in
anything more than a strong breeze. Lowering the yard would not
only reduce the sail area but, by dropping the centre of pressure,
lessen the chances of capsizing. Because of its limited stability and
the danger of swamping the boat it is unlikely that the sail would
have been fully unfurled in very strong winds. When running
with a 30 km/hr (8.33 m/s) wind, the apparent wind velocity
would have been $(8.33 - v_b)$ m/s, and the force on the sail
estimated from equation (9.11), assuming $C_T = 1.15$, is given by

$$F_T = 0{\cdot}085\,(8{\cdot}33 - v_b)^2.$$

This driving force, which decreases as the trireme travels
faster, is shown in Fig. 9.15. The sailing speed with a following
30 km/hr wind, obtained from the intersection of the driving force
curve with the resistance curve, is 13 km/hr (7 knots), or about
the same as the cruising speed under oars.

Steering and directional stability

Before the thirteenth century AD the steering of Western
vessels was accomplished with one or more large oars mounted
on the vessel's side, which is a steering method that is comparable
to the way a modern canoe is handled. The word 'starboard'
(literally, steering-board) comes from the northern European
custom of positioning the steering oar on the right-hand side of
the ship. On the earliest boats for which there are pictorial
records, the steering-oars were simply slung on the gunwales with
loops of rope. By the Fifth Dynasty (about 2500 BC) the
Egyptians were securing their steering-oars to posts rising well
above the hull and slightly forward of the gunwale fixing (Casson
1971:18). A tiller socketed to the steering-oar made the
helmsman's job easier. Apart from an Egyptian flirtation with a
stern position for the steering-oar, it remained positioned on the
side of the vessel in the Western world until Medieval times.

In contrast, the stern-rudder was adopted by the Chinese as
early as the first century BC (Needham *et al.* 1971:638, 639). To
some extent the construction of the junk may be responsible for
the early development of the Chinese stern-rudder. The typical

junk has neither keel nor sternpost; both the bow and stern are
square, and the rudder is suspended by rope tackles in a well at
the stern, rather than being mounted on a stern post (Needham
et al. 1971:632). Since it was an easy enough matter to raise the
rudder when the vessel was in shallow water it could be set well
below the level of the hull. The Western-style stern-rudder was
fixed to the hull and, to avoid damage, it did not project below
the level of the hull. It therefore had to operate entirely in the
turbulence of the vessel's wake. In this situation the side force, or
lift, generated when the rudder is turned is not nearly as large as
it can be if operated in water undisturbed by the vessel. For this
reason Western rudders had to be large. A further advantage of
the Chinese rudder was that it was balanced. That is, a portion of
it was positioned in advance of the pivot, so that it required a
comparatively small moment to turn it.[7] On the larger Western
ships of the seventeenth century as many as five or six men were
needed to hold onto the tiller during violent weather.

The steering-oar has some advantages over the Western
stern-rudder and its survival into recent history is hardly
surprising. A major advantage was that the steering-oar had an
ideal shape with a large aspect ratio. Also, it was operated from
the side of the boat and, because it could be easily raised, could
dip well below the bottom of the hull into water undisturbed by
the vessel's wake. The shape of the early steering-oar was not
unlike the rudder on today's popular racing catamaran, the Hobie
Cat, which also has a high aspect ratio and dips well below the
hull. The high aspect ratio of the steering-oar ensured that a large
lift or side force was generated by its aerofoil-like shape. The side
force F_s on a steering-oar can be expressed in terms of a side force
coefficient C_s (as can be done for a sail) so that

$$F_s = \tfrac{1}{2} \rho_w v_b^2 S_0 C_s. \tag{9.18}$$

Fig. 9.16 compares the side force coefficient of a steering-oar of
aspect ratio 5 with a rudder of aspect ratio 1. The narrow
steering-oar blade is about twice as efficient as a broad rudder at
the small angles of incidence that were probably used to keep the
boat on course. Large angles of incidence produce a large drag
and would therefore not be used, except for changing course.

Another advantage of the steering-oar was that it had
balance. The stock of the early steering-oars, like those on Cheop's
royal ship, was centred on the blade (Jenkins 1980:171). These
oars would have had imperfect balance because the centre of
pressure of a symmetrical aerofoil-like section is roughly one-third
of its width from the leading edge. On the other hand, the
steering-oar of Viking ships like the one found at Gokstad, had a
truly balanced blade with the stock positioned at about one-third
its width (Crumlin-Pedersen 1966). Little effort was required to
hold the tiller of a well-balanced steering-oar. In describing a
Roman superfreighter of just over 1000-tonne capacity the

---

[7] One of the earliest Western ships to
have a balanced rudder was Brunel's
Great Britain, built in 1843.

satirist, Lucianus of Samosato, probably did not exaggerate when he wrote: 'and all its cargo one little old man just now brought in safely, pivoting those huge steering-oars with a fragile tiller! They pointed him out to me; Heron was his name I think; woolley-haired little fellow, half bald' (Lucianus 6).

A replica of the newly discovered ninth-century Gokstad ship (Fig. 9.17) was built by the Norwegians and sailed to America for the Chicago exhibition of 1893. Since this exhibition was held to commemorate the 400th anniversary of the discovery of America by Columbus, the Norwegians wanted to show that it was quite feasible that Leif Ericson had preceded Columbus by some 500 years. Captain Magnus Andersen who commanded the replica of the Gokstad ship was sceptical of the efficiency of its steering-oar, but after his Atlantic voyage claimed that it was superior to a stern-rudder (Brøgger and Shetelig 1971:99–102). A replica of another Viking vessel, the Ladby ship, had a turning circle of four to six lengths. Even with only the starboard crew rowing, the ship could be made to turn to starboard, and it was possible to hold the helm in position with a single finger, despite the efforts of the crew to turn the ship the other way (Crumlin-Pedersen 1966).

The position of the mast also affects the steering of a boat. In Egypt the Nile boats of the Fifth Dynasty and earlier times had a mast stepped well forward of their centres, like on the ship depicted in a relief on Sahure's mortuary temple shown in Fig. 9.1 (Bowen 1960). Some illustrations even show the mast ahead of the waterline, but this is a stylistic over-

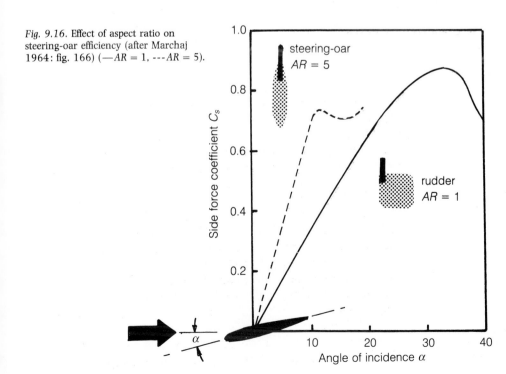

Fig. 9.16. Effect of aspect ratio on steering-oar efficiency (after Marchaj 1964: fig. 166) (—$AR = 1$, ---$AR = 5$).

emphasis of the hull's curvature. The river boats were sailed up the Nile with the prevailing north wind directly behind them. On the return journey, the mast and sail were lowered, and the boat allowed to drift with the Nile's flow. The well-forward sail position is suited to a following wind. When such a boat is tossed off-course by a sudden wind gust or a wave the forward sail quickly pulls the boat back to her original heading, in much the same way as a weathercock vane swings into the wind.

If a boat has a heeling force on its sail, it is necessary to steer slightly crabwise so that the hull makes a small angle to the boat's course and develops a hydrodynamic side-force or lift that can balance the heeling force of the sail. The hydrodynamic side-force acts through the centre of pressure of the hull, which is called the *centre of lateral resistance (CLR)*. With their symmetrical bow and stern sections the early boats had a centre of lateral resistance between a quarter and a third of their waterline length from the bow. The Egyptian boats had relatively flat bottoms that were inefficient at producing a side-force. Such boats have to sail

Fig. 9.17. The Gokstad ship.

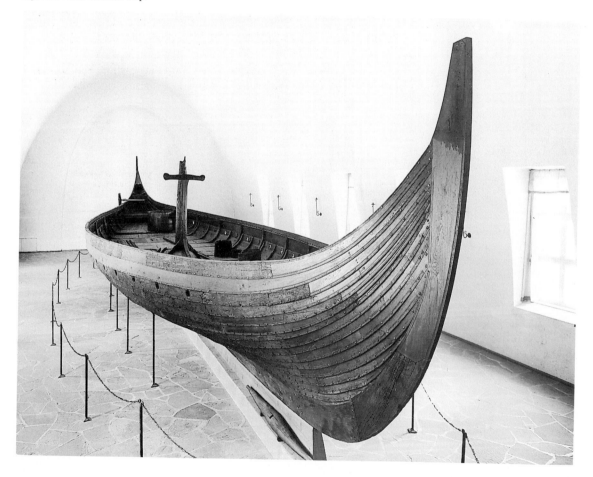

in a pronounced crabwise manner, which will cause a large increase in resistance. Their speed is reduced, and they are only able to sail on a very broad reach. It was the shape of the hull, rather than the sail, that prevented the early boats from making

Fig. 9.18. Effect of mast position on sailing efficiency.

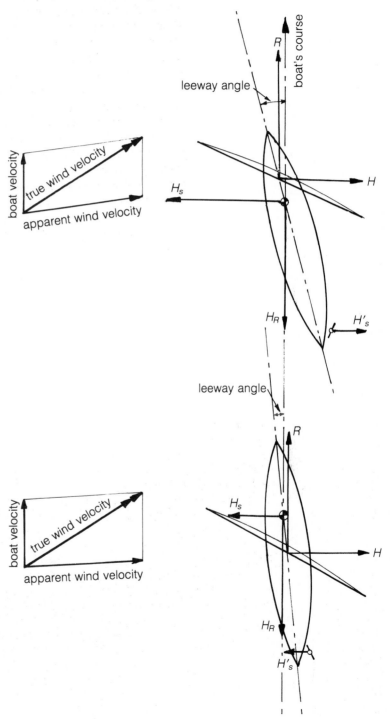

much headway into a wind, as anyone who tries to sail a
small boat without its centre-board will soon realise. It is
interesting that Viking boats did have small keels and deep knife-
like sections in the bow and stern which could have produced a
significant side-force. Without such a reasonably efficient hull the
Vikings would probably not have voyaged to the New World and
Columbus might truly have had the honour of being its first
European discoverer.

The mast on Egyptian sailing vessels after the Fifth Dynasty
was moved aft and, by the beginning of the New Kingdom
(*c.* 1500 BC), the mast was invariably located at the centre of the
boat, as it was on Queen Hatsheput's ships (Bowen 1960). This
shift reflects the increased sailing ability of the Egyptians who had
become adept at undertaking fairly lengthy sea voyages. On
single-masted square-rigged vessels, the mast stayed in a central
position until the present day because it is easier to sail a vessel
with a mast aft of the centre of lateral resistance. Let us compare
the forces on a boat with a forward mast sailing on a broad reach
to the forces on one with a centrally placed mast sailing on the
same apparent course (Fig. 9.18). With a forward mast it is
necessary to turn the steering-oar so that it holds the boat into
the wind. Unfortunately the side-force (H_s') on the steering-oar
adds to the heeling force (H) on the sail and these must be
balanced by the hydrodynamic side-force (H_s) on the hull. Such a
large side-force can only be obtained at large leeway angles,
causing an increase in the resistance of the boat. If the sail is
behind the centre of lateral resistance, as it is with a central mast,
then the steering-oar must hold the boat out of the wind. The
steering-oar can now provide a very significant part of the side-
force required to balance the heeling force on the sail.
Consequently the side-force that the hull must develop is much
reduced. The boat can be held on course with a smaller angle of
leeway, reducing its resistance and enabling it to sail faster. A
vessel with a central mast can be sailed more into the wind than
one with its mast forward of the centre of lateral resistance.

A modern yacht is also designed so that the centre of effort
of all its sails is behind the centre of lateral resistance of the hull.
However the distance between the centre of effort and the centre
of lateral resistance is kept small, because the hull with its keel or
centreboard can produce a large hydrodynamic side-force. The
rudder simply provides a small balance. In the early boats the
steering-oar made a much larger contribution to the total side-
force, which could only be utilised if there was a fair distance
between the centre of effort and centre of lateral resistance.

10

Musical instruments

In its broadest sense music, like speech, is a form of communicating by mutually understood patterns of sound. Appreciation of music is universal. It is so much part of human behaviour that it may well pre-date speech and all but the simplest of technology. In understanding the past, the study of ancient musical instruments and the music they made is surely important.

Over the years a good deal of effort has gone into reconstructions of musical instruments since they are rarely found intact and in good condition. Musical instruments were commonly made from perishable or delicate materials such as wood, bamboo, fibre, skin, horn or bone, and if they did survive their entombment or burial it was usually only just, with the more delicate parts long ago consumed by soil acids and microbes. Naturally the older the instrument the more likely it is to be poorly preserved. Most good finds are from undisturbed burials – the tomb of Tutankhamun, the royal tombs of Ur, and the western Han tombs at Zhangsha. One of the Han tombs opened up in 1972 contained a complete ensemble of dozens of musical instruments neatly laid out as part of a ghostly banquet for an aristocrat who had evidently been fond of the good life. The condition of these instruments was remarkable – even the strings on a 2000-year-old zither were preserved. However close inspection by archaeologists of the items revealed that a number of them were unplayable, cheap imitations that must have been specifically made as funerary goods. Obviously the gesture was thought to be enough to guarantee the occupant's needs in the afterworld.

Other details about the design and methods of playing ancient musical instruments come from illustrations on tomb walls, pottery vessels and cylinder seals, and from early written documents. It was not until an important find of cuneiform tablets in 1962 that Babylonian musical theory was first revealed. There is still much to learn from these different sources, especially about early Chinese music that in many ways was much more sophisticated than that of the civilisations to the west.

The nature of sound

Sound always originates as some kind of motion. The sound of a drum that has been struck, or a guitar string that has been plucked, can be immediately traced to the rapidly vibrating membrane or string. With wind instruments, where the air is the primary medium, the motion is not so obvious. To be heard these sounds have to be transmitted from that source to the ear and, unlike light, they need a medium through which to travel. The vibration at the source of sound sets in motion the air between it and the listener, a phenomenon that Robert Boyle (1627–91) was able to illustrate by placing a watch 'with a good alarm' inside a vacuum chamber. Because Boyle could not hear the alarm go off, he concluded that 'whether or not the air be the only, it is at least the principal medium of sounds' (Wood 1975:2). If the dog-fights between the spacecraft in the film 'Star Wars' had been real, the spectacular explosions would have taken place in a deathly silence.

A vibrating body alternatively compresses and expands the adjacent air. These undulations propagate outwards in much the same manner as ripples on a pond.[1] That sound needs time to travel is a common observation – lighting is followed by thunder and our voices echo off cliff walls. The first experiments to measure the speed of sound were performed by Pierre Gassendi (1592–1655), who measured the time interval between observing the flash and hearing the report of cannons and muskets (Wolf 1950:286). The velocity given by Gassendi, 1473 Paris feet per second (478 m/s), was much too high, as was that given by Marin Mersenne (1588–1648), the Franciscan friar who in 1636 published *Harmonie universelle* which gave the theory of vibrating strings and related the pitch of a note to the frequency of vibration. The actual speed of sound at 15 °C is 340 m/s. While the speed of sound is independent of pressure, it does increase with temperature at about 0·6 m/s for each degree centigrade (Duncan and Starling 1950:663). This phenomenon is noticeable with wind instruments which rise slightly in pitch as they warm

Table 10.1 *Power of various musical instruments*

Source	Power in watts
bass drum	25
trombone	6
piano	0·4
bass tuba	0·2
flute	0·06
bass voice	0·03
alto voice (softly voiced)	0·001
violin (softest passage)	0·000004

Source: Wood 1975:34

[1] The analogy of the ripples in a pool of water is an old one, cited as early as the second century BC by the Chinese scholar Dong Zhong-Shu (Needham and Wang 1962:202), and three centuries later by the Roman engineer, Vitruvius (V, 3, 6).

up – for this reason the woodwind section of an orchestra has a warming-up session prior to a concert. Extremely loud sounds, such as the report of a cannon, travel slightly faster than normal.

Musical instruments radiate energy as sound and the range in power that they emit can be enormous (Table 10.1). The intensity of sound, defined as the power passing a unit area perpendicular to the direction of propagation of the sound, decreases as it radiates outwards. If a source in mid-air radiates sound equally in all directions, the intensity at a distance r is the power of source P divided by the area of the spherical surface ($4\pi r^2$) over which it has spread. In practice, of course, sources are not usually in mid-air, nor do they radiate sound equally in all directions. Nevertheless the intensity of sound does decrease roughly in proportion to the square of the distance from the source. Human hearing is sensitive to the intensity of a sound and can register a remarkably wide range. Hearing varies from person to person, but its threshold is generally about 10^{-12} W/m^2, and for a short time we can tolerate sounds as loud as 1 W/m^2 without damage to our ears. It is obvious that the sensation of sound is not proportional to its intensity – a bass drum does *not* sound six million times as loud as a softly played violin. To most people, the sensation of loudness increases in steps that are roughly equal to a tenfold increase in intensity. Therefore two sounds are said to differ in sound level by one unit when their intensities are in the ratio of ten. This unit is called the *bel*, in honour of Alexander Graham Bell, the inventor of the telephone. From Table 10.1 it can be seen that a trombone is about two bels louder than a flute heard at the same distance. An intensity of sound at the threshold of human hearing of 10^{-12} W/m^2 is taken as having zero loudness, and the loudness L in bels of a sound intensity of I W/m^2 is defined by

$$L = \log_{10}(I \times 10^{12}).\qquad(10.1)$$

For practical purposes the bel is usually too large and a smaller unit, the decibel, which is equal to a tenth of a bel, is more commonly used.

We recognise only some sounds as musical notes. The reason for this selectiveness is that sound waves arising from a noise have no pattern in the sequence of compression and rarefractions arriving at the ear, whereas musical notes have a definite pattern.

The pitch and quality of a musical note

Over long distances a sound in which there is a sudden change of pitch can be heard more easily than an ordinary shout. In the European Alps it was yodelling that commanded attention of a person on the opposite side of a mountain valley, while in the Australian bush the cry 'coo-ee' was similarly a common long-distance signal. Some animal calls, such as the song of a bird, are a succession of notes of definite pitch. Other animal calls, such as for instance the hiss and growl of the Tasmanian Devil, we regard as noise. In most 'developed' music styles, and particularly in Western music, the most important pattern comes from the control of clearly distinguishable intervals of pitch. Rhythm often plays an important part, especially in African music, but since there is little to say about its mechanics, this aspect of music, though important, will not be discussed.

A musical note is a regular succession of waves of compression and expansion. The frequency, in cycles per second, or hertz (Hz), at which these waves impress our eardrums gives the *pitch* of the note. The idea of a note having pitch is as ancient as tonal music. Galileo realised that pitch depended on the frequency of vibration when he scraped a brass plate with a chisel and noticed that the note emitted was higher in pitch when the chattermarks were close together (Galileo 1638:144–5). Absolute standards in pitch are comparatively modern except in China where the pitch pipe that sounded the basic Huang zhong note was made the basis of not only musical standards but also those of length, volume and weight (Needham and Wang 1962:199).[2] Elsewhere musical instruments had to be adjusted to the local standard. With stringed instruments these adjustments can be done easily by changing the tension in the strings. Wind instruments can be a lot more difficult to tune. For instance, in the Solomon Islands, the vital statistics of the host's panpipes had to be sent to the guests well before an inter-village 'sing-sing' could be held.

When a single note is played on two different instruments it will have the same pitch. Yet each instrument has its own sound quality. The difference in quality between notes can be displayed visually if the output from a microphone is fed to an oscilloscope where the pressure signals are converted into electrical pulses. Tracings of such signals for instruments sounding the same note are shown in Fig. 10.1. The patterns of the notes are all repeated in the same frequency, but the shapes of the wave forms are different. While studying the conduction of heat the French mathematician, Joseph Fourier (1768–1830), discovered that any complex wave form could be broken down into simple forms (Taylor 1959:383; Wood 1975;68). The basic waveform is almost identical to one obtained from a tuning fork. The tone corresponding to this wave form, called a *simple harmonic wave*, is a pure tone. Although not unpleasant to the ear, a pure tone is lifeless. It is the characteristic complexity of the wave forms of the various instruments that gives each its distinctive quality.

The amplitude y of a simple harmonic wave at time t is given by

$$y = a \sin 2\pi f t \tag{10.2}$$

where a is the maximum amplitude and f the frequency. Many mechanical systems such as pendulums and weights attached to

---

[2] Before the relationship between pitch and frequency was known in Europe, standards of pitch were fixed by assigning distinct notes to organ pipes of different standard lengths. The first modern standard was suggested by Praetorius in 1619 whose standard corresponded to a frequency of 424 Hz for A in the treble clef. On the eve of World War II an international conference in London fixed A in the treble clef at 440 Hz (Wood 1975:47–9).

springs, as well as musical instruments have oscillations that are harmonic.

The great German physicist and mathematician, Herman von Helmholtz (1821–1899), applied Fourier's analysis to musical notes and showed that the amplitude of any note could be represented by a series

$$y = a_1 \sin 2\pi ft + a_2 \sin 2\pi(2ft) + a_3 \sin 2\pi(3ft) + \ldots \tag{10.3}$$

The first term in this series with the lowest frequency f is called the *fundamental note*, or first *partial* (Wood 1975:70). The other terms have frequencies that are whole number multiples of the fundamental frequency, and are called *overtones* or higher order partials. The amplitudes of the higher partials are usually less than that of the fundamental note and decrease with the order of the partial. A well-trained ear can identify these higher order partials. The Greeks appreciated that the note of a musical instrument contained higher notes, as problem 8 in book 19 of the Aristotelian *Problemata* indicates. The flute's clear and simple tone arises because its note is composed of even-order higher partials, only the first three of which are present to any degree. In

Fig. 10.1. Wave forms of a tuning fork and various wind instruments: (*a*) pure note; (*b*) flute; (*c*) clarinet; (*d*) obe (after Wood 1975: pl V).

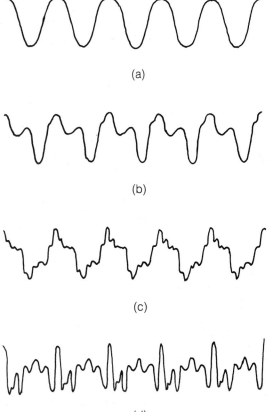

(a)

(b)

(c)

(d)

Fig. 10.2 we have drawn a hypothetical composite note which is the sum of a fundamental and an overtone of twice the fundamental frequency and three-quarters its maximum amplitude. Notice how similar this hypothetical note is to the note of the flute shown in Fig. 10.1. The clarinet's reedy tone comes from particularly strong eighth and ninth partials. The oboe is weak in the fundamental and strong in the fourth and fifth partials, a combination which gives it a characteristic haunting tone (Wood 1975:71).

The quality of an instrument's note, therefore, depends upon the strength of its partials which all combine to form a complex tone. It is the intrument-maker's job to ensure that the tone is pleasing. The fundamental note sounded by a violin made in Taiwan is the same as that of a Stradivarius, but its quality is completely different.

Harmony and musical scales

When two different notes are sounded together to form a *chord* the result can be either pleasing and harmonious or jarring and discordant. A person's judgement on the degree of harmony depends to a large extent on the regularity of the actual physical combination of the notes, though it also depends on one's personal interpretation. A worldwide comparison on tonal music has revealed that people regard certain frequency intervals, such as the octave, fifth and fourth, as pleasing. The ratios of the frequencies in these musical intervals are very simple; namely 2:1, 3:2 and 4:3 respectively. The Pythagorean philosophers perceived music as a mathematical system of harmoniously arranged numbers. Knowing that the octave, fifth and fourth could be obtained on a single-string instrument by dividing the string's length into a half, two-thirds and three-quarters, they

Fig. 10.2. A composite note formed by a fundamental and its first overtone (fundamental -—-, first overtone ---, composite note ——).

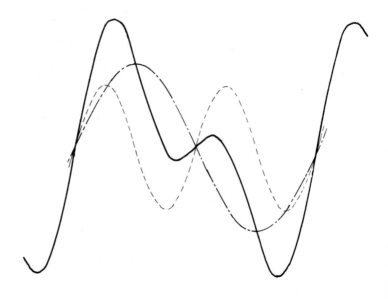

thought that the pleasing effect came from the beauteous simplicity of the ratios. The notion of harmony in numbers was a basic tenet in Pythagorean philosophy and it was thought that the distances of the planets from earth conformed to the musical intervals, so that they rang with 'the music of the spheres' (Aristotle, *De Caelo* II, IX).

Von Helmholtz believed that clashing of the fundamentals on their higher partials was the cause of dissonance. When two notes of slightly different frequency, f_1, and f_2, are sounded together, what we hear is a note of the average frequency $(f_1 + f_2)/2$, but with a variation in amplitude known as 'beating' (Wood 1975:158). In mathematical terms the composite sound is the sum of the two harmonic motions which, assuming that they have the same amplitude, can be written as

$$y = a \sin 2\pi f_1 t + a \sin 2\pi f_2 t,$$

which can also be expressed as

$$y = 2a \sin 2\pi \frac{(f_1 + f_2)}{2} t \cos 2\pi \frac{(f_1 - f_2)}{2} t. \tag{10.4}$$

The composite wave has a frequency of $(f_1 + f_2)/2$ with a slower variation in amplitude at a frequency of $(f_1 - f_2)/2$ as we show graphically in Fig. 10.3. Helmholtz suggested that the beating effect gave a rough unpleasant sound (Pierce 1983:74–81). Two notes a semitone apart appear harsh because their frequencies are close and we hear their beats. A perfectly tuned octave is the most consonant of intervals because all the higher partials of the notes correspond in frequency (Fig. 10.4). However, if the octave is even slightly out of tune, the beats that occur between all the higher partials make it sound harsh. When a chord with an interval of a fifth is played most partials correspond, and those that do not are too far from those of the fundamental to cause beating. Some beating can occur when a major third chord is played, because the third partial of the higher note is close to the fourth partial of the fundamental, as is the fifth partial of the higher note and the sixth partial of the fundamental. Hence a major third is not as consonant as an octave or perfect fifth. Von Helmholtz constructed a curve giving the degree of dissonance when the lowest C on the violin was held steady on one instrument while the other starting in unison glided slowly

Fig. 10.3. Beats formed by two notes of nearly the same frequency.

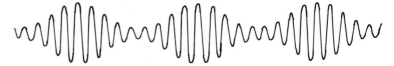

upwards in pitch (Fig. 10.5). However, if pure tones containing no upper partials are played, most people when asked to grade the degree of dissonance from 1 to 10 still match von Helmholtz's curve remarkably well. The perception of consonance and dissonance is not only the result of the nature of the sounds themselves but has to do with the way the mind recognises them. Since a person's appreciation of music is linked to wave pattern recognition, Pythagoras may have been right about the beauty of numbers – most people do seem to enjoy the simpler forms of perfect fifths and fourths.

Because of the subjectiveness in our perception of sound we can be deluded into hearing what is not actually there. Just as we have optical illusions, such as the fatigue effect that makes us see

Fig. 10.4. Partials present with an octave, fifth, major third and semitone.

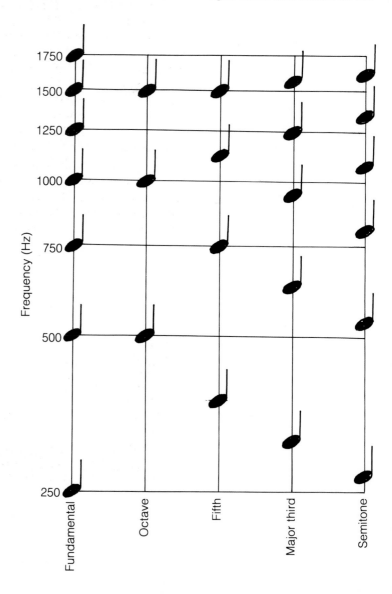

a green spot straight after looking at a bright red one, so too are there aural illusions. One of these aural illusions is revealed by our perception of 'white noise', a sound that has a random array of all the frequencies within the range of human hearing. If one listens to a noise which only has a single frequency filtered out, it still sounds like real 'white noise'. But if one immediately afterwards listens to a full complement of random frequencies the person will 'hear' the note belonging to the previously missing frequency (Taylor 1976:159). Aural illusion is probably important in our perception of the primary note of Western bells. The partials of bells, unlike those of string or wind instruments, do not form an harmonic series with the fundamental note. What is usually identified as the primary note of a Western bell is an octave below the fifth partial, a note that cannot be picked up by resonance (Wood 1975:153–4). The primary note of a Western bell has no physical reality; its existence is only in the listener's mind. As we shall see later, the ancient Chinese had a better understanding of bell construction.

The number of notes available for music composition is infinite, and yet even in the world's most complex musical forms only very few are selected. A series of such specially chosen notes is called a *scale*. Amongst non-literate peoples these scales are unconscious and the variation in pitch that is accepted is much greater than in Western music. The simplest scales, found in the Americas, India, Siberia and the Pacific, comprise only two or three intervals in an octave. With ethnic music the most common scale is pentatonic with five intervals to the octave. In southern China the pentatonic scale consists entirely of whole tones which

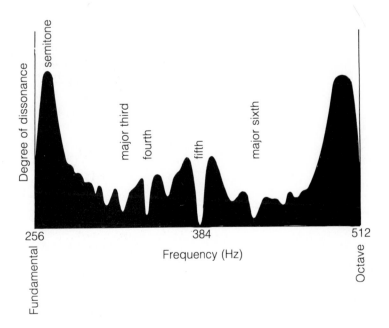

Fig. 10.5. Von Helmholtz's curve of dissonance.

roughly correspond to *do, re, mi, so, la* in the West's heptatonic *so-fa* (Needham and Wang 1962:155).[3]

    Musical scales are based on definite pitch intervals which are the ratio of the frequencies of notes. The theoretical scales first appeared in both Greece and China during the sixth century BC, and it is quite possible that they had a common origin in the Near East (Needham and Wang 1962:176–83). Pythagoras is said to have visited Babylon, and there exists a parallel story about a westward journey by Ling Lum, a minister to Huang Di, the legendary Yellow Emperor.

    The Greek scales were based on the tetrachord, a four-stringed instrument, whose range was a perfect fourth (4/3) (Taylor 1928:136–46). The intervals between the notes of the tetrachord were classified into three types: diatonic, chromatic and enharmonic (Wood 1975:173–5). In the diatonic type, which corresponds to modern Western music, there were two major tones (9/8) and a *limma* or 'remnant' (256/243) which is similar to our semitone (16/15). The scale was extended by adding a second tetrachord to the first, either with the last note of one corresponding to the first of the other, or disjunctively, so that the first note of the second tetrachord made a fifth (3/2) with the last note of the first one. With a disjunct tetrachord we have a heptatonic scale similar to the Western scale. Depending on the disposition of the semitone seven different modes are theoretically possible, though it is not certain that all of these were actually used. Plato (*Republic* III:398–9) only approved of the 'dignified' Dorian and 'persuasive' Phrygian modes, while condemning

Table 10.2 *Comparison of the intervals in various scales*

Equal temperament	Major key in Western just temperament	Greek Dorian Mode	Chinese	Indian Shadja grāma
1·000	1·000	1·000	1·000	1·000
1·059		$1·053(\frac{256}{243})$	$1·068(\frac{2187}{2048})$	
1·122	$1·125(\frac{9}{8})$		$1·125(\frac{9}{8})$	$1·125(\frac{9}{8})$
1·189		$1·185(\frac{32}{27})$	$1·201(\frac{19683}{16384})$	
1·260	$1·250(\frac{5}{4})$		$1·266(\frac{81}{64})$	$1·250(\frac{5}{4})$
1·335	$1·333(\frac{4}{3})$	$1·333(\frac{4}{3})$	$1·352(\frac{177147}{131072})$	$1·333(\frac{4}{3})$
1·414			$1·424(\frac{729}{512})$	
1·498	$1·500(\frac{3}{2})$	$1·500(\frac{3}{2})$	$1·500(\frac{3}{2})$	$1·500(\frac{3}{2})$
1·587		$1·580(\frac{128}{81})$	$1·602(\frac{6561}{4096})$	
1·682	$1·667(\frac{5}{3})$		$1·688(\frac{27}{16})$	$1·688(\frac{27}{16})$
1·782		$1·778(\frac{16}{9})$	$1·802(\frac{59049}{32768})$	
1·888	$1·875(\frac{15}{8})$		$1·898(\frac{243}{128})$	$1·875(\frac{15}{8})$
2·000	2·000	2·000	$2·027(\frac{531441}{262144})$	2·000

---

[3] Guido D'Arezzo, a Benedictine monk of the eleventh century, named the notes in the tonic set after the first syllables in successive half lines of a Latin hymn.

Lydian (which is similar to the major keys in Western music) and Mixolydian modes for their dirge-like harmonies, which he regarded as 'unsuited even for women'. The relative frequencies of the notes in the Dorian mode are given in Table 10.2.

The Chinese used their musical knowledge to construct tuned sets of chimestones (*qing*) and bells that could be played in more than one key. Even with pentatonic music twelve intervals, each of a semitone, are needed in an octave, just like in a modern piano which has an octave of eight white and four black keys to enable music to be played in any key. While the Greeks derived their scales from a single-string instrument (called a monochord), the Chinese used pitchpipes. The *Lü shi chun qiu* (239 BC) gives the earliest description of the way in which the lowest note engenders the others (Needham and Wang 1962:173). In the Chinese system the length of the pitch pipe is multiplied by either $\frac{2}{3}$ or $\frac{4}{3}$, so that the notes are kept within the compass of a single octave. The corresponding frequency ratios, taken as the reciprocals of the pipe lengths, are given in Table 10.2. In the Chinese system only the fifth is perfect; apparently even the octave is untrue. However it is inconceivable that the Chinese, who revered the musician able to detect small differences in pitch, would not in practice have had a perfect octave.

The classical Indian system of scales is similar to our Western one. Each note is associated with the cry of an animal: for example the sixth note, the *Dhaivata*, is likened to the croak of a frog excited by love (Wellesz 1957: 205–7). The ear is considered to be able to distinguish sixty-six intervals, or scrutis, in an octave, but in practice only twenty-two scrutis are used. According to the *Nātya Shāstra* and Matanga in his *Brihaddeshī*, both written sometime between the second century BC and the fourth century AD, the scruti is the difference between a minor (10/9) and a major tone (9/8). Three scales or *grāmas* were used in ancient Indian music. The main scale *Shadja grāma* is given in Table 10.2, and the second scale *Madhyama grāma* was the same as the major key in Western just temperament. A third scale *Gāndhāra grāma* was known in ancient times, but its nature has not been described in the texts (A. Daniélou, *Northern Indian Music* (Praeger, New York, 1969), pp. 29–52).

In Europe the development of harmony led to a scale that had simpler frequency ratios than either the Greek or Chinese scales. This *Just Temperament Scale* (Table 10.2), devised in 1560 by Gioseffo Zarlino of Venice, gives better consonance for most chords because more partials correspond (Wood 1975:185–6). The Just Scale is not perfect since the twelve semitones are unequal. Fixed note instruments such as the piano cannot be exactly in tune in every key. While an ordinary person would not be able to detect the very slight inaccuracies in pitch, they must have been a worry to the Chinese who were the first to use the *Equal Temperament Scale*.

In the Equal Temperament Scale, introduced by Zha Zai-Yu

in AD 1584, the octave is divided into twelve equal intervals so that all keys can be played with the same accuracy (Needham and Wang 1962:220–8). The equal temperament semitone has an interval of $2^{\frac{1}{12}}$. While it is very easy today to compute a twelfth root with a pocket calculator, it would have been a formidable task in the sixteenth century. Chinese algebraists could handle roots of high powers in the thirteenth century, but Zhu Zai-Yu was unaware of their work and had to resort to a method of calculation involving only square and cube roots. In the Equal Temperament Scale (Table 10.2) every interval is an irrational number that cannot be expressed as a ratio of two numbers no matter how large they are. Such a scale would have been an anathema to the Pythagoreans, believing as they did that ultimate reality existed in pure numbers. This principle was such dogma in the School's philosophy that one of its members, Hippasus, was expelled for revealing that the square root of two was an irrational number (Diels 1912:36–7). Quite possibly the Equal Temperament Scale was introduced to Europe by Simon Stevin, the man responsible for the adoption of another Chinese innovation, the land yacht (Needham and Wang 1962:227).

Musical instruments

In their classification of musical instruments the ancient Greeks had three major divisions: string, wind, and percussion. In our modern classification, which is identical to the traditional Indian one, percussion instruments are subdivided into idiophones, where the vibrating member is rigid, (as with xylophones), and membranophones, where it is a stretched membrane (such as on a drum). The ancient Chinese, following a completely different path, classified their instruments according to the eight materials from which they were constructed: metal, stone, earth, skin, silk, wood, gourd and bamboo (Needham and Wang 1962:142). We shall follow the modern classification and start with stringed instruments (chordophones) because their mechanical behaviour is the easiest to understand.

Chordophones or stringed instruments

The earliest stringed instruments may well have originated from the hunting bow since the musical nature of the sound emitted by a plucked bowstring can be immediately appreciated (Marcuse 1975:178–81). Unenhanced, the note remains weak, and for a musical bow to be effective it needs a resonator. The simplest resonator available is the player's open mouth, which, with changes of shape, can produce a few overtones. A second common form of resonator is the gourd (Fig. 1.2). A tuning loop makes it possible to divide the string into two parts to produce two separate notes, while a further note can be obtained by stopping the string with the back of a finger. A variation of the musical bow is the ground bow – again a very simple instrument. Its resonator is a pit covered with a piece of bark weighed down

with stones (Marcuse 1975:378–81). One end of the bow is fixed
in the ground beside the pit, and the other end tied to the piece of
bark with a string. The ground bow's note can be altered by
changing the tension on the string, giving a range of a fifth.
Another method used for special effects is to stop the string by
holding it between the thumb and forefinger.

Stringed instruments require a resonator of some kind that
is vibrated by the bridges or supports of the string to enhance
their sound. It is important that the resonator does not have a
predominant resonant frequency, as such a frequency would be
disproportionately loud. The resonators of primitive stringed
instruments have varied widely in their forms. During the
Classical Greek period the lyre had a tortoiseshell resonator with a
skin belly, as do some Ugandan lyres today (Marcuse 1975:363,
377). The larger lyre, or *kithara*, used by professional Greek
musicians, was designed with a wooden box-like resonator. In
South Africa the primitive folk guitar, called a *ramkie*, had a skin-
covered resonator; old tin cans are now used as a less aesthetic
but practical substitute (Kirby 1968:246–56).

A range of pitch is obtained from a stringed instrument by
either having multiple strings or stopping them. 'Primitive' music
usually has a small pitch range with few notes, and so most
simple instruments are played with open strings. Even in Classical
Greece, where the stopped monochord was used to establish
musical theory, most instruments had open strings. The only
fretted instrument the Greeks had was a three-stringed long-
necked lute, called the *trichordian*, which is thought to have
originated in the Caucasus region of southern Russia (Marcuse
1975:406–8). The earliest fretted instrument in China was the
long zither called the *qin*, which is documented from about
1100 BC (Marcuse 1975:193–7). This instrument had a single
melody string that was stopped, and six open strings for the
accompaniment.

All stringed instruments require some provision for tuning.
The tuning peg, with which we are familiar today, was developed
during the first millennium AD in Byzantium and was completely
unknown in earlier times. The lyres of Classical Greece were
tuned by wrapping the string around the yoke with a narrow
strip of rawhide (Marcuse 1975:364). This tuning ring, called a
kollops, was twisted to alter the tension, a method of tuning that
is still done in parts of Africa. Levers were used for tuning on the
Sumerian lyres (*c.* 3000 BC) discovered in the royal cemetery at
Ur (Rimmer 1969). The string was wrapped around the lever and
a number of turns taken around the yoke of the lyre so that the
friction between the string and the yoke was sufficient to hold the
string and tuning was attained by moving the lever. The strings
of the Sumerian and Indian arched harps were wound around the
neck without any special fastening device, whereas the Egyptian
harp had knobs to secure them (Fig. 10.6). Sachs (1940:93)
believed that the knobless harps evolved from those with knobs

Fig. 10.6. An Egyptian musician
playing an arched harp that has knobs
for fixing the strings.

because it was easier to tune a harp by simply pushing the string along the neck. A harp with knobs to fix the string could only be tuned by untying the strings, changing the tension and retying them. If Sachs' hypothesis is correct then the harp, as he points out, is an example of an artifact becoming more sophisticated but structurally simpler with time. However the strings on a knobless harp would perhaps become out of tune more easily during playing by the strings slipping down the neck, so we are not completely convinced by Sachs' argument.

The Greeks and the Chinese knew that the pitch of a string was inversely proportional to its length, though it was not until the seventeenth century that the quantitative relationship between the frequency of a string and its length, mass and tension were established by Mersenne. When the end of a slightly stretched rope is jerked, a wave travels down it and is reflected at the other end. Waves travel in a similar fashion along a vibrating string, but they are not apparent because a *standing wave* is established. In Fig. 10.7 two waves *a* and *b* of equal amplitude are shown propagating in opposite directions along a stretched string for half of the period of vibration $1/(2f)$. The total displacement of the string is the algebraic sum of these two waves which gives the standing wave that we actually see. We cannot perceive the propagation of the individual waves. Since the ends of a string are fixed in an instrument, the displacement here must always be zero. Mathematically we can express the two travelling waves by

$$y_a = a \sin \frac{\pi}{l}(x - ct)$$

$$y_b = a \sin \frac{\pi}{l}(x + ct)$$

where l is the length of the string and c is the velocity of propagation of the waves. These two amplitudes when added (see Appendix III) give

$$y = y_a + y_b = 2a \sin \frac{\pi x}{l} \cos \frac{\pi ct}{l} \tag{10.5}$$

which represents a vibrating string whose frequency of vibration is given by

$$f = \frac{c}{2l}. \tag{10.6}$$

It can be shown that the velocity of propagation of a wave along a string stretched to a tension T is given by

$$c = \sqrt{\frac{T}{m}}. \tag{10.7}$$

where m is the mass per unit length of the string. The fundamental frequency of a vibrating string is therefore

$$f = \frac{1}{2l} \sqrt{\frac{T}{m}}. \tag{10.8}$$

This equation was established empirically by Mersenne, and Galileo (1638) published the same result in his *Dialogues* two years later. Mersenne also noticed, what the Greeks long before had discovered, that a vibrating string produces overtones in addition to the fundamental note. However it was Joseph Sauveur (1653–1716) who first demonstrated that the overtones could be clearly produced by lightly touching the vibrating string at points

Fig. 10.7. Formation of a standing wave in a vibrating string (travelling wave——, stationary wave——).

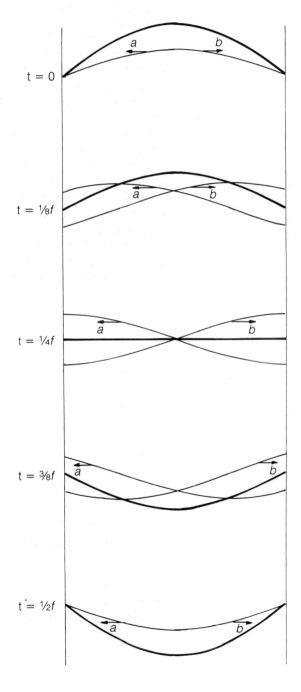

which divide it into simple ratios (Wolf 1950:283). The points where the string is at rest Sauveur called *nodes*. The frequencies of the higher order vibrations correspond to the fundamentals of strings of length l/n where n is the order of the partial (Fig. 10.8). Therefore the frequencies of the partials are given by

$$f = \frac{n}{2l}\sqrt{\frac{T}{m}}.$$ (10.9)

Higher order partials are always present and give quality to the note.

Aerophones, or wind instruments

The source of mankind's earliest music must logically have been the sounds of the human voice. By forcing a stream of air through our reed-like vocal chords we can create notes, their pitch depending on the length and tension of the chords. Just as with strings, the shorter the length of the vocal chords the higher the note. Women's vocal chords are about 12 mm long, compared with 20 mm for men. The speaking voices of men and women have average frequencies of 145 and 230 Hz respectively, which are in almost the inverse ratio of the vocal chord lengths (Wood 1975:132–3). In singing, we can vary pitch by changing the tension in the vocal chords. This provides a range of about four octaves from a bass singer's lowest note of about 66 Hz to a soprano's highest note of about 1056 Hz.

One can only speculate about the identity of the first wind instruments. Notes can be blown on conch shells, animal horns, or on almost any similar hollow resonator. Undoubtedly horns which give only single notes were employed initially as signalling

Fig. 10.8. Possible modes of vibration of a string (a) fundamental, (b) first overtone, (c) second overtone, (d) third overtone.

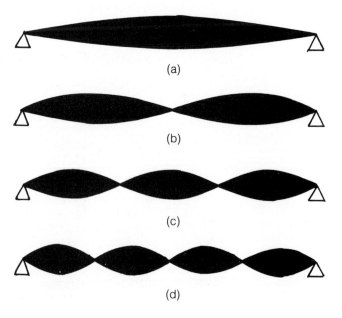

(a)

(b)

(c)

(d)

instruments. The possibility of overblowing, that is, blowing harder than normal so as to produce an overtone rather than the fundamental, gave these early horns a musical potential that must have soon been exploited. All the wind instruments can be separated into three major families on the basis of how the air is made to vibrate.

With the flute family of wind instruments the forced air flow impinges on a sharp edge to produce vortices that break away and excite the air in the resonator. The sounds of trumpet-like instruments are created by the player's lips vibrating against a mouthpiece. With reed instruments the player's breath excites a reed that sets the air in the resonator vibrating.

A Magdalenian rock painting in the Trois Frères cave in France is claimed to depict a sorcerer playing an end-blown flute (Seewald 1934:42–3). Fragmentary bird-bone flutes found in the Aurignacian III levels of the Isturitz caves in the Basses-Pyrénées show that comparatively sophisticated instruments were being made by the beginning of Upper Palaeolithic times (Megaw 1968). Side-blown flutes, such as the modern orchestral type, are thought to have originated somewhere in Central Asia during the first millennium BC (Marcuse 1975:554). Although once widespread, nose flutes, played with nasal rather than oral breath, are now only common in Melanesia and Polynesia where they have a religious significance – the belief being that nasal air is an expression of the soul (Sachs 1940:46). Another class of flute-like instruments are pipes that have a whistle mouthpiece, like the recorder or the toy tin-whistle. With these instruments the air is ducted so that it impinges on a sharp edge cut in the pipe just below the mouthpiece.

Flute-like instruments have cylindrical tubes and are usually open-ended. When blown, a succession of compression and expansion waves are reflected at the ends of the tube to set up a standing wave. The frequency of the instrument depends primarily on its length and whether the free end is open or closed. At a closed end, the momentum of a wave is destroyed, the pressure increases and the compression wave is reflected unchanged. The reverse occurs with a wave of expansion. A closed end therefore corresponds to the fixed end of a string and is a node, that is, a point where there is no motion. At an open end, a compression wave expands into free air. The pressure at an open end remains equal to the atmospheric pressure, which means that a compression wave will be reflected as a wave of expansion so that the two pressures annul each other. On the other hand, the motion of the air is greatest at an open end, because in a compression wave the air moves in the direction of propagation whereas the motion in an expansion wave is opposite to the direction of propagation. A position of maximum vibration is called an *antinode*.

When an open-ended tube is blown a compression pulse

travels from the mouthpiece down the tube and is reflected as an
expansion pulse. This pulse returns to the mouthpiece after a time
$2l/c$, where l is the length of the pipe and c is the speed of sound.
At the mouthpiece the expansion pulse is reflected as a pulse of
compression. If a second compression pulse is initiated at the
precise moment the first pulse arrives at the mouthpiece the
vibration will build up and repetition of the process will enable
resonance to be sustained. Therefore, the fundamental frequency
of an open tube is $c/2l$, and for A in the treble-cleft (440 Hz) we
can calculate the necessary length of tube from the velocity of
sound (340 m/s) to be 0·77 m. In the fundamental mode of
vibration, antinodes form at each end with the node positioned at
the centre. Overtones are possible in the same way as they are for
strings. If pulses are sent down the tube at intervals of l/c the air
can again be made to resonate at twice the frequency. A whole
range of partials are possible where

$$f = \frac{nc}{2l} \tag{10.10}$$

with n being the order of the partial. The vibrations of the air in
the tube are longitudinal, not transverse like those in strings.
Longitudinal vibrations are difficult to illustrate in a drawing, and
the modes of vibration in pipes we show in Fig. 10.9 are drawn
schematically as transverse waves.

If the tube has a closed end, that end must be a node. When
a compression pulse travels down the tube it is reflected as a
compression pulse, which on reaching the mouthpiece is
translated into an expansion pulse. If we are to sustain the
vibration we have to wait until the expansion pulse is reflected
back before supplying an additional pulse. The fundamental
frequency of vibration in a closed tube is therefore $c/4l$, or half

Fig. 10.9. Resonance in (*a*) open tubes, (*b*) closed tubes; the first four partials (conventionally shown as traverse vibration; N = node, A = antinode).

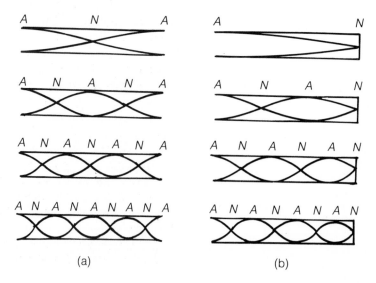

(a)   (b)

that of an open tube with the same length. A closed tube cannot be made to resonate at twice its fundamental frequency because if a second compression pulse were to be initiated after time $2l/c$ it would cancel the reflected expansion pulse. Therefore only the odd-order partials (Fig. 10.9) exist for closed tubes where

$$f = \frac{nc}{4l} \tag{10.11}$$

and

$n = 1,3,5,7,$ etc.

Whereas the simple expressions for vibrating strings are quite accurate, those for the frequency of a cylindrical wind instrument are far less so. The major source of error is that the pressure of the air at an open end does not fall to the atmospheric pressure exactly at the end, but at some distance away. As a consequence, the effective length of a tube is greater than the actual length by $0.58D$, where D is the diameter of the pipe (Duncan and Starling 1950:717). The culturally precocious Chinese probably understood this error in the pitch of pipes as early as Han times (Needham and Wang 1962:213). Another effect of diameter on frequency of vibration is a slight reduction in the velocity of sound in narrow tubes, which is mainly due to viscous forces (Duncan and Starling 1950:659). Variations in the temperature and humidity of a player's breath will also have an effect on the velocity, and consequently on the pitch of the sound.

Since the earliest flutes had no finger holes, a range of notes could be produced only by overblowing. With many early and simple flutes the bore was so narrow that it was impossible to blow a fundamental note (Marcuse 1975:554). Another way of producing notes is to completely or partially close the end with the hand, which is what is done by shepherds in many parts of the world to produce an octave lower. Panpipes made up of a set of tuned tubes enable a much greater range of notes to be achieved. In the southern Ukraine, panpipes made from bird-bones have been found that date to about 2000 BC and it is probable that this type of instrument has an even greater antiquity (Marcuse 1975:590).

The easiest way of achieving a full range of notes is by cutting finger holes into the flute – the number is usually at least four. An antinode forms near the open hole closest to the mouthpiece with the pitch of the notes being approximately given by the distance between the mouthpiece and the open hole. However the precise position of the antinode will depend on the size of the finger hole and whether the holes beyond it are open or closed. Since the pressure of the air passing through a small hole is not precisely constant, the antinode is displaced towards the open end.

In playing a horn or trumpet it is the vibration of the lips that causes the air to vibrate. The lips effectively form a closed end at the mouthpiece of a trumpet, unlike the blowing of the flute where the mouthpiece is open. Therefore theoretically only the odd-order partials are sounded. The resonance of a horn with a conical bore is somewhat different to that of a cylindrical trumpet. An antinode will exist at the mouthpiece of a true conical horn even though it is closed; a horn behaves like a cylindrical pipe with both ends open, and has all partials present (Wood 1975:112). However the performance of horns and trumpets is not simple, because they are never truly conical or cylindrical. Trumpets, however cylindrical their bore may be, usually have bell-mouths which amplify their sounds and smooth out their harsh strident tones. Even a perfectly cylindrical pipe can be made to resonate at other than its true harmonies. These extra notes are called *privileged frequencies* (Taylor 1976:67–8). Suppose we have a cylindrical pipe with a fundamental frequency of 60 Hz and which can produce the true harmonics listed in Table 10.3. If we vibrate our lips on the mouthpiece at 30 Hz it is possible that not only the fundamental frequency of 180 Hz will be heard but, because every second vibration is slightly reinforced by our lips, also a 90 Hz note. The partials of this first order privileged frequency may be excited by vibrating our lips more slowly. In fact the whole gamut of privileged frequencies and their partials shown in Table 10.3 is possible in theory, though only the true harmonies are strong and the lower privileged frequencies are not easily attainable. A mouthpiece has to be efficient to produce the privileged frequencies. When a modern mouthpiece is fitted to one of the trumpets found in the tomb of Tutankhamun it is possible to obtain a full scale, but only two notes can be produced if the trumpet is played in its original condition. While one can predict notes that are theoretically possible on a trumpet or horn, irregularities in their form and the shape of their mouthpiece determines the particular notes that can be achieved in practice. For this reason, the capabilities of horns and trumpets can really only be found by experiment.

Table 10.3 *Privileged frequencies for a closed pipe 1·4 metres long*

Partials	1	3	5	7	9
true partial frequencies (Hz)	*180*	*540*	*900*	*1260*	*1620*
1st order privileged frequencies (Hz)	90	270	450	630	810
2nd order privileged frequencies (Hz)	60	*180*	300	420	*540*
3rd order privileged frequencies (Hz)	45	135	225	315	405

Note: The true partials are in italics.

In early cultures horns and trumpets usually served as martial or magical instruments. Although the ranges of some European horns were extended by finger holes, it was rare for the horns of antiquity to sound more than one or two notes. The didjeridu (Fig. 10.10) of north Australia, one of the more fascinating wind instruments, is half-way between a trumpet and a horn. It consists simply of a tree branch, 1–2 m long, hollowed out by fire or termites. The inside diameter typically tapers from about 30 mm at the end which was blown to a maximum of about 50 mm at the opposite end (Fletcher 1983:28). The sound was often amplified by resting the end of the didjeridu inside a resonator – traditionally a bailer shell, but now more commonly a tin can. In playing, the fundamental note of the didjeridu is usually sounded as a continuous drone accented by pitch inflections or superimposed with a vocalised sound. A definite overblown tone anywhere between a seventh (15/8) or an eleventh (8/3) above the fundamental is also used as a structural element in the music of eastern Arnhem Land (Moyle 1981:323). Experienced players can produce other overtones, but the didjeridu is normally played only as a drone accompaniment to songs. Although these songs are usually traditional, one contemporary dance song of the Yuulngu tribe is about Donald Duck (Moyle 1981:329).

The last group of aerophones we will discuss have reeds that set the air in resonance. These reeds can either vibrate freely, or beat against a similar reed or a slightly smaller opening. While beating reeds vibrate the air in the tube they have little effect on the frequency of these vibrations. Air can only enter the tube at the moment of maximum pressure when the reed is compelled to open. This is exactly the reverse of what happens with a flute, which has air entering when the pressure is at a minimum.

In the ancient Mediterranean region and in the Middle East the reed pipe was far more popular than the flute. The most common type of reed pipe was the twinned form, consisting of either a parallel or divergent pair. The double reed pipe dates back to at least early Sumerian times, this fact being attested by the discovery of a magnificent pair of slender silver pipes about 300 mm long from the royal cemetery at Ur (Rimmer 1969). The Greeks were particularly fond of the double reed pipe which they called the *aulos*. Of all the surviving fragments of ancient Greek musical instruments it has been the broken pieces of *auloi* which have proved to be the most interesting to archaeomusicologists. Although *auloi* fragments have been the subject of careful study since the late nineteenth century, no one has yet been able to accurately reconstruct a complete instrument (Landels 1981). While there are many reasons for this lack of success, the most important is that small reed vibrators are very fragile and perishable; not a single specimen has been identified from an archaeological site.

Fig. 10.10. Didjeridu being played in
eastern Arnhem Land.

In pipes where a reed freely vibrates within a closely matched opening it is the reed's vibration that determines the pitch of the note, and the resonant frequency of the pipe is matched to the reed. It is thought that free-reed instruments originated at least 3000 years ago in southern China (Marcuse 1975:731–9), only appearing in Europe in the seventeenth century. In ancient China the most popular form of free-reed instrument was the *sheng*, or mouth organ. The *sheng* was made of a number of reed pipes inserted upright into a small bowl-shaped gourd. Each pipe had a hole just below the free reed. By stopping this hole with a fingertip a player could excite the reed by both exhaling and inhaling, which is exactly the same as is done today on its descendant, the European mouth organ.

Idiophones, or percussion instruments other than drums
Idiophones have more complex modes of vibration than chordophones or aerophones, and the partials produced by idiophones do not form a harmonic series. In this class the xylophone and the Indonesian *saron* and *gender* have the simplest modes of vibration. The xylophone originated in Southeast Asia, and was most highly developed in Indonesia where it is known as a *gambang*. From Southeast Asia the xylophone spread to Madagascar and Africa (Jones 1964): it was not known in Europe prior to the sixteenth century. In its simplest form the xylophone comprises a few wooden bars resting on firm bundles of grass laid over a resonator pit. This remarkably simple musical instrument still occurs in parts of Africa. A more-developed type, the trough xylophone, has an open-top sounding box as its resonator. In Indonesia the box was traditionally carved from a single block of wood, while in another variant of African design, split gourds with the membrane that protects spiders' eggs glued over their openings were tuned to the pitch of individual bars (Sachs 1940:54).

A later development of the xylophone is Indonesia's *saron* and *gender*. In these instruments, that belong to the metallophone family, the wooden bars of the xylophone are replaced by bronze or iron strips. The earlier variety, the saron, has a trough resonator much like the xylophone, while the *gender* has tuned bamboo resonators hung beneath the bronze strips.

The bars of xylophones and related instruments vibrate in a flexural mode. When a bar is sounding the fundamental note, nodes are formed at about two-ninths of the bar's length from either end, where the bar is usually supported. The higher partials are significantly damped by the supports. For example the third partial has an antinode position at about the node of the fundamental. Such damping is desirable because the partials are not harmonics.

The velocity of propagation of flexural waves depends on their length. For waves whose length is long compared with the cross-sectional dimensions of the bar, the velocity of wave propagation is given by

$$c \approx \frac{2\pi}{\lambda}\left(\frac{EI}{\rho A}\right)^{\frac{1}{2}}$$ (10.12)

where λ is the wave length, E the Young's modulus, I the second moment of area of the cross-section, ρ the density, and A the cross-sectional area (Kolsky 1963:51). The partials of a xylophone bar do not form an harmonic series because the velocity of wave propagation depends on the wave length and their frequencies are given by

$$f \approx \frac{(2n+1)^2\pi}{8l^2}\left(\frac{EI}{\rho A}\right)^{\frac{1}{2}}$$ (10.13)

where n is the order of the partial (Volterra and Zachmanoglou 1965:322). For a rectangular bar of length l and thickness t the frequency is proportional to its thickness and inversely proportional to the square of its length. The width of the bar does not significantly affect the frequency. In Indonesia and Africa the fine tuning of xylophone bars was accomplished either by paring down the thickness of the bar over its central portion, which reduces its stiffness and thus lowers its frequency, or by trimming the tips of the bar so that its mass is reduced and the frequency raised. The African *sansa* is somewhat like a xylophone, the main difference being in the method of vibrating the bars (Marcuse 1975:101–3). The *sansa* consists of a set of split cane or metal tongues clamped across two supports on a sounding box so that the projecting ends are free to vibrate like cantilevers. The instrument is played by holding it in both hands and using the thumbs to pluck at the projecting tongues. The tongues must vibrate with a node at the first support, the frequency being proportional to the thickness of the tongue and inversely proportional to the square of its length. Pitch can be adjusted by sliding the tongue in or out of the supports, with fine tuning accomplished by sticking small balls of beeswax under their free ends which has the effect of lowering their frequency. The *sansa* was first recorded in the sixteenth century, and its antiquity is unknown. Modern versions are now manufactured in European countries.

Flat stones, or lithophones, if of sufficient thinness, will vibrate to emit a bright clear tone that can reverberate for a considerable time. The Chinese chimestone (*qing*), dates back at least to the Shang Dynasty (*c.* 1520–1030 BC); they have a variety of shapes – clouds or fish for instance – though more usually they are L-shaped (Fig. 10.11). As a musical set (*bian-qing*) the chimestones ordinarily number no more than 16. A notable exception is an immense stand of 32 sonorous slabs of bronze (called a *dong-qing*) which has been recently unearthed from the tomb of the Lady of Zeng.

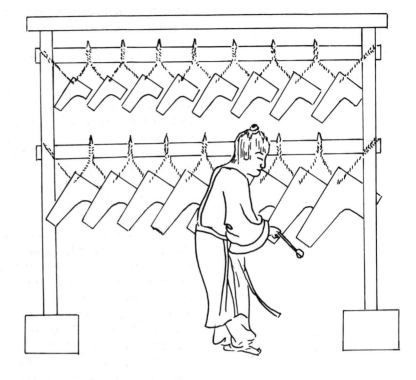

Fig. 10.11. A stand of L-shaped Chinese chimestones (after Needham and Wang 1962: fig. 304).

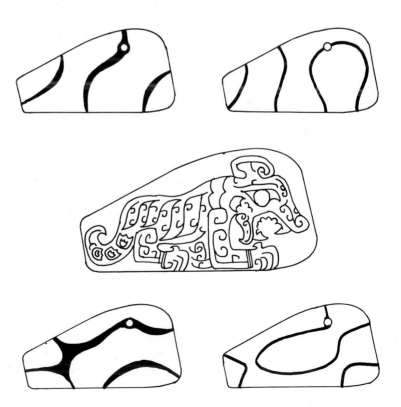

Fig. 10.12. Some nodal patterns obtained on a replica of an ancient Chinese chimestone dated to the Shang period (about 1400 BC).

The modes in which a chimestone can vibrate are complex but can be revealed by a simple method first used in the eighteenth century by Ernst Chladni (1756–1827) to study vibrating plates (Wood 1975:61–3). If a smooth horizontal plate with a sprinkling of fine sand is bowed on its edge, the sand grains bounce around until they gather at the nodes. By bowing at different points on the plate, and by stopping it with the fingers, different frequencies can be excited, each with its own nodal pattern. Fig. 10.12 shows some of the nodal patterns we obtained from a plate cut to the shape of a chimestone found in a royal tomb of the Shang period at Anyang. This chimestone would have been hung by a cord from the hole in its top portion. In our experiments the replica was clamped horizontally through this hole.

The first bells were probably mere noise-making instruments. However in China they quickly developed into sophisticated musical instruments. By the Shang Dynasty clapperless bronze *zhong* bells were being cast that made up chimes, or *bian-zhong*, of up to 65 individual bells, like the magnificent set found in the tomb of Zonghou Yi in Hubei Province (Shen 1987). The Chinese *zhong* (Fig. 10.13) differs considerably from the Western bell which is round. The *zhong* bell has an oval cross-section and the front and back faces meet in a ridge called the *xian*. The lip of the bell arches up from the *xian*, and the upper body has 36 bronze

Fig. 10.13. The features of a *zhong* bell (after Shen 1987).

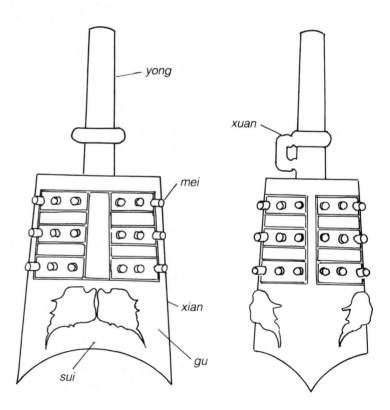

nipples or *mei*. In a *bian-zhong* each bell is suspended by a collar (*xuan*), and a counter-balance (*yong*) causes the bell to hang at an angle of about 30° to the vertical. This design not only gives the bell a strike note that is the fundamental but, even more surprisingly, two distinct pitches. When a *zhong* bell is struck low on the centre of the face (*sui*) one note is sounded, and when struck on the side (*gu*) near the *xian* a note, a minor or major third higher, is sounded. The Shang campanologists not only tuned their bells so that the two fundamental notes were harmonic, but also managed to ensure that the overtones were harmonic as well by the position and size of the nipple-like *mei*. What showed the great accoustic knowledge of Shang campanologists was their ability to tune their bells to two different pitches. Ordinarily a bell is tuned by removing some of the metal, but with this method it is seemingly impossible to tune for one bell pitch without altering the other. However the Shang campanologists knew the nodal lines of the two notes, and could alter the pitch of one note, without changing that of the other, by carefully paring away the metal along the nodal lines of the second note.

The *bian-zhong* is a highly developed musical instrument. The closest modern approximation is the carillon, which comprises a carefully selected group of bells that yields equal-tempered chromatic intervals. However some of the partials of the bells of a carillon are still in dischord and only a limited number of chords can be played. What is a mystery is that the skill and knowledge of the early Chinese campanologists was lost around 200 BC and the dual-pitch potential of the *zhong* was not recognised until 1978 (Shen 1987). The later Chinese and all other bells in the world have a single pitch.

Membranophones, or drums

This class of musical instrument is almost exclusively occupied by the drum. The distinctive sound of a skin drum can be largely attributed to the membrane; the body acts merely as a sounding box. In many parts of the world the drum was, and still is, an instrument of ritual importance, annointed at times with sacrificial blood or, as in South America, holy water. Even in Europe a certain mystique has surrounded the drum. In seventeenth-century Germany no one under the rank of baron was allowed to own a kettledrum, and to this day regimental drums have a significance rivalling the colours (Sachs 1940:329–30).

In Europe, until relatively recently, drums served only as rhythm instruments – for instance, Virdun's 'rumbling tubs' (Sachs 1940:329). The first introduction of a tuned kettledrum in a European orchestra was in the seventeenth century by Jean-Baptiste Lully, a merciless intriguer of the French Court (Marcuse 1975:167). Outside Europe the tuning of drums was an early accomplishment, effected by inserting wedges under the lacing, as with the Indian tabla, or by twisting the lacings on pegs (Sachs 1940:155). Sets of drums tuned to a musical scale are found in both Asia and Africa (Marcuse 1975:158).

A stretched membrane vibrates in the same manner as a string. The velocity of wave propagation is $\sqrt{\sigma/\rho}$ where σ is the tensile stress and ρ the density of the membrane. The frequency of the fundamental mode of vibration is given by

$$f = \frac{0 \cdot 765}{d}\left(\frac{\sigma}{\rho}\right)^{\frac{1}{2}}$$

(10.14)

where d is the diameter of the membrane (Volterra and Zachmanoglou 1965:289). As with idiophones the partials do not form a harmonic series.

Archaeomusicology

While archaeomusicology has existed for more than a hundred years – François Fétis (1869:25–6), a director of the Brussels Conservatorium of Music, observed that a Bronze Age antler pipe was capable of producing four notes of a diatonic scale – it is still a rather obscure field of study. Although the mechanics of music is well understood it has had little application to the study of ancient instruments. One reason is that it is difficult to use theory to accurately reconstruct ancient instruments. Unlike the other topics that we have treated, where usually an order of magnitude answer suffices, reconstruction of ancient music demands an almost precise answer which cannot be obtained from simple theory. For example attempts have been made to determine the scales of some *auloi* from fragments, using only the simple theory of pipes (Landels 1981). These reconstructions are at best very approximate because they fail to take into account variables such as the sizes of the *auloi*'s finger holes and bore, and the complex and powerful effects of the reed's structure. In music there is a greater need for actual reconstructions of ancient artifacts than there is in other areas of material culture. However even with reconstructions it is difficult to be certain of the capabilities of the instruments. Megaw (1968:338), in discussing the tonal range of seven bone-pipes dating from the fifth or sixth to the twelfth century AD, has noted that it is impossible to judge the cross-fingering, partial fingering or overblowing that may have been used.

Fortunately interest in archaeomusicology, which has been very much a European-based discipline, is now widening with the inauguration of an archaeomusicological study group of the International Council for Traditional Music. Perhaps in time the music of the past will again be heard.

11

Epilogue

The purpose of our book has been to illustrate the role of
mechanics theory in the study of ancient and traditional material
culture. A large amount has been written already on a wide
range of mechanics of traditional artifacts but those who have
carried out such studies are usually specialists within particular
disciplines and are concerned with quite specific topics. This book
is the first review of the interdisciplinary field of mechanics in
archaeology and in the wider field of material culture studies.
Many of the most significant intellectual advances occur when
scholars and scientists look beyond the boundaries of their own
disciplines. Archaeologists in particular need to be acquainted
with much that is not within the normal scope of the discipline
because almost every other discipline interfaces with some facet of
the subject. Archaeologists are often trained in more than one
field, or they have sufficient grasp of other areas of knowledge to
be able to collaborate with non-archaeologists. However there
seems to be a general lack of awareness of the contribution
mechanics can make to the study of material culture. It is this
lack of mechanics in the description of ancient relics, a great
lapse, that has provided the opportunity for frauds and lunatics to
beguile even well-informed people with stories about extra-
terrestrials and supernatural forces shaping human history.

Mechanics is a field that deserves renewed interest by
archaeologists and others who study material culture. That it has
not in recent decades is partly because of a relative decline in the
popularity of studies on the material culture of non-industrial
societies. The percentage of material culture studies as a
proportion of general anthropological research has continued to
fall since about the turn of the century. After 1920, in North
America, the slide took a sharp turn, while in Europe it was not
so drastic and the research field remains strong in countries like
Britain, Germany and Sweden (Fenton 1974:28; Sturtevant
1969:626). During the past 40 years theoretical studies on
material culture have been few and far between but there is now
a resurgence of interest in material culture studies (Fenton 1974;
Oswalt 1976) and research funding into this field is returning.
Institutions that are in the forefront in sponsorship are the
Australian Institute of Aboriginal Studies and the Wenner-Gren

Foundation for Anthropological Research, as well as all the major museums of the world that have ethnological collections.

Even if one cannot perform the mechanical analyses it is important to be aware of the information mechanics can provide. Given the broad scope of mechanics in archaeology and in material culture it has only been possible for us to cover some of the territory. There are many mechanical issues in archaeology that we have barely touched upon and others that we have not even mentioned, such as the functioning of irrigations systems, snow skis and hunting traps, or ship construction, about which much new data has been provided by marine archaeologists. More research needs to be done on major issues, such as reconstructing the technology of the Easter Islanders to understand how they built their extraordinary edifices. The implications of the technological feat of transporting and erecting the monolithic statues on Easter Island are still a matter of debate that we believe only the combination of field archaeology and mechanical study can fully resolve.

The data base for the mechanical analyses of artifacts is limited by the small amount of basic research that has so far been carried out. For instance much of the information on human ability that we used in this book did not come from modern archaeology or engineering but from a melange of nineteenth- and even eighteenth-century sources. There is a need for more information about the properties of the natural materials used to make artifacts, since not uncommonly these materials have little or no commercial value and are therefore little studied by researchers in other scientific fields. For instance we have encountered this difficulty in trying to assess the performance of some Australian Aboriginal weapons, which are usually made of wood. Whereas the Aborigines had utilised perhaps more than 500 species of trees to make their various artifacts, only a few have commercial value and consequently the physical properties of only about a third of these timbers are known.

We hope that practitioners of the physical sciences are made more aware of the opportunities available to them to further our understanding of the human past. The range of relevant experiments that can be performed by the archaeologist, engineer or the informed lay person is truly vast, but as with the properties of materials that were formerly utilised there are great chasms of missing data that are needed for modelling performances of artifacts (cf. Kamminga 1985:21). Often enough in archaeological and ethnological reports the important functional features of an artifact are not fully recognised or appreciated and so the report is of limited value in assessing performance. This is not to belittle the work of some ethnologists of the nineteenth and twentieth centuries who have provided meticulous accounts of traditional material cultures (e.g. Kluckhohn *et al.* 1971; LeBar 1964; Osgood 1940; Spier 1928, 1930, 1933). But the quality of ethnologies has been and still is uneven because collectors are selective in their observance of artifacts in use and in the scope of their collecting which at least in part can be attributed to the fact that functional attributes of many artifacts are not fully understood. Collectors should attempt to be comprehensive in seeking artifacts that have short working lives, in that they are made for particular purposes and often quickly discarded – such as rattan needles and bark thread, and wooden pounders for softening bark cloth which we have seen in use among the Agta of Luzon. These kinds of artifacts are equivalent to the disposable wooden chopsticks and plastic knives and forks of fast-food outlets. Similarly we have observed that spring traps are ordinarily not collected by ethnologists, which is most unfortunate since it is difficult to determine the mechanical performances of such traps from literary and pictorial sources alone. It is important to be aware of the types of attributes of an artifact that need to be recorded to provide the essential data for determining its performance.

Despite the efforts of many scholars over the last hundred years mechanics in archaeology as a field of study is still in its infancy. The mechanical applications that can be developed are countless, and future research will undoubtedly generate more questions. What is to be gained from mechanics is a firmer basis for theory building, and a better understanding of both human adaptation to the environment and the development of material culture.

APPENDIX I

Glossary of mechanical terms

See also entries in index

acceleration – angular (α)
Unit: rad/s²
Rate of change in angular velocity of a rotating body.

acceleration – linear (a), centripetal (a)
Unit: m/s²
Rate of change in velocity. Centripetal acceleration is the acceleration of a rotating body towards its centre of rotation due to its angular velocity.

amorphous – *see* crystalline

antinode – *see* node

aspect ratio (*AR*)
The length/breadth or height/breadth ratio of an oar, sail, etc.

boundary layer
The thin layer of fluid adjacent to a moving body, that is subject to viscous forces.

buoyancy force (*F*)
Unit: N
The upwards force exerted on a partially or fully submerged vessel by a fluid. The force is equal to the weight of the fluid displaced.

centre of buoyancy (*B*)
The point through which the buoyancy force acts; the centre of the volume of a boat's immersed part.

centre of effort (*CE*)
The centre of pressure of a sail.

centre of gravity (*CG*)
The point in a body through which the force of gravity acts.

centre of lateral resistance (*CLR*)
The centre of pressure of a vessel's hull.

centre of pressure (*CP*)
The centre in a body through which the aerodynamic forces act.

centroid
The centre of area of a plane geometric shape.

chord
Two or more notes sounded together.

cleavage planes
In crystalline solids certain planes can be cleaved more easily than others; these are the cleavage planes.

crystalline, amorphous
The atoms in a crystalline solid are arranged in regular patterns. In an amorphous solid there are no long range regular patterns in the atoms though there may be short range patterns.

density (ρ)
Unit: kg/m^3
Mass per unit volume.

drag (D) – eddy, form
Unit: N
Resistance to the motion of a body through a fluid. Eddy drag is caused by the formation of eddies in a vessel's wake. Form drag is caused by the boundary layer breaking away from the surface of a body and is a function of its shape.

drag coefficient (C_D)
Unit: non-dimensional
The drag divided by the dynamic force $\frac{1}{2}\rho v^2 S$.

efficiency – mechanical (η)
Unit: non-dimensional
The ratio of the mechanical work performed *by* a machine to the work done *on* it.

elastic deformation
A body is elastic if it returns to its original configuration when unstressed. In a linear elastic body the strain is proportional to the stress.

energy – kinetic (T), potential (V)
Unit: J
Energy is the capacity of a body to perform work. Kinetic energy is the energy of a body due to its motion. Potential energy is the energy of a body due to its position or state of strain.

equal temperament
A musical scale where the interval between each semitone is exactly the same and is $2^{\frac{1}{12}}$.

equilibrium – stable (unstable)
A body is in equilibrium when stationary or in uniform motion under balanced forces. A body in stable equilibrium will return into its original orientation if given a small displacement.

force (F)
Unit: N
Mechanical action that produces or acts to restrain the motion of a body or is responsible for its deformation.

fracture toughness (K_{Ic})
Unit: $Nm^{-3/2}$
A measure of a material's resistance to fracture.

frequency – pitch *(f)*
Unit: Hz
The number of vibrations a note forms in a second.

friction – coefficient *(μ),* angle *(λ)*
Units: μ non-dimensional, λ degree or radian
The friction coefficient μ is the ratio of the friction force F to the perpendicular contact force between the two surfaces. The friction angle λ is the angle the total force between two sliding surfaces makes to the perpendicular to the surface, that is, $\mu = \tan \lambda$.

friction – force *(F_f)*
Unit: N
The force resisting sliding or rolling between two surfaces.

Froude number (F)
Unit: non-dimensional
The ratio of kinetic to potential energy in wave-like motions. The Froude number for a boat of waterline length *l* sailing with a speed v_b is given by $F = v_b/(lg)^{\frac{1}{2}}$.

fundamental – frequency, note
The note of lowest frequency present in a harmonic composite note.

gravitational acceleration (g)
Unit: m/s^2
The acceleration that a free-falling mass experiences because of the earth's gravitational field. $g = 9\cdot81 \; m/s^2$.

gravitational constant (G)
Unit: $m^3/kg \; s^2$
The gravitational force F between two masses m_1 and m_2 a distance r apart is given by

$$F = G\frac{m_1 m_2}{r^2}. \; G = 6\cdot67 \times 10^{-11} \; m^3/kg \; s^2.$$

gravitational force (F)
Unit: N
The force of attraction between two masses. When it is the force between a mass and the earth, the gravitational force is called the weight of a mass.

heptatonic – *see* pentatonic

isotropic material
A material whose physical properties are directionally independent.

just scale
A musical scale devised in the sixteenth century which has simpler ratios than the Greek scales.

laminar (turbulent) flow
In laminar flow the streamlines are steady without any appreciable mixing. Turbulent flow is unsteady and involves mixing.

lift (L)
Unit: N
The aerodynamic force perpendicular to the motion of a body.

lift coefficient (C_L)
Unit: non-dimensional
The lift divided by the dynamic force $\frac{1}{2}\rho v^2 S$.

load (W or F)
Unit: N
A force due to gravity exerted by a mass on an object. See also gravitational force.

mass (m) – see also virtual mass
Unit: kg
Quantity of matter.

maximum and minimum (mathematical)
A mathematical maximum (minimum) exists in a function of a particular variable when for any change in that variable the function decreases (increases).

metacentre (M)
The intersection between the line of symmetry of a slightly heeled vessel and a vertical line through the centre of buoyancy.

metacentric height (GM)
Unit: m
Height of the metacentre above the centre of gravity of a vessel.

modulus of rigidity (G)
Unit: Pa
The ratio between shear stress and shear strain for a linear elastic solid.

modulus of rupture (σ_B)
Unit: Pa
The maximum hypothetical bending stress a beam can withstand without failure assuming that the material is linearly elastic.

moment (M)
Unit: Nm
The twisting action of a force about an axis is the product of the force and the perpendicular distance of its line of action from the axis.

moment of inertia (I)
Unit: kg m²
The inertia a body presents to angular acceleration.

momentum – angular
Unit: kg m²/s
The product of moment of inertia and angular velocity.

momentum – linear
Unit: kg m/s
The product of mass and linear velocity.

musical interval
The ratio of the frequencies of two notes.

musical scales – enharmonic, chromatic, diatonic
The three Greek scales where the octave is divided into eight notes of varying intervals.

Node, antinode
At a node in a standing wave there is no vibration. The maximum vibration in a standing wave is the antinode.

overtone – partial
The overtones of a note are the frequencies present that are higher than the fundamental frequency. The partials of a note are all the frequencies that make up a composite note.

orifice – coefficient of contraction (C_c)
Unit: non-dimensional
Ratio of area of the jet to area of the orifice. For sharp-edged orifices $C_c \simeq 0.7$.

overblowing
A technique of obtaining extra higher notes on trumpet-like instruments by blowing harder than normal.

partial – see overtone

pentatonic (heptatonic)
A scale with 5(7) intervals to the octave. Much Chinese music is pentatonic, whereas modern Western music is largely heptatonic.

plastic deformation
Deformation that is due to permanent flow of a material and which is not recovered on the removal of the load.

Poisson's ratio (υ)
Unit: non-dimensional
The ratio between elastic lateral strain and axial strain in a stretched rod.

power (P)
Unit: W
The rate at which work is done.

pressure, absolute (relative) *(P)*
Unit: Pa
Force per unit area exerted by a fluid on either an internal or external surface. Absolute pressure is measured from a vacuum and relative pressure from a standard atmospheric pressure.

principal axes of rotation
The three mutually perpendicular axes of rotation of a body that contain the maximum and minimum moments of inertia. A free body has stable rotation only about the maximum or minimum principal axes.

privileged frequency
Notes obtained in trumpet-like instruments by vibrating the lips at lower than the fundamental frequency.

radian
An angle can be measured in degrees or radians. The magnitude of an angle in radians is obtained by dividing the arc of the circle it subtends by the radius.

residual resistance
Unit: N
The drag on a boat other than skin friction. Primarily the wave-making resistance of a boat.

resilience
Unit: J/m^3
The ability of a solid to store energy by deforming elastically.

Reynolds number (R_e)
Unit: non-dimensional
The ratio between the dynamic pressure of a fluid and its viscous shear stress.

$$R_e = \frac{\rho v d}{\mu}.$$

scalars and vectors
A scalar quantity needs only magnitude to define it, whereas a vector requires a direction as well.

safety factor
A number by which the strength of a solid is divided to obtain a safe working stress.

second moment of area (I)
Unit: m⁴
The sum of all the infinitesimal portions of the area of a beam's cross-section multiplied by the square of their distances from an axis passing through the centroid.

shear modulus (G)
Unit: Pa
The ratio of shear stress to shear strain for a linear elastic solid.

simple harmonic motion
A body oscillating about an equilibrium position in such a way that its acceleration towards the equilibrium position is proportional to the distance from that position is in simple harmonic motion.

skin friction (F_f)
Unit: N
The drag imposed on a body by a thin boundary layer.

skin friction-coefficient (C_F)
Unit: non-dimensional
The skin friction divided by the dynamic force $\frac{1}{2}\rho v^2 S$.

specific work of fracture (G_{Ic})
Unit: J/m²
The work required to extend a crack by a unit area.

standing wave
A wave composed of two waves of equal amplitude travelling in opposite directions which does not apparently move.

strain – normal (ε) shear (γ)
Unit: non-dimensional
The normal strain is the stretch per unit length. The shear strain is the angular distortion in an orthogonal element of the body.

strain energy density (U)
Unit: J/m³
The elastic energy stored in a strained solid per unit volume.

strength – yield (σ_y), ultimate tensile (σ_t), compressive (σ_c)
Unit: Pa
The yield strength of a material is the stress that just causes non-elastic deformations. The ultimate tensile strength is the maximum stress that a material can withstand without breaking. The compressive strength of a material is the maximum compressive stress it can withstand without crushing or fracturing.

stress concentration factor
The ratio of the local stress at a notch or defect to the average stress.

stress intensity factor (K)
Unit: Nm$^{-3/2}$
A measure of the stress field that exists at the tip of a crack.

stress – normal (σ), shear (τ)
Unit: Pa
The normal (shear) stress is the perpendicular (tangential) component of the force acting on a unit area of the surface of a body.

stresses – principal (σ_1, σ_2, σ_3)
Unit: Pa
The perpendicular stress acting across a surface orientated so that the shear stress is zero. There are three principal stresses at a point that are mutually at right-angles, one of which is a maximum and one a minimum stress at that point.

surface energy (γ)
Unit: J/m^2
The difference between the energy level of surface atoms to that of atoms within the bulk of the material.

turbulent flow – *see* laminar flow

vector – *see* scalar

velocity – angular (ω)
Unit: rad/s
Rate of change of angular displacement of a body about an axis.

velocity – linear (v)
Unit: m/s
Rate of change of spatial position.

velocity ratio (VR)
Unit: non-dimensional
The ratio between the velocity of a machine's driving force and its output.

virtual mass (m_v)
Unit: kg
That hypothetical mass which, if moving at the velocity of a projectile, has the same kinetic energy as the projector at the moment of release.

virtual work
The work done when a body is given a small hypothetical displacement from its position of equilibrium.

viscosity
A measure of resistance to the flow of a fluid.

viscosity – coefficient (μ)
Unit: Pa s.
Shear force per unit area necessary to produce a unit velocity gradient in a fluid.

voussior
One of the stones that form part of an arch or vault, usually having its sides slightly inclined.

Wave length (λ)
Unit: m
The distance from one crest of a wave to the next.

wave propagation velocity (c)
Unit: m/s
The velocity at which a wave passes through a fluid or solids.

weight – *see* gravitational force

work – mechanical (W)
Unit: J
Mechanical work is done by a force when it moves or deforms a body. The work is the product of the force and the distance moved in the direction of its line of action.

Young's modulus (E)
Unit: Pa
The ratio between normal stress and strain for a linear elastic solid.

APPENDIX II

Symbols

WITH PAGE NUMBER OF DEFINITION

H horizontal thrust, 119

I moment of inertia, 79; second moment of area, 110; intensity of a sound, 267

k stiffness, 205

K stress intensity factor, 138

K_I mode I stress intensity factor, 138

K_{II} mode II stress intensity factor, 139

K_{Ic} plane strain fracture toughness, 138

l length

L lift force, 171; loudness, 267

m mass, 20

m_v virtual mass, 164

$\mathbf{M}, M$ moment, 77, 178

MA mechanical advantage, 75

M_b bending moment, 106

N normal force, 171

p pressure, 48; length of walking pace, 195

p_a atmospheric pressure, 49

P power, 35

q quantity of fluid, 50

Q rate of discharge, 52

r radius, distance

R reaction force, 81; radius of curvature of a bent beam; 109, radius of roller or wheel; range of a projectile, 162

R_e Reynolds number, 59

R_E effective change in radius of curvature of a bow, 186

s distance

S length of bow string, 183; surface area

t time

T kinetic energy, 35; second order term in the stress field at the tip of a crack, 139; a duration of time; tension

u displacement in the x direction, 70

U strain energy density, 72

v speed, 29; displacement in y direction, 72

V potential energy, 34

V volume

VR velocity ratio, 75

w	weight per unit length, 106; width of hull of a multihulled boat; 242
W	work done, 33; weight; width of a boat
x	distance along X axis, 20
X	an axis of the cartesian systems of axes, 20
y	distance along Y axis, 20
Y	an axis of the cartesian system of axes, 20
z	distance along Z axis, 20
Z	an axis of the cartesian system of axes, 20
α	angular acceleration, 79; a particular angle
β	a particular angle
γ	shear strain, 70
ε	normal strain, 70
η	coefficient of efficiency, 75
θ	a general angle
λ	friction angle ($\mu = \tan \lambda$), 29; wave length, 288
μ	coefficient of friction, 29; coefficient of viscosity, 57
ν	Poisson's ratio, 71
ρ	density, 49
σ	normal stress, 69
σ_c	compressive strength, 105
σ_t	tensile strength, 72
τ	shear stress, 57, 69; non-dimensional time, 173
φ	a general angle
ω	angular velocity, 32
Ω, Ω	angular velocity, 178, 247

Useful mathematical formulas

Trigonometric functions

$\sin \theta = a/c$

$\cos \theta = b/c$

$\tan \theta = a/b$

$\cot \theta = b/a$

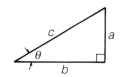

Trigonometric relationships

$\sin^2 \theta + \cos^2 \theta = 1$

$\sin (A+B) = \sin A \cos B + \cos A \sin B$

$\sin (A-B) = \sin A \cos B - \cos A \sin B$

$\cos (A+B) = \cos A \cos B - \sin A \sin B$

$\cos (A-B) = \cos A \cos B + \sin A \sin B$

$\cos 2\theta = \cos^2 \theta - \sin^2 \theta$

$\qquad = 2 \cos^2 \theta - 1$

$\qquad = 1 - 2 \sin^2 \theta$

$\sin A + \sin B = 2 \sin [(A+B)/2] \cos [(A-B)/2]$

$\sin A - \sin B = 2 \cos [(A+B)/2] \sin [(A-B)/2]$

$\cos A + \cos B = 2 \cos [(A+B)/2] \cos [(A-B)/2]$

$\cos A - \cos B = -2 \sin [(A+B)/2] \sin [(A-B)/2]$

Sine rule

$$\frac{\sin \theta}{a} = \frac{\sin \psi}{b} = \frac{\sin \Omega}{c}$$

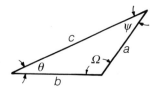

Intersection of chords

$AO \times OB = OC \times OD$

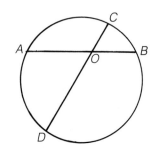

REFERENCES

Aiston, George 1922. Unpublished letter to W. H. Gill, dated 31 June 1922. Mitchell Library, Sydney.

Alexander, R. McN. 1976. Mechanics of bipedal locomotion. In P. Spencer Davies (ed.), *Perspectives in experimental biology*. Vol. 1, *Zoology*. Pergamon Press, Oxford, pp. 493–504.

1982. *Locomotion of animals*. Blackie & Sons, Glasgow.

Altshuller, G. S. 1984. *Creativity as an exact science. The theory of the solution of inventive problems*. Translated by Anthony Williams. Gordon and Breach Science Publishers, New York.

Ambrose, W. 1973. 3000 years of trade in New Guinea obsidian. *Australian Natural History* 11:370–3.

Ambrose, W. and R. C. Green 1972. First millennium B.C. transport of obsidian from New Britain to the Solomon Islands. *Nature* 237:31.

Anderson, R. C. 1962. *Oared fighting ships from Classical times to the coming of steam*. Percival Marshall, London.

Anonymous 1838. The boomerang and its vagaries. *Dublin University Magazine*, February, pp. 168–71.

Aristotle, *De Caelo*. Translated by J. L. Stodes, 1922. Oxford University Press, Oxford.

Physics. Translated by W. D. Ross, 1966. Clarendon Press, Oxford.

Aristotle (School of), *Mechanical problems*. In *Aristotle's minor works*, translated by W. S. Hett, 1936. Heinemann, London.

Problemata. Translated by W. S. Hett, 1957. Heinemann, London.

Arnot, D. B. 1928. Timber extraction in Johore. *Empire Forestry Journal* 7:233–7.

Athenaeus of Naukratis, *The deipnosophists; or Banquet of the learned*. Translated by C. D. Yonge, 1854. Henry G. Bohn, London.

Atkins, A. G. and D. K. Felbeck 1974. Applying mutual indentation hardness phenomena to service failures. *Metals Engineering Quarterly* 14:55–61.

Atkinson, J. C. 1956. *Stonehenge*. Hamish Hamilton, London.

Baker, P. E., F. Buckley and J. G. Holland 1974. Petrology and geochemistry of Easter Island. *Contributions to Mineralogy and Petrology* 44:85–100.

Balfour, Henry 1890. On the structure and affinities of the composite bow. *Journal of the Anthropological Institute* 19:220–50.

Barker, Herbert 1964. *Camels and the outback*. Pitman, Melbourne.

Barnaby, Kenneth C. 1969. *Basic naval architecture*. Hutchinson, London.

Bass, G. (ed.) 1972. *History of seafaring*. Thames and Hudson, London.

Beakley, G. C. and E. G. Chilton 1973. *Introduction to engineering design and graphics*. Macmillan, New York.

Beck, Benjamin B. 1980. *Animal tool behavior: the use and manufacture of tools by animals*. Garland STPM Press, New York.

Bellwood, P. 1978. *Man's conquest of the Pacific. The prehistory of Southeast Asia and Oceania*. William Collins, Auckland.

Bekker, M. G. 1956. *Theory of locomotion*. University of Michigan Press, Ann Arbor.

Bernoulli, Daniel [1738] 1968. Hydrodynamics. In *Hydrodynamics by Daniel Bernoulli and Hydraulics by Johann Bernoulli*. Translated by T. Carmody and H. Kobus. Dover Publications, New York.

Birdsell, J. B. 1977. The recalibration of a paradigm for the first peopling of Greater Australia. In J. Allen, J. Golson and R. Jones (eds.), *Sunda and Sahul: prehistoric studies in Southeast Asia, Melanesia and Australia*. Academic Press, London, pp. 113–167.

Blyth, P. H. 1976. Some technical considerations. In R. Hardy (ed.), *Longbow: a social and military history*. Patrick Stephens, Cambridge.

Boas, Franz (ed.) 1938. *General anthropology*. Heath, New York.

Borchardt, L. 1920. Die Altägyptische Zeitmessung. In E. Von Basserman-Jordan (ed.), *Die Geschichte der Zeitmessung und der Uhren*, Vol. 1. Walter de Gruyter, Berlin.

Bordaz, J. 1970. *Tools of the Old and New Stone Age*. Natural History Press, New York.

Bordes, François 1968. *The Old Stone Age*. Translated by J. E. Anderson. Weidenfeld and Nicolson, London.

Boreux, C. 1925. Études des nautiques Égyptienne: l'art de la navigation en Egypt jusqu'à la fin de l'Ancien Empire. *Mémoires de l'Institut Français d'Archeologie orientale du Caire 50*, Cairo.

Boulton, W. H. n.d. *The pageant of transport through the ages*. Low, Marston and Co., London.

Bowden, Frank P. and David Tabor 1950. *The friction and lubrication of solids*, Part I. Clarendon Press, Oxford.

1964. *The friction and lubrication of solids*, Part II. Clarendon Press, Oxford.

Bowen, Richard le B. 1949. Arab dhows of eastern Arabia. *American Neptune* 9:87–111.

1953. Eastern sail affinities. *American Neptune* 13:81–117, 185–211.

1960. Egypt's earliest sailing-ships. *Antiquity* 34:117–31.

Brøgger, A. W. and H. Shetelig 1971. *The Viking ships*. Twayne Publishers Inc., New York.

BS 2052:1953. *British standard specification for ropes made from coir, hemp, manila, and sisal*.

Bulliet, R. W. 1975. *The camel and the wheel*. Harvard University Press, Cambridge, Mass.

Burford, Alison 1960. Heavy transport in classical antiquity. *Economic History Review* 13:1–18.

Burstall, Aubrey F. 1963. *A history of mechanical engineering*. Faber and Faber, London.

Butler, Brian M. and Ernest E. May (eds.) 1984. Prehistoric chert exploitation: studies from the midcontinent. *Occasional Paper, No. 2*, Southern Illinois University at Carbondale, Centre for Archeological Investigations.

Butzer, K. 1976. *Early hydraulic civilization in Egypt; a study in cultural ecology*. University of Chicago Press, Chicago.

Cannon, Michael 1971. *Who's master? Who's man? Australia in the Victorian Age*. Thomas Nelson Ltd, London.

Carrier, D. R. 1984. The energetic paradox of human running and hominid evolution. *Current Anthropology* 25:483–95.

Carter, Howard 1927. *The tomb of Tut·Ankh·Amen. Discovered by the late Earl of Carnarvon and Howard Carter*, Vol. II. Cassell and Co., London.

1933. *The Tomb of Tut·Ankh·Amen. discovered by the late Earl of Carnarvon and Howard Carter*, Vol. III. Cassell and Co., London.

Carter, Howard and Percy E. Newberry 1904. *The tomb of Thoutmôsis IV*. A. Constable and Co., Westminster.

Casson, Lionel 1964. *Illustrated history of ships and boats*. Doubleday. New York.

1971. *Ships and seamanship in the ancient world*. Princeton University Press, Princeton.

Cato, Marcus Porcius, *On agriculture*. Translated by W. D. Hooper, 1947. Heinemann, London.

Cauchy, Augustin L. 1829. *Exercises de mathématique*, Vol. IV. De Bure, Paris.

Chevrier, Henri 1970. Technique de la construction dans l'ancienne Egypte, II. Problèmes posés par les obélisques. *Mitteilungen des Deutschen Archäologischen Institute Abteil ung Kairo* 26:15–38.

Chives, Keith 1976. *The Shire horse: a history of the breed, the society, and the man*. J. A. Allen and Co., London.

Chuang, Tze-Jer and Yiu-Wing Mai 1989. Flexural behaviour of strain-softening materials, *International Journal of Solids and Structures* [in press].

Clagett, Marshall 1961. *The science of mechanics in the Middle Ages*. University of Wisconsin Press, Madison.

Clark, D. K. 1878. *Manual of rules, tables and data for mechanical engineers*. Blackie and Sons, London.

Clark, Graham 1965. Traffic in stone axe and adze blades. *Economic History Review* 18:3–28.

Clark, Graham and Stuart Piggott 1970. *Prehistoric societies*. Penguin, Harmondsworth.

Clark, J. G. D. 1963. Neolithic bows from Somerset, England, and the prehistory of archery in north-west Europe. *Proceedings of the Prehistoric Society* 29:50–98.

Clarke, Somers and R. Engelbach 1930. *Ancient Egyptian masonry. The building craft*. Oxford University Press, Oxford.

Cooper, J. M. and R. B. Glassow 1968. *Kinesiology* (2nd edn). Mosby, St Louis.

Cotterell, Brian 1965. Velocity effects in fracture propagation. *Applied Materials Research* 4:227–32.

1966. Notes on the paths and stability of cracks. *International Journal of Fracture Mechanics* 2:256–33.

1968. Fracture propagation in organic glasses. *International Journal of Fracture Mechanics* 4:209–17.

1978. The split nut: a more efficient fastener. *Chartered Mechanical Engineer* 73–86.

Cotterell, B., F. P. Dickson and J. Kamminga 1986. Ancient Egyptian water-clocks: a reappraisal. *Journal of Archaeological Science* 13:31–50.

Cotterell, Brian and Johan Kamminga 1979. The mechanics of flaking. In Brian Hayden (ed.), *Lithic use–wear analysis*. Academic Press, New York, pp. 99–112.

1986. Finials on stone flakes. *Journal of Archaeological Science* 13:451–61.

1987. The formation of flakes. *American Antiquity* 52:675–708.

Cotterell, Brian, Johan Kamminga and F. P. Dickson 1985. The essential mechanics of conchoidal flaking. *International Journal of Fracture* 20:205–21.

Cotterell, Brian and James R. Rice 1980. Slightly curved or kinked cracks. *International Journal of Fracture* 16:155–69.

Coulomb, C. A. 1785. Théorie des machines simples en ayant égard au frottement de leurs parties, et la roideur des cordages. *Mémoires de Mathématique et de Physique de l'Académie Royale* 10:161–324.

Coulton, J. J. 1977. *Ancient Greek architects at work*. Cornell University Press, Ithaca, N.Y.

Crabtree, Don E. 1968. Mesoamerican polyhedral cores and prismatic blades. *American Antiquity* 33:446–78.

Crumlin-Pedersen, Ole 1966. Two Danish side rudders. *Mariner's Mirror* 52:251–61.

Cundy, B. J. 1980. The Australian spear and spearthrower technology: an analysis of structural variation. Unpublished MA thesis, Australian National University.

Dampier, W. C. 1968. *A history of science* (4th edn). Cambridge University Press, Cambridge.

Davidson, D. S. and F. D. McCarthy 1957. The distribution and chronology of some important types of stone implements in Western Australia. *Anthropos* 52:390–458.

Davison, C. St C. 1961. Transporting 60 ton statues in early Assyria and Egypt. *Technology and culture* 2:11–16.

De Morgan, F. 1894. *Fouilles à Dahchow*, Vol. I. Holzhausen, Vienna.

de la Hire, Philippe 1699. Examen de la force de l'homme pour porter ou pour tirer. *Histoire de l'Académie Royale des Sciences*, Tirés des registres de cette academie, 1699–1790. Paris,1702, pp. 96–8.

Defoe, Daniel [1772] 1974. *A tour through the whole island of Great Britain*. Dent and Sons Ltd., London.

Demes, B. 1982. Resistance of the primate skulls against mechanical stresses. *Journal of Human Evolution* 11:687–91.

Desaguliers, John T. 1734. *A course of experimental philosophy* (3rd edn), Vol. I. Printed for J. Senex, London.

1743. *A course of experimental philosophy*, Vol. II. Printed for W. Innys, London.

des Noëttes, R. J. E. C. Lefebvre 1931. *L'attelage et le cheval de selle à travers les âges; contribution à l'histoire de l'esclavage* (2 vols.). Picard, Paris.

Dibner, Bern 1970. *Moving the obelisks*. John Wiley and MIT Press, Cambridge, Mass.

Dickinson, H. W. and R. Jenkins 1927. *James Watt and the steam engine*. Clarendon Press, Oxford.

Dickson, F. P. 1972. Ground edge axes. *Mankind* 8:206–11.

1981. *Australian stone hatchets*. Academic Press, Sydney.

Diels, Hermann 1912. *Die Fragmente der Vorsokratiker* (3rd edn). Weidmann, Berlin.

Doran, Edwin 1981. *Wangka. Austronesian canoe origins*. Texas A. & M. University Press, College Station.

Dowson, D. 1979. *History of tribology*. Longman Group Ltd., London.

Drabkin, I. E. and Stillman Drake (translators) 1960. *Galileo, Galilei. On motion and on mechanics*. University of Wisconsin Press, Madison.

Drachmann A. G. 1932. *Ancient oil mills and presses*. Levin and Munksgaard, Copenhagen.

1958. How Archimedes expected to move the earth. *Centaurus* 5:278–82.

1963. *The mechanical technology of Greek and Roman antiquity: a study of the literary sources*. Munksgaard, Copenhagen.

Dransfield, J., J. R. Flenley, S. M. King, D. D. Harkeness and S. Rapu 1984. A recently extinct palm from Easter Island. *Nature* 312:750–2.

Du Bois, Augustus Jay 1902. *The mechanics of engineering*, Vol. I. *Kinematics, statics, kinetics, statics of rigid bodies and elastic solids*. Wiley and Sons, New York.

Duby, Georges 1969. *Medieval agriculture, 900–1500*. Collins, London.

Ducos, Pierre 1975. A new find of an equid metatarsal bone from Tell Mureibet in Syria and its relevance to the identification of equids from the early Holocene of the Levant. *Journal of Archaeological Science* 2:71–3.

Duncan, J. and S. G. Starling 1950. *A text book of physics* (2nd edn). Macmillan, London.

Durnin, J. V. G. A. and R. Passmore 1967. *Energy, work and leisure*. Heinemann, London.

Durrani, G., S. A. Khan, C. Renfrew and J. Taj 1971. Obsidian source identification by fission track analysis. *Nature* 233:242.

Dyson, G. H. G. 1962. *The mechanics of athletics* (6th edn). University of London, London.

Eluere, Christiane 1980. Fabriquer des liens et cordages préhistoriques. *Dossiers de l'Archéologie* 46:68–71.

Engelbach, R. 1922. *The Aswan obelisk; with some remarks on the ancient engineering*. L'Institut Francais d'Archéologie Orientale, Cairo.

Evans, Sir John 1872. *The ancient stone implements, weapons, and ornaments of Great Britain*. Longmans, London.

1897. *The ancient stone implements, weapons and ornaments of Great Britain* (2nd edn). Longmans, Green and Co., London.

Falkenberg, A. J. 1968. *Spyd og Kastetraer fra Murinbataena i Nord-Australia*. Universitetes Ethnografiske Museum, Aabok, Oslo.

Faulkner, Aleric 1972. Mechanical principles of flint working. Unpublished PhD dissertation, Washington State University. University Microfilms, Ann Arbor.

1974. Mechanics of eraillure formation. *Newsletter of Lithic Technology* 3:4–11.

Fenton, William N. 1974. The advancement of material culture studies in modern anthropological research. In M. Richardson (ed.), *The human mirror. Material and special images of man*. Louisiana State University Press, Baton Rouge, pp. 15–39.

Fétis, François J. 1869–76. *Historie générale de la musique dupuis les temps les plus anciens jusqu'à nos jours* (5 vols.). Firmin Didot, Paris.

Finney, Ben R. 1977. Voyaging canoes and the settlement of Polynesia. *Science* 196:1277–85.

Flenley, J. R. and S. M. King 1984. Late Quaternary pollen records from Easter Island. *Nature* 307: 47–50.

Fletcher, N. H. 1983. Acoustics of the Australian didjeridu. *Australian Aboriginal Studies* (1983):28–37.

Flood, Josephine 1983. *Archaeology of the dreamtime*. Collins, Sydney.

Forbes, R. J. 1956a. Power. In C. Singer, E. J. Holmyard, A. R. Hall and T. I. Williams (eds.), *A history of technology*. Vol. II, *The Mediterranean civilizations and the Middle Ages*. Clarendon Press, Oxford, pp. 589–622.

1956b. Hydraulic engineering and sanitation. In C. Singer, E. J. Holmyard, A. R. Hall and T. I. Williams (eds.), *A history of technology*. Vol. II, *The Mediterranean civilizations and the Middle Ages*. Clarendon Press, Oxford, pp. 663–94.

1957. *Studies in ancient technology*. (6 Vols.). E. J. Brill, Leiden.

Francis, J. R. D. 1969. *A text book of fluid mechanics for engineering students*. Edward Arnold, London.

Frere, John 1800. Account of flint weapons discovered at Hoxne in Suffolk. *Archaeologia* 13:204–5.

Frenzel, B. 1973. *Climatic fluctuations of the Ice Age*. translated by A. E. M. Nairn. Case Western Reserve University Press, Cleveland.

Frith, H. J. and J. H. Calaby 1969. *Kangaroos*. Cheshire, Melbourne.

Frontinus, Sextus Julius, *The aqueducts of Rome*. Translated by C. E. Bennett, 1925. Heinemann, London.

Fugl-Meyer, H. 1937. *Chinese bridges*. Kelly and Walsh, Shanghai.

Fullagar, Richard L. K. 1982. What's the use? An analysis of Aire Shelter II, Glenaire, Victoria. Unpublished MA (qualifying) thesis, La Trobe University, Melbourne.

Galileo [Galilei] [1638] 19XX. *Dialogues concerning two new sciences*. Translated by H. Crew and A. de Salvico. Northwestern University Press, Evanston, Illinois.

Gibbs-Smith C. H. 1953. *A history of flying*. Batsford, London.

Gilberg, Rolf 1974. Changes in the life of polar Eskimos resulting from a Canadian immigration into the Thule district, North Greenland, in the 1860s. *Folk* (Copenhagen) **16–17**: 159–70.

Gille, Bertrand 1956. Machines. In C. Singer, E. J. Holmyard, A. R. Hall and T. I. Williams (eds), *A history of technology*. Vol. II, *The Mediterranean civilizations and the Middle Ages*. Clarendon Press, Oxford, pp. 629–58.

Girard, P. S. 1810. Introduction. In James Smeaton, *Recherches expérimentales sur l'eau et le vent*. Paris.

Gol'dstein, R. V. and R. L. Salganik 1974. Brittle fracture of solids with arbitrary cracks. *International Journal of Fracture* **10**: 507–25.

Gordon, J. E. 1968. *The new science of strong materials. Or why you don't fall through the floor*. Penguin Books, Harmondsworth.

1978. *Structures. Or why things don't fall down*. Plenum Press, London.

Gorringe, H. H. 1885. *Egyptian obelisks*. Nimmo, London.

Gramberg, J. 1965. Axial cleavage, a significant process in mining and geology. *Engineering Geology* **1**: 31–72.

Greenwell, William 1865. Notices of the examination of ancient grave-hills in the Nort i Riding of Yorkshire. *Archɩeological Journal* **22**: 95–105.

Griffith, Alan Arnold 1920. The phenomena of rupture and flow in solids. *Philosophical Transactions of the Royal Society of London* A221: 163–98.

1921. The theory of rupture. *Proceedings of the 1st International Congress for Applied Mechanics*. Delft, p. 55.

Haddon, A. C. and James Hornell 1936. *Canoes of Oceania*. Vol. I, *The canoes of Polynesia, Fiji and Micronesia*. Bernice P. Bishop Museum, Special Publication 27, Honolulu.

1937. *Canoes of Oceania*. Vol. II, *The canoes of Melanesia, Queensland and New Guinea*. Bernice P. Bishop Museum, Special Publication 28, Honolulu.

1938. *Canoes of Oceania*. Vol. III, *Definition of terms, general survey and conclusions*. Bernice P. Bishop Museum, Special Publication 29, Honolulu.

Hall, A. R. 1956. Military technology. In C. Singer, E. J. Holmyard, A. R. Hall and T. I. Williams (eds.), *A history of technology*. Vol. II, *The Mediterranean civilizations and the Middle Ages*. Clarendon Press, Oxford, pp. 695–730.

Hardy, Robert 1976. *Longbow: a social and military history*. Patrick Stephens, Cambridge.

Hart, I. B. 1925. *The mechanical investigations of Leonardo da Vinci*. Chapman and Hall, London.

Hartley, N. E. W. and Rodney Wilshaw 1973. Deformation and fracture of synthetic α-quartz. *Journal of Materials Science* **8**: 265–78.

Hayden, Brian 1977. Stone tool function in the Western Desert. In R. V. S. Wright (ed.), *Stone tools as culture markers: change, evolution and complexity*. Australian Institute of Aboriginal Studies, Canberra, pp. 178–88.

1979. Snap, shatter and superfractures: use-wear on stone skin scrapers, in B. Hayden (ed.), *Lithic use-wear analysis*. Academic Press, New York, pp. 207–29.

Hayden, Brian and Johan Kamminga 1978. The first CLUW: an introduction to use wear. In B. Hayden (ed.), *Lithic use–wear analysis*. Academic Press, New York, pp. 1–13.

Hayden, Martin 1976. *The book of bridges*. Marshall Cavendish, London.

Heath, E. G. and V. Chiara 1977. *Brazilian Indian Archery*. Manchester Museum, Manchester.

Heath, T. L. 1897. *The works of Archimedes*. Cambridge University Press, Cambridge.

Heizer, Robert F. 1966. Ancient heavy transport, methods and achievements. *Science* **153**: 821–30.

Henderson, Yandell and Howard W. Haggard 1925. The maximum human power and its fuel. *The American Journal of Physiology* **2**: 264–82.

Herodotus, *The histories*. Translated by Aubrey de Selincourt, 1977. Penguin Books, Harmondsworth.

Herrmann, F. 1967. *Völkerkunde Australiens*. Bibliographisches Institute, Mannheim.

Hertz, Heinrich 1896. *Hertz's miscellaneous papers*. Reprinted, Macmillan, London. [Originally published 1882: *Verhandlungen des Vereins zur Beförderung des Gewerbefleisses* **61**: 449.]

Hertzberg, H. T. E. 1972. *Engineering anthropology, human engineering guide to equipment design*. H. P. Van Cott and R. Kinkade, US Printing Office.

Hess, Felix 1968. The aerodynamics of boomerangs. *Scientific American* **219**(5): 124–37.

1973. A returning boomerang from the Iron Age. *Antiquity* **47**: 303–6.

1975. *Boomerangs aerodynamics and motion*. Verenigde Reproduktie Bedrijven, Groningen.

Heyerdahl, Thor 1957. *Sea routes to Polynesia*. George Allen and Unwin, Ltd, London.

1958. *Aku-Aku. The secret of Easter Island*. George Allen and Unwin Ltd, London.

Heyman, Jacques 1966. The stone skeleton. *International Journal of Solids and Structures* **2**: 249–79.

1967. On shell solutions for masonry domes. *International Journal of Solids and Structures* **3**: 227–41.

1969. The safety of masonry arches. *International Journal of Mechanical Sciences* **11**: 363–85.

1972. 'Gothic' construction in ancient Greece. *Journal of the Society of Architectural Historians* **31**: 3–9.

Hickman, C. N. 1937. The dynamics of a bow and arrow. *Journal of Applied Physics* **8**: 404–9.

Higham T. F. and C. M. Bowra (ed.) 1938. *The Oxford book of Greek verse in translation*. Clarendon Press, Oxford.

Hill, D. R. 1984. *A history of Engineering in Classical and Medieval times*. Croom Helm, London.

Ho Ho Classification and Nomenclature Committee Report 1979. In B. Hayden (ed.), *Lithic use–wear analysis*. Academic Press, New York, pp. 133–7.

Hodge, A. Trevor 1960. *The woodwork of Greek roofs*. Cambridge University Press, Cambridge.

Hoerner, Sighard F. 1965. *Fluid dynamic – drag*. Published by the author, Brick Town.

Hoerner, Sighard F. and Henry V. Borst 1975. *Fluid dynamic – lift*. L. A. Hoerner, Brick Town.

Holloway, P. G. 1973. *The physical properties of glass*. Wykenhan Publications, London.

Homer, *The Iliad*. Translated by A. T. Murray, 1937–9. Heinemann, London.

Hooke, Robert 1676. *A description of helioscopes, and some other instruments*. John Martyn, London.

1678. *Lectures de potentia restitutiva; or, Of spring, explaining the power of springing bodies: to which are added some collections*. John Martyn, London.

Hopkins, H. J. 1970. *A span of bridges*. David and Charles, Newton Abbott.

Horne, G. A. and G. Aiston 1924. *Savage life in Central Australia*. Macmillan and Co., London.

Hornell, James 1970. *Water transport, origins and early evolution*. David and Charles, Newton Abbot.

Huffman, Michael A. 1984. Stone play of *Macaca fuscata* in Arashiyama B troop: transmission of a non-adaptive behaviour. *Journal of Human Evolution* 13:725–35.

Isaac, G. L. 1984. The archaeology of human origins. Studies of the Lower Pleistocene in East Africa 1971–1981. In F. Wendorf and A. E. Close (eds.), *Advances in World Archaeology* 3:1–87. Academic Press, New York.

James, T. G. H. 1979. *An introduction to Ancient Egypt*. British Museum, London.

Jenkins, Nancy 1980. *The boat beneath the pyramid. King Cheop's royal ship*. Holt, Rinehart and Winston, N.Y.

Johanson, D. C., M. Taieb and Y. Coppens 1982. Pliocene hominids from the Hadar Formation, Ethiopia (1973–1977): stratigraphy, chronology and paleoenvironmental contexts, with notes on hominid morphology and systematics. *American Journal of Physical Anthropology* 57:373–402.

Johnstone, Paul, 1980. *The sea-craft of prehistory*. Routledge and Kegan Paul, London.

Jones, A. M. 1964. *Africa and Indonesia. The evidence of the xylophone and other musical and cultural factors*. E. J. Brill, Leiden.

Jones, Rhys 1977. The Tasmanian paradox. In R. V. S. Wright (ed.), *Stone tools as cultural markers. Change, evolution and complexity*. Australian Institute of Aboriginal studies, Canberra, pp. 189–204.

Jope, E. M. 1956. Vehicles and harnesses. In C. Singer, E. J. Holmyard, A. R. Hall and T. I. Williams (eds.), *A history of technology*. Vol. II, *The Mediterranean civilizations and the Middle Ages*. Clarendon Press, Oxford, pp. 537–62.

Josephus, Flavius, *Bellum Judaicum*. In *Complete works*, translated by W. Whiston, 1960. Pickering and Inglis, London.

Kamminga, Johan 1979. The nature of use-polish and abrasive smoothing on stone tools. In Brian Hayden (ed.), *Lithic use–wear analysis*. Academic Press, New York, pp. 143–57.

1982. *Over the edge. Functional analysis of Australian stone tools*. Occasional papers in Anthropology, No. 12, Anthropology Museum, Queensland University, Brisbane.

1985. The pirri graver. *Australian Aboriginal Studies* 1985/II:2–25.

Kamminga, J. and B. Cotterell 1984. The pollen record and Easter Island statues. *Nature* 312:289.

Kamminga, Johan and Thomas J. Hudson 1982. The modified Los Angeles abrasion test. In J. Kamminga, *Over the edge. Functional analysis of Australian stone tools*. Occasional Papers in Anthropology, No. 12, Anthropology Museum, Queensland University, p. 108.

Kamminga, Johan and R. V. S. Wright 1988. The Upper Cave and the origins of the Mongoloids. *Journal of Human Evolution* 17: 739–67.

Kawai, M. 1965. Newly acquired pre-culture behaviour of a natural troop of Japanese monkeys on Koshima island. *Primates* 6:1–30.

Keeley, Lawrence H. 1980. *Experimental determination of stone tool uses. A microwear analysis*. University of Chicago Press, Chicago.

Kerkhof, Frank 1962. Bestimmung de maximalen Bruchgeschwindigkeit verschiedener Gläser nach der Ultraschall-Methode. *Glastechnische Berichte* 35:267–72.

Kerkhof, Frank and Hansjürgen Müller-Beck 1969. Zur Bruchmechanischer Deutung der Schlagmarken au Steingeräten. *Glastechnische Berichte* 42:439–48.

Khruschov, M. M. 1974. Principles of abrasive wear. *Wear* 28:69–88.

Kirby, Percival R. 1968. *The muscial instruments of the native races of South Africa* (2nd edn).Witwatersrand University Press, Johannesburg.

Kisch, Bruno. 1965. *Scales and weights – a historical outline*. Yale University Press. New Haven.

Klopsteg, Paul E. 1943. Physics of bows and arrows. *American Journal of Physics* 11:175–92.

1947. *Turkish archery and the composite bow*. Published by the author, Evanston, Illinois.

Kluckhohn, Clyde, W. W. Hill and Lucy W. Kluckhohn 1971. *Navaho material culture*. Belknap Printers, Cambridge, Mass.

Kolsky, H. 1963. *Stress waves in solids*. Dover Publications, New York.

Kosambi, D. D. 1967. Living prehistory in India. *Scientific American* 216:105–114.

Landels, J. G. 1978. *Engineering in the ancient world*. Chatto and Windus, London.

1981. The reconstruction of ancient Greek auloi. *World Archaeology* 12:289–301.

Lane Fox, Augustus Henry 1858. On the improvement of the rifle as a weapon for general use. *Journal of the Royal United Service Institution* 2:453–93.

1906. *The evolution of culture*, ed. J. L. Myres. Clarendon Press, Oxford.

Langford-Smith, Trevor (ed.) 1978. *Silcrete in Australia*. Department of Geography, University of New England, Armidale.

La Pérouse, J. F. de G. 1797. *Voyage de la Pérouse autour du monde*. Paris. (English translation 1978, Johnson, London.)

Lawn, Brian R. 1967. Partial cone crack formation in a brittle material loaded with a spherical indenter. *Proceedings of the Royal Society of London* A299:307–16.

Lawn, Brian R. and D. B. Marshall 1979. Mechanics of microcontact fracture in brittle solids. In Brian Hayden (ed.), *Lithic use–wear analysis*. Academic Press, New York, pp. 63–82.

Lawn, Brian R., A. G. Evans and D. B. Marshall 1980. Elastic/plastic indentation damage in ceramics: the mean/radial crack system. *Journal of the American Ceramic Society* 63:574–81.

Lawn, Brian R. and Michael V. Swain 1975. Microfracture beneath point indentation in brittle solids. *Journal of Materials Science* 10:113–22.

Lawn, Brian and T. R. Wilshaw 1975a. *Fracture of brittle solids.* Cambridge University Press, Cambridge.

1975b. Indentation fracture: principles and applications. *Journal of Materials Science* 10:1049–81.

Lawrence, Robert A. 1979. Experimental evidence for the significance of attributes used in edge-damage analysis. In Brian Hayden (ed.), *Lithic use–wear analysis.* Academic Press, New York, pp. 113–21.

Layard, A. H. 1850. *Ninevah and its remains* (5th edn). John Murray, London.

1853. *Discoveries in the ruins of Ninevah and Babylon.* John Murray, London.

Leakey, M. D. and R. L. Hay, 1979. Pliocene footprints in the Laetoli Beds at Laetoli, northern Tanzania. *Nature* 278:317–23.

Lebar, Frank M. 1964. *The material culture of Truk.* Yale University Publications in Anthropology, No. 68.

Lepsius, Richard 1859. *Denkmaeler aus Aegypten und Aethiopen.* Nicolaische Buchhrandlung, Berlin.

Lhote, H. 1953. Le cheval et le chameau dans les peintures et gravures rupestres du Sahara. *Bulletin de l'Institute Francais d'Afrique Noire* (Dakar) 15:1138–228.

1966. La route des chars de guerre Libyens Tripoli – Gao. *Archéologia* 9:29–36.

Liddell Hart, B. H. 1970. *History of the First World War.* Pan Books, London.

Littauer, Mary A. 1968. The function of the yoke saddle in ancient harnessing. *Antiquity* 42:27–31.

1972. The military use of the chariot in the Aegean in the Late Bronze Age. *American Journal of Archaeology* 76:145–57.

Littauer, Mary A. and J. H. Crouwel 1979. *Wheeled vehicles and ridden animals in the ancient Near East.* E. J. Brill, Leiden.

Little, William, H. W. Fowler, Jessie Coulton, C. T. Onions and G. W. S. Friedrichsen (eds.) 1978. *The shorter Oxford English dictionary* (2 Vols.). Clarendon Press, Oxford.

Lloyd, H. Alan 1957. Mechanical timekeepers. In C. Singer, E. J. Holmyard, A. R. Hall and T. I. Williams (eds), *A history of technology.* Vol. III, *From the Renaissance to the Industrial Revolution.* Oxford University Press, Oxford, pp. 648–75.

Lloyd, Seton 1954. Building in brick and stone. In C. Singer, E. J. Holmyard and R. A. Hall (eds.), *A history of technology.* Vol. I, *From early times to the fall of ancient empires.* Clarendon Press, Oxford, pp. 456–90.

Lourandos, Harry 1983. Intensification: a late Pleistocene – Holocene archaeological sequence from southwestern Victoria. *Archaeology in Oceania* 18:81–94.

Loy, T. H. 1983. Prehistoric blood residues: detection on tool surfaces and identification of species of origin. *Science* 220:1269–71.

Lu, G-D., R. A. Salomon and J. Needham 1959a. The wheelwright's art in ancient China. I. The invention of dishing. *Physis* (Florence) 1:103–26.

1959b. The wheelwright's art in ancient China. II. Sciences in the workshop. *Physis* (Florence) 1:196–214.

Lubbock, B. 1975. *The best of sail.* Patrick Stephens Ltd, Cambridge.

Lucas, Alfred 1962. *Ancient Egyptian materials and industries* (4th edn). Revised by J. R. Harris. Arnold, London.

Lucianus, The ship: or, the wishes. In *The Works of Lucian of Samosata* Translated by H. W. and F. G. Fowler, 1905–1935. Clarendon Press, Oxford.

Luebbers, R. A. 1975. Ancient boomerangs discovered in South Australia. *Nature* 253:29.

McCall, Grant 1979. Kinship and environment on Easter Island: some observations and speculations. *Mankind* 12:119–37.

MacCalman, H. R. and B. J. Grobbelaar 1965. Preliminary report of two stone-working Ova Tjimba groups in northern Kaokoveld of South West Africa. *Cimbebasia* 13.

McCoy, P. C. 1979. Easter Island. In J. D. Jennings (ed.), *The prehistory of Polynesia.* Harvard University Press, Cambridge, Mass., pp. 135–66.

Mach, Ernst [1883] 1942. *The science of mechanics.* Translated by T. J. McCormack. Open Court Publishing Co., La Salle, Illinois.

[Originally published as *Die Mechanik in iber Entwickelung.*]

McWhirter, Norris and (ed.) 1982. *Guinness book of records* (29th edn 1983). Guinness Superlatives Ltd, Enfield.

McWhirter, Norris and A. Ross McWhirter (eds.) 1974. *Guinness book of world records* (13th edn). Guinness Superlatives Ltd, Enfield.

Magie, William F. 1963. *A source book in physics.* Harvard University Press, Cambridge, Massachusetts.

Mandeville, M. D. 1973. A consideration of the thermal treatment of chert. *Plains Anthropologist* 18:177–202.

Marchaj, C. A. 1964. *Sailing theory and practice.* Granada, St Albans.

Marcuse, Sibyl 1975. *A survey of musical instruments.* David and Charles, Newton Abbot.

Margaria, R. 1968. Positive and negative work performance and their efficiencies in human locomotion. *Internationale Zeitschrift für angewandte Physiologie einschliesslich Arbeitsphysiologie* (Berlin) 25:339–51.

Marsden, E. W. 1969. *Greek and Roman artillery – historical development.* Clarendon Press, Oxford.

1971. *Greek and Roman artillery – technical treatises.* Clarendon Press, Oxford.

Mason, Otis T. 1895. *Origin of inventions.* Scott, London.

Mazière, Francis 1969. *Mysteries of Easter Island.* Collins, London.

Megaw, J. V. S. 1968. Problems and non-problems in palaeo-organology: a musical miscellany. In J. M. Coles and D. D. A. Simpson (eds.), *Studies in ancient Europe.* Leicester University Press, Leicester.

Métraux, Alfred 1940. Ethnology of Easter Island. *Bernice P. Bishop Museum, Bulletin,* No. 160.

1963. Weapons. In J. H. Steward (ed.), *Handbook of South American Indians.* Vol. 5, *The comparative ethnology of South American Indians.* Copper Square Publishers, New York, pp. 229–56.

Minty, E. J. 1961. The physical properties of aggregates used for road works in NSW. Unpublished MSc thesis, University of New South Wales.

Mohen, Jean-Paul 1980. Aux prises avec des pierres de plusieurs dizaines de tonnes. *Dossiers de l'Archéologie* 46:58–67.

Mookerji, Radha Kumud 1912. *A history of Indian shipping: a history of the seaborne trade and maritime activity of the Indians from the earliest times*. Longmans, Green, Bombay.

Moritz, L. A. 1958. *Grain-mills and flour in classical antiquity*. Clarendon Press, Oxford.

Morrison, J. S. 1980. *The ship: long ships and round ships*. HM Stationary Office, London.

Morrison, J. S. and J. F. Coates 1986. *The Athenian trireme*. Cambridge University Press, Cambridge.

Morrison, J. and R. Williams 1968. *Greek oared ships*. Cambridge University Press, Cambridge.

Moyle, Alice M. 1981. The Australian didjeridu: a late musical intrusion. *World Archaeology* **12**:321–31.

Mulloy, William 1968. *Preliminary report of archaeological field work, February–July, 1968*. Easter Island Committee, International Fund for Monuments Inc., Bulletin No. 1.

1970. A speculative reconstruction of the techniques of carving, transporting, and erecting Easter Island statues. *Archaeology and Physical Anthropology in Oceania* **5**:1–23.

Mulloy, William and G-H. Gonzalo Figueroa 1978. *The Kiva-Vai Teka complex and its relationship to Easter Island's architectural prehistory*. Asian and Pacific Archaeological Series, No. 8. Social Sciences and Linguistics Institute, Honolulu.

Needham, J. and Ling Wang 1959. *Science and civilisation in China*. Vol. 3, Sections 19–25. *Mathematics and other sciences of the heavens and the earth*. Cambridge University Press, Cambridge.

1962. *Science and civilisation in China*. Vol. 4, *Physics and physical technology*. Part I, *Physics*. Cambridge University Press, Cambridge.

1965. *Science and civilisation in China*. Vol. IV, *Physics and physical technology*. Part II, *Mechanical engineering*. Cambridge University Press, Cambridge.

Needham, Joseph and Gwei-Djew Lu 1960. Efficient equine harness: the Chinese inventions. *Physis* (Florence) **2**:121–61.

Needham, Joseph, Ling Wang and Gwei-Djen Lu 1971. *Science and civilisation in China*. Vol. IV,

Physics and physical technology. Part III, *Civil engineering and nautics*. Cambridge University Press, Cambridge.

Neugebauer, O. and R. A. Parker 1960. *Egyptian astronomical texts*. Vol. I, *The early decans*. Brown University Press, Providence.

Newberry, Percy E. 1897. *El Bersheh – part I, the tomb of Tehuti-hetep*. Archaeological Survey of Egypt, Special Publication of the Egypt Exploration Fund.

1900. *The life of Rekhmara*. Constable, London.

Newton, Isaac [1686] 1922. *Philosophiae naturalis principia mathematics*. Trans. by F. Carjori. 2 Vols. University of California Press, Berkeley.

Noetling, Fritz 1911. Notes on hunting sticks (lughrana) spears (perenna), and baskets (tughbrana) of the Tasmanian Aborigines. *Papers and Proceedings of the Royal Society of Tasmania*, for the year 1911, pp. 64–98.

O'Connell, A. L. and E. B. Gardner 1972. *Understanding the scientific basis of human movement*. Williams and Williams, Baltimore.

Oda, S. and C. T. Keally 1973. Edge-ground stone tools from the Japanese preceramic culture. *Material Culture*, No. 22. Society for the Study of Material Cultures, Tokyo.

Odell, George H. 1981. The mechanics of use-breakage of stone tools: some testable hypotheses. *Journal of Field Archaeology* **8**:197–209.

Oliphant, J. N. 1937. The development of more intensive use of mixed tropical forest. *The Empire Forest Journal* **16**:29–39.

Osgood, Cornelius 1940. *Ingalik material culture*. Yale University Publications in Anthropology, No. 22.

Oswalt, Wendell H. 1973. *Habitat and technology*. Holt, Rinehart and Winston, New York.

1976. *An anthropological analysis of food-getting technology*. John Wiley and Sons, New York.

Palter, J. L. 1977. Design and construction of Australian spearthrower projectiles and hand-thrown spears. *Archaeology and Physical Anthropology in Oceania* **12**:161–72.

Parish, W. F. 1929. Lubricants. In *Encylopaedia Brittanica* (14th edn), p. 453.

Parker, R. A. 1950. *Calendars of ancient*

Egypt. University of Chicago Press, Chicago.

Parsons, W. B. 1968. *Engineers and engineering in the Renaissance*. MIT Press, Cambridge, Massachusetts.

Perlès C. 1979. Des navigateurs méditerranéens il y a 10,000 ans. *La Rescherche* **10**:82–3.

Perrot, Georges and Charles Chipiez 1882. *Histoire de l'art dans l'antiquité*. Hachette, Paris.

Pierce, John R. 1983. *The science of musical sound*. Scientific American Books, New York.

Piggott, Stuart 1979. The first wagons and carts: twenty-five years later. *Bulletin of the Institute of Archaeology* (University of London), Number 16.

Philostratus, Flavius (The elder), *The life of Appollonius of Tyana* (translated by F. C. Conybeare, 1912). Heinemann, London.

Plato. *Republic*. Translated by A. D. Lindsay, 1976. Dent, London.

Gorgias. In E. Hamilton and H. Cairns (eds.), *The collected dialogues of Plato*. Bollinger series 71, 1961. Pantheon Books, New York.

Pliny (the Elder), *Natural history*. Translated by H. Rackman, 1945. Heinemann, London.

Plutarch, *Lives, Marcellus*. In *Agesilaus and Pompey, Pelopidas and Marcellus*, Vol. 5. Translated by B. Perrin, 1917. Heinemann, London.

Pope, Saxton, T. 1909. *A study of bows and arrows*. University of California Press, Berkeley.

Popper, Paul 1948. Cane bridges in Asia. *National Geographic* **94**:243–50.

Pratt, P. L. 1976. The arrow. In R. Hardy (ed.), *Longbow: a social and military history*. Patrick Stephens, Cambridge.

Premi, S. C. L. 1979. Performance of bullocks under varying conditions of load and climate. Unpublished Master of Engineering thesis, Asian Institute of Technology, Bangkok.

Proske, U. 1980. Energy conservations by elastic storage in kangaroos. *Endeavour* (NS) **4**:148–53.

Rankine, W. J. M. 1889. *Useful rules and tables relating to mensuration, engineering, structures, and machines*. C. Griffin and Co, London.

Rausing, Gad 1967. *The bow. Some notes on its origins and development*. CWK Glerups Förlag, Lund.

Ravi-Chandar, K. and W. G. Knauss 1984. An experimental investigation into dynamic fracture. III. On steady state crack propagation and crack branching. *International Journal of Fracture* **26**:141–54.

Rawson, K. J. and E. C. Tupper 1968. *Basic ship theory.* Longmans, London.

Renfew, C. E., and J. R. Cann 1966. Obsidian and early cultural contact in the Near East. *Proceedings of the Prehistoric Society* (NS) **32**:30–57.

Reynolds, Terry S. 1983. *Stronger than a hundred men: A history of the vertical water wheel.* John Hopkins University Press, Baltimore.

Richmond, Ian 1982. *Trajan's army on Trajan's column.* The British School at Rome, London.

Rich, John, W. and Sylvia Chappell 1983. Thermal alteration of silica materials in technology and functional perspective. *Lithic Technology* **12**:69–80.

Rimmer, Joan 1969. *Ancient musical instruments of western Asia in the British Museum.* British Museum Publication, London.

Ritter, August 1879. *Elementary theory and calculation of iron bridges and roofs* (3rd edn). Translated by H. R. Sankey. Spon, London.

Rogers, Everett M. 1962. *Diffusion of innovations.* Free Press of Glencoe, New York.

Roggeveen, Jacob 1722. *Extracts from the official log of Mynheer J. Roggeveen (1721–1722).* Translated by B. G. Corney. Hakluyt Society, Second Series, Vol. 13, 1908.

Rooke, P. P. and D. V. Cartwright 1976. *Compendium of stress intensity factors.* HM Stationery Office, London.

Roth, H. L. 1899. *The Aborigines of Tasmania.* Facsimile of 2nd edn, Fullers Bookshop [originally published by F. King and Sons. Halifax].

Roth, W. H. 1904. *Domestic implements, arts and manufactures.* North Queensland Ethnography Bulletin, No. 7. Home Secretary's Department, Brisbane.

Rougé, Jean 1981. *Ships and fleets of the ancient Mediterranean.* Translated by S. Z. Frazer. Wesleyan University Press, Middletown, Connecticut.

Rouse, Hunter and Simon Ince 1963. *History of hydraulics.* Dover reprint, New York.

Russell, Alan and Norris D. McWhirter (eds.) 1987. *Guinness book of records.* Guiness Superlatives Ltd, Enfield.

Russell, Mary D. 1985. The supraorbital torus: the most remarkable peculiarity. *Current Anthropology* **26**:336–60.

Sachs, Curt 1940. *The history of musical instruments.* Norton and Co., New York.

Satterthwait, L. D. 1980. Aboriginal Australia: the simplest technologies? *Archaeology and Physical Anthropology in Oceania* **15**:153–6.

Schindler, D. L., J. W. Hatch, C. A. Hay and R. C. Bradt 1982. Aboriginal thermal alteration of a central Pennsylvanian jasper: analytical and behaviorial implications. *American Antiquity* **47**:526–44.

Schmidt, E. F. 1953. *Persepolis I.* Oriental Institute Publication, Chicago.

Schnitger, F. W. 1964. *Forgotten kingdoms in Sumatra.* E. J. Brill, Leiden.

Schwedler, J. W. 1851. Theorie der Bückenbalkensysteme. *Zeitschrift für Bauwesen*, Vol. 1:26–31.

Schuster, B. G. 1969. Ballistics of the modern-working recurve bow and arrow. *American Journal of Physics* **37**:364–73.

Scofield, John 1976. Life slowly changes in a remote Himalayan kingdom. *National Geographic* **150**:658–83.

Scottsberg, Carl 1956. *The natural history of Juan Fernandez and Easter Island*, Vol. I. Almqvist and Wiksells, Uppsala, pp. 193–438.

Seewald, Otto 1934. *Beiträge zur Kenntnis der steizeitlichen Musikinstrumente Europas.* A. Scholl and Co., Vienna.

Semenov, S. A. 1964. *Prehistoric technology.* Cory, Adams and Mackay, London.

Shen, Sinyan 1987. Acoustics of ancient Chinese bells. *Scientific American* **256**:94–102.

Simmonds, N. W. 1959. Archery in South East Asia and the Pacific. *Royal Asiatic Society* **32**:67–104.

Skjölsvold, A. 1961. The stone statues and quarries of Rano Raraku. In T. Heyerdahl and F. N. Ferdon, Jr. (eds.), *Archaeology of Easter Island*, Vol. I. George Allen and Unwin, London, pp. 339–79.

Smith, Carlisle S. 1961. A temperal sequence derived from certain ahu. In T. Heyerdahl and E. N.

Ferdon (eds.), *Reports of the Norwegian Archaeological Expedition to Easter Island and the East Pacific.* Vol. I, *Archaeology of Easter Island.* Monograph of the School of American Research and the Museum of New Mexico, No. 24, Part I, pp. 181–219.

Smythies, B. E. 1952. Extraction by kuda-kuda in Sarawak. *Empire Forestry Review* **31**:42.

Snow, Charles, P. 1962. *The two cultures and the scientific revolution.* Cambridge University Press, Cambridge.

Soedel, Werner and Vernard Foley 1979. Ancient catapults. *Scientific American* **240**:120–8.

Sommer, E. 1969. Formation of fracture lances in glass. *Engineering Fracture Mechanics* **1**:539–46.

Sordinas, Augustus 1974. The âi or šfondéle: a beam press from the island of Corfu, Greece. In M. Richardson (ed.), *The human mirror. Material and special images of man.* Louisiana State University Press, Baton Rouge, pp. 135–73.

Spangler, Merlin G. 1966. *Soil engineering* (2nd edn). International Book Co., Scranton.

Spencer, W. B. 1928. *Wanderings in wild Australia* (2 Vols). Macmillan, London.

Spier, Leslie 1928. *Havasupai ethnography.* Anthropological Papers of the American Museum of Natural History, 29, 2.

1930. *Klamath ethnography.* University of California Publications in American Natural History, Archaeology and Ethnology, 30.

1933. *Yuman tribes of the Gila River.* University of Chicago Press, Chicago.

Spruytte, J. 1983. *Early harness systems.* (Translated by M. A. Littauer). J. A. Allen and Co., London.

Starr, D. 1983. Plastic megaliths. *Omni*, Feb., pp. 52, 91–2.

Straub, Hans 1952. *A history of civil engineering.* Translated by E. Rockwell. Leonard Hill, London.

Sturtevant, William C. 1969. Does anthropology need museums? *Proceedings of the Biological Society* **82**:560–619.

Surirey de Saint Rémy, M. 1745. *Mémoires d'Artillerie* (3rd edn). Joubert, Paris.

Tada, H., P. C. Paris and G. R. Irwin 1973. *The stress analysis of cracks handbook.* Del. Research Corp., Hellertown.

Taylor, A. E. 1928. *A commentary on Plato's Timaeus*. Clarendon Press, Oxford.

Taylor, Charles 1976. *Sounds of music*. British Broadcasting Commission, London.

Taylor, Lloyd, W. 1959. *Physics, the pioneer science*. Vol. I, *Mechanics, heat, sound*. Dover Publications, New York.

Thomson, R. H. G. 1954. A note on Stonehenge. In C. Singer, E. J. Holmyard and A. R. Hall (eds.), *A history of technology*. Vol. I, *From early times to the fall of civilizations*. Clarendon Press, Oxford, pp. 490–4.

Thucydides, *History of the Peloponnesian War*. Translated by R. Warner, 1954. Penguin, Harmondsworth, Middlesex.

Timoshenko, Stephen and J. N. Goodier 1951. *Theory of elasticity* (2nd edn). McGraw. Hill, New York.

Tindale, N. B. 1965. Stone implement making among the Nakako, Ngadadjara and Pitjandjara of the Great Western Desert. *Records of the South Australian Museum* 15:131–64.

Tixier, Jaques 1974. Glossary for the description of stone tools. Translated by M. H. Newcomer. *Newsletter of Lithic Technology. Special Publication*.

Todhunter, I. and K. Pearson 1886. *A history of the theory of elasticity and of the strength of materials*. Vol. I, *Galileo to Saint-Venant*. Cambridge University Press, Cambridge.

  1893. *A history of the theory of elasticity and of the strength of materials*. Vol. II, *Saint-Venant to Lord Kelvin*. Cambridge University Press, Cambridge.

Toyoshima, Shintaro and Mitsumasa Miyashita 1973. Force–velocity relation in throwing. *Research Quarterly* 44:86–94.

Tsirk, Are 1979. Regarding fracture initiations. In Brian Hayden (ed.), *Lithic use-wear analysis*. Academic Press, New York, pp. 83–96.

Valde-Nowak, Pawel, Adam Nadachowski and Mieczyslaw Wolsan 1987. Upper Palaeolithic boomerang made of a mammoth tusk in south Poland. *Nature* 329:436–8.

Vitruvius, *The ten books on architecture*. Translated by M. H. Morgan, 1960. Dover, New York.

Von Däniken, E. 1970. *Return to the stars. Evidence for the impossible*. Translated by M. Heron. Souvenir Press, London.

Voltaire, François Marie Arouet de 1785. *Oeuvres complètes de Voltaire*. De l'Imprimerie de la Sociète Litteraire-typographique.

Volterra, Enrico and E. C. Zachmanoglou 1965. *Dynamics of vibration*. Merill Books, Columbus, Ohio.

Wallner, H. 1939. Linien Strukturen und Bruchflächen. *Zeitschrift für physik* 114:368–78.

Weaver, Kenneth, F. 1986. Meteorites. Invaders from Space. *National Geographic* 170:390–418.

Wellesz, Egon 1957. *Ancient and oriental music*. Oxford University Press, Oxford [Vol. I in the Oxford History of Music].

Whipple, Squire 1847. *An essay on bridge building*. Utica, New York.

White, Carmel 1967. Early stone axes in Arnhem Land. *Antiquity* 41:149–52.

White, J. Peter 1968. Fabricators, outils écaillés or scalar cores. *Mankind* 6:658–66.

White, T. D. 1980. Evolutionary implications of Pliocene hominid footprints. *Science* 208:175–6.

Williams, Max L. 1957. On the stress distribution at the base of a stationary crack. *Journal of Applied Mechanics* 24:109–14.

Willms, Christoph 1983. Obsidian in Neolithikum und Äneolithikum Europas. Ein Uberblick. *Germania* 61:331–43.

Wilkie, D. R. 1960. Man as a source of mechanical power. *Ergonomics* 3:1–8.

Wolf, A. 1950. *A history of science, technology, and philosophy in the 16th and 17th centuries* (2nd edn). Allen and Unwin, London.

Wolff, W. 1949. Three mysteries of Easter Island. *Scientific American* 180(2):50–5.

Wood, A. 1925. *Joule and the study of energy*. Ball and Sons, London.

Wood, Alexander 1975. *The physics of music*. Revised by J. M. Bowsher. Chapman and Hall, London.

Woodson, Wesley E. 1981. *Human factors handbook*. McGraw Hill, New York.

Wright, R. V. S. 1972. Imitative learning of a flaked stone technology – the case of an orang-utan. *Mankind* 8:296–306.

Young, Thomas 1845. *A course of lectures on natural philosophy and the mechanical arts* (2 Vols.; new edition). Taylor and Walton, London.

Zeuner, Frederick E. 1963. *A history of domesticated animals*. Hutchinson, London.

INDEX